To

Roxane

Happy, happy
70th birthday

to a sister grandmother!

with affection,
Gayle

Ethics for Jessica

Ethics for Jessica

Meditations on Living

GAYLE GRAHAM YATES

Gayle Graham Yates
Jessica Scherer

WIPF & STOCK · Eugene, Oregon

ETHICS FOR JESSICA
Meditations on Living

Wipf & Stock
An Imprint of Wipf and Stock Publishers
199 W. 8th Ave., Suite 3
Eugene, OR 97401

www.wipfandstock.com

ISBN 13: 978-1-60899-065-8

Manufactured in the U.S.A.

For
our first grandchild,
Jessica Leigh Scheerer,
and
her cousin,
Sage Schultz Yates,
and
her brothers,
David Forest Scheerer
and
Justin Rain Scheerer

. . . as we gazed into the blossom of a flower . . . [we found] the crucible of beauty, if not art, and maybe even a glimpse into the meaning of life, . . . the contending energies of creation and dissolution . . . both transcendence and necessity. Could that be it—right there, in a flower—the meaning of life?

—Michael Pollan, *The Botany of Desire*

Contents

Acknowledgments

MY GRATITUDE IS MANYFOLD to those who inspired and encouraged me to write this book—my favorite of all my writings. The subject began forming for me with my students in the first-year classes I taught on "Ethics and the Arts in the University" at the University of Minnesota the last years before my retirement. We worked on the very personal development of each student's plan for her or his own ethical framework and finished each semester with a project in which these largely 18- and 19-year-olds wrote a letter to each one's as-yet-unborn child expressing their own individual ethics. I thought with them of my own ethical perspective for my yet-to-be-born grandchild, and I appreciate what those students and I learned together, as well as my education with all my students over my 38 years of university teaching. Thus, I first of all acknowledge my former students as sources of knowledge and understanding that fed into this book.

One former student in particular, Pauline Brunette Danforth, who worked with me on her PhD dissertation using the Ojibway elder Ignatia Broker's *Night Flying Woman*, I thank for adding to my insights on that book and helping to educate me in general about Native American writings, spirituality, history, and practices that were useful to my writing here.

For the book's setting and my increasing engagement with nature and the out-of-doors, I must first express my gratitude to the memory of my mother for her bequest that enabled me to buy our Wisconsin house in the woods. Next, I thank my husband, Wilson Yates, who saw to the building of that house that is my writing place and who has supported my writing along with all the parts of our life together over the years. Similarly, our children, Natasha Yates and Stiles Yates, and our son-in-law, Ian Scheerer, have been staunch supporters of my literary ambition.

When Jessica, our first grandchild, was born, it was time for me to put pen to paper with the ideas, information, and stories that I had imagined making up this book; and before I could get the writing done, Jessica was joined by her cousin Sage and her brothers David and Justin in our brood of grandchildren. They have all been an inspiration for my defining and articulating my own ethics and what I want to convey to them of what I think to be of lasting value.

As the book unfolded, some friends, colleagues, and family members read parts of the manuscript or the part I had finished, vetted sections for accuracy and propriety, and helped me by their commentary as readers. First among them is Pamela Mittlefehldt, who read it first and most thoroughly, as I had read her PhD dissertation some years ago. Bill and Susan Sands, Sue Ebbers and Carolyn Pressler, Robin Jensen, and Shirley M. Clark also read portions of what I had written and provided feedback to me. Natasha Yates read parts several times, once declaring my writing on erotic love unsuitable for Jessica to read—that is, you understand, my daughter to her mother about her daughter—and not okaying that section until about its fourth iteration, though Natasha finally read the whole finished manuscript and approved.

Others who read the entire manuscript and offered assessments to my great benefit are Sally Vardaman Johnson; Maggie Brockman; Deborah Haynes, who read it as a critical colleague; and Jean Brookins, who read it as a professional editor. Finally, I thank all the editors and staff at Wipf & Stock Publishers, especially Christian Amondson who accepted my manuscript and shepherded it through its initial steps and Greg Teague, my copy editor.

I acknowledge and thank Robin Jensen for permission to quote in this book from a December 19, 2005 e-mail message from her to me, and, also, I acknowledge and thank Nathaniel Danforth for allowing me to use in full his unpublished poem "the lake sits silent," which he wrote in 2005 when he was eight-years-old. In addition, I acknowledge for two lines from "View with a Grain of Sand" and 4 ½ lines from "The Joy of Writing" by Wisława Szymborska permission from the publisher Houghton Mifflin Harcourt; and for quotation of two lines by Liesl Mueller from her poem "Hope" permission from Louisiana State University Press.

Errors herein, as a writer needs to say, are my own. I hope there are few or even none; but I am only mortal and perception of correctness or mistakes is finally relative. Thus, I will end my acknowledgments in the same spirit I end the book: on hope, hope that what I have written is as error-free as it can be.

Preface

I WRITE THIS BOOK in first-person and in epistolary form. It is at once a memoir and an extended letter to my eldest grandchild, Jessica, and all the members of her generation as they become adults. That is, my first-person speaking voice is addressing Jessica directly and, with her, her brothers and cousin and every other reader whose interest I may attract.

The book has four threads: *nature writing* by a very amateur naturalist; *storytelling* from my heart and mind about many of the subjects that I know, including theater, poetry and fiction, art and architecture, philosophy and spirituality, and our family; *reflections* on living in the frame of my understanding of ethics; and *advice* once in a while about what I have learned about loving as the bedrock of living. The thematic core is ethics. However, it is no "how-to" book, but rather a book of deliberations on what I have learned and what living has given me.

Aspects of my experience that inform my writing are my feminism as one of the founders of Women's Studies; my consciousness of the need for us all to participate in environmental protection; my commitment to local, national, and world citizenship; and my continuing openness to new avenues of spirituality. I use the tree as the central image or metaphor for my focus in the book on both my growing appreciation of nature and the change I seek in the growth of persons in society as unified with nature. From the outset, I try to establish and develop the dominant image of the tree: the setting at our Wisconsin place, Coventry-in-the-Northwoods; and my voice as environmentalist, reader, feminist, and grandmother.

This book has four parts: I. Living, Learning, and Doing Nothing; II. On Learning; III. On Loving; and IV. On Hoping. Each part has a seasonal trope, the first one autumn; the second, winter; third, spring; and culminating with summer—each trope a metaphor for a feature of a person's development. I think of autumn as the season of abundance, of fruition, of promise fulfilled, the season when nature is vividly multicolored. Here I will use autumn images and experiences from nature as suggestions of abundance of human possibilities in the chapters that they head. Winter to me is the season of waiting, of thoughtfulness and, in Minnesota and Wisconsin, of a cold and silent white landscape. I write of the season here as a metaphor for hibernation, for germination, for internal development within nature and ourselves. Spring is the time of greening and blossoming, of course, and for many of us it suggests happiness and rebirth. Here I will use spring images and descriptions of experiences of spring to signify times of growth. Finally, summer is the time of maturity and fulfillment, and in Part IV it will be the image of the full, rich life of the person and the community.

Within each major section or part of the book there are several short chapters, each containing (1) one or more short nature passages written as journal entries from my recent experience through the seasons with four actual years collapsed into one cycle; (2) passages of storytelling or explication on the chapter topic; and (3) sometimes direct commentary or counsel for the reader. Often I include epigraphs from writers whose lines have meanings important to me. The book's voice is my voice, the experience described—intellectual, social, cultural, and personal—my own. The setting of the book is our Wisconsin lakeside cottage, which we have named Coventry-in-the-Northwoods.

I interweave here nature and ethics, love and learning, storytelling, and spirituality in a way that reveals new configurations of meaning from my intellect and affection to the intellect and affection of my reader, particularly my firstborn granddaughter, Jessica.

Begun: October 6, 2004   Completed: December 10, 2008
Coventry-in-the-Northwoods   Virginia Street
Hayward, Wisconsin   Berkeley, California

Introduction

LOOKING OUT THROUGH WIND-TOSSED yellow birch leaves, the still-green pin oaks, and the glistening red-pine needles, in the near distance I see Callahan Lake, "our" lake. The leaves blow above tall scaly reddish-brown trunks of pines, black-marked white birches, and the few gray oak tree trunks between me in my loft perch and the water I see below. The lake sparkles with early autumn midday sprinkles of sunlight, and I delight in the view from my loft at Coventry-in-the-Northwoods, my special solitary writing place. A woodpecker hammers outside as if it were door-knocking. Chickadees swirl around the bird feeder on the deck two stories below. In this happy-making place where your granddad made sure I had what I wished for—a writing place—I have a book he gave me standing beside my table with its cover as room decoration, a kind of logo: *A Room of Her Own: Women's Personal Spaces*.

I also have fine memories of going with your granddad to a one-woman show in New York drawn from the feminist literary classic by Virginia Woolf, *A Room of One's Own*, from which that title was derived. In the book Woolf writes that for the independence and self-reliance needed to write, a woman needs "five-hundred pounds a year and a room of her own" —financial security and her own private space. I also remember with pleasure my many readings of Virginia Woolf's books, that one and the even more powerful lyrical presentation of feminism, *Three Guineas*, both on my own and with my students. Who I am these days, in these "ripening" years of my life, as writer Meridel Le Sueur called our years of aging, includes being writer, feminist, amateur naturalist, environmentalist, family member, engaged citizen of the United States and of the world, professor emerita, and spiritual seeker. I am free now no longer to duck or dodge or to make apologies for who I am at my core. I think what I am becoming as I write this book on behalf of you and your generation is a contemplative—a twenty-first century contemplative—free to be on my own terms.

At this wonderful cottage and in this special place, I sit seeing out of doors in every direction. Through my skylight above my comfortable chair that both rocks and reclines, I can see the cloudless sky. Through the rails around my safe, cozy, and small second-story spot, which extends out a bit over the living room and has a small quilt from my maternal Grandmother Jones that I treasure hung over one railing, I can see through the double-windowed entry door on the side of the house to the cedar-mulch path going to the lake. Beyond the path I see the small oak, white spruce, sugar maple, and white pine trees I have planted. And through the three heights of windows that make up the front wall, I look out any time I want and see the lake through the trees. From every room in the house, glimpses of the lake are possible and the trees are ever visible. The light, too, I enjoy constantly. Sunlight comes in from the skylight and the large windows all around the house and illuminates my pages and my heart. It makes bright patterns and contrasting shadows that change through the day from eastern morning sun to western sunset across the lake, from summer long-day brilliance through winter's meager light. Nights when the moon is full the trees stand black in the mellow light, the shimmering waves on the lake reflect the moon's light, and indoors looking out it seems an eerie daylight out of doors.

You, Jessica, and the rest of our family members have come here several times with me since we built the house when you were a small baby. In fact, you and your mother, Natasha, Uncle Stiles, and Aunt Tina came here the weekend the moving truck brought the furniture and you helped me settle in—well, your adults did. The very next weekend all of you, along with your dad, Ian Scheerer, and your granddad, Wilson Yates, and his father, Herschel Yates, your great-granddad, came and spent Thanksgiving here—the best Thanksgiving I have ever had. The week between settling in and Thanksgiving I stayed here and watched the lake freeze over for the first time, seeing patches of ice, then a thin crust over the whole lake, then a snowfall covering the entire lake with white. In the spring we have also watched the ice-freezing process reverse: liquid water appears around the edges of the lake, then after a while cracks break through and some puddles appear on top of the ice surface, then some floes of ice appear in chunks, and finally the lake is open water again.

In this chair in my loft, I have rocked you and your cousin, Sage, and your twin brothers, David and Justin. Once when you were just over a year old and still the only grandchild, your Uncle Stiles tiptoed up here very quietly and took a picture of you in my arms, both of us fast asleep in this chair. We already have many family memories in this place, as well as my having my own remembered times of coming here to write, to rest, to restore, to heal, and to become revitalized. I always feel ecstatic as I arrive, driving through the trees that seem to hug the road and to hug my car and me within it; and, when I unlock the door to the house, my spontaneous thought is always, every time, "I love this place!"

Living as close to nature as I do in this house, even though I am mindful that I have all the comforts I need and want of domestic technology and contemporary conveniences, I find myself enjoying simplification and wanting fewer material things. In this more uncomplicated life, I am able to let go of much that distressed me in the past. I have gradually become satisfied with the life I have lived all of my years, able to let many of the disappointments and sadnesses of my earlier life slip away, able to let failed ambition and difficult times at work and in public life fall into place in the past where they belong. I find myself content to enjoy and love our family, my friends, our environment, our communities, our world, and even, paradoxically, to some extent, anyway, to love or to seek understanding with the individual people, the community and government leaders, and the nations and movements that have hurt us or who are our enemies.

So, in this place where I am happy, supremely content, and at a time of life when nature and experience have helped me gain some perspective on living, when I was sixty-four-years old and you were four years old, I began a book for you on what I have learned about living. I finished it at sixty-eight when you were eight.

The idea for this book came from a first-year seminar I taught at the University of Minnesota for several years on "Ethics and the Arts in the University." It was held in the university's Weisman Art Museum, a building that I love very much and was designed by internationally acclaimed architect Frank Gehry. For the class, I used visual art and literary materials, Aristotle's ethics, and Ojibway elder Ignatia Broker's narrative, *Night Flying Woman*, with the students for us to think together about how we learn ethics, how we come to hold our ethical convictions, and how we decide our ways of behaving, the choices we make, and what we will do and be. The course culminated in the students' writing their own ethical credos or papers on their own ethical ideas. One year a student suggested that this assignment take the form of a letter to each one's as-yet-unborn child—most of the students were eighteen- or nineteen-years old. I liked her proposal so much that I used it for all my subsequent classes. You were not yet born and I always intended to write my own paper along with my students on my own ethics for my as-yet-unborn grandchild.

Now I publish it as a book for you. Though you are a young child now, I write for you when you become a young woman. I hope this book will be read by you and by many other young people of your generation, as well as by people of all ages who are interested in learning from reading. It is a book in which I hope to combine writing from my heart as well as from my mind about my love of nature; my love of our family; my intellectual discoveries from reading, travel, research, and observation over the years; and my political, cultural, economic, and environmental concerns for the world. I want to write of the ecstasy of learning to read, as you are experiencing now, and I want to write of the ecstasy of making love, the ecstasy of discovering a new city, a new artist, a new idea, a new morning's snowfall, a new friend, ecstatic experiences that are all of a cloth for me, and not separable realms of knowing, of being. I want to write of mistakes and hurt and failure, as well, for I want you and my other readers to understand that disappointments and broken hearts, sickness and loss of loved ones can be avenues to victorious living that you may assimilate with grace and turn to your advantage, if you so choose.

My previous writing has been scholarly with some features of autobiography—hybrid literature. This book for you from me is wholly autobiographical, drawing on what I have learned from living a scholarly life, and, indeed, from living the whole of my life, the parts that were both defeats and victories, that were mistakes and resolutions, research and common sense, laughter, pain, and especially tears: tears from grief and tears from joy.

PART I

Living, Loving, and Doing Nothing

Autumn

The environing world of a forest clearing is calm and unjarring,
living its own familiar life, so unlike the threatening, unpredictable
environment of the artifact world.

—Erazim Kohak, *The Embers and the Stars*

(From Professor Kohak, the spring of 1963, when I was pregnant with
your mother, I took a course at Boston University on "Existentialism and
Phenomenology"; and he wrote on my term paper, "You are smarter than
the average bear." I have puzzled over his paradoxical comment all the
years since: What on earth did he mean?)

—Nature in Autumn—September sun slants lower in the sky.
Schoolchildren return to their desks and farmers harvest corn.
Blackberries ripen and gourds dry on the vine. A nip cools the air, and
tall-standing maple trees show glimmers of reds among their green
leaves.

1

Living Well

I saw the world as a tree, a gigantic poplar, and myself as a green leaf
clinging to the branch with my slender stalk. When God's wind blew, I
hopped and danced, together with the entire tree.

—Nikos Kazantzakis, *Report to Greco*

**—Nature in Autumn—Last night it rained hard. This morning on my
walk down to the Chief River the ground was wet underfoot and more
leaves had fallen. Also the autumn color was more brilliant than it was
yesterday. On this early October date last year the color was at its peak
of golds and auburns and rosy-reds. Then, trees were full-leafed and
wholly colorful, and greens were to be seen only on the pines and firs
along the roadside. Today there is still green in many oak and maple
leaves but the trees look splotched with orange and yellow all over. Fall
will be a few days later this October than last, and because of the winds
of the last few days, the dazzling colors may not be as fulsome.**

O NE OF THE THINGS I love about my life now is my ability to observe
more keenly. I pay attention to nature in many of its aspects at our
house on the lake, and I enjoy looking up information or identifications in
my unabridged dictionary, my science dictionary, or one of my naturalist
guidebooks to birds, trees, wildflowers, butterflies, or the seasons. I love
reading books of nature writers about this region of the Upper Midwest,
such as Aldo Leopold's *A Sand County Almanac,* John Bates's two volumes
of *A Northwoods Companion,* and Sigurd F. Olson's *The Singing Wilderness
and Listening Point.*

Reading Olson's books, I cannot disregard my feminist self, however, who notices his era's lack of gender-inclusive pronouns and the sexism, albeit of a gentle and unaware kind, when he is exuberant about his young son catching a big trout and then is similarly thrilled when he catches two large fish himself with his wife watching. I want to read pronouns that acknowledge both him and her, and I want women to fish, too, not just watch, as you, Jessica, love to fish with your dad. Yet, I have mellowed since my hottest-headed feminist days of absolutistic judgment to being able to identify cultural sexism and to enjoy as well the lyrical writing and authenticity in articulation of joyful experience in nature as Olson's are.

I also, of course, have near at hand Henry David Thoreau's *Walden,* which I read as a student, though perhaps now I read it more for its message of close appreciation of nature, whereas before I read it for its beauty as literature. Recently, I discovered and read another nature book that I like very much. It is *The Outermost House: A Year of Life on the Great Beach of Cape Cod* by Henry Beston, which is like Thoreau's *Walden* in being set in New England and written as one year's progression through the seasons. Like both those books, this one for me is a movement through a year's seasons of weather and of understanding.

While I read avidly about nature in this new phase of my life—it used to be a running joke about me that if I wanted to know about something (sex, cooking, canoeing, term-paper writing, whatever) that I would get a book about it—I don't have to be an expert to enjoy living in nature. Still, I do want to have an accurate understanding of what I am seeing and perceiving, and I want to know what is required for me to be respectful, conserving, and faithful in my enjoyment of nature as well as in my behavior toward nature.

I speak of living in nature here at the cottage; but, of course, that's a kind of foolish logic, for we live in nature wherever we are. We are a part of nature. Our human bodies are a variety of animal bodies. Our senses of taste and smell and hearing and seeing have kinship with those of other animals. Our responses to sunshine and water and nutrients are related to responses made by plants and animals, made by all other living things, to those elements that sustain and nurture. Likewise, our human reactions to deprivation, to thirst and hunger, to attacks and blows and poison, to sickness and injury and deformity bring suffering and even death as they do to other creatures, indeed, to all of the earth.

Whether we are in humanmade places like crowded cities, isolated hovels, or incarcerating fenced enclosures, or whether we are in forbidding natural places like scorching deserts, frozen tundra, or threatening wet bogs, we are in nature, a part of nature, relating to nature, always in nature. The unpleasant places people make as well as the delightful ones like fine city architecture, beautiful monuments, well-landscaped parks, and this house in the woods are all akin to nature, derived from nature, or made from materials in nature.

Even though we have bad weather at times and once had burst pipes from a freeze, in general, the nature I enjoy at the cottage is the most pleasant of nature, among the most agreeable of nature from a human point of view. Thus, it behooves me to pay attention to nature's needs, not only to observe and to enjoy, but to give back, to care for, to maintain, to honor and respect, to replenish and conserve, to return more than I take from nature.

I have a particular appreciation for trees. We chose this spot as the location for our cottage because of the many trees on the one-acre place. The red pines reminded me of the long-leaf pines in the South where I grew up and which my father planted on our land where he farmed. The birches and aspen were new to me when I came to live "up north" more than half a lifetime ago, and I found them very attractive. Maples and oaks I had known in various places. When the builders cut down and damaged far more trees than needed to build our house, I was quite unhappy, and I set out to replace them manyfold. Each spring I have bought bundles of little indigenous trees from a county agency for planting on our acre: white pines and sugar maples, canoe birch, balsam fir, blue spruce and white spruce, tamarack, plum, high bush cranberry, crabapple, elderberry. Planting trees was new to me in the year 2000, but I have found it exhilarating to see the new growth on the surviving small trees each summer and even more thrilling when dozens of pin oak volunteer seedlings, baby firs, and tiny, tiny white pines have appeared. Though a number of my small trees don't survive, many do; and I will leave on this acre of lakeside land more trees than I have taken away—more trees, and trees that are healthy, well cared for, watered, fed, thinned and pruned, having taken only trees cut for firewood and Christmas decorations, and leaving trees replaced, restored, and replenished.

The trees surrounding this cottage and the house itself are your inheritance—yours, Sage's, David's, and Justin's. I do not mean that I want to limit you to coming to this particular place and only revering these particular trees—I mean I hope you also love the trees, these trees and all the other trees that you will see and know. Loving the trees can be a very powerful part of loving life. Paying attention to trees necessarily means paying attention to light and water and nutrients that sustain the trees and all other forms of life.

In 2004 the Nobel Peace Prize was won by Wangari Maathai (pronounced wan-GAH-ree mah-DHE-YEE), an environmentalist from Kenya. The first African woman to receive the Nobel Peace Prize, she was described in a *New York Times* headline, "Like a Tree, Unbowed," and she was cited for "starting an environmental movement that has planted 30 million trees in Africa," as well as having campaigned aggressively for women's rights and for greater democracy in Kenya, efforts for which she had been persecuted, attacked, and even jailed at times. Understanding the implications of deforestation all over Africa, she started the tree-planting effort in Kenya as beneficial both for the environment and for women's rights. After all, as she likes to point out, it is African women who go out each morning with small axes to cut and gather wood for the fuel for preparing the morning's food for their families.[1]

Thinking of African women, I remembered when we visited your mother when she was a Peace Corps Volunteer in Letlhakeng, Botswana and saw the women walking down the dusty roads toward the village carrying bundles of sticks on their heads. It was not at all exotic as my tourist mind first saw it, but totally practical daily wood-gathering work for cooking food. Another of my tourist viewpoints expressed in Africa that now brings an embarrassed blush to my cheeks was my saying to Natasha soon after we arrived in the Botswana capital, Gaborone, in August, which is winter in southern Africa, "Oh, someone has a wood fire burning here! I love the smell of wood smoke!" Natasha replied with indignant feeling, "Mother! Everyone has a wood fire here!"

---

1. Marc Lacey, "Like a Tree, Unbowed." *The New York Times*, October 9, 2004, p. A5.

2

Love Is Born, Love Lives On

All life contains the secret of Life. "In this acorn," the mystic Julian of
Norwich said, "is everything there is."

—Joan Chittister, *Illuminated Life:*
Monastic Wisdom for Seekers of Light

**—Nature in Autumn—Tonight I listen to the rain. It has rained all af-
ternoon. The last two days were unseasonably warm and sunny. I spent
most of both of them out-of-doors. I swept leaves, trimmed plants,
brought in wood, and, most especially, dipped water out of and cleaned
out the canoe.**

IN JANUARY 2001, WE lost the last of all four of our parents with the
death of your great-grandfather Yates, or Dad to me. Your granddad
Wilson Yates and I thus became the older generation. For me the year just
gone before was momentous. I had passed my sixtieth-birthday milestone
with upbeat celebrations and supportive greetings and gifts from family
and friends. I had resolved to set in motion a phased retirement plan
from my University of Minnesota professorship and, paradoxically, with
an end-time in sight, I had a really satisfying year of teaching. And I had
the unqualified new joy of your being born, daughter of my daughter,
firstborn of my firstborn, Jessica.

The year that you were born there were enormous changes in the
world. Scientists and thoughtful people like your mother began to realize
the urgency of rescuing our environment from the pollution and greed
and abuse that have poisoned or limited or destroyed our earth's supplies

of clean water, fresh air, nutrients, and shelter for people and creatures and trees. Political power is sometimes overwhelmed by commercial and corporate power, and leaders of both governments and international businesses sometimes serve their own self-interest, personal aggrandizement, ownership, and accumulation of wealth rather than the global network of humankind to which their officeholding in governments and business should obligate them.

The year that you were born, religions, the traditional carriers of ethical values and spiritual meaning, had also changed dramatically from the time of your great-grandfather's birth in 1910 until his death in your first year of life. Outright wars or military skirmishes like war were carried out in the name of religions—Protestant versus Catholic, Muslim opposing Jew, Orthodox Christian in conflict with Muslim, anti-Buddhist, anti-Hindu—in many world locations. In the United States by 2000 and to the present, there is an unprecedented mix of religions, the faithful practicing their religions or at least maintaining features of their religious cultures as they blend with other Americans in their educational, social, and political settings. There are also bigotry, antagonism, and sometimes violence against groups singled out for their religion, and damage is thereby done to the whole society.

But also in the year that you were born there was, and continues to be, love. You were born of love, the lovemaking of your parents, and into love—the delight and care and teaching and watchfulness of your mother and father, your four grandparents, four great-grandparents, two couples of uncles and aunts, godparents, and many more family members, friends, and relatives. You were born into the love that is personal and individual, and you are much loved; but you were also born into the love that is principled and universal. For some people that Love is spelled with a capital letter and seen as deity. For others it is the highest form of connection and communication between and among human beings. For everyone it is necessary to life itself, literally to staying alive.

Love is not simple, nor is it easy. Love is always in combat with hatred, perpetually threatened to be overcome by greed, abuse of power and resources, selfishness, isolation, narrow-mindedness, neglect, negativity, unconcern, or even lack of awareness.

In all our years to come, I intend to grow with you in love, explore all the ways that love is possible, and to search for ways, both ordinary and unorthodox, to be respectful, open-minded, unselfish, gracious, aware and engaged, and mutually supportive with you. And alongside you, I want us to be loving toward our world, our family, nature, and our country, our friends, people we don't know, people we don't like very much, people we don't understand, and people who don't treat us well. I want us to learn together to be tolerant, peace-making, and generous. I want to teach you what I know that is good, and I already know that I have much to learn from you.

More than anything else, oh, my dear Jessica, what I most want to give you is love, my love for you and support for your own ability to love deeply—uncomplicated, unmeasured, sustaining love. Already I receive a bounty of love from you, more than I could have imagined was possible before you were born!

3

Gold Standard of Love

Then God said, "Let the earth put forth vegetation: plants yielding seed, and fruit trees of every kind on earth that bear fruit with the seed in it."

—Genesis 1:11

—Nature in Autumn—Warm and sunny October days yesterday and today. I take my morning walk down to the Chief River with a bounce in my step. As the stream runs off from the lake on one side of the road through a huge culvert, the water pools on the other side after draining over a rock face into a waterfall of a few feet. In this pooling of the river water, there is usually wildlife. A few days ago I saw three otters swimming around the pond, diving in and coming up several feet away. One day I saw the great blue heron flying over just beyond that pool and I thought a little regretfully that it will be gone, will have flown south before long. That large blue-gray bird with its long curving neck, fringe of black flight feathers and pointy black plumes over its eyes I often see at this place on the river all through the summer. It seems to live here. Today there was no wildlife in sight, but I did see changing foliage that gladdened my heart. Individual big brown oak leaves fell in my path and I wondered at their symmetry. I walked by the special enormous maple that I love standing alone in a clearing and noted that it now has only a few leaves at the bottom and they are subtle, very beautiful pinks ranging from mauve to cerise. Having hoped to catch the "peak" of the autumn leaf color, I realize that I have been a kind of perfectionist—a failing of mine I have to watch and scotch. Seeking the "peak" is relative. Now that many leaves have fallen, the chokecherry on our acre and all the birches having lost nearly all their leaves, the "peak" may have passed, but the colors of the remaining leaves are still very beautiful. Perfectionism can be a downfall characteristic—autumn leaves are beautiful at all their times.

A T LEAST A PART of my enjoyment of trees comes from the influence of my beloved father-in-law, your great-granddad Yates. Dad was a woodworker. He made beautiful wooden boxes and wooden lamps, candlestick holders, chess pieces, bowls, and other items turned on the lathe. All our family members treasure having them, especially since his death, for we know there will be no more. He loved the wood he worked, as his father had before him, and he also loved the trees from which the wood came.

One memorable day after autumn had come, when he lived in the assisted-living complex on Bryant Avenue in Minneapolis, he phoned and asked if I would take him out in the car to find an oak tree, the bare high-reaching branches that he could see in the distance from his third-floor window. I went immediately, of course, for I loved learning about trees and other aspects of nature from him. It did not take us long to find the tree, and we enjoyed sitting beside its huge trunk and looking skyward through the tracery of its many branches.

After Dad died, I realized he was our gold standard of love.

One of our favorite family pictures is of him holding you in the birthing room at the hospital within an hour of your birth, your uncle Stiles's hand protectively positioned just below Dad's hand under your small head, which was engulfed in one of those silly little hats hospitals put on newborns. Dad's radiant face has a smile only for you, his firstborn great-grandchild, daughter of his much loved only granddaughter. The rest of us—your new parents, grandparents, uncle—might as well not have been in the room.

Dad's smile, though, that smile of singular focus on the person to whom he is giving his full attention, we all knew. It was the joyous experience of us all: family, neighbors in his small Missouri town, lifelong friends, acquaintances old and new. My sister-in-law Mary Ellen explained him to one of the other guests at your parents' wedding this way, "Our father-in-law is very easy to love!"

In Alice Walker's novel, *The Color Purple*, what the character Celie says of Shug, her beloved woman friend who orchestrates Celie's liberation, was true of Dad: "[H]e know how to love somebody back!"[1]

Dad's overpowering love was different from mere charm. We all know people, men especially, in my opinion (former President George W. Bush comes to mind), whose pleasantness, personal warmth, nick-naming, delightful teasing, name-remembering, unwavering eye-contact, humor, focus totally on you with attention to and comment on your appearance or your achievements or your interests and behaviors are mere charm. They are all behaviors meant to serve these people's own self-centered goals. These are the men that the debauched privileged character in the television series, *Brideshead Revisited*, adapted by John Mortimer from the novel by Evelyn Waugh, called, "Ch-ch-ch-ch-charming!" Such people's captivating attentiveness is charming, but superficially so, even emotionally fraudulent.

Dad was charming, all right; but his delight in whomever he was talking to reached to his core and was fully sincere. His charm was genuine. His humanity and care for others were a lifelong development of love of all those people around him and all with whom he came into contact.

Dad lived with his wife, Gertrude Wilson Yates, more than sixty years in Matthews, Missouri, a tiny town in a small region of Mississippi River delta country in southeast Missouri called the Bootheel because it sticks down into Arkansas in a bootheel shape as if it should be a part of Arkansas. Dad's legendary father-in-law, "Papa Wilson" to his grandsons, your granddad and his brother Marshall, had brought cotton farming as far north in the delta region as it had come. He was revered for his pioneering agricultural work that, along with President Franklin D. Roosevelt's Little River District Drainage Project, brought abounding prosperity to the area. A blustery and demanding man, the senior Wilson must have been—I did not ever meet him, for he died before your granddad and I were married—a contrast to his kindly, gracious, and soft-spoken son-in-law.

Dad had come to Matthews originally as a weekend college-student Methodist minister to serve the church to which the Wilson family belonged. He was quite handsome, a delightful, talented, dashing young man, and soon he was wooing Miss Gertrude Wilson, three years his se-

---

1. Alice Walker, *The Color Purple*. Boston: Harcourt Brace Jovanovich, 1982, p. 139.

nior. Before long, the young Herschel Yates and schoolteacher Gertrude Wilson eloped, apparently out of fear of the disapproval of her father, though the record is not clear and the collective family memory is vague as to the reason why. Nevertheless, the young couple settled in Matthews early in their married life, into the house next door to the Wilson home and lived there the rest of the lives of the older Wilson couple and of Gertrude Wilson Yates. Herschel and Gertrude brought up their two sons in Matthews next door to Dad's in-laws, and Dad variously taught school, served as a social worker, and farmed, as well as continuing to be a lay minister, and was even the town mayor for one term. Over those years, he endeared himself to everyone in Matthews, becoming the "town priest" as someone called him. He not only served the Methodists, but everyone in the town and some throughout the county as confidante, counselor, informant, officiant at weddings and funerals, sharer of his garden vegetables, and eager conversationalist about Democratic politics, economics, all forms of government, farming, and religion. Well read and well informed about the issues of the day, he kept up with current affairs and current intellectual life in the United States. He was an unpretentious man, very dignified, flexible, knowledgeable, and confident, though not a bone in his body was arrogant or smug. Although a "small-town man," he had a poised sophistication that wore well everywhere he went.

Wilson remembers his father particularly, and with pride, as the minister who spoke out on controversial issues of the time, issues of racial equality, world peace, and international cooperation. Though he was "different," as his wife might have said, his genial disposition and genuine loving kindness toward everyone won even the hearts of those who deeply disagreed with him. And his was a time and place where the "other" to his Methodist and Democratic stances might be Baptists and Republicans. I remember that, after my mother-in-law's funeral, Dad said with some amazement that one of the men in town was willing to be a pallbearer at his wife's funeral, "and he is a Republican!"

It always seemed a little poignant to me, though, that Dad stayed in southeastern Missouri where his well-to-do father-in-law was a town pillar and where Dad seemed to have lived in the shadow of the older man. Dad did not ever go to seminary, as he clearly had wanted to when he set out to be a minister, and he read theological and religious books voraciously. (It seemed perfectly clear to me that your granddad was fulfilling his own father's ambition when he went to a theological seminary and studied to be a minister, and nobody had a bigger smile than Dad's as late in his life he sat on the front row at Wilson's installation as seminary president.) It also seemed to me, for many years, that Dad was unfairly dominated by his wife and her father as they stayed on in the town where E. W. Wilson had accumulated wealth and influence. He seemed to have been too agreeable, too easy to sway. Yet it was Dad, without any question, who was most beloved by both family and townspeople.

In her last years, I was very close to my mother-in-law; but the first years Wilson and I were married, I was awed by her rather formal manner and kept a little distant from her. I thought of her as rather authoritarian, circumscribed, and limited by her provincial attitudes and values of her small town. She was—always—outspoken, definite in her opinions, and insistent that other people share her opinions or puzzled if they didn't. She was not dogmatic or hostile, though; but she was "proper," not self-revelatory, and she did not share her own feelings at all well. I remember her once saying of Natasha as a teenager, and I realized she was also speaking of herself, "Just because she doesn't express her feelings very readily doesn't mean she doesn't have them!"

Dad was "easy to love," as Mary-Ellen said much later, but I had to take a while to figure out my mother-in-law. Clearly I was marrying her golden boy, her firstborn son and heir, and I had to find my place with her; though, on the other hand, the first time Wilson took me to Missouri to meet them—*after* we had gotten engaged—he pushed me through the front door first, and my future mother-in-law met me at the door and hugged me. Our relationship in those first years took some work on both our parts, but in the end my mother-in-law and I understood one another as together beloved members of our family.

I remember at the time of Dad's death, the chaplain at Dad's residence phoned our house and engaged me in what turned out to be a very helpful counseling session. She mentioned that Dad had said to her he had needed to take care of his wife during her last years. The chaplain felt she must have been a frail and needful person. "What? My mother-in-law?" I said in astonishment. "My mother-in-law was loving and kind, but, as our kids said of her, 'She is a very take-charge kind of person.' She was much the dominant partner in the marriage! Her father had the money and land, and she was his 'boy', he not having a son. She was a very determined, decisive person." And the wise young chaplain replied, "But in their intimate life, he may have been the leader, he may have been in charge." Gulp, I thought, like the child learning with initial sex education that its parents must have had sex if they had children, my parents-in-law had good sex? And he was the leader?

Of course! Clearly, they loved one another very, very deeply. Wilson remembers their giggling in the next room to his and Marshall's when everyone had gone to bed. And I remember the countless times one would phone us with great concern and solicitude when the other spouse was ill or injured. I remember the mountains of presents one would have for the other under the Christmas tree and the delight they would each have about finding just the right gifts for the other. And I remember the love mantra between my parents-in-law that has become a routine in our next generation families that started with the two of them. "I love you the most," one of them would tease, sounding almost like an adolescent. "No, I love you the most," the other one would retort quickly. And your uncle Stiles, beloved grandson, has taught his small daughter the exchange: "I love you the most, Sage!" "No, I love you the most, Daddy!"

It was a special privilege for me to be Dad's caregiver the last two-and-a-half years of his life. I became a better person, I felt, from having been close to him during those last of his years. We moved him out of his Matthews home, cleaned it up and sold it, and brought him to live near our Minneapolis house at Walker Place, a seniors complex. It was the summer of your parents' wedding. My own parents had died and my mother-in-law had been dead for three years. I would never have expected to play the family role of between-the-generations caregiver those years, so busy had I been with my career with its teaching and publishing and officeholding, its travel opportunities and times abroad on faculty exchanges. Instead, I found this period of family caregiver to be among the happiest of my life.

First, when your parents, Natasha and Ian, fell in love and decided to marry, I applied my organizational skills, my management ability, and even my literary skills to helping the two of them have a spectacular wedding ceremony and reception at the Weisman Art Museum. Likewise, that same summer, I again took the lead in finding a place for Dad to live and helping persuade him to move near us. For two years before that I had taken responsibility for packing up and "taking Christmas" to Dad in the Missouri house, organizing from Minnesota the food, the decorations, and the presents. Now I was able to help him make the change to living in Minnesota.

When Dad lived at Walker Place, we all pitched in—Wilson, Natasha, Ian, Tina, Stiles, and I—but it fell to me to do the details of making it all work. I really cared that he be happy and that he felt his needs were met. Wilson bought his groceries, but I went by often to check on his household requirements, to defrost his refrigerator, to take him food he particularly liked, to bring him postage stamps and note cards to write, to persuade him to get his laundry done, or to have dinner with him at least every Thursday night. It turned out in that period, though he was financially comfortable, his cost of living was much greater in Minneapolis than it had been in his little town and that worried him. He didn't want to pay what it cost, for example, to have the nurse check on him, to have his laundry done, or, the sticking point, to eat in the building's lovely subsidized restaurant. Finally, I just bought meal tickets—along with inviting myself to dinner every Thursday night—and told him he would be wasting my money if he didn't go downstairs to dinner. He was chagrined—but went to his dinners. We had him come to our house for family events, and we all showed up for every one of the special events for families at Walker Place. Once I had him over to our house to help me repot plants, but he tired quickly and was very frustrated with himself, so I regretfully took him home to Walker Place. The first year I offered to give him a birthday party for "about 12 or so" of his new friends at the residence plus our family. "Just 12?" he exclaimed, "but I wouldn't know how to pick them!" I ended up posting an invitation with a sign-up sheet on the central bulletin board for people who wanted to come—and served birthday lunch in the building party room to 59 people!

The next year I just offered coffee and cake to everyone in Walker Place for Dad's birthday party, and it did seem as if nearly everyone came! Similarly, at the memorial service we held in the building's chapel after we returned from Dad's funeral and burial in Missouri, the place was packed and people commented that the usual crowd there for such services was only about a dozen.

When Dad died, I was not at his bedside or in the hospital as I had been for my mother and for my mother-in-law, and my grief was deep; but I also had a sense of satisfaction or peacefulness that I had not had with the other parental deaths. I had done what I could for him; and Wilson, his beloved son, was in Minneapolis and had spent long happy, companionable hours with Dad in his hospital room. That was very good for the two of them, father and son. Also, at Walker Place where Dad had returned from the hospital to hospice care just two days before his death, Wilson reported that when he brought Dad into his hospice room and found Stiles, Tina, Natasha, Ian, and you as a nine-month-old baby, Jessica, waiting there to welcome him, a big smile lit up his face. We all knew how much he was loved and were all together in our returning our love to him.

I have never been happier doing something. My caring for Dad was authentic and real, "genuine" as my mother would have said. To this man of enormous kindness, gentle manner, generosity, and love, I had been able to mirror back to him a bit of his spirit with my homely tasks of seeing to his care and of facilitating our family's being with him. At his last birthday party when he turned 90 and I had invited his sister Jane, his other son Marshall, and other grandchild Michael to come from out of town as a surprise for the weekend's partying, he told the people at his table at dinner with that wonderful twinkle in his eye, "She did all this! It was her idea! We don't say that 'in-law' any more. She is my daughter!"

4

Ways of Learning

I can't imagine a wilderness that would have as much to say to me as
Grandpa's garden did: the floral scents that intimated something about
the ways of ladies as well as flowers, the peach tree that made legible
the whole idea of fruit and seed, the vegetables that had so much to say
about the getting of food and money, . . .

—Michael Pollen, *Second Nature: A Gardener's Education*

—Nature in Autumn—Yesterday, early in the morning, as I went out to
town in my car there were snowflakes in the air. It had rained most of
the last two days, and the colors of leaves still on the trees had darkened
from the brilliance of their cherry-reds, bright oranges and yellows,
magenta and golden to more somber shades of cinnamon, umber, bur-
gundy, copper, burnt orange, and rusty brown. I still had a few small
trees at the house from my last spring's county-source lot. Because they
were spruce and fir, I decided to plant them in pots for the winter when
I came back from town and give them to our family households to use as
little Christmas trees to be planted here next spring. I put out birdseed
for the chickadees, blue jays, woodpeckers, and sparrows I have seen at
my feeder in view below my loft; and I made a mental note that the loons
I have heard these nights may soon go south for warmer dwellings.

Later in the day yesterday, as I walked by my favorite maple tree
alone in its clearing, it was bare: no leaves at all.

Today, a day later, I watch the leaves fall. There are only a few, yellow and brown, just one falls now and then, or a few at a time, from

the birch trees and oak I see through my high windows from my loft writing spot. It is a gray day and a north wind is strong. The waves are white-capping on the lake and blowing unusually southerly, making the water look a fluid silver and slate gray. I think of the two huge bur oaks at the bottom of our garden in Minneapolis, which are a part of a grove along our alley in our neighborhood yards and are said to have been there before houses 150 years ago or more. I rely on those oak trees for images of strength and endurance, just as I count on these red pines, birches, and pin oaks before me in my writing loft at the cottage to provide reassuring images of seasonal order and change.

M Y BROTHER WAS A forestry major at his college. I was a philosophy major. Once he came to visit me when we were both students, and he asked, somewhat disdainfully, "In my lifetime, I am going to plant about a million trees. What are you going to do with philosophy?"

My brother did indeed plant trees, probably many millions of trees, as a ranger for the U.S. Forest Service and later in his private business as a rose nursery owner. He has been very successful. I became a professor and planted ideas, so I felt successful, too; but I have told my brother recently that now I am planting trees. I believe my one acre can make a difference, and I love my tree planting.

However, my particular education made a difference too. By both my example and what I hope I can teach you and Sage, David, and Justin, I urge you to become educated as much as you possibly can and in as many ways as you can. For me, college itself opened up the world to me. I loved college. I sang in the college choir, I acted in college theater, I worked on the newspaper. Doing those things made me understand music, theater, and journalism better for the rest of my life. I studied subjects I hadn't known existed before—anthropology, sociology, psychology, even philosophy, which I chose to emphasize. I studied languages: Latin, French, and German. Before college I did not have the opportunity to study a language other than English, and it was too late for me to become as fluent as I wished to be. I hope you will learn languages other than your own soon, while you are a young child. Your mother and father already are beginning to help you learn Spanish and German. You went to a language camp last summer. I have loved learning German and your father, his father, and grandmother, your great-grandmother Freda, speak German, Freda having spoken German in her home as a child. All of us in your family who know some German would enjoy speaking German with you. I also want you to learn Spanish, for Spanish is the first language of an increasingly large number of Americans, and it would benefit us all to speak Spanish as well as English. Knowing another language helps a person think differently, helps one better understand the people for whom it is their first language. My studying German at Millsaps College many years before was directly pertinent to my desire to go to Germany as an exchange professor, which I ended up doing three different semesters in 1989 and the 1990s.

My reasons for studying both philosophy and German as a college student were reasons of affection and friendship along with inquiry into the subjects. When I chose my philosophy major, it was as much because I adored the philosophy professor, Bond Fleming, as a man as that I liked the subject. I appreciated and trusted him very much from the first course I took with him. When I decided to take German, it was at the urging of a good friend of mine, Kent Prince, who had greatly enjoyed German before I had. He pointed out that our German professor's method was conversational and that we had available to us a language lab and *Deutsche Tische*, a table in the college cafeteria where students and the professor regularly spoke German. I had confidence in my friend's opinions, so it was quite easy to take his suggestion. Of course, one needs to enjoy the field of study for its own sake when one makes a commitment to it, but reasons of affection and trust in another person's judgment are not bad reasons for making educational choices. The benefits for me were enormous in studying both philosophy and German, the subjects we came to share; and I am still in touch with my ninety-five-plus-year-old beloved philosophy professor whom I visited this year in Atlanta and my college contemporary friend Kent who persuaded me to take German.

Formal education has great benefits, but there are many other kinds of education as well. Travel and observation, paying attention, exploring, asking questions, getting involved, seeking new experiences all can provide education. When I was a teenager, I was very fortunate to be involved in both the 4-H Club and the Future Homemakers of America (FHA) at the state and national levels. In my cosmopolitan, urban setting in the present, people tend to joke about these organizations for rural children; but for me growing up, I learned from 4-H and FHA invaluable lessons of public life, of leadership, and about the lives of people quite different from my family and me. In the 4-H Club, I made cupcakes in one state conference cooking competition and did not win a thing; but another time I won the state public-speaking contest. As state president of the Future Homemakers of America, I traveled with a small group of official delegates by train in sleeping compartments from Jackson, Mississippi to Chicago for a national convention. I had to dress up and wear a hat to board the train, thus learning the proper travel etiquette of the time—the 1950s. The next summer in an FHA delegation, I went to Ames, Iowa, for a convention. With delegates from each state in the nation, these conventions opened my eyes to many different ways we could be Americans and how different our cultures in states and regions are. I remember that the delegates from Hawaii brought leis to the leaders, which fascinated me and alerted me to the fact of different flowers flourishing in different climates. I also remember meeting another "Gayle Graham" from Kansas. One of the other Mississippi delegates in our group, Mary Ann Mobley, a state president two years before I was, became Miss America not long afterward and later became a professional actress, giving our local people a celebrity to enjoy having known.

Also, both as a teenager and a young adult, I was deeply involved in my church; and the Methodist Church was probably the single greatest influence on my life, particularly my education. From the leaders with whom I worked in the Methodist Youth Fellowship (MYF) and the Methodist Student Movement (MSM), I learned variations of religious thought that gave me comparisons for the conservatism and even fundamentalism that were a part of my childhood. I learned early openness, tolerance of people, respect for the wider world, theological liberalism, and social activism from church-related experiences; and these influences were greatly beneficial for me as I grew to be the person I wanted to become. I served as the national president of the MSM and traveled a great deal to numerous U.S. settings in that office, which also allowed me to meet and work with students from colleges and universities all over the country. New York and Washington became familiar places to me; and through the MSM council I made friends from around the country. I spent a summer in a Methodist student "work camp" in Jersey City in 1958, which introduced me to the New York City environment as a summer resident. I had spent the previous summer at a church-related theater in Ohio and enjoyed acting with students from several states and being a part of a professional company that survived on a shoestring budget. This experience taught me that acting is not only the work of glamorous stars from Broadway and Hollywood but also that of trained and dedicated people who work hard at their art and achieve marvelously without necessarily receiving great monetary rewards or public acclaim.

After I completed the advanced degrees necessary for my profession, I realized I learned at least as much from experience as I had learned in the classroom. When Wilson, Stiles, Natasha, and I went to live in England for our first sabbatical, we learned most from just being there. Within weeks both five-year-old Stiles and nine-year-old Natasha spoke with beautiful English accents from their playground experience on Mulberry Close in Cambridge. Their elders learned British English and British culture more slowly perhaps but very surely by living in our Cambridge neighborhood, making friends with local people, eating scones, and drinking tea for "elevenses"—what Americans would call morning coffee break—with local professors in the university library cafeteria, and riding the red double-decker bus to the "city centre" to do our shopping.

That first sabbatical summer—never having been to Europe before and eager to experience the historical sites, the art and architecture, the people of different nations and their languages, foods, and customs—Wilson and I put the two young children into our newly purchased little VW station wagon and went to Amsterdam, France, Switzerland, Germany, and Belgium, seeing all the art museums we could find with Stiles and Natasha in tow. A few months later in Edinburgh, on entering the National Museum of Scotland, we burst our buttons with pride when five-year-old Stiles went straight up to a guard and asked, "Do you have any Van Goghs in this museum?"

We also learned about architecture and art by traveling around East Anglia that sabbatical year. Wilson's and my "free time" activity was driving—on the unfamiliar left side of the roads—out to ancient parish churches in villages—March and Isleham, Abingdon, Lavenham, and Saffron Walden, and more—or going down to London on the train to see more church architecture and to visit more art museums. Down on our hands and knees we did brass rubbings of some thirteenth-, fourteenth-, and fifteenth-century monumental memorial brasses set into the cold stone floors of numerous English churches, cathedrals, and colleges, thus learning history in that unusual way.

On the children's autumn school holiday we took a trip to England's Lake District; on spring holiday, we went to Florence and Rome. When we went back to Cambridge for a term when Stiles was ten and Natasha was fourteen, we went to Russia, to what were then Leningrad and Moscow, during the fall school holiday, which coincided with Stiles's eleventh birthday. We have birthday dinner pictures of Stiles and Natasha, the only children in the tour group, looking somewhat puzzled as they were surrounded with lots of empty adult-drink bottles for wine and beer and sitting before a cake with one big candle. Our Intourist guide, also named Natasha, had scoured Moscow to find a candle, because birthday candles were not a customary part of Russian birthday celebrations.

On the spring trip to Italy during our first European stay, Stiles, by then six years old, balked at the front of the Academia in Florence after a few too many visits to architecture and art galleries and insisted he was not going one step farther. Coaxing him to come in and see Michelangelo's sculpture of the biblical David, Wilson told Stiles the story of the boy David becoming a hero by fighting the giant Goliath. Stiles finally agreed to see only the sculpture of David; so, with his arms folded and pouting, the boy walked right past all the other works, a whole aisle of Michelangelo masterpieces, and came to David. He stood quietly and then walked all around, looked and looked and then asked his dad to tell him the story again. He was captivated. A few days later, back at our home on Mulberry Close, I went up to his room at bedtime when he was supposed to be dressing for bed. What I saw as I stood in his doorway was my young son, dressed in his pajama top only, posing in front of the full-length mirror in his room in the stance of the statue. "Mum," he said when he saw me, in his wonderful full-blown British accent, "I look a bit like David, don't you think?!"

(The summer after that year, however, when we were back in the United States and going South on family visits, Stiles and Natasha insisted they wanted to go to Disney World in Florida: "We haven't been *anywhere* this year," they whined!)

I learned much over my lifetime through many different ways of finding out, observing, studying, doing research, and living thoughtfully—as well as making some mistakes and trying to correct them. My hope for you is that you will take advantage of all the ways you have available to you to learn all that you possibly can. We are fortunate in our family to be privileged in ways that allow us to travel, to take special lessons in the subjects we want to learn, like dance, art, and gymnastics that your mother has arranged for you in recent years, as well as to go to formal schooling. I believe the price we need to pay for participating in such privilege is both to take as much advantage of it as we possibly can and then to share freely what we have learned with all the people we touch.

5

Aristotle and the Ojibway

In search of my own reality, I seek the power of the rock,
the magic of the water, the religion of the tree, the color of the wind,
and the enigma of the horizon.

—George Morrison, artist who was Ojibway

—Nature in Autumn—The week before Thanksgiving of 2000, the year
our cottage was just built, I literally watched the lake freeze over outside
our cottage windows. First it was open water. Then patches of ice appeared. Falling snow piled up on the ice patches but melted on hitting
places where the deeper water had not yet frozen. Before long there was
a skim of ice over the whole lake but it was still patterned in sections of
snow white and ice gray. Our boat and dock were still stuck in the lake's
ice and needed to be broken free and brought ashore. By Thanksgiving
Day, our lake was entirely frozen over and completely covered with
snow.

As you plan for your adult commitments as a young woman, Jessica,
choose a philosopher or a poet or another important thinker to believe in, to study thoroughly, to learn well. Oh, you don't need to pick
just one, but start with one. And choose a culture other than your own
to learn about, to engage with, and to be excited about. It is all right to
change your mind and pick a different thinker or culture, abandon one
or both, or add more to your first ones after you have learned more and
become better informed. What is important is to study deeply and hard
about what at first might be a challenge.

The philosopher I was first attracted to was Plato. I liked the literary dialogue form of his work, and I was attracted to his philosophy of idealism. Plato was the originator of the idealistic tradition, the understanding that primary reality comes as ideas or forms or abstract notions. Later I was enamored with twentieth-century existentialist philosophy, particularly that of Jean-Paul Sartre and Albert Camus, both of whom were creative writers as well as philosophers. Existentialism turned previous philosophy on its head with its assertion that primary reality is meaning, not something outside human cognition, neither abstract principles of the idealists nor natural substance or material reality of the contrasting empiricist tradition, but the positing of meaning. "Existence precedes essence" is a kind of encapsulation of existentialism, meaning that a person or thing has to be living, to exist, before ideas or understanding can be applied to it, essence gleaned or attributed.

When I studied the German language, I wanted to learn about the literature and music and history of the German-speaking countries, Austria and Germany, about how people behaved and what was important to German-speaking people. For me learning another language opens up the culture or cultures of the people whose language it is. It gives one a fuller view of the possibilities of being human, a basis of comparison of one's own language and culture, and a wider knowledge of choices people have made and of differing patterns of lives people live under conditions, in climates, and in circumstances that vary in different places in the world.

The summer after I was a college sophomore, I became immersed in urban New York area culture, particularly that of the Puerto Ricans whose neighborhood church was served by the work-camp project in which I participated. Coincidentally for me, that was the summer that Leonard Bernstein's Broadway musical set in New York Puerto Rican culture, *West Side Story*, was running for its last weeks. I was able to see this soon-to-be-contemporary-classic play derived from Shakespeare's *Romeo and Juliet* on its last night on Broadway. It was fun that night to learn the theater culture detail that the curtain does not close on the last night of a new play's run as it normally does other nights, signaling the play's ongoing life even as this run of it closes.

It was also fun to be reminded that in the art of the theater the power of the dramatized story can reinforce a simple truth we need to hear over and over again: in this case the victory of love over all the odds of hostility and bigotry and discord. The tragic story of Romeo and Juliet from

Shakespeare is replicated on the streets of New York in Puerto Rican fac-
tions of ethnic gangs in the *West Side Story* musical version. It is the classic
portrayal of young lovers from warring communities who are fated from
the start to separation over their devotion to each other across culturally
forbidden lines of clan or race or tribe or faith. In this case, they are from
the rival gangs of Sharks and Jets. Nevertheless, theirs is the same story of
love bravely fresh and hopeful in a young man and woman who choose
death together rather than separation and the thwarting of their love. The
promising love song melody of "I just met a girl named Maria . . ." joined
my romantic vocabulary alongside Juliet's balcony scene with "Wherefore
art thou, Romeo?"

When I first planned my seminar for my first-year students on
"Ethics and the Arts in the University," the philosopher I chose for them
to study deeply was Aristotle, the culture other than their own, that of the
local Native Americans, the Ojibway. None of the students that particular
year was Native American, and the Greece of Aristotle was so far back in
history that we were distantly separated by time as well as by people. We
connected our focus on ethics with the classic Greek philosopher and the
Ojibway people's narrative, along with some literature we read and art we
saw in our museum meeting place through our own thinking, writing,
and discussion of what we were learning together.

Aristotle's ethics is one of the foundational frameworks for considering behavior in European cultures and all those cultures derived from
Europe, including ours in America. Aristotle's ethics is familiar to many
educated people from the generalized principle known as the Golden
Mean—the idea that one's choice of action should be in the middle
ground between extremes. For example, courage is the mean between
rashness or impetuousness and cowardice. The Golden Mean that courage exemplifies, as well as the courageous behavior that follows from
practicing it, Aristotle calls a virtue. Rashness in one extreme—tilting
forward to action without enough forethought or preparation—and cowardice as its opposite—shrinking from taking action or shirking choosing
responsibility—are the vices that contrast on the extremes with the virtue
of courage.

The ancient Greek philosopher Aristotle (384–322 BCE) was the
student of Plato (427?–347? BCE), whose *Dialogues* precede Aristotle's
work in establishing Western philosophy as it has been passed down
through the centuries. Aristotle in turn was the tutor of Alexander the

Great (356–323 BCE), who became the very influential conqueror and ruler from Macedonia in what is now Greece. Alexander the Great carried Greek culture, language, and learning to many other parts of the known world of his time and ushered in what is known as the Hellenistic Age or the period of worldwide Greek influence. It is this chain of intellectual and political effects that led in part to the European-shaped regions of the world having the basic cultural forms they do today.

In Plato's *Dialogues*, through dramatic interactions written as teacher-student conversations, the philosopher purports to record the wisdom of his teacher, Socrates, whose famous dictum is "The unexamined life is not worth living." Plato wrote of metaphysics, nature, politics, and education with the point of view always being on abstract ideals as more basic to reality than material forms. Ultimate reality is ideas in Plato's scheme of things.

Plato started the Academy near Athens in 386 BCE, wrote and taught there for the rest of his lifetime, and Aristotle studied with him at the Academy. Through the history of Western philosophy, Plato is thought of as the founder of philosophical idealism and Aristotle as the founder of philosophical empiricism. Aristotle came to reject Plato's abstract theories of ideas and developed far more practical systems of analysis of nature, science, human psychology, aesthetics, social behavior, and politics by means of observation, language, and logic. He worked out the first systematic scheme of logic, a rational tool that still forms the base of the complex discipline of logic today, as well as his thoroughgoing system of ethics.

In recent years the Greek philosophies of Socrates, Plato, and Aristotle have become greatly amplified for me by travel. I have visited Greece three times, twice to attend conferences at Aristotle University in Thessaloniki as the guest of my friend Youli Theodosiadou, and most recently on a small-ship adventure with your granddad to Athens, Delphi, and the Cycladic Islands in the Aegean Sea. To visit the sites of classical antiquity in Greece, Jessica, was so very exciting for me after studying philosophy long ago as a college student with my beloved professor, Dr. Bond Fleming, and having graduate seminars at Vanderbilt University in both Plato and Aristotle when I was barely twenty-one-years old. I would love to take you to Greece someday, Jessica.

When I first went to Greece with my conference group as Youli Theodosiadou's guest, we professors lectured in an Aristotle University lecture hall in Thessaloniki where a sculptural bust of Aristotle sat in a place of honor in the auditorium. Though our topics were thoroughly modern ones of American Studies—my talk was on images of sexuality in a story by Eudora Welty compared with those in Nikos Kazanzakis's *Zorba the Greek*—the presence and liveliness of Aristotle were more vivid than ever before to me in this place where he had lived and worked.

Youli took us on an excursion to the nearby excavated tombs and museum of King Phillip II, father of Alexander the Great; and she pointed out from the tour bus the site of a road where St. Paul probably traveled on his visit to the region—hence his subsequent letter writing and the biblical texts of St. Paul's Epistles to the Thessalonians. In the museum on the site of the tomb of King Phillip II, a poster showed a statue of Alexander with his head tilted to one side and text explaining that he suffered from torticollis, a congenital twisting of the neck and head musculature. Oh, my goodness, I thought, your brother Justin had torticollis at birth! Your mother and his physical therapist expended great effort to train him to develop his infant neck to stretch in the other direction from the one he favored in order to avoid his having a tilted neck and pointed head later in life. To think that our Justin had this problem in common with Alexander the Great! It made the historical Alexander much more human to my mind.

When your granddad and I were in Athens, one of the places we visited was the Agora. The Agora is the location of ruins of the Athenian ancient market, the government buildings of the first democracy in the world, and the stone paths called Philosophers' Way. In preparation for our seeing the ancient government and market sites of the Agora, our excellent tour guide took us by the contemporary government buildings and into the meat, fish, and produce markets of today. She did this to help us contrast in our imagination their parallels from antiquity, which she was to show us shortly. Seeing their modern counterpart sites before touring the Agora made our walking about the archaeological ruins of marketplace, government buildings, and walkways more meaningful. This place, now covered with low shrubs of oregano and sage, gravel walkways, and slabs of marble ruins, was the original area where Socrates, Plato, and their students strolled. I remembered being told in my college philosophy class of this site where the earliest Western philosophers practiced their "peripatetic method" of walking together with their students and teaching with questions and answers driving even more questions and answers.

It was October when we were in Greece and plants were blooming, leaves and grass were green, the sea was emerald blue, and I thrilled at knowing what I had known for four decades of ancient Greek philosophy, religion, and mythology and now was experiencing through the sights and sounds and tastes of old. I sent Dr. Fleming a letter telling about my pleasure in at last being in Athens and imagining the presence there in this scene of their history of the philosophers whose ideas I had first learned about from him.

I also remembered the tutelage I received on Greek and Roman mythology in college as but a girl in my late teens when we went to Delphi and saw the temples to the god Apollo with the statue of the sphinx. Now Delphi is one of the most important archaeological sites in Greece, along with a town of the same name. It is located on Mount Parnassus in southern Greece; the well-maintained ruins show the power and respect given to the ancient deities of Greece. It has ruins of the temple of Apollo, ruins of "treasury" buildings where offerings were brought from many outlying settlements of Greeks, steep stone pathways to a theater site and, highest of all, to the stadium.

The temple to Apollo on this site honors Apollo, son of the god-king Zeus and of Leto, as the god of the oracles, the lead god of the far-flung Greek colonists, the leader of the muses, and the god of poetry and of music. The temple site at Delphi was revered in ancient times as one that honored all the gods, a panhellenic site. Delphi was believed to be the center of the earth and still holds a stone marker that was believed to designate the earth's center. Like the marker, an eternal flame burned inside the Temple of Apollo that signified its central importance to the gods. Because of its great value for all the Greek colonies, athletes came from all over Greece to compete in the incomparable Pythian Games every four years.

The sphinx was a very important figure at Delphi, and there is a prominent statue of her in the museum there today. She is a winged figure with a woman's head and a lion's body. The sculptural figure originally stood on a tall Ionic column and may have represented the wise virgin oracles who spoke in riddles to forecast the future for those who entreated them for advice in the temple. The sphinx is seen to be a monster and, also, a bearer of wisdom, though arbitrary in her dispensing of what she knows.

According to mythology, the sphinx gave mysterious and ambiguous advice. Although she was sought for her understanding, she was not to be trusted. When your granddad and I were traveling in Greece, I sent you a picture postcard of the statue of the sphinx at Delphi. I wanted you to have that image, Jessica, for, she, being female like you and me, can serve as both edification and warning: she had great power, and, also, could do great harm. We too as female people are potentially powerful and, also, could do great harm if we abused our power.

Aristotle saw his work on ethics as a prolegomena, or preparatory text, to his politics, which like ethics, he thought, is a moral philosophy. In Aristotle's time there was not nearly as much emphasis on the individual human being as there has been in the modern era, so he thought of ethics as primarily for society, as showing the ways for behaving well as a society. Political philosophy in turn provides ways of organizing and conducting society's affairs for the welfare of all. He wrote, "Our task is to become good men, or to achieve the highest human good. That good is happiness." (Click! goes my feminist brain: there is that non-gender-inclusive "men" generic word. At long last I have learned not to turn it off, always to acknowledge that click of sexism to my students and in my own mind, but to point out that both the writer and the translator "meant" the word to include all humans by that generic male reference, and, also, to acknowledge that Aristotle and the very text of his I am presenting appreciatively show several deeply held sexist biases, including that women are not fit for leadership, which I can point out and then skip over but not ignore.) My ruminations, however, should not obscure the validity of Aristotle's claim, which I have followed as my own, that the highest human good is happiness. His caveat, and my own, still warrants attention: human happiness as the highest good is not merely for an individual person, but for the whole of society, shared happiness of the entire community, arrived at by shared good values and behaviors.

The title of Aristotle's ethics volume is *The Nicomachean Ethics*.[1] Nicomachaeus was Aristotle's son. The philosopher does not mention this fact in the body of his text. He shows none of the sentiment than many a contemporary author, including me, would display in dedicating a book to a loved one. In fact, this was not a dedication in the modern sense, for Aristotle did not publish this material, but his notes were gathered and put together by his son, and this is why the ethics volume is known by his

1. Aristotle, *The Ethics of Aristotle: The Nicomachean Ethics*, London: Penguin Classics, 1976. Tr. J. A. K. Thomson. Thomson translation first published by Allen and Unwin, 1953.

son's name. Still, this sense of the ethics book being "for" Aristotle's son is the basis for my student's idea of our writing, as Aristotle did, for the next generation, an idea that I used for my subsequent first-year seminar students. And it led me to choose to write our own ethics for our child or grandchild, for the young, as you become adults in the next generation, for you, Jessica.

Happiness is the goal of life, Aristotle believed; but to achieve happiness the person must develop and practice both moral goodness and intellectual goodness. The good is not an abstraction, and happiness is not a personal emotion. Rather, goodness is a goal, which a person can work toward both intellectually and ethically and become "habituated" to practicing, he says. In his *Ethics*, Aristotle advances a set of principles very systematically, very carefully, and sometimes very tediously—my students occasionally thought it a drag to read the book—that can guide behavior toward what Aristotle calls the "habituated" practice of virtue as the pattern of one's life. In the translation of Aristotle's book that my students and I used, the translator provided a table of virtues and vices from Aristotle's text, giving columns showing twelve virtues in four columns for (1) the situation; (2) the virtue that embodies the mean; and (3) and (4) the two opposing vices that are on the extreme sides of that virtue. This corresponds to some contemporary psychological theory that suggests a person's best characteristics—"virtues"—are the reverse or the flip side of the same person's worst characteristics.

The virtues Aristotle names are (1) courage (between rashness and cowardice in a situation of fear and confidence); (2) temperance (between licentiousness and insensibility when choosing pleasure or pain); (3) liberality (regarding acquisition and spending money, between prodigality and illiberality); (4) magnificence (between vulgarity and pettiness in one's attitude toward spending); (5) magnanimity (between vanity and pusillanimity [or sniveling] when choosing honor or dishonor); (6) proper ambition (between being overly ambitious and unambitious); (7) patience (controlling anger between being irascible and having lack of spirit); (8) truthfulness (between being boastful and understating one's accomplishments); (9) wittiness (in conversation between buffoonery and boorishness); (10) friendliness (in social conduct, between being obsequious or flattering and being cantankerous); (11) modesty (between being too shy and being shameless); and (12) righteous indignation (expression between envy and malice).

Although I will not precisely follow Aristotle's list of virtues or goals for behavioral goodness in what I am writing here, Aristotle's points are embedded in my thinking and many will emerge in what I describe and endorse as good for your consideration.

Aristotle's is one system of ethics for you and me to consider, Jessica. Now let's turn to another framework for thinking about ethics, the one we can elicit from studying the narrative of the Minnesota Native American people, the Ojibway, in *Night Flying Woman*, written by Ignatia Broker.

In Minnesota and Wisconsin where we live, the Ojibway are one of the tribes of Native Americans who lived here for some centuries before white people came, before "contact" between Native Americans and European Americans.

The Ojibway are known as Chippewa in U.S. government sources, but they know themselves as the Anishinaabe, or "Original People." Reservations where some Ojibway people live now are here in northern Wisconsin and northern Minnesota, and some families and individual urban people who are Ojibway live in Minneapolis and St. Paul and other cities. Our cottage is located near the Lac Courte Oreilles (LCO) reservation, and it has a school, a community college, a radio station, a casino, and a Catholic church that was formerly a mission parish. In fact, the land where our cottage stands was Ojibway land before the loggers came in the nineteenth century and took it by authorization of the U.S. government.

One year my university graduate seminar students went on a weekend field learning trip to the Ojibway reservation at Leech Lake in Minnesota, a workshop planned and hosted by two American Indian students in the group, one who is Ojibway, Pauline Brunette Danforth, and another, Linda Oxendine, who is Lumbee and who had worked for the Minnesota Ojibway tribal organization. The remarkable seminar group was made up of two Chinese students, one student from Brazil, one from Germany, one from Indonesia, three white Americans, and three Native Americans from three different tribes—Oneida, Lumbee, and Ojibway. The resort owner and one of our experts was my colleague from American Indian Studies, Ron Libertus, also an Ojibway. We had an amazing experience of visiting the tribal Bug-o-nay-ge-shig school; listening to the elders talk about tribal traditions, their ceremonies, and their medicine bundles; visiting with the tribal newspaper editor; and going to a tribal cemetery where the graves were covered with small wooden houses in varying states of freshness and decay. When I asked if I might go into the cemetery, my host said gracefully, "I choose not to," instantly giving me understanding of the sacredness of the place and the particular way honor is paid the dead. We were told that people put food and knick-knick, tobacco, a sacred ceremonial substance, at the entries of the small houses for the deceased's sustenance on their journey, and they respectfully allow the artistic and interesting wooden structures on the graves gradually and naturally to deteriorate and blend into the soil.

The Ojibway woman, Pauline Brunette Danforth, who led the seminar group wrote her PhD dissertation as my student on the Ojibway narrative *Night Flying Woman* by Ignatia Broker, as a spiritual text, and I learned much from her as we worked together. *Night Flying Woman* was a book I repeatedly chose to read with my students in the "Ethics and the Arts in the University" seminar. I emphasized with the students the ethical principles that could be derived from *Night Flying Woman* and also pointed out that the book could just as readily be interpreted as good storytelling, historical information, or cultural studies.

This storytelling approach to presenting and learning ethics contrasts with Aristotle's logical, rational approach; but both ways of learning are helpful to us in discovering morally appropriate behavior, both from the past and as a guide for our own lives. I am eager for you, Jessica, to learn both of these ways of learning—and more.

The story of *Night Flying Woman* takes the reader through the cycle of the lifetime of a woman, Ni-bo-we-see-gwi, "Night Flying Woman," who is nicknamed Oona. At the beginning of the story, Oona is born an only child "after the blueberry gathering and before the wild-rice harvesting," showing the seasonal way of the people's registering time, and at the exact moment of an eclipse of the sun. A wise woman of the tribe, A-wa-sa-si, meaning "Bullhead," was asked to name the child; and she chose Ni-bo-we-see-gwi to signify the importance of the instant of her birth, the eclipse. Her birth moment was a sign, her people believed, since she was "born of love and joy" in this temporary daytime darkness, that she was "born a person who became strong and gave strength, who became wise and lent this wisdom to her people, who became part of the generation of chaos and change."[2]

Oona goes through the ceremonial times of her development as the chosen woman, going into the woods to consider the responsibility of-

2. Ignatia Broker, *Night Flying Woman*. St. Paul, MN: Minnesota Historical Society Press, 1983, pp. 14–16.

fered her before accepting it. Hers is the generation of Ojibway people's first coming into contact with European-Americans, and she has visions of men rolling logs on the water, foretelling her people's need to move deeper into the forest and then their need to interact with the loggers in their lumber camp wooden houses. Oona's people have not made houses from the trees, and this strange practice is one Oona has to help her people reluctantly accept along with the white people's cutting down parts of the forest for their building. The Ojibway people also have to accept the practice of dividing up the land into units for ownership, something unknown before to them, for they thought of the land, the earth, as their partner in life along with the plant life and other animal life, not something divisible or owned. Eventually the people in the story move to what is now the White Earth Reservation in northern Minnesota. At the end of the narrative, a child comes to the elderly Oona. "My name is Mary in the English way," she tells Oona, "but in the language of our people, I am called A-wa-sa-si." She is Bullhead like the revered old woman who had named and taught Oona.

On being asked what she wants from the old woman, young A-wa-sa-si replies, "I should like to hear the stories of our people."

Oona has an heir as her people's wise woman.

The writer of the foreword of *Night Flying Woman*, Paulette Fairbanks Molin, summarizes the ethical views that can be detected in the book. "It describes a philosophy of living . . . ," she writes. "One of the tenets is sharing. . . . Another tenet is respect—for the earth, for plant and animal life, and for one another. . . . The story also tells of many traditions, always in the context of their places in the lives of the Ojibway people . . . for example, of the custom of the Ojibway to be guided throughout their lives by dreams and of the importance of giving thanks and honoring elders."[3]

Sharing, respecting the earth and all creatures and all people, honoring traditions, attending to dreams, giving thanks or showing gratitude, honoring elders are Ojibway principles of ethics as revealed in *Night Flying Woman*. On the Ojibway Web site on the Internet, Harold Flett elaborates by writing that honesty, humility, truth, wisdom, love, respect, and bravery are Ojibway ethical characteristics. As evaluation of an Ojibway person's character, he suggests that the sacred tobacco, knick-knick, is used as a preparation for speaking to the spirit world, saying the tobacco

---

3. Pauline Fairbanks Molin, Introduction, *Woman*, p. xiii.

travels ahead of words to show the goodness of the person, to show one to be honest, kind, and respectful.[4]

Once at an art opening at the Weisman Art Museum (WAM) when some Ojibway artists' work was being shown, I heard my colleague Ron Libertus tell in a matter-of-fact way a very moving story from his Ojibway boyhood. He said he loved to go out and hunt deer with his father, but his father taught him that they had to prepare correctly, to plan to take only the deer that were needed for food, and to begin their hunt with a ceremonial prayer to the deer. In this prayer they honored the deer, which they called brother, and thanked him for the life they both, human and deer, were living and thanked him for the food the deer would provide for sustaining the people's lives.

On another occasion, I observed the Ojibway's reverence for nature and understanding of its sacredness at an exhibition that included some of the works of George Morrison at the WAM. An internationally known modernist abstract painter, Morrison draws from nature and sometimes blends Anishinaabe feeling and understanding into his work. The works themselves are vibrant expressions of color and line, shapes and form— abstract. Yet the viewer can feel and understand the dynamic of nature Morrison explores.

George Morrison (1919–2000) was internationally acclaimed as a major twentieth-century American abstract expressionist artist, the only Native American person so recognized. When the National Museum of the American Indian opened in Washington, DC, in 2004, Morrison was one of the two artists whose work was featured. Working in abstract form, Morrison nevertheless conveyed the powerful connectedness with nature that he and many others of his Anishinaabe people feel. He sometimes worked in wood and created standing or hanging sculptural pieces. One done in 1974 and now at the Minneapolis Institute of Art is a driftwood collage in a rich variety of earth and wood colors, size 60 1/8 x 168 ½ x 3. He collected the pieces of wood and also shaped the design to suggest the horizon line of his familiar Lake Superior, on whose northern shore he had been born and beside which he lived his last years.

Numerous paintings from Morrison's later years also have that subtle horizontal line seen in the wood sculpture, a third or less from the top of the painting, giving the art piece a kind of Lake Superior signature of

4. Harold Flett, Objway "Customs and Beliefs," www.nald.ca/CLR/chickiken/titleiii/ktm.

the artist. The bold reds and blues and greens of many of them call out their nature origins. One 1997 work, called "Red Rock Variation: Lake Superior Landscape," is dominated by red streaks with gray and black, suggesting a dark evening sunset sky.

A wood sculpture by Morrison called "Red Totem," made in 1980, stands 20 feet tall and is now in the Heard Museum in Phoenix, Arizona, though there are several variations of this piece. The work is a construction of stained cedar puzzle pieces fitted together. Its verticality and mass suggest the traditional totem pole of some West Coast Native American peoples, while the simplicity of the single red natural wood color and the elegance of the undecorated design convey a generalized beauty. Connectedness to earth and air, trees and sky is suggested by the use of the plain cedar wood. It is possible for the viewer to feel harmony with nature and harmony with particular Native American people, as well as generalized spiritual harmony within oneself as one looks at "Red Totem."

Morrison's work dramatizes what he meant when he wrote, "In search of my own reality, I seek the power of the rock, the magic of the water, the religion of the tree, the color of the wind, and the enigma of the horizon."[5]

The traditional Ojibway and other Native Americans in the past had a notion of time that was cyclical, or that circled from season to season, spring through summer, fall, and winter to spring again, from day through night to day again, from birth and growing to maturity to decline and decay, circling back to new birth. In thought dominated by written history and logical thought, such as Aristotle's, time is structured as linear. There is a past, present, and future. Time proceeds forward on a continuum.

Although apparently oppositional, the cyclical or seasonal and the linear or historical ways of viewing time need not necessarily be contradictory ways of considering time. As we reflect upon what has gone before or what we anticipate, what has taken place in history or what we want to plan, as we consider choices based on known precedents in our lives or in the world, as we go about thinking analytically, as Aristotle did, a linear view of time serves us as a useful tool. However, if we want to think about human health and heat and food and shelter, if we want to understand and make judgments about cleanliness and safety, growth

5. George Morrison, quoted in "The Art of George Morrison and Allan Houser," by Gregory Schaff, *Native Peoples Magazine*, 1 September 2004. Found on-line at www .nativepeoples.com.

and physical change, about our environment and using or conserving natural resources, we must think in cyclical time to understand and make decisions about what is best to do and to refrain from doing.

In the seemingly contradictory understandings of time as circling and time as linear of the Ojibway and Aristotle, we learn that the contradiction is not real at all, but complementary. Similarly, Aristotle's base for determining ethics from rationality and the Ojibway base for deriving ethics from nature, while appearing to be conflicting, can also be complementary. For me as a person in shaping my life and for participating in the communities to which I belong, both using thoughtful, reasonable means to understanding and observing, intuitive, responsive harmonies with nature are helpful ways to think about what I should do. For you, Jessica, I recommend you use both your good mind's thought processes and your engagement with nature as equally good and complementary sources for deciding who you will be and what you will do.

6

On Doing Nothing

Bird migrations, the rising of the winter stars out of the breakers and
the east, night and storm, the solitude of a January day, the glistening of dune grass in midsummer, all this . . . is a meditative perception
of the relation of "Nature" (and I include the whole cosmic picture in
this term) to the human spirit. . . . I . . . believe Nature is a part of our
humanity and without some awareness and experience of that divine
mystery [the hu]man ceases to be [hu]man.

—Henry Beston, *The Outermost House*

—Nature in Autumn—The first night I stayed in our cottage, the plumb-
er and electrician had not finished their work and the house was cold,
but I had a glorious night's sleep upstairs in the bedroom off the loft.
I awakened to snow in the upper branches of the white pine treetops
outside my window on the side of the house opposite the lake. When I
looked out, a big cottontail rabbit hopped about on the grounds, making fresh tracks, and I thought I saw bald eagles in the red pines near the
lakeshore. That weekend Stiles, Tina, Natasha, and you, baby Jessica,
came to help me settle in with the precious pieces of newly refinished
old oak and walnut wood furniture from our Mississippi and Missouri
family homes—tables and cedar chests, a highboy, a dresser, chairs,
and a washstand—and new couches and chairs. The house was ready
for Thanksgiving with a bottle of champagne on our kitchen island
from our realtor and builder; and our household furnishings, dishes
and cookware, art works and family quilts made by aunts and grandmothers were carefully put into their places. When our entire family

arrived, Dad walked in the front door and said almost offhandedly of the newly repaired and polished cedar chest sitting in the center of the living room, "Papa made that chest for Mama." That was the first we knew of its origin.

OUR FRIEND BILL SANDS wrote in our cottage journal one New Year's Day when he and Susan had come to lunch with us at Coventry-in-the-Northwoods, "This is a unique place to find solitude and do absolutely nothing, which really is doing a lot."

"Doing nothing" is this way of being open to whatever may arise: resting, stopping activity, being richly alone in finding solitude, rather than lonely in aloneness. It has long been a cherished state of mine. I recommend it to you, Jessica, as an ethical position for being open to the right thing to do, for being courageous enough to remain alone with yourself and quiet, expecting nothing at all to happen, doing utterly nothing. Paradoxically, in so doing, you will find the strong center of yourself, find your self. Then, you can come away refreshed, renewed, ready for your choices and actions, ready to be who you are, authentic, in the world. I first understood this concept a long time ago from reading a 1978 children's book, *Aloneness*, by the important African-American poet and fiction writer, Gwendolyn Brooks, in which she contrasts in language for a child the difference between being alone and lonely and being alone to discover a rich solitude.

This position is akin to one of Buddhist meditation for seeking enlightenment, I think. It also reminds me of Hindu yoga spirituality that is disciplined with body exercise and health awareness along with meditation. Too, it is like Christian silent reflection in the monastic tradition over centuries of practice. For me, it is most wholesome and fully vitalizing in the midst of nature, hearing the winds blow through the pine trees as the Ojibway people did at this place before me in Wisconsin and Minnesota, watching the sun blaze across the sky, listening to the rain, gazing at the water as seaside Africans have been known to do for spiritual sustenance for centuries. It is a spiritual practice most profound, which I invite you to share with me and also to learn to practice in your own way.

A Confucian example of the value of "doing nothing" is given by the expert writer on world religions, Karen Armstrong. She quotes a story from the fourth-century BCE contemplative Daoist named Zhuangzi. According to the story, Yan Hui, Confucius's favorite student, told

Confucius that he has been able to achieve the mental emptiness about which his mentor had taught. He said, "I sit quietly and forget!" Pleased, Confucius told him that he had indeed found the way to enlightenment, "The Way is found in emptiness. Emptiness is the mind's fast."[1]

Poets and artists stare out their windows first. My friend Sam King, known by her formal name Susan Deborah King in her public life as a poet, commented offhandedly at a poetry reading one night that poets and artists do a lot of staring out of windows and that is an important part of their work. I have read the same kind of notion in the more revelatory writings of several authors. And, where, I ask myself, did those horizon lines on all those marvelous abstract and colorful paintings by George Morrison first originate? I suspect they came first to Morrison's "mind's eye" as he looked out over his beloved horizon of Lake Superior. For my writing, it is very constructive time well spent for me to sit alone in my writing place, perhaps with pen and paper in hand, looking out over whatever is in view—in my cottage loft, the lake through the trees beyond the surrounding windows; in my small third-floor university office, the brick protective railing that runs around the outside of the building, the tops of campus trees in the distance, and flags flying from flagpoles on other buildings; from my desk in front of our second-story apartment window during our stay in Berkeley, the orange tree with its bright fruit I could see across the street through the nearer maple leaves; and, in my second-floor study in our Minneapolis home, the oak limbs and fir trees and neighbors' close-by houses visible outside the window beside my home desk. Sitting at the desk I face the wall where I have the *Organic Gardening* calendar hanging in front of me with its pictures of fresh flowers and vegetables of the month, beside it my small ceramic tree frog plaque from Puerto Rico and another pottery tablet that proclaims, "Saturday's child works hard for its living." With no real focus but the distance and no precise idea except my writing in general, the restfulness of the solitary gazing beyond the place and the moment provides refreshment, intellectual renewal, and often the very words or thoughts or images that were unavailable just a while before.

For me, that is what meditation amounts to: solitary quiet and openness combined with mental letting go of structures of place and time and circumstance. For me, a suggestion from Buddhism is helpful, that of

1. Karen Armstrong, "The Power of Forgetting." *Guardian Weekly*, Vol. 175, No. 10, August 25–31, 2006, p. 5.

emptying out preconceptions, prior content, emptying as preparation for readiness for glimmers of enlightenment, approaches to wholeness. It is all right with me, Jessica, if you or someone else doesn't want to call that meditation—some people, including me, don't like labels like "meditation" for what they do. It works for me, and I like to call it "doing nothing." It feels good to me. It feels like a fine approach to life. Try it out in your own way with your own language in your own time.

There can also be collective approaches to such internal gathering up of thoughts, feelings, and spirit. Once in 1973–74 when we lived in Cambridge, England, an Indian woman, Kanta Agrihotri, who was a practicing Hindu, asked a small group of us neighborhood women on Mulberry Close to come to her home every week and do yoga with her. She did not invite us into the spiritual dimensions that yoga held for her, but she taught us yoga exercises, illustrating and leading with her beautiful sari-clad body. After we had done yoga positions and movements for an hour or so, every week she would feed us: marvelous, nutritious vegetarian Indian food. None of the rest of us ever thought we might reciprocate and provide food or invite the group to our houses. It was sufficient to gratefully receive her hospitality and yoga lessons. We went to our Hindu friend's home with great appreciation and satisfaction one morning every week and practiced yoga and enjoyed our camaraderie and her leadership. Back in the United States, I have periodically taken a course in yoga, have sporadically done yoga exercises on my own, or done yoga with other women for short periods of time. But while my body is stretched and limbered and I find some physical comfort in my activity, I have not felt the warmth and fullness of yoga practice since those days in Cambridge when I first learned to fold my legs in a lotus position or to stretch and bend for a sun salutation in my little international neighborhood women's community in Cambridge. There may have been nothing orthodox about it; we may have each learned something different from it; but in my case it provided a kind of unified spirituality blending body, mind, spirit, and community in one almost-ritualized weekly repeating experience.

A similar story of shared meditative experience comes from the beginning times of the Weisman Art Museum. It connects this variation on spirituality in shared experience for me. I love the story that in 1934 the University of Minnesota president at the time, Lotus Coffman, set aside a space in the new university auditorium building, the Northrop

Auditorium, some third-floor rooms for a small art gallery called the Little Gallery. He wanted university students, many of whom came from Midwestern farms and had never seen original art, to learn about and experience good art, and he even designated some funds for the purchase of original art for the museum. The founding documents suggested that one small room be set aside for the silent viewing of "one beautiful object" and was to be a place where students could go and "contemplate beauty."

A museum director was chosen by an unlikely and serendipitous method: a university administrator had died unexpectedly, and in an effort to provide for his wife, Ruth Lawrence, university officers offered her the choice of being a dormitory housemother or the director of the new museum. Lawrence chose the museum in what was one of those "the rest is history" moments. She proved to be a very skilled arts administrator and the first art she bought included two large oil paintings by Georgia O'Keeffe. One has become almost the signature of the museum, now the Weisman Art Museum, a much-larger-than-life double image of poppies named "Oriental Poppies." The other, the first piece she bought, paying $1500 for it from Alfred Stieglitz's New York sales gallery, was similarly enlarged from nature into giants of their natural selves, depicts two oak leaves, and is titled "Oak Leaves, Pink and Gray." Both these paintings illustrate O'Keeffe's lifelong pursuit of painting from nature with attention to processes of birth, maturation, decay, and regeneration. The poppies are shown at the height of summer fruitfulness, while the oak leaves are very beautiful images of autumnal decay.

Both these works provide wonderful art experiences, and I can imagine students in the 1930s, straight from their farms and city homes, coming to the university and finding themselves in the Little Gallery's small space with one art work on which to "contemplate," that piece at first being "Oak Leaves, Pink and Gray." Or, maybe later, that work was "Oriental Poppies." I can imagine that student being changed forever by the impression left from the bold colors, the gorgeous abstract suggestions of lines, the vivid images, and the ruminations of their own imagination as they stood or sat with the paintings, and I hope drinking deeply of the suggested meanings and the glorious power of the images before them. (The facts from the gallery's history don't bear out these ruminations of mine, following the one of the founding president, for items began to "disappear" from the room and by 1940 it had to be closed because students began to use the space "for purposes other than the contemplation of art." Nevertheless, I can still hold up the ideal, can still foster President Coffman's dream and hope that some students followed it!)

Georgia O'Keeffe is one of my favorite artists. She is now considered one of the twentieth century's greatest painters, but in her earliest professional years, she had to work hard to get the attention of other, mostly male, artists. She once said the reason she made her flowers so big in her now-famous series of flower paintings was so that the men would notice them.

When I have taken groups of students through the museum in my role as tour guide or professor and we have looked at the brilliant orange-yellow-red-black-red-red-red "Oriental Poppies," my students have liked the work very much. Some of them immediately see "passion" in it. Some see "fire." Some just want it to be the flowers big enough to see. Some are brave enough to say they see electric sexual feeling. Some see danger of passion or fire or heat. A few even can imagine the potency of the opium drug that can be derived from poppies. Some think of the high summer sunshine and blossoming the painting indicates. Some see the bug's-eye view that it presents. Everyone likes it.

It seems to me that both the practice of yoga exercises with my Cambridge friends and neighbors and the viewing of Georgia O'Keeffe's paintings at my university museum can be understood as meditation. Both are ways of delving deeper inside oneself by viewing or doing something outside. They are "meditation" in two different ways—one with either lone or shared physical focus, the other either a lone or group aesthetic experience in which one finds depths of pleasure and resources of understanding by visual means. Each one is a way I have a wonderful time "doing nothing."

My experience with yoga can be replicated for you by your figure skating or your dancing or some other essentially solitary activity for close attentiveness to your body and mind and their harmony. My experience with Georgia O'Keeffe's paintings could be replicated with close attention to sculpture or architecture or other forms of art. The dimension of physical or aesthetic experience as meditation, as "doing nothing" for spiritual renewal, for the return of refreshment to the whole person I heartily recommend. I have found it a joy to take you as a small girl to see the Georgia O'Keeffe "Poppies" painting at my university museum, Jessica, and I look forward to many more times together experiencing art and enjoying artistic body movement with you as you grow and learn and come into your own.

7

Knowing, Loving, and Hoping

"Hope" is a thing with feathers—
That perches in the soul—
And sings the tune without the words—
And never stops—at all—

—Emily Dickinson, "Poem 254"

—Nature as Winter Begins—We get ready for Christmas with all our family, adult children, and grandchildren coming to be with us over the holiday weekend in our Minneapolis house. It has been frigid cold with nights near zero and single-digit temperatures for the daytime. We enjoy the merriment of Christmas preparation—cooking, shopping for gifts, and bringing an eight-foot balsam fir tree indoors to decorate with lights and ornaments that have long been in our family: one glittering ball your mother made when she was a Brownie Girl Scout; one with his name written on it in sparkling letters Stiles made a few years later; some we bought in England when we lived there; some we found in Germany and Austria during our Christmastime spent there. Other evergreens, too, we select with the fir tree and make festive wreaths for our door and fence gate. We hang swags of cedar with big red bows along the fence and put more green branches with red bows in big pots on the steps going down to our sidewalk. There has been some snow, but not as much as we often have for Christmas; still, the festive bringing in of greenery from out of doors is one of the delights of Christmas time.

We look forward with eager anticipation to our family being with us, to sharing our family love in the tangible ways we do at Christmas, to what you, Jessica, called at three years old the "river of Christmas gifts" under our tree, the festive foods of cookies and bread and pies homemade for Christmas, turkey and dressing to eat on our candle-lit Christmas dinner table. We have ready stockings to hang on Christmas Eve, anticipate Christmas storytelling before bedtime as we do every year, and Christmas morning we will delight in bright-eyed children opening presents before a roaring wood-fire in our fireplace.

The attention to light and the customary bringing indoors of evergreen trees and branches are important signifiers at Christmas. Just before Christmas, around December 21, is the shortest day of light in the Northern Hemisphere, the winter solstice; and all religions over time have had some kind of celebration or recognition of this time of least light before "the sun begins to return." There is historical speculation that the Christian feast of the birth of Christ was set at this time, the actual date of Jesus's birth being unknown, based on a pre-Christian nature celebration around the return of the light. Also, Christ is represented in scripture as "the Light of the world."

This year in this season one of our family friends, Robin Jensen, has been going through a severe illness with her son Bobby, culminating with his receiving a bone marrow transplant from his sister, Libby. He was going to have the transplant on December 20, the day before the winter solstice. Robin wrote in an e-mail to some of her friends just before the day of the dangerous procedure, "One of you reminded me that is the darkest day of the year, with the light beginning to return on the 21 (or maybe the 22). I think of the familiar expression, 'It's always darkest before the dawn' and think how real that might be for us this year. We think, too, of the light coming into the world as told in the prologue to the Gospel of John. This year, as ever, our present is this light, just as Libby's special gift to her brother is her perfectly matched marrow."

OH, JESSICA GIRL, MY Jessica Bean, as your dad sometimes called you affectionately when you were small for reasons known only to him. Jessica, Jessica, Jessica Leigh, as your mother named you after her choice of a name for herself, you are loved.

Love received is a precious trust.

Love makes no demands. Love exercises no authority.

Love is love.

And when one is loved, one is freed to love in return, one is freed to be oneself most fully, one is empowered to give large returns.

Love cannot be divided into fractions, added to or subtracted from, rather love has the effect of multiplying.

Love is leaven for one's growth in spirit.

Love is food and water for one's sustenance.

Love dances and sings.

Love bears sorrow.

Love is constant.

Invisible to the naked eye, love is really real, yet love unseen vitalizes the physical body.

My beloved granddaughter Jessica, I wish for you great love. As you are much loved by your family and friends, may you love greatly.

I wish for you great joy, laughter, play, and work.

I wish for you as a child playmates and schoolmates who are children you can love deeply and who will love you equally in return.

I wish for you the continuing love, protection, and discipline your parents give you so unstintingly, and I wish for you unbounded, reciprocated love from all your family's relatives and friends. I wish for all our love, protection, and discipline to take root and grow inside you until they mature as your own.

I wish for you as an adult steadfast friends, and I wish for you to be a good and loyal friend.

I wish for your love to expand beyond your people to your community and nation, to our natural environment, and our world.

When the time is right, I wish for you a beloved life partner with whom you both can be fully loving of yourselves and one another.

I wish for you good health, both physical and mental.

I wish for my adult Jessica to revel in work, to delight in play, to embrace difficult challenges, to use your intellectual ability fully, to participate vigorously in politics and government, in arts and high and popular culture, in religious life, in education, in family life.

I do not wish for you a life free of sorrow or pain or disappointment. Rather, I wish for you to learn when young to understand and work with pain and loss, both physical and psychological, both personal and institutional, so that you can learn better to take care of yourself and to empathize with others.

I wish for you the ability to admit your mistakes when you have made them, and to ask forgiveness when you have done wrong.

I wish for you the ability to fall down, even to fall on your face, and to pick yourself up, dust yourself off, and start over.

I wish for you self-confidence, but not arrogance.

I wish for you good judgment, but not harsh or hurtful judgmental acts against other people. Still, I want you to have the strength to face wrongdoing, judge it, and stand up to its perpetrators.

I wish for you a life of creativity and goodness, and I wish for you a lifelong pursuit of these good possibilities.

When you are grown, on your own, and in the world, I wish for people to say of you as they see you, "There is Jessica Leigh Scheerer, a woman of grace." To me the word grace epitomizes all the qualities of goodness of loving humanity.

The components of the life I wish for you are loving, learning, and hoping. While there are many particular ways on the path to goodness, they all come together in love, I believe. Honesty, loyalty, integrity, respect, courage, and truthtelling are bound together by love of other people, love of self, and love of communities and nations. Love, though, is not simplistic. You must be intellectually alive to find right ways of loving. Aristotle wrote of an equal measure of intellectual virtues and moral virtues. You must know the good before you can do the good. You must work just as hard at learning and knowing as you work at loving.

And, finally, there is hope. You must hope that life will be good, hope that you can achieve what you desire, hope that you can live well. The light goes out in a life in which there is no hope.

A play that I have remembered with appreciation for almost 50 years after I saw it on Broadway when I was a student, the 1958 verse drama *J.B.* by Archibald MacLeish, is a play about hope. *J.B.* is a modern-day retelling of the biblical book of *Job*, a story of a person and a family having bounty followed by utter loss and catastrophic degradation following a bombing. They move again to restoration of their lives through faithfulness. A line about hope from *J.B.* has stayed with me as a metaphor of promise through all of my adult life. It is, "Blow on the coal of the heart, and we'll see by and by."

In the plot line of *J.B.*, two characters who represent cosmic good and evil, or God and the devil, are the narrators and the mockers of J.B., whom they sometimes call Job. The affluent and comfortable J.B. and his wife, Sarah, are prosperous, happy, contented, and religiously faithful. They live in urban America in a time following World War II with its recent history of protracted violent warfare and atomic bombing. Nevertheless, J.B. claims that the world is "new and born and fresh and wonderful." Soon, though, like the biblical Job, J.B. and Sarah lose one important part of their life after another. In this post-World War II time setting, though the war is over, they lose each of their children in violent deaths, they lose their home and surroundings. The city is reduced to ashes, Sarah disappears, J.B. believes she has left him, and a bomb's explosion leaves J.B. badly injured. Still he refuses to give up hope. He says, "The end is the acceptance of the end."

At last a light appears outside and J.B. opens the door to see Sarah holding a fresh twig with new leaves and flower petals on it. She says, "I found it in the ashes . . . All that is left is ashes. I broke the branch . . . "

He has come to doubt everything. He has come to believe there is no future. He asked her why she left him, and she says, "Yes, I left you. I thought there was a way . . . [but] even a green leaf on a branch stopped me." She tells him that she loves him, and he says mournfully that he has no light.

She replies, "The candles in churches are out. The lights have gone out in the sky. Blow on the coal of the heart, and we'll see by and by. . . . We are, and that is our answer. We suffer. What we are suffers. . . . In doubt, in dread is ignorance. . . . Still [we] live. . . . Still [we] love."

The symbolic light, the symbolic new life in the green new growth of the sprouting twig, and the symbolic fire of the embers of the coal of the heart provide great power for otherwise ephemeral declarations of love. Yet, that is all there is. "We are." Human life finds warmth and growth and thereby power to go on only through love. And love is enough to foster hope.

Christmas Day—The Christian Love holiday comes now in our family and in the world. In our Minneapolis home, we wake early but soon sunlight is streaming in. Loving husbands on Christmas morning, your dad and granddad make tea and Ian takes your mother an early

morning tea tray to her in bed and your granddad brings my pot of tea upstairs to me on my tray.

Last night you and Sage and David and Justin hung your stockings by the fireplace just before your bedtime on Christmas Eve. Sage's and your stockings have a princess design, the boys' a reindeer and a snow-man. You were full of giggles as you each found just the right places for your stockings to go.

Earlier, with smiles on our faces, we had read aloud by turns our traditional Christmas Eve reading, "A Child's Christmas in Wales," as we have done as a family all of your mother's life; but last night was extra special because you took your turn reading aloud with us for the very first time. We all held our breath with excitement and joy as we heard your clear bell-like young girl's voice take your turn at reading.

After your bedtime, your granddad and I slipped away and crunched over the ice into church for the candlelight service at Hennepin Avenue United Methodist Church where at midnight we held up across the hushed congregation brightly lighted candles and sang softly together "Silent Night" as the night ushered in a new Christmas Day.

This morning you children bounded out of bed and, happy-faced, you dressed yourselves independently in good-looking Christmas clothes with no prompting or help from your adults. The four of you dashed to the Christmas tree and your stockings by the fireplace, where your uncle Stiles already had a fire roaring. In front of the fire's glow in our cozy inglenook on this Christmas morning, you children empty your stockings of their goodies. Each stocking has in it a big apple and a big orange, small toys, and nuts just as those of Natasha's and Stiles's had when they were children. You are soon taking bites out of your apples, and someone brings in fresh juice and hot muffins. We distribute gifts, open them and exclaim over them. Soon we are in a sea of wrapping papers and ribbons, gifts and contentment. The fire begins to die to embers as you try out your new nutcrackers, huge doll-sized red-painted wooden figures your granddad had brought from England. The boys held theirs out in front of them like toy soldiers, while you cradled yours as if it were an infant child. So much for our efforts to avoid gender-stereotyped behaviors!

We slow down enough to eat our breakfast later in the morning, and then we eat our turkey dinner in the afternoon. You play with your toys and climb on our laps and give us hugs. You volunteer, "I love you!"

into grandparent ears. We tell stories of when Stiles was a boy, when Natasha was a girl. We ask Ian to tell about his boyhood Christmases. We have tea and sweets, greater and greater pleasure creeping over us. We look at the baskets of Christmas cards and holiday letters from friends and family far and near and think and speak of our loved ones, telling their stories to one another, telling what has happened in their lives this year according to the Christmas letters.

Later in the afternoon, we all go out for a walk in the still and shining sunlight, some of us walking on the path all the three-mile way around the frozen edges of Lake Harriet. Our red cheeks and frosty breath glisten in winter happiness, for on this one afternoon with its clear blue sky, children and laughter in our lives, we experience in our family the fragile peace that is Christmas.

PART II

On Learning

Winter

One must have the mind of winter
To regard the frost and boughs
Of the pine trees crusted with snow . . .

—Wallace Stevens, "The Snow Man"

—Nature in Winter—The golden rosy color blazing through the trees takes my breath away as I look up from my writing. At this late afternoon time of day on December evenings in Wisconsin, darkness creeps right up on us; and, even though I have to turn my head only slightly to see the western sky through my windows, I almost miss the moment of sunset colors, just almost. I glance across the snow-covered deck and through the blackening snow-laden branches of oak and birch trees. I see farther beyond them darkening red pines with their armloads of snow and see ever so briefly the southwestern sky full of bold nightfall colors. Gorgeous, splendid rosy light splashes pink, yellow, and orange beams on the horizon, across the snow-blanketed lake, and around the tree trunks; and the gray comes down from above and black dark drifts up among the trees. When I turn my head away again, again just slightly, and then look back westward, the sun's last blast of brilliant rosy rays has gone.

8

Goodness as Both Intellectual and Moral Excellence

It was so easy, thought Isabel. It was so easy dealing with people who were well-mannered, as Paul Hogg was. They knew how to exchange those courtesies which made life go smoothly, which was what manners were all about. [Manners] were intended to avoid friction between people, and they did this by regulating the contours of an encounter. If each party knew what the other should do, then conflict would be unlikely. And this worked at every level, from the most minor transaction between two people to dealings between nations. International law, after all, was simply a system of manners writ large.

—Alexander McCall Smith, *The Sunday Philosophy Club*

—Nature in Winter—at the New Year—Most years since we have had the cottage, your granddad and I have come to Coventry-in-the-Northwoods over the New Year's holiday. It is usually quite cold and clear with deep snow on the ground and the lake is frozen under a glistening frosty white snow.

Our first task on arrival is to carry in wood and to build a good fire in our fireplace. As soon as the fire is putting out steady warmth, we stop and make a pot of tea to enjoy in front of it; and we put our feet up, for we are usually tired from the busy pace of the holidays just past. Time spent before the fire at Coventry-in-the-Northwoods is at last time to do nothing. To do nothing in the coldest depths of winter is time to recover from the effort of the preceding days and weeks and time to be still and chill out for readiness for the new time that is to come and whatever our new time might bring.

This year on New Year's Eve when your granddad, Sage, Stiles, and I were here, Stiles recovering from his and Sage's mother Tina's recent divorce, it rained. Puddles collected on portions of the solid ice atop the whole lake below the house where only the evening before Sage, Stiles, Wilson, and the dog Isaac had walked and skidded and played on the rock-hard lake surface between our shore and the island. For several days it has been gray with a little rain, very little snow, and even bare brown ground in a few spots, unusual in northern Wisconsin for late December and the holidays. But, as our New Year's Eve guests, Susan and Bill Sands, left for their house early in the evening, it had begun to snow and they feared that the road would become slick from the rainwater freezing underneath it, yet were happy with us that at last snow was coming.

Since snow fell in the night, on the morning of New Year's Day, we had a fresh coat of four inches or more on the ground, on the deck and on the metal deck chairs and table, on the skylight above my loft and on the roof, on the shed's roof and the neighbors' houses, on the branches and around the trunks of the trees, on the path and the steps sloping down to the shoreline and on the pristine ice surface of the lake. As we got out of bed and started making our breakfast, we enjoyed the snow-surrounding silence, the utter silence of the snow-filled New Year's morning.

The dawning rays of New Year's morning sunlight spread across fresh snow, heralding the New Year with white fluff hanging on all the tree branches and covering the grounds and the deck of the house. This sunlit snow is happy-making, gladdening to the spirit. It bodes well for a New Year filled with rising good feeling, new promise and new prospects along with the joy-giving weather.

At New Year's time in northern Wisconsin when we go out of doors, we soon have ruddy cheeks and visible cold silvery vapors of breath. The packed frozen surface of the snow crackles underfoot, and heavy-laden pine branches sometimes dump snow on our hats and down our collars as we walk through the woods. Silence is broken only by the shrill call of a single bird, and sunlight warmth barely reaches through the gray shadows of leafless tree limbs standing above the frozen ice-locked lake shore. Bracing walks in the snowy woods are another way to do nothing in the depths of winter.

Silence on this morning is one of its greatest pleasures. Sitting in the quiet and stillness looking out at the snow, my inner eye sees peace, comfort, and assurance of life's steadiness and of my own reliability. Inside my warm house, in my near woods and beyond it my winter-solid lake with the snowfall outside and the noiseless calm everywhere, I find in my inner vision imagery sufficient to light the future days of the year to come. If this is meditation, I do it best with untracked snowfall.

In the late afternoon, I go out for a jubilant, solitary walk and see only bird tracks ahead of mine on the snow-filled road.

At sundown, a small fiery orange ball of light peeks through the white-clad branches, and streaks of pale blue and golden pink illuminate the sky's horizon as the unmarked covering of white still lies softly blanketing the frozen earth and lake for the night to come.

Sage and the dog run out to meet me, Sage's hat flaps flying. Sage takes my hand and smiles up at me and we walk back to the house hand-in-hand.

THE FIRST YEAR WE lived in England when I was in my thirties I did a research project on the nineteenth-century English intellectual, writer, and journalist, Harriet Martineau. I was interested in what she had written about women and the feminism of her day, but I also became intrigued with how she went about her work, her method. Eventually, I published a collection of Martineau's writings about women, but one of her books that I learned most from is called *How to Observe Manners and Morals*. She wrote this essay on board ship in 1834 as she sailed to the United States, where she was to travel, observe, and eventually write her well-known two-volume work, *Society in America*. While as a student I had studied ethics, the discipline addressing morality, I had never before connected *manners* and morality in my mind.

Manners to a girl growing up in the South was about using the correct silverware at dinner, or, indeed, setting the dinner table properly with the silver handles one inch from the edge of the table, the forks on the left, knives and spoons on the right, set from outside in toward the plate according to use in the sequence of the meal. Manners was about the dresses one should wear and what design and length and dress materials were fitting for which time and situation—somber and plain and with only gold jewelry for funerals, light-colored frocks that always covered the knees in the springtime, "fall colors" of browns and oranges and grays in the autumn (never mind what the weather was like), shiny materials like taffeta with sparkly beads or sequins only in the evening, and never, never white shoes after Labor Day. Manners decreed white shirts for men after six, and spit-polished men's shoes at all times. Manners were about being cheerful and kind and friendly, but not too friendly as to be forward with one's elders or the opposite sex. It was about "deportment"—for which there was a place on elementary school report cards for a "grade," presumably telling parents how children behaved in school. Clearly, it was bad deportment to get into fights, say rude words, insult people, or talk back to the teacher. That carried into adulthood: stay out of fights, use agreeable language, be considerate of other people's feelings and respect your elders and people in authority.

Until I read Harriet Martineau's *How to Observe Manners and Morals*, I really had not thought about the continuum from manners—everyday personal behaviors—to morals—public and principled behaviors that speak to respect for the shared needs within society of both persons in our daily lives and groups of people in public gatherings, indeed, of the needs and agreeable relationships of all of humankind. As the prolific fiction writer and medical law professor, Alexander McCall Smith, writes in his novel *The Sunday Philosophy Club*, "If each party knew what the other should do, then conflict would be unlikely. International law, after all, was a system of manners writ large."[1]

Respect is a key word for manners. However silly some of the rules of etiquette might seem, the reason for their being is to have an agreed-to understanding of the ground rules of behavior within any group so that interaction will have basic boundaries. The same is true of fundamental principles of morality, of ethics. This is true of any individuals or cultures, though some of the rules of etiquette—manners—and even some of morality—ethics—vary in different cultures. Thus, diplomats and national leaders, and even people who are simply travelers, are well served by learning the mores, or expected practices of manners, and ethical assumptions, along with languages and local dialects when interacting with people away from home. And, also like language, some practices and some rules of manners and ethics change and modify over time as cultures change and peoples change.

---

1. Alexander McCall Smith, *The Sunday Philosophy Club*. New York: Pantheon Books, 2004, p. 140.

Thinking of respect as the guideline principle, I consider the conflict that swarmed in the winter of 2006 between the West and the Muslim world. It was started by the publication in a Danish newspaper and subsequently in others of cartoons depicting the Prophet Muhammad in a derogatory fashion, one with a lighted bomb fuse rising out of his head. Protests raged in many cities of the world in Muslim communities, in Muslim countries, and among friends of Muslims. Violence occurred in numerous places and even deaths in some. Cartoonists, newspaper editors, and many people in the West insisted that the publication is defensible as a matter of free speech and of freedom of the press, important principles in democracies. The outraged Muslims argued, sometimes with violent protest, that the cartoons are blasphemous and are a desecration of their religion, and that those people and countries contributing to such attitudes should be punished. Some, if not all, of the anger was over the unpopular U.S. war in Muslim Iraq, and the U.S. flag was burned in demonstrations along with the Danish flag. Once all the fury was ignited, the protest and violence seemed to multiply, and there was no going back to origins of the conflict or reasons for the inflamed feelings. Lost on both sides seemed to be knowledge of the consequences their actions might bring, along with the inciting reasons for the controversy. In Islam, drawn or painted figures of all kinds, including representations of Muhammad, are not allowed to be made or published, for they are seen as religiously disrespectful. Political cartoonists' sustenance, though, is satire, so it might be hard for cartoonists to retreat from making fun of what is held in political, military, or religious regard. Even so, their picturing Muhammad and other representational items from Islam was a serious offense against their faith in the eyes of Muslim believers.

It seems to me that a knowledgeable and ethically sensitive understanding of what is held to be sacred by Muslims—respect for the religion of Islam and its people—might have given the cartoonists second thoughts about satirizing Muhammad. Indeed, the argument made in defense of such satirization that parallel pieces poking fun at their religions are usually taken in stride by the Christian or Jewish faithful in the West is not good enough. One needs to be aware that the ethical standards in Islam and in Islamic-majority countries are not at all the same ones held in a secular country or in a Christian or Jewish religious community. In my view, Jessica, these cultural standards of what are appropriate and what are violations of people's sacred views should be respected by outsiders as well as held by the faithful when both sides of a misunderstanding are trying to decipher and interpret behavior.

In the controversy over the cartoons showing Muhammad engaged in violence, both sides might have shown tolerance and avoided the unfortunate consequence. For instance, the cartoonists could have considered ahead of publication that Muslims reject any pictorial representation of what they deem sacred; and in objecting to the inflammatory cartoons, Muslims and their supporters could have forgiven the act of their publication in the knowledge that satire is not usually meant to be taken literally. Such responses might have shown awareness of both understanding and empathy, learning and loving.

Learning and loving are the twin parts of goodness, of ethics, it seems to me. A person must learn all she or he can to gain both the knowledge that facts and information bring and the understanding that developed reasoning, judgment, and interpretation offer.

If the aim of ethics is goodness, goodness for the person and goodness for society and the world, then individuals and communities must seek both learning and loving, must find ways to have both abundant learning and expansive loving. Learning well along with clear comprehension, both rationally and intuitively, is one part of goodness; and full-fledged loving with its components of generosity, respectfulness, and empathetic understanding is the other part of goodness. The same guidelines apply to both individuals and communities or nations. They work for everyday life and ordinary behavior, and, also, for major decision-making in public life on the domestic and world scene.

"Being good," as I learned from reading Martineau's *How to Observe Manners and Morals*, is not just behaving oneself. It does not mean just doing what seems right in one's own context or following unreflectively what some leader or authority figure has suggested. Rather, being good involves a commitment of a person and her community to understanding people and circumstances and the value systems out of which other people are working. The pursuit of goodness is to learn fully and to love fully as the components of living fully.

Respect that buttresses both learning and love intertwines the natural and the intellectual spheres, making the cycle of the seasons integral to the development of persons and societies as they grow in understanding, or, indeed, as we learn to let go of passions or engagements that limited us in our past. Loving the earth and taking care of my trees on my one acre at Coventry-in-the-Northwoods is one way I can take responsibility as a citizen of the world. Living harmoniously with nature in our time and in our place with the best rules we can discover and agree upon for both our personal deportment and the comportment of national and international affairs is the first step to realizing goodness.

9

Learning

... it doesn't matter where you watch life from if your gaze takes in the whole world.

— Verlyn Klinkenborg, "Donald Hall, Poet Laureate," *New York Times*

—Nature in Winter—Last night in Minneapolis as we were at a sixtieth birthday party for Kathi Austin Mahli in a downtown restaurant, we saw swirls of snow begin to fall outside the big windows right beside us. Snow spiraled and flew and heaped up on the ground, only to be blown again into thick circles of snowflakes in the air. It had not snowed for a while, so we thrilled at its snowing all evening. Snow came down all night and through the next morning, accumulating several inches. It was like a birth long anticipated—very little snow so far this winter, but then finally it came.

LEARNING COMES ALL SORTS of ways, systematized or stylized, haphazard, overwhelming or comforting, empowering or disabling. Learning in and of itself is just what happens to us as we go through our daily lives and the elevated times of our lives. If we are wise, we structure and take advantage of learning in ways that best serve our human growth. For me, reading, observing, and listening have been the best ways to learn.

READING

"Reading is funner than playing!" you announced one day near the end of kindergarten, Jessica, when your younger brothers and cousin were going out to play and you stayed behind with the adults to read aloud to us. I was overjoyed with both your new skill of reading and also with your priorities! When I was a child, I learned to read when I was three—I hardly remember not knowing how to read, but I do remember taking my brother's school books to my Aunt 'Cile and asking her to teach me to read. I don't think I had yet stopped drinking my milk from a baby bottle at that time, for I do remember filling up my own bottle and putting the nipple on it for myself and being teased by family members for that as somehow connected to my learning to read.

It was my teacher-mother who provided lots of books for me to practice reading; and, following my mother's lead, I soon thought reading was the most important activity one could pursue. As a rather isolated farm child, I could experience by reading much about other places and times and kinds of people that I would not have otherwise been exposed to. When I didn't quite trust what was going on around me, I learned to trust reading as giving me a greater truth than I could find in my immediate surroundings. There were some flaws in that viewpoint, of course. The rhyme "April showers/ Bring May flowers" was puzzling to me because we had spring flowers in southern Mississippi in February and March, long before May. My children's magazines that came to my rural Mississippi mailbox were full of stories about children playing in the snow in the winter and having to wear hats and mittens and heavy coats to go out of doors. We sometimes needed lightweight coats in December, January, and February; but we didn't have hats and gloves at all except for the ladies to dress up in to go to church or the men to do farming field work in the sun; and we never had snow. "White Christmas" was a song about somewhere else, for on Christmas Day, temperatures in the 70s were not unusual at my Mississippi home place, and we could run outdoors in our bare feet on the green grass and sometimes pick still-growing vegetables from the garden and cut fresh roses from the rose bushes. Oh, once every three or four years there might be a little snow for an hour or two or a more treacherous ice storm for a couple of days in the winter, or our small pond froze over on a few sub-freezing nights only to thaw in the daytime, but we did not usually have any ice or snow. I only read about frigid climates and how the children dressed for them. My experience of snow and ice, of boots and heavy coats and mufflers, of making snow forts and snow angels, and skating on ponds was only known to me by reading. I learned other weathers only by reading along with many facts and ideas that were other to my childhood location—and, actually I felt deprived or regionally inferior when every winter there were snow and ice to sled and skate upon in my magazines but not on our farm's grounds or our pond and creeks. As in the Wallace Stevens poem, "The Snow Man," I did not have access to "the mind of winter" to know the "pine trees crusted with snow." I did not know *real* winter, my child's mind concluded.

The negative side of my magazine-taught impression of winter was, of course, that cold winters became normative in my child's mind and I generalized that the places in the world that had snow were altogether better places than mine when the fact was merely that the writers and publishers of my reading material were Northern. Your experience with winter, Jessica, and the other seasons as a Minnesota child is the opposite of mine as a child, so you could think erroneously, conversely, that south Mississippi winters with Christmas green grass, bare ground, and an eleven-month growing season is some kind of enviable warm paradise— or an unpleasantly hot place—not just the way it is in another geography. You, too, can learn, though, about different climates and locations, as I did, by reading. Judgments good or bad do not need to follow gaining information.

You have many different kinds of opportunities to learn in your life, and I wondered when you were a very young child if you would enjoy reading as much as I did. However, I should have known: your parents and all of your surrounding adults have provided many, many books of your own; and your mother has taken you regularly to the library since you were a very little girl. Thus, even though it was not a surprise that you would enjoy reading, your announcement that "Reading is funner than playing!" gave me great delight. Child of my heart, daughter of my daughter, I can understand you and, with reading to share, we are big leaps ahead in understanding each other for the rest of our lives.

"Be a reader" is a kind of first rule to me for being a good learner. Still, there are countless other ways to learn, and I invite you to explore many, many of them.

OBSERVING

Another enjoyable way of learning is to be an observer. An observer is a watcher, one who pays close attention to what is around you. An observer looks for details, subtleties, and variations, as well as at the big picture and for logical progression. When you were just barely two and the ball you were playing with rolled under the couch, you exclaimed laughingly, "I wasn't paying my 'tention!" You learned early that you need to pay attention!

In her autobiographical essay, *One Writer's Beginnings*, Eudora Welty, a writer I admire very much, tells of paying attention as the beginning point for her as a storyteller and as her link to finding out the truth: "the *scene* (ital hers) was full of hints, pointers, suggestions, and promises of things to find out and know about human beings. I had to grow up and learn to listen for the unspoken as well as the spoken—and to know a truth, I also had to recognize a lie."[1]

She also writes about observing as she learned to do photography as a child. Her father had a camera, which her family would use on trips, and she learned that her father could capture images of what they saw on their travels and then they could hold them for later viewing. When she had her own little box camera, she learned for herself to catch images on film and have them as pictures to know in future observation as likenesses to the people or places in the moment she had photographed them. In the 1930s Welty made photographs all over Mississippi as a Works Progress Administration (WPA) worker, getting a start as a semiprofessional photographer. While her publications and reputation as an author increased over the years, and writing is the area in which she is widely known, she published books of photographs in the latter years of the twentieth century, and that work of hers, too, is considered fine art.

When I was a college student, anthropology was one of the subjects new to me that I enjoyed studying very much. In the field of anthropology, being a participant-observer is one method of doing serious scholarly work. It is based on watching and paying attention. An anthropologist lives among people and tunes in to everything visible, suggested, and spelled out in the culture and among the people she or he is studying. Participant-observation involves noticing what people eat and drink, what they do for fun and for work, what people do for money or compensation, how their families function, what they take seriously, what they scorn, and what they celebrate. The scholar pays attention to what the people hold sacred or religious and what is mundane, which possessions are treasured, which are readily disposable. It is a very specific look at one group of people in one time and place.

1. Eudora Welty, *One Writer's Beginnings*. Cambridge: Harvard University Press, 1983, p. 16.

In the late nineteenth and early twentieth centuries, participation-observation was one of the methods that developed with the founding of the field of anthropology. Franz Boas (1858–1942) is considered the founder of American anthropology and the accompanying branches of that field: cultural anthropology, physical anthropology, linguistics, and social theory. Some new ideas that came into shared educational prominence along with and developed within anthropology by the turn of the twentieth century were cultural relativism, social dynamism, and cultural egalitarianism. For these notions to be operative, a science of culture and society was needed, not just a philosophy or system of thinking. Cultural relativism is the belief that the way human lives and societies are organized is not set or static, but mobile and interactive over time and place. Its concomitant, social dynamism, suggests that through time and in locations societies and people change and reshape themselves. Their patterns of behaviors and beliefs are fluid rather than set. The third conceptual principle, cultural egalitarianism, holds that all societies are equivalent or parallel in values or structures of behavior. Thus, no one "civilization" or society or group of "civilizations" is superior to or the standard for others, but all cultural groups are comprehended as equally complex and equally valuable in and of themselves, even though their characteristics might differ considerably. Anthropologists' social theory emerged as they searched for ways of explaining their new understandings of peoples, societies, and cultures. Among the first of the scientific methods developed by anthropologists to shape and test these new ideas of what cultures and societies are was participation-observation.

Franz Boas taught anthropology at Columbia University, and both his own work and that of his students helped fashion anthropology as a new academic discipline, as a new approach to science, and as a bold new way of routine thinking. Ordinary observation, for example, with a consciousness of cultural relativism rather than a preconception of an established viewpoint, can lead a person to new and imaginative ways of seeing her everyday world.

Two of Boas's women students, both Columbia University PhDs in anthropology, were to be major contributors to changing American intellectual life with studies they did as participant observers. Ruth Benedict (1887–1948) finished her PhD in 1923 and soon published *Patterns of Culture* (1934), a work that has given future generations the tenets of a new way of looking at culture. Benedict used death rituals as her subject to provide cultural characterizations of three different groups: Pueblo Indians from the U.S. Southwest from her own field research she called "placid and harmonious"; Dobu Islanders in Papua New Guinea from fellow anthropologist Rio Fortune's research were characterized as "paranoiac and mean spirited"; and the Kwakiutl, Native Americans from British Columbia, from her professor Franz Boas's studies, were labeled "self aggrandizing and megalomaniacal."[2] Margaret Mead (1902–1978), whose PhD year was 1929, published her graduate student participant-observer work as *Coming of Age in Samoa* in 1928 and *Growing Up in New Guinea* in 1930. From her field learning focused on childhood and adolescence, Mead published these widely influential books that had long-lasting effects both on academic life and on public examination of prevailing customs and mores around maturation of children and about teenagers' sexual behavior.

Some of the conclusions of these anthropologists and even their research methods have been challenged by subsequent scholars, and debates about them go on. However, when I was an undergraduate student studying anthropology for the first time, I found both Benedict's and Mead's books stimulating and enlightening, and they still have prominent places in our cultural history, as well as in my memory of my developing new ways to think as a young student. I invite you also, Jessica, to think of their intellectual contributions and what you can gain from them. These anthropologists' professional observations and reports on it have made immense contributions to knowledge and to helping us think about what we know and can understand in different ways. To be a good observer, though, Jessica, you need not be a professional anthropologist. Observing well can be a very useful part of ordinary life for a child or for an adult. Paying attention, close observation can be a part of your everyday life, now and all of the time. Practicing being an observer means to notice everything, to keep your eyes and ears and mind open, especially to the subtlety of detail or innuendo or apparent contradictions.

Anthropology with its head start on studies through observation was a field that was ready early to be a home for a form of feminist studies. Sherry B. Ortner has been one of the leaders of feminist studies in anthropology. She, like earlier American anthropologists, first studied people from economically underdeveloped nations and regions of the world

2. www.webster.edu/-woolflm/ruthbenedict.html

and U.S. minority populations. In her case, her first work was among the Sherpas of northeast Nepal. Her second book was a very influential work on gender, *Female to Male as Nature Is to Culture* (1974), a work asserting male dominance in cultures worldwide, a position she modified in later works to show more cultural gender-flexibility.

Recently, though, she has turned more definitely to her own group and did a book on class, race or ethnicity, and gender from research among her high school graduating class at Weequahic High School in Newark, New Jersey. *New Jersey Dreaming: Capital, Culture and the Class of '58* was published in 2003. She calls it a "social and cultural genealogy," and her subsequent research has been about Generation X, the children of these middle-class subjects who were her classmates.

Once I met Sherry Ortner when she was a guest at my university; but, more important, she and I shared the goals of many scholars of our generation of wanting to study more seriously and more deeply the particulars of our own lives and the lives of women in our past, our societies, and worldwide. Ortner's field of anthropology had perhaps a head start on other disciplines by having methods like participant observation and by their having experience studying individuals within groups and collectivities to reach analytic conclusions about cultures. Anthropologists also had learned how to use their social-scientific findings to advocate beneficial social changes.

Along with Ortner, during my early years as a professor in the 1970s and 1980s, many of us feminist scholars began to look at our own academic fields for both biases against women and underrepresentation of the subject of women and women's gender-specific culture. This often was followed by a deeper look at contemporary cultures and lives through the lens of feminist understanding of paying attention to women; women's points of view; the particular ways women worked, behaved, and spoke; women's lives; women's interactions with other people, and what we came to call women's culture. Previously, it had often been assumed that women and men were "alike," or no assumption at all was made about women as a group separate from men, or, conversely, women were assigned social roles based on gender that went without much examination or contestation. In many different ways we recovered women's works in literature and art and sciences. We studied social biases against women or laws, speech patterns, or social and cultural expectations that set women apart in harmful or judgmental ways and hampered women's full humanity.

We searched for more realistic views of how women and men are different and how alike. Together we started the new field of Women's Studies with its feminist scholarly methods in the 1970s. It gives me pleasure to know that I was one of the early group of American women scholars who helped re-shape intellectual, educational, and cultural understanding of women.

For my sixtieth birthday, in your voice as a one-month-old baby, your parents wrote a tribute to me that showed their perception of my shared professional goals with those of Sherry Ortner and other feminist scholars. I was honored that they understood what was professionally important to me and what my college anthropology professor, George Maddox, called my "preferred self-concept." In "An Ode to My Grandma," Natasha and Ian wrote to me for their baby Jessica:

> She loves to inspire others to think
> with precision and passion.
> She writes about people and places
> that make a difference in our world.
> She took an important role in increasing opportunities
> for members of my gender
> so that we may lead more equal and equitable lives, . . .

"Be a watcher, an observer!" is indeed an important suggestion for a manner by which to learn and to learn well. I am pleased that your parents' observation of me is such an appealing one and one that is the way I want to be known.

LISTENING

Listening is another tool for learning that is enormously important. Sometimes listening requires the discipline of being quiet and attending to what other people are saying and also being clear about what people you are listening to mean by what they are saying. Listening in other ways informs and teaches you. You learn by hearing sounds in nature, distinguishing bird calls, differentiating with your eyes closed the gentle waves on the lake from rapidly lapping wave sounds, hearing wind blow fiercely or slowly, and perceiving signals from whistles or bells in the distance. Listening to music opens up languages of sound and rhythm, harmonies, dissonance, counterpoint, and tension resolution. Music evokes emotional stimulation and attachments and it reveals mathematical appreciation of its design. Hearing is an altogether thoroughgoing and helpful form of learning. Yet, mere hearing is different from listening. Listening is paying attention with your mind and heart as well as your ears.

On the subject of listening, I again especially recommend Eudora Welty's autobiographical essay *One Writer's Beginnings* along with her fiction and essays, from which I enjoy learning. *One Writer's Beginnings* is an account, not only of how she became a writer, but also of how she learned as a child and what she learned that carried her well into adulthood and her amazing career as a world-renowned fiction writer. I had an advantage beyond many readers of Welty, perhaps, because she was from my home state of Mississippi and many of the places she wrote about, the people she created as characters in her fiction, and the atmosphere and attitudes she turned into fiction in her Mississippi settings were familiar to me from my growing up time. Also, the dialects her characters spoke were usually familiar to me from the one I spoke as a child and the ones I heard surrounding me in southern Mississippi.

Even so, she uses the particulars and cultural nuances and landscape and language of our shared home state to fashion creative writing that addresses profoundly shared human dilemmas, foibles, and celebrations. Her work is far from simply about Mississippi. Readers of many nationalities, regions, and affinities enjoy Welty's work and scholars translate it and study it and hold conferences about it. I once attended a conference in Dijon, France, on "The Southernness of Eudora Welty's Writing" that was sponsored by Danièlle Pitavy, a French professor who had just published a book in French on Welty's work and who had been instrumental in having stories by Welty added to the nationwide French-required secondary school curriculum. All of the 35 or so scholars from several countries who attended the conference had published books or articles on Welty or were French and Japanese translators working on texts by Welty. Youli Theodosiadou from Greece, Elsbieta Oleksy from Poland as well as Danièlle and her husband, François, from France, and several Americans were among the Welty scholars whom I met at that Dijon event, and we have all become professional friends of each other's since that time. Some of us have even visited each other's countries as professional guests of one another. I mentioned before my visits to Greece sponsored by Youli Theodosiadou, and I also had a marvelous lecture trip to Łodz and Krakow in Poland as Elsbieta Oleksy's guest. It was fun to hear my lectures on Eudora Welty translated into Polish as I gave them in

Elsbieta's classes! All of us have seen each other several times subsequently at Eudora Welty Society conferences or European American Studies Southern Studies meetings and have enjoyed listening to one another's talks and papers on Eudora Welty.

Welty divided her short memoir into three parts: Listening, Seeing, and Finding a Voice. In the first section on listening, Welty describes from her earliest childhood the familiar sounds that have remained in her memory and enriched her life and her writing: the clocks in the Welty home striking—"a mission style oak grandfather clock" that had "gong-like strokes," a smaller striking clock "that sometimes answered it," a cuckoo clock "with weights on long chains"; her mother and father early in the morning humming or whistling as they got ready for the day, phrases from "The Merry Widow" going back and forth to each other while the small girl tried to button her shoes; and the toy trains her father loved to run, whose "elegant rush and click . . . could be heard through the ceiling, running around and around its figure eight."[3]

From the sounds from her childhood, Welty drew imagery, as any of us can from what we have heard and seen. The sound imagery's meanings in the memoir suggest pictures and sounds to our imagination as readers. Welty also writes about being read to in what her father called "the library" and being shown the barometer and the night sky from which she learned to love reading and what she called her "meteorological sensibility, " which later fed her writing. She also enjoyed listening endlessly to the women's conversations when other Jackson women came to call on her mother or when the seamstress came to sew. She loved listening to the treadle of the sewing machine clacking up and down, listening to what the adults had to say, and making what she would of what they meant, both by what was said and what was left unspoken.

My own memory of early childhood resonated with the sound of the sewing machine as I first read *One Writer's Beginnings*. I remember sitting on the floor beside Aunt 'Cile's treadle Singer sewing machine and hearing the rhythms of the treadle as she pressed it up and down, making the needle on the surface go "tack-tack-tack-tack-tack-tack" through the fabric under Aunt 'Cile's deft fingers. And then my mind moves me in memory to under the quilting frames in winter where Aunt Bessie and Aunt 'Cile spent many hours, their needles coming down to where I could

3. Eudora Welty, *Beginnings*, p. 51.

see them under the quilt and then quickly being pushed back up out of my view by their skillful hands, then down again in an instant. Sometimes my two aunts talked to each other as they quilted, but my warmest memories of those wintertime hours under the quilting frames and the beautiful quilts being stitched on them was their teaching me orally Bible verses, psalms, and prayers they had memorized from the King James Version of the Bible.

Welty said that she had learned after she became an experienced writer that she could tell if her writing "sounded" right from reading it over in her head and mentally hearing how the lines read. And hearing Welty read her own work was an incomparable experience. There are recordings of her reading some of her stories, which I will someday play for you, Jessica.

Listening in one's regular life, listening carefully at all times is a very important way to learn. Informed listening I have learned to do as a scholar, as in the case of our listening to one another's talks and papers at the Welty conferences. Such listening is a fine way to develop deeper understanding.

In a way, listening connects to "doing nothing": freeing one's mind totally of stimuli and activity to be utterly at rest, to be carefree, to let go. Listening often has a focus, like observing does; it is sometimes deliberate attention to sound. However, it can be, like "doing nothing," devoid of intention, plan, or concentration. The palimpsest or opposite of one quality can be its reinforcement.

Once I told one of my friends that I don't enjoy symphony orchestra music as much as I think I should, though I go often to orchestra performances with Wilson because he enjoys them so much. She said, "Oh, I just sit in Orchestra Hall and let the music flow over me, and I learn all I want!" I tried that approach and it worked. So it can be with listening in general. Not listening can paradoxically be good listening, if one is open to what might come to one's ears. I had been trying too hard to "know" the orchestra music, to analyze it according to some academic formula I did not quite understand; but, when I opened myself to simply experiencing the music, to enjoying it however it came, I was suddenly free to delight in it.

The learning attributes, skills, or tools, then, that I recommend most highly your practicing well, Jessica, are reading, observing, and listening. They are at the same time everyday and easy and, also, can be highly developed, complex, elaborate, and sophisticated. There are, of course, more attributes of learning, more ways of learning, and many applications. For example, you can think of learning modes in application to language, the arts, or science and mathematics.

Using your tools for learning, involve yourself first and most wholly with language. Language is the learning tool I most enjoy playing with and developing my ability in its use. Early in your life you were very good with language and you can already be very creative, very precise, and very engaging with the way you speak and think with language. You enjoy learning the exact word for a thing or situation, and with your quick mind, you remember and use new words that you hear. When you were barely six, you broke your arm and your mother taught you to say you had a "fractured ulna." She had not meant anything pretentious by this, simply giving you the exact word. However, after you had said that often and impressed and astonished adults, she told you maybe you should just say you have a broken arm! But that language accuracy of yours I greatly admire and share appreciation of it with you and your mother.

Also, involve yourself with the arts. Practicing an art form is very good for your learning; and, if you become expert in it, so much the better. However, just learning for the pleasure of it alone is good. Learning how to do a certain kind of art makes you understand that art for the rest of your life, both that art form itself and understandings about life itself that you can come to through that art's conveyed knowledge. The best example of this from my life is playing the piano. Although I am a very pedestrian pianist, the many years of piano lessons my mother insisted I take have paid off in my understanding and enjoying the playing by accomplished pianists—and, indeed, of my understanding a great deal about music and the music-making of many instrumental musicians.

In addition, do math and science, Jessica. Throw yourself as fully as you can into these subjects. I favored the arts and literature. Your mother had an inclination for the sciences, and she is a science teacher. Whichever direction you go—the arts or the sciences—and who knows, you may be one of those balanced people who does equally well in the arts and the sciences—give a great deal of time to learning about science and math, alongside learning arts, ways of thinking such as philosophy and literature. They are building blocks for vast areas of knowledge and enjoyment whatever eventually becomes your area of expertise. Of course, it is entirely possible to combine these branches of knowledge. The artistic skill you already show as a child you might one day use for science as an illustrator of medical textbooks, for example, or at making botanical art for investigating plant species in an endangered forest.

As you read, observe, and listen, be diligent with your investigations for learning. Be persistent! Challenge yourself! Steady attention pays off in lifelong satisfaction with having learned and in knowing how to keep on learning! Too few people realize that learning is an endeavor for one's entire lifetime.

10

Knowing Science and Knowing Art

Poetry is as necessary to comprehension as science. It is as impossible to live without reverence as it is without joy.

—Henry Beston, *The Outermost House*

—Nature in Winter—I built a fire in the fireplace on arrival at the cottage the day before yesterday, then made chicken soup for my supper. In the mornings yesterday and today I took walks up the road in the frigid weather with snow waist deep and higher on the roadside, two and three feet solid on the ground. Each night I saw the first star, shining bright about 30 or 40 minutes after sundown in the high western sky just above where the red sun had gone down. Seeing the first star reminded me happily of rocking your uncle Stiles in the rocking chair in his nursery at his bedtime when he was a toddler just learning words. I would see with him the first star appear and teach him the familiar nursery rhyme, "Star light, star bright/ First star I see tonight/ I wish I may/ I wish I might/ Have the wish I wish tonight."

This morning the sun shines on a white landscape of complete stillness. Yesterday's untouched snow cover on the lake now shows tracks from midnight snowmobilers, but this morning there is no motion at all in the soft light that glows gently over the white landscape, that illuminates the snow caught in the crevices of bare tree branches and glances over the pine treetops.

SCIENCE WAS YOUR MOTHER'S choice of subject for studying and teaching, Jessica. At Beloit College, she majored in psychology and minored in biology. After graduation she did primate behavioral research on tamarin monkeys for a summer in the Panamanian rain forest in a project of the Smithsonian Tropical Research Institute. The research findings were used to try to convince the Panamanian government to stop deforestation.

After that, she taught science in Letlekeng in Botswana as a Peace Corps volunteer. When she came back to the U. S., she worked for a few months in a biochemical laboratory at 3M, and then moved to New York where she earned an M.A. in science education at Columbia University. Upon graduation she stayed in New York City and for the next seven years taught middle school science, math, and health at the United Nations International School. She particularly liked environmental biology, and she continues her engagement with environmental concerns in practical ways in her lifestyle choices and her advocacy work in your Mississippi River town of Red Wing as she takes care of you and your brothers as young children and participates in your community life.

In the broadest sense, science is an attempt to understand the physical and natural worlds by the exploration of natural phenomena. In scientific fields, events, or trends, living things or inanimate objects in nature can be observed, analyzed, and explained; and facts from them can be proven and verified by tried and true methods of testing. Thus, biologists, astronomers, physicists, chemists, or biochemists can get at knowledge, discover new knowledge, or, indeed, sometimes refute previous scientific findings as untrue, by replication of each other's observations, experiments, analyses, and conclusions.

Science is about explaining nature. Arts subjects are about showing and interpreting human meanings.

Although science begins with observation of nature and ideas about testing explanations of a natural phenomenon, art involves making something that was not there before. Art, like science, begins with ideas and imagination but the shape of art takes form from human creativity, while science involves testing ideas about nature with various procedures of measurement. The ideas that give rise to scientific study are questions and formulations aimed at understanding and explaining nature. The material for science is all of nature. The materials for art are words or rhythms, sounds or objects of metal or wood and chisels or paints, canvases and brushes, or other components. Making art, just like doing science, requires discipline and training, either formal training with expert teachers or self-teaching with a considerable amount of ambition and self-control. The products of art might be literary, poetic, musical, operatic, architectural or sculptural, or even philosophical or sociological. An artist might depict the moon in bronze or silver or paint the stars with oils. A scientist might ask, How far away are the moon and the stars? How hot or cold is the moon? The stars and the planets? And where did the bronze, the silver, and the paints come from?

The genesis of either art or science might well be the same, however, might be the budding of an idea in a person's thoughts and the desire to pursue that idea to an end of understanding some reality of nature or humanity. It might be a collective or cultural beginning when a need cries out in a community for a problem to be solved, a device to be made, or a source of human suffering to be addressed. Creativity is also involved in both science and art, as is the function of intuition, or a hunch that something might work, that something might be understood in a new light. Still, art and science run alongside each other in humankind's wit and wisdom as two paths that lead to knowing.

11

Architecture as Both Science and Art

There is simplicity of nature, and there is simplicity of wisdom. Both of them evoke love and respect.

—Leo Tolstoy, *A Calendar of Wisdom*

—Nature in Winter—Snow had fallen yesterday when I arrived at Coventry-in-the-Northwoods and the temperature spiraled downward all afternoon and night. When I turned on our little weather-warner radio this morning, its mechanical voice told me the temperature was barely above zero degrees Fahrenheit. More snow had come in the night, a light and fluffy snow, big crystals that looked almost like separate snowflakes piled high with lots of lacy pattern in the puffy mounds on the ground. When I bundled up in my boots and coat, hat and gloves and ventured outdoors to brush the snow off the mailbox and put in my outgoing letters and to go to the woodpile to get in more wood for my fireplace fire, I had the impulse to lie down and make snow angels beside the road, so magical was the soft, icy covering of the earth, but I refrained, going back into the house to my wood fire and my work.

THERE IS A THRILL I have, a rosy feeling rising in my chest—intuitive; irrational; glowing; bubbly—that comes when I read a poem that I find magnificent, when I meet the eyes of an adored person, when my team wins the World Series, when my political party wins the election, when I have agonized over a problem and then its solution comes, when I complete a really hard task and know I have done well, when my beloved asks me to make love with him, when I walk across the Washington

Avenue Bridge and look up and see the shining stainless steel Weisman Art Museum in front of me, when I am served chocolate mousse cake with raspberry sauce, when I have searched for the precise word numerous times and then the exact one appears, when I hear the ocean waves rush and splash on Boca Raton beach, when I bring in the *New York Times* in its blue plastic wrapper off the front steps of our Minneapolis home first thing in the morning, when I see the snow blowing in big spirals over Callahan Lake and I am safely indoors in front of my wood fire in our cottage's stone fireplace. This feeling, elation, is in the top two percentile of pleasures for me. It is stimulation and satisfaction for me intellectually, aesthetically, and emotionally. And elation is what I feel in the presence of good architecture.

The practice of architecture, as well as architectural interpretation and history, forms a discipline that is a blend of both science and art. A course in the history of American architecture taught by Professor Donald Torbert was one of the best parts of my graduate education. Until I took that course I had paid little attention to architecture as a subject or to buildings on the landscape of my life. After that year-long course, pilasters and dormers and hipped roofs and steel trusses; Corinthian, Ionic, and Doric capitals; Carpenter Gothic, board-and-batten, and Richardsonian Romanesque styles; bricks and wood and stone, stainless steel and glass and plaster materials; cedar and walnut and oak and grade-one white pine lumber became terms in my vocabulary; and experiencing architecture more knowledgably became a new delight for me. Where before buildings and bridges, houses and skyscrapers had just been there, vaguely in my vicinity, now I enjoy them, appreciate them, revere some of them even, or criticize them with new awareness and with a much wider range of applicable words and arena of comprehension.

As a professor of interdisciplinary American Studies, I taught architecture topics as cultural material in some of my classes. I taught about the early twentieth century organic architecture of Frank Lloyd Wright, how Wright led in the Prairie School of architecture that had its beginnings when Wright worked as a young man with Louis Sullivan in his Chicago studio. I taught about Louis Sullivan's role in the 1893 Chicago World's Fair, known as the World's Columbian Exhibition, in which most of the buildings were painted white and were in a style that referred back to mid-century French Ecole des Beaux-Arts influence. McKimm, Mead, and White, the "White City" architects for the fair had studied at the

Ecole des Beaux-Arts; and among their white buildings Sullivan's highly decorated Transportation Building with its bright colors of red, orange, and yellow, receding arches and a gold-leaf overlay, stood out like a sore thumb. In a short time, though, it became clear that Sullivan, and not the "White City" architects, was setting a new direction in American architectural practice.

It was Sullivan's work that anticipated modernism and his early dictum "form follows function" provided modernism's rationale. A gem of his late work is a bank building in Owatonna, Minnesota; and Professor Mulford Sibley and I took a class of graduate students we were team-teaching to visit that building one spring day. We drove to Owatonna from Minneapolis through farmlands with black soil newly plowed, and as we enjoyed the baby green of new leaves on trees and opened our car windows to breathe in the fresh spring air, it was not hard to understand the organic principle of these architects. It was clear they wanted their buildings to appear to be one with the earth, to seem to rise unbroken from their foundations in nature like rocks rising out of the soil or timbers patterned to stand alongside trees.

The Owatonna bank has been called the most beautiful bank building in the world. In this small town, Sullivan's gem of architecture shines like a miniature monument across the street from a park. It is a great brick cube of oranges, browns, and tans with huge arches in which are set sparkling abstractly patterned stained-glass windows. Blue and green tiles decorate the arches and the circumference of the bank, and Sullivan's characteristic leaf-and-vine patterned terra cotta ornamentation finishes the corners. The building is said to be Sullivan's finest work and is called a masterpiece, a treasure, and a jewel. Its visitors come from far distances, other countries, and many states in our nation. Many people, including our students, Mulford and I, find it breathtaking and are very pleased to have visited it.

After we visited the bank, we were invited to the home of a former student of socialist Mulford Sibley's for supper. Though I was the initiator of our focus on architecture, Mulford, who had been my PhD thesis advisor and was much loved by us all—leftists, moderates, regular Democrats, partisan Republicans, and right-wingers alike—was the contact with his former student and became a lesson in graceful acceptance whatever one's politics. The woman who hosted our group for supper was a former Republican national committeewoman and had a picture of former President Ronald Reagan on her sunroom wall. Unfortunately, some of us, as we ate supper in her sunroom as her guests, almost got the giggles as we saw left-wing student Paul Carrizales seated under Reagan's portrait. Mulford, however, retained his full dignity and respectfulness as we received the hospitality of his former student in her town where we visited its architecturally iconic bank.

Architecture also became an integral part of my travel after I took Donald Torbert's class and I visited important and lowly buildings alike in the United States and abroad. When we spent our first sabbatical year in England, Jessica, when your mother was nine and Stiles five, I took the lead in family excursions to English parish churches and cathedrals. I was soon learning the period designations of ancient and medieval English architecture and developing a new repertoire of visual architectural images.

We went to see the Anglo-Saxon tower of St. Bene't's Church in Cambridge, the building where the "little priest" monumental brass is housed, our rubbing of which hangs on our dining room wall in Minneapolis. The brass lies in the stone floor of an aisle and we made several rubbings from it, and, also, we returned again and again to see the brass as well as the building on many visits back to Cambridge. We went to the Norman church in the village of Iffley near Oxford and saw this near perfect example of Norman style, St. Mary's Parish Church, built in 1170 and known as Romanesque almost everywhere except in England. We later bought a copy of an architectural drawing of the Iffley church that also hangs in our Minneapolis home.

We drove our car the few miles from Cambridge to the cathedral town of Ely and enjoyed seeing the glorious Norman structure, built in the eleventh century by William the Conqueror soon after he came to England in 1066 on the site that had long been a church and dedicated as a cathedral in 1109. Ely Cathedral rises out of the region of the flat fen land of East Anglia as if it were a ship on waters. The cathedral's enormous octagonal central tower has a Gothic dome, the only intact octagonal one still in existence today. The present-day cathedral stands on a site of a Saxon church and a monastery built in 673 and set up for an order of nuns led by the feisty and independent St. Etheldreda after the end of her second marriage. For a while I adopted St. Etheldreda as my personal "matron saint" in appreciation of her independence and leadership of women, and she continues to be a special saint in our household. We have returned to Ely many times, once hearing a concert in the cathedral conducted by Leonard Bernstein and more than once visiting the Lady Chapel where stone images remain defaced and broken from the ravages of Oliver Cromwell's seventeenth-century Puritan revolution. Now that our friends Virginia and Stephen Watkinson live in Ely beside the River Ouse, we combine our visits with going to this favorite cathedral of ours with them. When Stiles and five-year-old Sage went with us to England, Ely Cathedral was Sage's first major religious architectural site to see.

While in England for that first sabbatical year, we took our first trip across the English Channel on the ferry in our little Volkswagen station wagon. With the children in the back seat, we arrived in France, drove to Paris, and made our first visit to the Cathedral of Notre Dame de Paris. All of that church's architectural glories of beauty, delicacy, and monumentality are still present in our memory, but its renowned stained glass rose window is the most cherished of our visual memories of it.

With architecture, then, as one of my great arts loves, when the University of Minnesota contracted with highly renowned architect Frank Gehry to design and build its new Weisman Art Museum, I was thrilled. The museum opened in 1993, and as we prepared for its opening, I volunteered to the museum's education director, my former student Colleen Sheehy, to train to be a tour guide. By means of Colleen's tour guides class and learning about the new museum's holdings and the design and plans for the building, I got in on the ground floor to watch the construction and opening of the WAM building. We tour guides are called Weisguides, and that first group of Weisguides enormously enjoyed going on a hardhat tour of the building as it was in process of being built. We also delighted in meeting the workers as they did their jobs and in meeting Gehry himself at the opening events. Someone made a photograph of me with the great architect that I cherish like a starstruck schoolgirl.

The abstractly sculptural stainless steel building towering above the rock face of a bluff on the Mississippi River is a favorite of Frank Gehry himself and is widely appreciated. At the time of its opening, the *New York Times* architecture critic said that the building has "five of the most gorgeous galleries on earth." Gehry himself has said that our museum, the first he designed in its entirety, as opposed to simply adding onto, was the beginning work for his series of enormously successful, large and expensive, and world-acclaimed sculptural buildings, including the

Guggenheim Museum of Bilbao, Spain, and the Los Angeles Disney Concert Hall.

John Cook was the local project architect for the Weisman and I served with him on the museum board. After that, Jessica, it was, of course, gratifying to be able to work with John Cook and his partner, Joan Soranno, toward the building of the architecture award-winning Bigelow Chapel at your granddad's institution, United Theological Seminary. I volunteered to be on the chapel planning committee and successfully nominated my Weisman advisory board colleague and his partner to be the architectural team for the chapel building project.

Joan Soranno and John Cook introduce themselves by saying that Joan is the art part of the team and John is the science team member. Joan does the design work, and John does the technical planning, the implementation of the design, and the oversight of the construction. It was clear from the way they present themselves that they see their work as melding art and science. Over the months of watching the plan develop and the building go up, I was fascinated to see the truth of this blend in their practical and very beautiful application after the initial months of thinking, designing, consulting, and working out the physical site-specific engineering, technical, and aesthetic prospects for the building.

At the beginning of its process, the chapel planning committee held a typical architectural competition with five architectural firms or teams presenting their proposed plans. Joan and John presented her plan and a small wooden model featuring a circular design for the building was presented by them; and, though Joan and John as a team might have had a bit of a lead because of John's and my previous association, the committee, especially its women members, liked the circular building arrangement of Joan's design very much. By contrast, the other four competitors, all first-rate architects, proposed rectangular and vertical structures that matched the rather boxy modernist shapes and vertical and horizontal straight lines of the library building and classroom wing at United Seminary that would form two sides of a quadrangle with the projected chapel.

After John and Joan got the commission, therefore, we were disappointed when they brought to the committee the first models for the project with exterior lines that were straight, tall, and flat, no longer curvilinear. We women had liked the suggestion of the feminine that the round chapel model conveyed, in contrast with the very masculine-seeming verticality of the other campus buildings. However, Joan eventually won us over—and probably secured the dozen or so awards given to the finished building—with a stunning, magical curvilinear interior design. It features very thin curved translucent panels of a golden-toned quilted maple that banks in front of solid windows and rounds upward just beneath the glass ceiling. There the translucent panels soar across the sanctuary and create a warm, enveloping, and nurturing inside environment.

At the start of construction of the Bigelow Chapel, Jessica, you were a part of the groundbreaking ceremony! With me on the committee and your granddad at the helm as president, we asked that you be a ground-breaker as a three-year-old child among the dignitaries, as your mother had been when she was twenty-months-old at a groundbreaking for a church in Framingham, Massachusetts, where Wilson was a graduate student assistant minister. We have a picture of Natasha holding a little shovel that day in Framingham—and another of adult Natasha digging into the ground for the Bigelow Chapel with your little gold-painted trowel with your three-year-old's head on her shoulder. Apparently, you had turned a little shy and had asked her to "help" turn the soil with the little golden trowel in front of all those people.

The glorious finished chapel—now pictured on lots of glossy covers of magazines and in multipage spreads of architecture publications—is made of glass, precast concrete stone formed in patterns of Italian Travertine marble, and stainless steel. The chapel features a bell tower at the south end that reaches the height of the library opposite the building and a cantilevered extension of the flat roof on the north end that balances in length the height of the tower. The west wall is a curtain wall of glass and stainless steel with heavy glass fins or perpendicular extended panels that might be interpreted to mimic buttresses on traditional churches. The east wall is stone, and the roof is glass with a rubber layer of water-proofing. On the south end, there is an entrance to the building from the parking lot, and this entrance vestibule adjoins a hallway where there is a new office for the seminary chaplain, the sacristy (storage for liturgical garments and vessels), rest rooms, and entryway pegs for hanging coats. One enters the building from the south into a processional aisle carpeted with soft green covering that first becomes a narrow hallway with glass panels entirely on the west through which we see the meditation garden with its sedum ground cover, musclewood tree, and dark stones, then moves forward beside the main sanctuary space.

The processional aisle is atypically on a single side of the sanctuary, not down the middle or on two sides of the worship space as aisles often are. It descends at a slight angle all the way down to the narthex on the north end and is separated from the central space by only a low balustrade made of wood like the floors and like the curvilinear west panels over the windows and ceiling. The east wall beside the processional aisle is solid, a white plaster surface covering the stone wall, with high clerestory windows of translucent glass.

The central worship space under the flowing curved wood panels has light wood furniture as well. The chairs are movable so that services may be conducted with the congregation facing any direction. Looking toward the south, the view is a solid stone wall with a large concave cross hollowed into it and a window to the congregation's left with a view of the meditation garden featuring its musclewood tree. If it should face toward the west, the congregation has a view of and through the maple panels and glass and to the out of doors beyond them and can see sunsets in the western evening sky. There are endless possibilities of arranging the beautifully designed Annika chairs and other furniture, east, west, north, or south, but these two have proven the favorites of the chaplain and other clergy who have overseen services and events in the building.

The millwork for the Bigelow Chapel was done by a company called Wilkie-Sanderson; and when Joan Soranno, not able to bear the thought of machine-made pulpit furniture possibly contrasting with her beautifully designed wood interior, volunteered to design the pulpit furniture, as well, and Wilkie-Sanderson volunteered to make it, as they had the cabinetry and other millwork for the chapel, as well as their having fabricated the maple panels.

I especially enjoyed learning from all the skillful people who worked on the chapel how they did their work, Jessica. In addition to the pair of talented senior architects and their younger colleague Steven Dwyer from Hammel, Green and Abrahamson (HGA), the uniform pride in their work and expertise at accomplishing it were shown by everyone: the Mortenson Construction Company's management representative Scott Ganske; the construction worker superintendent of the building project Tom Schwab; the Wilkie-Sanderson millwork company led by Marc Sanderson; the creators of the precast concrete stone blocks at the ArtStone company including owner-designer Marc Rolle; the stonemason Jim Suprelle; indeed, all the workers on the project. They all amazed me, as did the lead donor Mollie McMillan in whose parents' memory the building was named and who worked tirelessly as an active building committee member. The seminary staff members and officers worked diligently, also, and with increasing excitement as the building became a reality.

I have great memories of several decisive moments in the chapel building process that it was fun to be a party to. The first had to do with pew seats.

One day John and Joan brought to the committee several graceful and attractively designed chairs to consider choosing for the pew chairs. We took our turns sitting in them, and the men pronounced them uncomfortable, too small, not fitting their backs very well. Your granddad and seminary vice-president Jon Morgan led this objection. Most of the women, including me and including Mollie McMillan, liked the Annika chair very much and thought it fit our bodies perfectly; and, besides, we thought it the most handsome. After we had expressed our opinions, particularly Mollie, the committee voted for the Annika chairs. I don't know whether this had more to do with our being women and in the majority or with Mollie's being the major donor!

Just before the opening of the building, retired communications professor Gene Jaberg and I got to do a video for a public television broadcast about the chapel. Thus, with my interviews with all the principals, planning the narration for the video, and serving on the planning committee, I learned and enjoyed many insider stories about the building's construction. One was how the convex cross on the exterior of the building came to be clad in stainless steel. Joan's original design had the cross on the bell tower in modest stone relief. She thought the subtlety of such a cross very appropriate. It faced out and above the building so that viewers could, on being seated inside the building, contrast it with the cross incised into the north wall of the interior. There had been a debate in the planning committee with some members thinking that, because the chapel is nonsectarian, there should not be a cross at all—there is always some detail like this for a group to get excited about; but the members who pointed out that the seminary has a Christian context held sway and the cross remained and was built onto the front of the tower. One day, though, in the midst of the construction when the tower had been finished with its slightly protruding stone cross, a somewhat conservative and influential member of the planning committee went outside to look at the tower and huffed that you couldn't see the cross. That led Tom Schwab, the construction superintendent—and everybody's hero problem-solver as the project went on—to spend his own time on the weekend laying out a stainless steel covering to scale for the exterior stone cross, placing it on the tower on Monday, and saving the day from the controversial little tempest of the exterior cross.

Tom Schwab said in his video interview that this building was one of the two or three most memorable on which he had ever worked. He noted that his most enjoyable and important work did not show, particularly work on the foundation slanting south to north with its installations of heating, plumbing, and electrical materials that needed to emerge as a flat floor slab for the building's interior. John Cook told of Tom's need to work out problems of physics and engineering on his own computer, proving the architects wrong by a small fraction of an inch that was crucial to the foundation's being installed properly!

The originality of the building was exciting in every way through the design and construction stages, but I didn't expect to realize that the materials themselves, their origins and production, would be the most fascinating parts of all to me. The two most noteworthy were the precast concrete "stones" and the light-transmitting curved wooden panels on the building's interior.

At the opening ceremonial events, when someone acknowledged that the blocks that appeared to be stone were precast concrete, the woman behind me tapped me on the shoulder and whispered, "They are not Travertine marble?"

Joan had wanted them to be Travertine marble and had to be convinced through hard argument that the budget just would not allow the soft off-white Italian stone to be imported for the building. Instead, Marc Rolle of the small New Ulm, Minnesota company named ArtStone oversaw creating the precast concrete blocks that can be mistaken for the real thing. First, they got some actual pieces of the Italian stone and made molds of them from which thirty-nine different ones turned out to be usable. Of those thirty-nine, ArtStone made blocks in three different hues, turned the molds at four different angles, sifted sand into the surface of a few of the castings, and thereby made a large variety of Travertine-appearing pieces. Each one weighed 72.5 pounds and there was a total of 3,850 in the building. There was no mortar used between the pieces, but rather they were attached with stainless steel clips.

At one inaugural party, I made a point of sitting beside the stone-mason, Jim Suprelle, and asked him how he made his plan so that the concrete stones appeared to have the infinite variety of quarried stone. "I just do it!" was his reply. "I can't tell you how this one fits with that one or which color to put where! I just know!" Like any truly creative artist, he saw that they just "fit" for him! He "just did it"!

The particular maple tree for the curved panels and the travels of that tree make up another amazing story in the chapel's design and construction saga. HGA's Steven Dwyer was in charge of finding just the right tree for the job after the architectural firm had worked with Marc Sanderson of Wilkie-Sanderson on the testing of the "quilted maple" that Joan Soranno had found and requested be used for the panels. The project had never before been done in this country, and the job started with Steven Dwyer locating the right tree, a large diseased big-leaf maple in Washington state.

The tree was cut in Washington, shipped to Germany where Germans have the right saws for peeling the bark and cutting the timber in a circular motion (John Cook described it as cut "like a toilet paper roll") into a 1/32" thickness. This wood was sent to a company in Indiana where it was laminated between two layers of acrylic, then shipped on to Wilkie-Sanderson where it was made into the panels specified by the architects and then delivered to the chapel site. Though there were more finishing touches to be done after the curvilinear panels were raised and secured in place, the crowning glory of the building was brilliantly achieved when the new and original, never-before-made quilted maple pieces soared in their grandeur, letting in the Minnesota light through their own soft golden filter.

Like Tom Schwab, I felt that the Bigelow Chapel's creation was one of the very small number of projects I had been a part of in my lifetime in which I am most proud to have participated. Tom was proud as a building contractor superintendent and I was proud as a planning committee member. The award-winning building is a superb example of architecture at its finest. The finished chapel that we already loved is a product of both art and science coupled with the contributing talents, intelligence and skills, commitment, industry, and diligence of all the workers on the building.

12

Science, Acid Rain, Radioactive Fallout, Wetlands, and Global Warming: the Life Work of Eville Gorham

Nature—there is my country.
The work—to celebrate, to reveal the mystery,
the beauty, and the rites of Nature, of the Visible World.

—Henry Beston, *The Outermost House*

—Nature in Winter—Icicles hang in a row of hard spikes from the eaves of the house as I start out for a morning walk bundled in my coat, hat and scarf, heavy boots, and warm gloves. Briefly, I imagine the horror of one of those sharp brittle picks of ice striking my head as I walk by. After I crunch safely beyond the icicles and look back to see their beauty as they reflect the dazzling sunlight from their frozen crystals, I walk on with happier thoughts, mind and body now well protected against dangers in the icy air.

I DELIGHT IN CALLING Eville Gorham my friend, Jessica, for I admire him as a dedicated scientist and offer him as an example to you as a person who prepared well to do his job as a scientist and then followed his imagination and his findings where they led him—and has literally made the world a better place by doing so.

Joan Sorano and John Cook's field of architecture is both science and art. Eville Gorham's field is biology, a science discipline, but his practice of it seems to me to be artistic. In the hands of its most excellent practitioners, either art or science is a melding of both. For the scientist, perhaps, the art of her or his work is the informed imagination that makes the idea of the possible apparent to the scientist's mind.

Eville Gorham is among the best of scientists. He has been called the "grandfather of acid rain" or "the discoverer of acid rain." He prefers the more modest designation, "an expert on acid rain." No, he did not "discover" acid rain, he insists when I blunder into that commonly held assertion. "Acid rain was discovered in Manchester in 1852 by Angus Smith, Her Majesty's Inspector of Alkali Works and the prototype of the scientific civil servant," Gorham gently corrects my mistake in crediting him with the discovery. "It took me quite a while to find out how much he knew about it," he continues. "See his book *Air and Rain*." Eville acknowledges that he worked on the subject of acid rain for 40 years, after having "discovered that acid rain acidified lakes owing to long-distance transport of air pollution from urban/industrial areas." This is his major contribution to science.

I see my friend Eville Gorham every month or so at meetings of what your granddad calls my "old men's club"—my faculty dining club, Gown in Town. It was for many years for men only, and it is a group that does indeed have a number of retirees active in it, hence Wilson's name for us, but it also has young and midlife faculty members in their most active academic lives. (I am asserting, you see, that we retirees are not inactive!) The membership of Gown in Town includes some of our faculty from many different fields who have achieved at a high level of originality and have contributed new knowledge to their disciplines. Speaking of their own research at our monthly meetings, a surgeon might demonstrate a new procedure for the operating room, an engineer might show new possibilities for aerospace technology in the use of wind tunnels, a rural sociologist might discuss housing options for poor people in small towns and on farms, a clothing expert might discuss African fabric design, or a cancer research scholar might discuss new strategies for detecting and treating prostate cancer. I heard Eville speak at Gown in Town with both passion and authority on our need to address environmental protection on a global level.

Eville Gorham's primary achievements, both in research and advocacy for worldwide scientific understanding and practical government policy changes, were summarized when he was awarded the Benjamin Franklin Medal in Earth Science in 2000: "Dr. Gorham studied the impact of acid rain on water systems, the spread of radioactive fallout in the food chain, and the effect of sulfur dioxide pollution on forests. In simple terms, Dr. Gorham's work has helped clarify precisely where all the 'stuff' that we put into the air, land, and water goes, and what it does when it gets there."[1]

Eville Gorham's contribution to the understanding of acid rain plus carefully crediting the work of a predecessor scientist on which he built his own work, as Eville did for Angus Smith, are typical of him. Still, Gorham himself did, indeed, make a significant contribution to the field of acid rain. He and three other scientists wrote a report in 1978 for President Jimmy Carter's Council on the Environment. The report laid the foundation for the president's Second Environmental Message in 1979 and for his legislative mandate enacted as Public Law 96-294 concerning the imperative to clean up acid rain. This law brought about an effort at industrial cleanup that is ongoing. Although other environmental problems continue, widespread reversal of sulfuric acid content in rain has been accomplished in many nations.

Nowadays Eville is retired, but he continues to be actively engaged in the study of ecosystems. Lately his research has focused on the huge stores of carbon in northern peatlands and what might happen to it under the stress of global warming. He was a Regents' Professor at the University of Minnesota, the highest honor bestowed by our university on a faculty member. A botanist by training, he became what is now known as a biogeochemist and is a respected scientist throughout the world. His long list of honors includes membership in the National Academy of Sciences and, along with the 2000 Franklin Medal, the 2005 Society of Wetland Scientists Lifetime Achievement Award, and many others.

Eville Gorham's current scholarly work on the subject of peatlands is attested to by a quotation on the front page of the 10 January 2008 Minneapolis *Star Tribune* on the threat of global warming posed by peatlands in northern Minnesota. It reads, "'Northern peatlands are the wild card in global warming,' said Eville Gorham, a retired University of Minnesota Regents' professor of ecology who has studied peatlands around the world."[2]

In Eville Gorham's case his colleague Clarence L. Lehman quotes him as saying modestly that his accomplishments came largely by chance.

1. "Thursday, April 27—The Franklin Institute Awards," Franklin Fact Archive at www.whyy.org/tv12/franklinfacts.

2. Minneapolis *Star Tribune*, January 10, 2008, p. A1.

Lehman, however, counters in something like an argument with himself—which he seems to have learned from Gorham—that Louis Pasteur said "Chance favors the prepared mind" and that Eville Gorham was indeed prepared intellectually, educationally, and imaginatively to do scientific work that has literally changed the world.

Gorham's own telling of his story of his life in science is the best version of all. Even though the World Wide Web, his colleagues' testimonials, and papers in both scholarly journals and popular science publications have many accounts of his achievements, he dismisses some as "Exaggerations!"

Just as Clarence Lehman speaks of Eville Gorham's opportunities as coming by chance, Eville accounts his own life's work, especially his most important research projects, as being "serendipitous." He likes to say that there are two extremes of doing science. One is rule-based, by which the scientist posits a hypothesis, tests it, and if its postulate works out, proposes a second hypothesis, with tests following it and results studied in a progression of hypotheses, tests, and findings.

Eville says his own scientific method is a kind of "serendipity," the other extreme from the mode of proceeding from rules. He suggests that the "serendipitous" scientist says when gathering information, "something will turn up," meaning, "let's get some data and see what they will tell us." Chance encounters or chance results have led him to scientific explanations that had not been at all the point of the initial project. Both of the projects for his graduate degrees, he tells me, yielded unanticipated results through serendipity that were much more useful to science than his initial directions would have been. His MSc thesis work for Dalhousie University in Halifax in his native Nova Scotia, and his PhD project for University College, London, both had such unanticipated outcomes and, thus, findings that did not directly follow from the questions that informed the original projects. Yet they proved to be more valuable to science in the long run.[3]

For Eville's master's thesis research, he began a project on "the effects of temperature on a secretory organelle, the Golgi body, in the cells of salmon embryos at different stages of development over time." His very words. Even though I consulted my science dictionary and thought I understood enough to imagine the little cellular packets of cytoplasm in the

---

3. Eville Gorham, phone conversation with the author, April 7, 2007.

small bodies, try as I may, I couldn't discuss Golgi bodies and salmon embryos in my own words. So I give you his very words.[4]

As Eville did his work, growing salmon eggs in baths of water at different temperatures, he felt loath to kill the beautiful creatures as his research required: ". . . one could see their little hearts beating and the red cells circulating through their veins." Nevertheless, Eville carried out the research as planned—and it failed. After his initial alarm at not reaching the desired results of the experiment, he noticed that the changing temperatures of the water had distorted the sequence of body changes of the small embryos even within their normal temperature range. Temperatures outside that range led to their becoming "'monsters', such as fish with curved backs or two heads!" Also, Eville learned that the "most extreme temperatures resulted in early death." Thus, he was able to write his thesis after all, and what he found out about fish subjected to thermal pollution was of much more significance than what he might have contributed to his field from the initial project.[5]

Similarly, Eville's PhD project for University College, London—for which he had moved to the botany side of biology so he no longer had to anticipate killing beautiful creatures—yielded an unexpected result. Eville started out to investigate the mineral uptake of some species of plants in the English Lake District. As he studied the soils in which the plants were growing, however, he noticed that as the organic matter of the soils increased so did their acidity, while "saturation of the ion-exchange capacity of the soil with bases (chiefly calcium) declined." Again by chance observations in Eville's initial work, he developed a different project and one that would have wider-reaching implications, "the acidification of woodland and wetland soils as they accumulated increasing amounts of organic matter."[6]

His colleague Lehman describes another aspect of the convergence of Eville's research findings and law and government policy changes that resulted from what he published. Early in Gorham's career, Lehman recounts, when nations were still doing open-air testing of nuclear weapons and creating radioactive fallout, Gorham quite accidentally became involved in its study. While he was working in the English Lake District in

4. Eville Gorham, "The Ways in Which I Have Pursued Scientific Investigations over 60 Years," paper, April 3, 2007, np., page 2 of 5.

5. Gorham, "Investigations," np, pp. 1–2.

6. Gorham, "Investigations," np, pp. 2–3.

1957, an accident happened at the Atomic Energy Authority's Windscale plutonium facility that deposited large amounts of various fallout isotopes over the district. At the urging of a friend, the county medical officer, Eville first studied lakes and ponds, but his findings were insufficient to prove contamination. This failure led him, by a stroke of inspiration, to study sphagnum moss and lichens in the region and he found them to contain extraordinary amounts of radioactivity compared with other sorts of plants in the area. Knowing that arctic caribou and reindeer eat lichens and that indigenous native people eat the caribou and reindeer meat, he concluded that radioactivity would then become widespread in their human tissue.[7]

Four years later in 1961, Gorham was pleased to learn that his reporting on nuclear fallout in the food chain from lichens to caribou and reindeer to humans had played a small but significant role in Alaskan Inuit populations successfully protesting a project of the U.S. government intending to use nuclear devices to blast a harbor in northwest Alaska. Local research in Alaska confirmed and greatly extended Gorham's research in the English Lake District, leading to the Inuit protests that caused the project to be dropped.[8] This also gave considerable impetus to the call for a moratorium on nuclear testing in the atmosphere, finally accomplishing the treaty to ban it.

As definite as he is about his scientific work, Eville is as equally precise with language. His writing is quite painstaking and clear, and he likes to give full expression to his reasons for using certain language. For example, he has made a theme of serendipity as the central focus of his professional life. In a short essay about his work, Eville begins with attribution of the term he has chosen with the 1754 coinage of the word "serendipity" by Horace Walpole, taking it from a Persian fairy tale, "The Three Princes of Serendip," who continually chanced upon information they were not looking for.[9]

Pointing out that even his activism as an environmentalist came about by chance, Eville says that in Britain, where he was trained, it was not then at all acceptable for a scientist to go out and talk to the public

---

7. Gorham, "Investigations," np, page 3; "Windscale, Ferry House and Alaska: An Unlikely Connection: Eville Gorham tells us why," FBA News, No. 34, Summer 2006, pp. 12–13.

8. Gorham, "Windscale," p. 13.

9. Gorham, "Investigations," np, p. 1.

about scientific work. "Applied science" was looked down upon. After he came to the University of Minnesota in 1962, however, a colleague at the university needed someone to go to the Minneapolis Park Board and talk about Dutch Elm Disease, a sickness that was beginning to spread among the thousands of elms in the city and which was beginning to be treated with DDT, the worst possible treatment in the eyes of the scientists. Because Eville had taken a seminar on Rachel Carson's book *Silent Spring*, Eville went to the Minneapolis Park Board on behalf of his colleague, then to the Minnesota House of Representatives to protest the inappropriate use of DDT for Dutch Elm Disease. These and other expert testimonials led to a change of policy, and the experience led Eville finally to become an environmentalist.[10]

In 2007, based on research done decades ago and casual conversations nearly as far into the past, Eville and four colleagues published a paper that he considers the best work he has done in years. More than twenty years ago, Eville and his research associate Jan Janssens had started collecting from the literature considerable data about ages and depths of North American peatlands. At that time he conjectured in a casual conversation with Jan that if they could put together enough of this information about peatlands and their initiation it might "tell us something." Much later, by joining forces and combining data with a Canadian Geological Survey expert on the retreat of the Laurentide ice sheet, and a highly skilled mathematical modeler, Clarence Lehman, they were able to draw important conclusions in a paper about the invasion of the landscape by peatlands over time as they followed in the wake of glacial retreat. Of this work, Eville writes, "Because we know the average amount of peat in a cubic meter of peatland and its average carbon content, we are now following up with a paper on the accumulation of carbon in North American peatlands, an important reservoir in the global carbon cycle over thousands of years."[11]

For the science and thinking required to identify and clarify certain major changes resulting in damage to the environment—radioactive fallout entering the food chain from plants through animals to humans, acid rain damaging lakes and forests, and now the amount of carbon accumu-

10. Eville Gorham, phone conversation with the author, April 7, 2007.

11. Gorham, "Investigations," np, p. 3; Eville Gorham et al. "Temporal and spatial aspects of peatland initiation following deglaciation in North America," *Quaternary Science Reviews* 26 (2007): 300–311.

lated in peatlands following glacial retreat over North America—and at times for efforts to identify national and global remedies for the damage and advocacy of legal action to apply them, Eville Gorham bears great responsibility. He says he was just doing his job—and enjoying it fully. "Isn't it fun to be paid to do whatever you please?" he quips.

After several communications back and forth between us, with me trying to understand what he was saying and just what he has done and what he makes of science, Eville wrote me a note saying, "It occurred to me recently [to mention] the very real thrill that comes with adding a building block, however small, to the edifice of our understanding of nature and how it works, knowing that it will fit with others' building blocks steadily to improve that understanding. By this means one leaves a legacy for others, and develops a feeling that one has lived a useful life—a feeling that I am sure animates those in the arts as well."[12]

Eville Gorham's life and work is indeed a useful legacy for humankind and the earth.

12. Note to the author from Eville Gorham, May 19, 2007.

13

The Museum of Modern Art

The artist, perhaps more than the grocer or the ice-man, is natively inclined to try to peer into the truth of things. In a way, it might be said that he has a vested interest in the truth.

—Ben Shahn, *Masters of Modern Art*

—Nature in Winter—Last summer Ian cut into lengths of firewood some fallen trees on our land. I also persuaded the four grandchildren to pick up sticks for one cent apiece. Justin especially took this task very seriously and picked up more sticks than the others. There is always a fresh stick supply on the ground under our trees, and the children picked up a goodly number to which I added. Though we had had to buy some firewood in the past, this winter we were prepared with both a full woodpile and several baskets of kindling sticks for our fireplace. The whole process of building a fire is an enjoyable practical task in cold weather. First one of us must go to the woodpile and carry in armloads of wood. Then, we must stack the fire just so with kindling and logs and light it carefully. I often think of my having taught Stiles to build fireplace fires when he was about seven, for I reasoned that a boy would be safer around a fire if he knew how to build one. Starting a fire might take a couple of tries or a bit of blowing the beginning coals with the bellows for the fire to flame up; but when it has started, a live fire in the stone fireplace warms our spirits along with our hands and faces as we gaze out at bare trees and wintry weather outside and feel warm inside.

ALTHOUGH I ADMIRE THE work of scientists and architects and work at being a literary artist myself, the scholarly, creative, or inventive work in the arts about which I know least as a participant, but which I have reveled in all of my adult lifetime is visual art—painting, graphic arts, prints, sculpture. As a museumgoer, traveler, seeker after knowledge of art, art book devourer, artists' studio visitor, and museum tour guide, I have loved the visual arts. Even though "the arts" as a term covers opera and orchestra and other forms of music, poetry, and fiction and other literary forms, architecture and other building practices, "art" in our common parlance means the art we see. That more narrow sense of visual art is the way I am talking about art here.

My first serious immersion in art in its American capital, New York City, is also tied to my romance with and engagement to your grandfather. I was a senior at Millsaps College and had already presided over a "Religion and the Arts" week at my college. Now as a national officer of the Methodist Student Movement, I was charged with planning a conference on art in New York City for two delegates from each U.S. state. The national staff person—the real organizer of the conference with the New York contacts and knowledge about its art—was B. J. Stiles and he invited his friend, Wilson Yates, to join the committee, saying it "has a pretty chairman [we used sexist language in those days]!" Wilson and I served on the committee in its planning meeting in Nashville, the Methodist headquarters, in October; and we got engaged at the arts seminar itself in New York in March. (Before the conference started, he took me to a little restaurant in Greenwich Village named Le Cave Henri Quatre and then we whizzed away in a taxi to the Top of the Sixes bar and restaurant at 666 Fifth Avenue. Here, seated in the bar before a drink wholly new to me, Benedictine and Brandy, he asked me to hold out my hand for him to tell my fortune. I held out my left hand, ring finger up. He put my engagement ring on my outstretched finger.)

Wilson's wedding present to me for our July wedding that summer was the Museum of Modern Art book, *Masters of Modern Art*, the first art book in my collection; and art education has been a joint venture in our marriage from then until now.

That spring 1961 National Methodist Student Movement seminar was the time and its setting, the Museum of Modern Art (MoMA), the place of the beginning of my lifelong romance with art along with the parallel one I have had all these years with your granddad. At that spring

gathering of eager students, we were hosted by none other than the original curator and director of MoMA, Alfred H. Barr, Jr., a man who had
enormous influence in the interpretation of modern art, the spreading
of knowledge far and wide about modern art, as well as assembling and
exhibiting MoMA's incomparable collection.

With Alfred Barr as our guide, I came to "know art" that week in
New York. This art education gave me my beginning confidence in art
interpretation and aesthetics for my lifelong learning about and enjoyment of art, and I came to realize that art for me is a primary entry into
understanding life and ever deeper and more profound aspects of life's
surprise and delight. Naturally, it was modern art of the mid-twentieth
century around which I came of age as an art aficionado.

On our tour of MoMA with Alfred Barr, as well as many times later,
I saw Alberto Giacometti's (1901–1996) long, skinny bronze sculptures
of human figures. Their surreal disproportion and rigidity and elongated
height both repelled and fascinated me that day and for years to come.[1]

I saw Willem de Kooning's (1904–1997) abstract expressionist oil
"Woman, I" made of wild and heavy brushstrokes, big black marks, and
bold white streaks lined with reds and blues. Big eyes, whites centered
with large black dots, black nostrils, and bared teeth along with large
white-covered breasts are the most expressive parts of the painting. Legs
apart and feet akimbo in abstract high-heeled sandals, the woman of the
central seated figure seems at once alone and settled and, also, accompanied by extra hands and female bodies and a facial expression that only
terrorizes. This painting is one of my most vivid memories of MoMA on
my first seeing it.[2]

Another memorable painting that returns and returns to my awareness after my first seeing it is "Echo of a Scream" by the Mexican social
realist artist David Alfaro Siqueiros (1898–1974). We have a lithograph by
Siqueiros in our collection that your granddad bought in San Francisco
some years later, a large image of a Mexican woman carrying a wrapped
infant and apparently running away from something.

I later saw Siqueiros murals on a trip to Mexico City; but nothing has
been more gripping or tormenting than MoMA's "Echo of a Scream." The
work pictures at the top a large disembodied head of a screaming black baby

---

1. *Masters of Modern Art*, Alfred H. Barr, Jr., ed. New York: Museum of Modern Art,
distributed by Doubleday and Co., 1958, pp. 150–151.

2. *Modern Art*, 176–177.

with a full-bodied black child somewhat to its right and front also screaming. In the background and foreground appear rubble, metal triangles,
what seem to be parts of guns and ammunition. From the front the scene
is brightly lighted and the children's faces are in harsh full light, but a dark
cloud covers the top background. It pictures horror in a single image.[3]

We must have seen the Russian Jewish artist Marc Chagall's (1887–
1985) "I and the Village" and "Birthday"[4] on that Alfred Barr tour of
MoMA, for my *Masters of Modern Art* book has plates of them in it; but
I don't remember so clearly seeing them on that visit. I remember better
receiving from your granddad more than once postcards of "Birthday"
showing the domestic scene of a man and a woman, the woman holding
a bouquet of flowers and the man floating up in the air with his neck bent
totally the wrong way around as he flies above the woman to face her and
give her a kiss. Chagall is associated with impressionism and surrealism
with his figures floating in the air and improbable sizes of tiny buildings
and giant faces, but his work conveys to me none of the terror or fear of
some of the other surrealists. Rather, his paintings suggest joyfulness. He
is a favorite artist of both Wilson's and mine. One Christmas when I lived
in Munich and your granddad, your mother, and uncle Stiles were coming to spend Christmas with me, I was able to buy a Chagall lithograph
print from the *Kunsthaendler*—art dealer—on the street near my office
building for my Christmas gift to Wilson. You have seen it, Jessica, hanging over the mantle in the inglenook of our Minneapolis home. It is a
favorite of all of our art in our home.

What we did see and remember well from MoMA and Alfred Barr's
tour is the "drip painting" or "action painting" by Jackson Pollock (1912–
1956), "Number I."[5] Jackson Pollock's form of abstract expressionism
emphasized his process of working with his materials of paint on canvas
by dripping colors of lavenders and pink and blue with lots of white drips
and lots of black drips to create a work that was no picture at all but rather
an exhibition of the skilled control of the artist over his materials. We have
seen paintings by Jackson Pollock many times in other cities' museums,
most notable of which are several large ones at the Peggy Guggenheim
Museum in Venice.

3. *Modern Art*, 156–157.

4. *Modern Art*, 132–133.

5. *Modern Art*, 178.

Most memorable of that first time to MoMA was our viewing of Picasso's "Guernica." We saw other pieces by Pablo Picasso (1881–1973) that day—"Three Musicians," "Girl Before a Mirror," "Three Women," works that are still there—but none of them made the impression that "Guernica" had on us.[6] That mural, which has now moved permanently to the Prado Museum in Madrid, was featured at MoMA in 1961 when we were there. Called by some the greatest painting of the twentieth century, "Guernica" is a monumental antiwar work painted by Picasso in response to the 1937 Nazi bombing of the Spanish town of Guernica at the behest of the Spanish dictator Francisco Franco in the Spanish Civil War.

The work is largely black and white and seems like a gigantic, tumultuous drawing. At the center top is a light bulb with what may be a sun around it that emits no light and is circled with dead rays. Near it a hand holds up a lamp, but the lamp too does not shine. There are a bull's head with misplaced eyes and horns and a horse's head with bared teeth and a missile-pointed tongue. All eyes of animals and humans protrude and show fright. There are people's hands with fat distended fingers and feet, sometimes vaguely attached to arms and legs, sometimes not. Human bodies with big faces and wide-open mouths lie trampled on the painting's floor or surge upward from compromised positions or toward the oddly triangular shafts of light on the right, distant from any logical light source. Chaos reigns, yet the figures refer to life—to animals and people and light. I am willing to believe that this is one of the world's great paintings. The utter ruin of war, the horror, terror, and blinding pointlessness of such destruction stays with me all these years since I first saw "Guernica."

The Museum of Modern Art was a superb place for me to start enjoying profoundly and learning deeply about art on that March day of 1961 with all of my adulthood before me, and it has continued to be over the decades since when I have paid it visits. MoMA is one of the places at the top of our list, Jessica, when I take you to New York City.

Art in its most visible forms and in its many other forms, science in its pure and its applied forms, and art and science in forms in which they combine I commend to you, my highly intelligent and inquisitive granddaughter! Knowing science and knowing art are important components for knowing life.

6. *Modern Art*, 67–71, 80–83, 87–89, 92–93, 97. "Guernica" not illustrated in book, used postcard image for discussion.

14

Truthtelling

Tell all the truth, but tell it slant . . .

—Emily Dickinson, "Poem 1129"

—Nature in Winter—When I opened the blinds this morning, the bright sun flooded in through the windows. It shone on the white-blanketed landscape and on the snow-covered lake beyond the trees. It is a gorgeous winter morning. Outside, silence and utter stillness prevail. The temperatures have risen from their subzero iciness of the past two days and nights, and indoors the furnace does not have to work so hard to keep me warm—I even closed the fireplace flue and refrained from making wood fires the past two nights so the house's warm air would not be sucked up the chimney.

Holiday—Mardi Gras
Today is Shrove Tuesday, Fat Tuesday, *Mardi Gras, Carnevale, Faschingsdienstag,* Pancake Tuesday, the day in the Christian calendar that is the day before Ash Wednesday, the beginning of Lent. Many Christians in our time pay little attention to this date. However, certain cities, especially ones with large Catholic populations or that were originally Catholic, have Shrove Tuesday celebrations, some lasting for several days prior to the beginning of Lent. Historically in Christendom everyone observed this day as one of the many feast days of the Church. It provides a continuity in the Christian calendar from Christmas, the feast day for the birth of Christ, to Easter, the feast day celebrating the death and resurrection of Christ, the movement of the people from the

observance of the humble beginning and anonymity of Jesus at his birth to what the faithful believe is Christ's victory over death, worldwide establishment of his glory, and thus the universal promise of life for all. In nature, this season follows from the deepest of winter to the arrival of spring. As in many parts of Christian history, it is believed that Christian practice and celebrations were originally overlaid onto earlier nature revelries and observances.

Shrove Tuesday means "to shrive" or to hear confession. *Carnevale,* the earliest word used for the period before Lent, comes from the Latin "carne vale" meaning "farewell to the flesh," Lent being a period of fasting, circumspection, confession, and repentance for sins, as well as obedience to abstinence from meats, fats, eggs, and dairy products. The Carnival season begins on Epiphany, or Three Kings' Day, twelve days after Christmas and lasts until the stroke of midnight on Shrove Tuesday. It is a season of revelry, abandon, partying, often of overindulgence in rich food and drink. There is often outlandish dress-up, masking, parading, dancing in the streets, and merrymaking. In some places, drunkenness and brawling occur. All this is in the name of preparation for the fasting, sacrifice, confession, and decorum expected for the forty-six days leading up to Easter (the first Sunday after the first full moon after March 21, the vernal equinox).

Fat Tuesday, the most used label for the holiday in American English, comes from the historical last day before the Lenten restrictions, a day that in some early European Christian settings a fattened calf was slaughtered and eaten. In England the day is known as Pancake Tuesday, pancakes having been made historically to use up all the fats, eggs, and milk products in people's kitchens. In some English homes Pancake Tuesday is still observed with pancake suppers.

The world-renowned festivals that culminate on Shrove Tuesday include *Carnevale* in Rio de Janeiro, Venice, and other Italian cities and *Mardi Gras* (which means "fat Tuesday" in French) in New Orleans, in towns across the Mississippi Gulf Coast, and in Mobile, Alabama, all American settings that were first settled by French Catholic people. In German *Faschingsdienstag* is the word for Fat Tuesday, and one city where it is celebrated most exuberantly is Munich. Once when I was spending the spring semester in Munich, my German-speaking friend, Karin, took me into the city center to the *Vicktualienmarkt,* the open-air food market, for the traditional *Faschingsdienstag* celebration.

There Muenchners dress up and cavort, drink hot spiced wine and eat sausages, parade and dance. The finale for *Faschingsdienstag* at the *Vicktualienmarkt* is a bawdy dance by the city's washerwomen, who dress up in peasant dirndls and aprons and dance around and around on a raised platform, kicking up their heels together in the market square.

I watch the Shrove Tuesday broadcast of the *Today* TV show from New Orleans where, six months after the devastation from Hurricane Katrina, the city of New Orleans is bravely and jubilantly celebrating its 150th anniversary year Mardi Gras with floats, parades, parties, and its famous rituals of plastic bead-tossing and outlandish costuming. Smiles are on faces there once more after months of horrible hardship; and reveling in the streets looks like fun, though homes of many people, especially the poor, are still piles of rubble and debris.

One facet of truth is the nugget of religious understanding that high celebrations and their opposites in revelry and abandon illustrate—in this example, Mardi Gras. This religious example suggests these are two parts of the truth of human nature. Humans must cultivate both the depth, reverence, and solemnity that high holidays command; Mardi Gras or Carnival celebrations tell us, as well, the capacity for playfulness, for letting go, and for fun the pre-holiday that parties allow are necessary aspects of being human. Even the fact that some people celebrate Mardi Gras to excess with drunkenness, gluttony, and sexual abandon illustrates this point. The opposite of Mardi Gras will come through Lent and Easter, when decorum, sacrifice, and self-control are exhibited in the behavior of people and in the celebrations in churches as they observe these somber seasons of constraint.

There are other ways of getting at the truth, of course, than in those religious ones of high celebrations or festivals. People find truth in many ways both in person and in public groups, but the routes to truth portrayed in religious festivals give one path.

FINDING THE TRUTH

Small children have a hard time sorting out truth from fantasy, truth from wishes, truth from the many possibilities that are the objects of their desires. Kindergartners and other young children have to summon a goodly amount of courage to tell the truth when they know they have been naughty or when they know there will be consequences of an action of theirs that they didn't anticipate when they took it. I remember once when I was in sixth grade—and normally I was an exemplary, well-behaved child—two friends of mine and I decided at recess to walk around our classroom on top of the desks with our shoes on. When the teacher, Mrs. Massey, came back into the room and saw the dirty shoe prints on the desks, she asked me indignantly who did that, and I replied, "Edmund did it!" I am sure I lowered my eyes and innocent Edmund looked startled.

Obviously, I told a lie, compounding my bad behavior, and I am sure I was duly punished, but, interestingly, I don't remember how I was punished, I just remember how terribly guilty I felt in being caught misbehaving and then lying. Dealing with bearing the consequences of not telling the truth or sorting out from the available information what is true or untrue, separating truth from fantasy or wishes are all part of the "work" of being a child and of parents' and caregivers' teaching responsibility to children. (You once told a babysitting couple that you were a little adopted Mexican girl, that your parents had gone to China trying to find a little girl to adopt and couldn't find one, so they went to Mexico and got you. Your mother's response when she heard about your story was, "So all that pregnancy bed rest was for nothing!" Nobody needed to tell the babysitters that you were articulating a fantasy, which even you as a five-year-old knew was just that.) It is just as hard for teenagers, college students, and young and old adults to tell the strict truth all the time.

A child's first encounter with the concept of truthtelling usually comes at a very young age when one of their adults inquires suspiciously, "Are you telling me the truth?" The way my mother said it, with a very grave voice, was, "Are you telling me a story?" It is hard enough to be sure about the truth as a child, but truthtelling as adults is a far more complex process and over the centuries much thought, philosophical and otherwise, has gone into defining truth.

What is the truth? Is truth constant, solid, and established? Or is truth fluid, flexible, and ever changing? From those two poles—absolutism and relativism—flow the central premises of most intellectual debates on many subjects. Is what is really real ideal? Or is it material? Are numbers and measures fixed and set? Or are they infinite and maneuverable? Is the universe created and permanent? Or are the patterns of nature and physical and natural life adaptable and mutable? And, as to ethics, is the right thing to do clear-cut, undeniable, and certain for all possibilities, or are there options and variations and changing conditions that influence the right decision? In other words, is right always right and wrong always wrong without deviations? Or is "it depends" a good idea?

In his *Ethics* Aristotle says that the object of human life is happiness to be gained through goodness, but his position is not happiness for the individual person but for the community. Aristotle's time did not have nearly the developed sense of individualism that has risen with modernity to the point now that elevation of the human individual has become extreme at times, I think, and in the extreme a detriment to people in groups, the nation, and the community. Such radical individualism is damaging or belittling to common principles or shared values. I would tell my university seminar students that anyone who said, as many inevitably did, "It all depends on the individual!" that he or she would suffer grave consequences—like a grade of failure—in the class for saying such a thing because it is a false assertion. Aristotle, as well as many major thinkers and thoughtful political leaders with him over time, argued that seeking goodness was a goal in service to community, the whole group, the people; and that two equally important routes would lead to that goal of social happiness: searching for moral goodness and searching for intellectual goodness. Thus, in this unified system of thinking, trying to find the truth intellectually is a moral task just as much as trying to find the truth ethically as a basis for decision-making and for taking action is moral.

To tell the truth, I think, means working very hard to find out as much as you can know about the subject, what has been known about it in the past, and what the best minds of the present are saying about it. It means paying attention and solving problems with the best intellectual tools you can develop, with your whole being including your emotions, and with the help of whoever might be knowledgeable about the subject. For me it has always meant reading books and articles and newspapers; for others it means having conversations with trusted people, but both are important. To find your way to tell the truth means taking the time to think through exactly what the problem is you are dealing with, to look at as many sides of the question as you can, and to consider as many potential decisions as you might make. It also means consulting other people who have good judgment, and, finally, following your heart and your imagination as well as your rational mind in deciding what to think or what to do: to tell the truth.

There are many definitions of truth abroad in our time, including the assertion that truth is not possible, that it is a chimera. My own approach to truth is a commonsensical rather than an academic one. Of course truth is relative. Of course truth changes through cultural, social, and political circumstance. Of course knowledge added or subtracted about a topic alters something of the truth of it. Still, in my core, I believe that there is a brightly lighted center, a nub, a kernel that gets to the heart of the matter of most questions asked if we work hard enough to find it; and that kernel, that nub, that brightly lighted center, that core is truth, that beyond which no more questions can probe, no more qualifications can change, no more aspects can modify. Truth is the center of meaning.

Still, over time, in different circumstances, with new knowledge, in different places, the truth of one time or place, one circumstance or set of facts can change. Truth is mobile. Truth is dynamic. Truth is nubile.

It is very easy to be mistaken about what truth is, very easy to jump at some conclusion and believe it to be true when it is false, easy to want something to be true so badly that one deceives oneself into believing it is, easy to stay on the surface of wishes and desires and commonly held opinion without making the effort to try to be sure about what is true. But is truth all that difficult to ascertain? Sometimes. Sometimes a scientist has to search and search, try to prove and disprove, think and study, probe and argue about some point in pursuit of truth, though truth continues to elude. Sometimes a scholar spends years of life in a quest for a specific truth and ends with still more questions. But there are times, too, when in an instant's inspiration, in a flash of insight, in a brief moment, a person can come to the knowledge of sure truth. In all these ways truth is sought and truth is known.

TRUTH ON THE STAGE

On October 5, 2005 the TV news carried an obituary of playwright August Wilson. He was sixty years old and had completed a cycle of ten plays chronicling the history of African Americans. The director Timothy Douglas who had staged his last play, *Radio Golf*, at Yale Repertory Theater the spring before and was readying it for Broadway the next season, compared August Wilson with Shakespeare, saying Wilson had retold African-American history in drama as Shakespeare had retold English history in his history plays. An actor called August Wilson the greatest American playwright of his century. A clip was shown of the playwright himself being interviewed in recent years, replying to a question of whether he wanted to be known in the future as "August Wilson, African-American playwright" or "August Wilson, playwright." He said in a voice that mixed humility and passion that "August Wilson, playwright" would do, that he was an African-American man, so that's what he knew: he didn't know anything else, so that's what he wrote about. Left unsaid, but pertinent, is the fact that William Shakespeare was a sixteenth-seventeenth century Englishman (1564–1616) and English history and Elizabethan-era culture were what he knew, too. The genius was turning his intimate knowledge of his people and his culture into plays. August Wilson, playwright, would do. August Wilson turned what he knew into plays, as did Shakespeare.

Your mother and I went to see Wilson's play, *Jitney,* in New York when she lived there. She had bought the tickets, very good seats, up near the front. The then-mayor of Minneapolis, Sharon Sayles-Belton, and her husband, both African-Americans, sat just behind us. I am sure we white people and black people alike enjoyed and learned from the play. It spoke to our shared humanity of the classic conflicts, struggles and fears of being human. Of Wilson's plays, I have seen *Ma Rainey's Black Bottom, The Piano Lesson, Gem of the Ocean,* and *Joe Turner's Come and Gone.* I hope to be able to see all the works of the cycle on stage before long. The Penumbra Theater Company in St. Paul, under its founder and director Lou Bellamy, was the location where Wilson himself was a member and did much of his early writing and seeing his plays produced. Bellamy has vowed to stage all ten of August Wilson's cycle of plays in Minneapolis-St. Paul in the years to come. I share the opinion of other admirers of Wilson's work that he is a great American playwright—maybe on the top rung, one among Eugene O'Neill, Arthur Miller, Tennessee Williams, and Edward Albee, but, surely, a great American playwright.

The ten plays in August Wilson's ambitious cycle are set over the twentieth century, one for each decade, and most of them in the Hill District of Pittsburgh where Wilson grew up as one of six children in a family abandoned by his father when he was young. He learned much that he knew from self-education in the Carnegie Library. He was very bright, having learned to read by four; but he was not challenged by school. The other part of what he learned was from his observation and participation in his Hill District neighborhood. The Hill District people were deeply deprived economically, felt a continuous threat from the police, and lived perpetually in unstable social conditions. The Hill District of Wilson's boyhood was a site of much poverty among the large number of African-Americans, Jews, and Italian immigrants who lived there. He made characters out of the taxicab drivers, the blues musicians, and the garage mechanics who were the descendants of slaves, and black single mothers in crowded small apartments who cleaned other people's houses and found their hope in occasional black athletes and black preachers.

Known as the Twentieth Century Cycle or the Pittsburgh Cycle, Wilson's ten loosely connected plays portray African-American experience of each decade of the century, though they were not chronologically written. The second to last play he wrote, for example, *Gem of the Ocean* (2003), is set in 1904 and shows the beginning point of the story. However, audiences of Wilson's work from earlier written and produced plays were already familiar by the first production of *Gem of the Ocean* in 2003 with the legendary Aunt Ester, the central character of the play about whom there had been frequent references—sometimes oblique, sometimes matter-of-fact, sometimes suggestive of mystery in others of the plays. Throughout the cycle, Aunt Ester has a kind of mythic presence; and though there are other characters in other Wilson plays who have heroic and even oracular status, Aunt Ester's role hovers above them all. Telling is the fact that, when *Gem of the Ocean* opens, Aunt Ester's age is given at 287 years old, roughly the age of African slavery in the Americas in 1904, establishing her as standing for the foundational figure of origin of the African-American people.

Themes of losses—financial, personal, social—permeate the ten plays. Death is as vivid as life in each story as the characters struggle to make their lives work, always seeming to struggle hand-in-hand with death. In *Seven Guitars,* for example, the 1940s play, one says, "Everybody got a time coming. Nobody can't say they don't have a time coming."[1]

Seven Guitars presents a blues musician, Floyd Barton, known as Schoolboy, newly released from prison and returned home, trying with some urgency to start up his recording career again by trying to gather a group of his Hill District friends to go with him to play music in Chicago, where he believes he has a contract waiting. At the same time, he is trying to rekindle his love relationship with Vera. The play opens with Barton's

---

1. Quoted in Ben Brantley, "Weaving Blues of Trying Times and Lost Dreams," Theater Review of Signature Theater Company production of *Seven Guitars* in *The New York Times,* Aug. 25, 2006, p. B1.

funeral and then moves back quickly to the last days of his life and what can be made of it, including the death.

The character of the neighborhood older man, Hedley, plays against the story of the younger man and the group of musicians as sick and disappointed Hedley asserts his own pride, ambition, and defeats in trying to be a larger-than-life, Bible-quoting, and avuncular elder. Hedley claims that the time will come, and soon, when black people will come out on top, will be in charge. There is a kind of wildness to his prophesying.

In *Seven Guitars* there is music-making, shooting, mourning, gossiping, quarreling, and moaning in the Hill District back yard in which it is set. There is no resolution, only mystery, even about who was shot and who did the shooting; and the conversation is essentially mundane; but as the lives evolve on the stage, the characters become vivid with life, with survival, each an instrument of vitality—as the title suggests, "seven guitars." The play is about making music, it is about dying and about living the best one can, and it is about each person trying to make a life. It is about disappointment and failure and standing up again and going on, all essentially put forward in small talk. The people in it are black people, though, unmistakably. The religion in it is the African-American version of Christianity mixed with black experience; and the music in it is black music—blues and jazz and soul—made up out of black people's experience in America.

Ma Rainey's Black Bottom, is set in Chicago rather than Pittsburgh and is one of Wilson's earlier plays. It is the 1920s play. Focused in music like *Seven Guitars,* its action also takes place largely in small talk. The first part of the play has musicians hanging around waiting for Ma Rainey to arrive for a session of playing and literally nothing happens. Yet the audience sees the power of the music in the lives of black people, as well as the significance of the pivotal figure and of the human transcendence of making music. Everybody is waiting for Ma Rainey and the suspense gives her an aura, a larger-than-life persona. However, she as a figure is more human scale and not as overarching as the prophesying Hedley and especially not the generative Aunt Ester. Yet, she is one of Wilson's life-modeling characters.

When Ma Rainey does arrive for the last part of the play, the extraordinary power of the music in her presence brings everyone to life. Although an amusing pun, the "black bottom" in the title does not refer to Ma Rainey's anatomy but to a popular 1920s dance. Ma Rainey's ability to make music and make souls sing is what the play is really about.

Gem of the Ocean was staged in the spring of 2008 at Minneapolis's premier theater, the Guthrie Theater, produced by The Penumbra Theater, and directed by Lou Bellamy as the first show in Bellamy's plan to present all ten of August Wilson's plays in the following five years. I attended and found it a spectacular evening of theater. The superb acting and directing provided full musicality to Wilson's words, a spellbinding story in Wilson's plot, and a soaring epic rendition of African-American history and spirituality in the stratospheric layer of Wilson's drama.

Aunt Ester is sought, as the play opens, by a young man named Citizen Barlow. The 287-year-old woman is known to be able to "wash people's souls," and Citizen Barlow is in spiritual distress as he comes to the house at 1839 Wylie Avenue in Pittsburgh's Hill District where Aunt Ester is known to live. Aunt Ester's household includes Black Mary, a young woman who keeps house for her and Eli, her friend who oversees her schedule of sustenance-seeking visitors. Aptly named Caesar, who happens to be Black Mary's brother, he is the local constable and landlord.

Citizen Barlow's anguish is over his being responsible for a man's death. Barlow, on not being paid for his work at the local mill, stole a bucket of nails. Another man is accused of the theft and drowns himself rather than live with the false accusation, the death that Citizen takes upon himself. Further unrest comes when the workers at the mill go out on the street in protest over the unjust accusation. Citizen has been so named by his mother after emancipation in trust that he will live to become a citizen. Now he fails his name.

Aunt Ester takes Citizen into her home and takes a liking to him, saying that he reminds her of one of her former husbands; but, she tells him, she cannot wash people's souls: "God the only one can wash people's souls. God got big forgiveness."[2]

After a waiting period and a test for Citizen (finding and bringing back two pennies found side-by-side, a test only of his sincerity), Aunt Ester takes him on a journey to the sepulchral City of Bones. First she makes a paper boat out of the document that is the slave bill of sale for her, Ester Tyler. She insists he believe that the tiny paper board will carry

2. August Wilson, *Gem of the Ocean*. New York: Theatre Communications Group, 2006, p. 20.

him, and in time he begins to rock with the waves. Soon they see the City: "Head bones and leg bones and rib bones. The streets look like silver. The trees are made of bones. The trees and everything made of bone."[3]

But Citizen is blocked from going in. A Gatekeeper appears and stops him. "Who is the Gatekeeper, Mr. Citizen? Is it somebody you know?" asks Aunt Ester.

It is the man who jumped to his death in the river. "You got to tell him, Mr. Citizen. The truth has to stand in the light. You got to get your soul washed."

Citizen admits to the theft of the bucket of nails and, now free, is allowed to enter the City of Bones. It is intensely clear, made so in the production I saw at the Guthrie by the beautiful choreography, that the passage is African-Americans' Middle Passage, the coming on slave ships, this one named "Gem of the Ocean," and the City of Bones is the ancestry of broken and damaged, yet surviving, people out of Citizen's and African-Americans' past.

Black Mary too has had a moment of self-definition; and she tells Citizen, with whom she has had the beginning of a love relationship, "You got to be right with yourself before you can be right with anybody else."[4]

Aunt Ester, the catalyst, is the indomitable wise spirit of the African-American people. The symbolism of her age, of her slave document, and her unafraid access to the City of Bones all suggest her being the embodiment of the people. Her name, too, has multiple possible referents. As in so much of August Wilson's writing, on the surface her name is just a name and serves as what she should be called. Yet, there are biblical sources that are powerfully close. It could be a folk misspelling of Esther, the beautiful and powerful queen, who through her influence with her Persian king saved the captive Israelites from cruel treatment. Or, Aunt Ester's name could refer to the Christian high holiday of Easter, the holiday celebrating Christ's resurrection from the dead and the coming of new life out of death. Or, Ester could be a symbolic rendering of the chemical ester, the fat or essential oil left after the removal of hydrogen. Whatever her name might indicate, Aunt Ester is the channel through which one can come to know truth, truth of Citizen's or Black Mary's own lives and truth of their people.

3. Wilson, *Gem*, p. 68.
4. Wilson, *Gem*, p. 73.

THE ELUSIVENESS OF TRUTH

As August Wilson is a truth-telling playwright whose work I greatly admire, nineteenth-century poet Emily Dickinson is a favorite poet of mine
whose overt subject is often truth. Her incomparable lyricism, rich and
enticing metaphors from nature, elliptical truthtelling, and bright language
surprise, delight, and inform me. Her poem that begins "Tell all the Truth
but tell it slant—" puts truth in a nutshell for me. With her second line,
she suggests that a roundabout way is the best path to truth: "Success in
Circuit lies." Then throughout the poem she uses the natural image of light
to convey the nonmaterial reality of truth, hinting that straight-out truth
would overwhelm. She says truth is "[t]oo bright" and is "[a]s lightening" if
not shown slowly. She says that children must be "eased/With explanation
kind" rather than be given a full blast of truth outright. With a final contrast
of light imagery with "dazzle" against darkness or blindness, she writes that
truth "must dazzle gradually/Or every man be blind—."[5]

Dickinson's poem helps me understand that truth is a cumulative
effect of knowing, that truth comes in dollops or waves before I can know
any unity of truth, any wholeness. The poem gives hope that truth is out
there if I seek with my vision and with my understanding until I find it in
the unifying of what I know.

Still, truth doesn't come firing at me in my face full-force. Rather,
one can see glimmers of it and then a picture more and more clear until it
shines as a steady light—for a time. After a while there are new glimmers
from a new understanding and the light that is truth changes, modifies,
refocuses to become a new clarity.

5. Emily Dickinson, Poem 1129, *The Poems of Emily Dickinson*, Vol. II, Thomas H.
Johnson, ed. Cambridge: Belknap Press, Harvard: 1951, 792.

15

Knowing the Earth and Knowing the World

And all this beneath a sky by nature skyless
in which the sun sets without setting at all

—Wisława Szymborska, "view with a grain of sand"

—Nature in Winter—Ice storms are the worst weather in Wisconsin, maybe anywhere northerly. It is usually too cold too quickly for an ice storm here, but we had one yesterday. Sleet mixed with rain fell as if in sheets from a slate-gray sky in the daytime, and by nightfall tree limbs were encased solidly in ice. The deck, road, and paths had hard, thick ice coverings, dangerous for attempts at walking upright. Even on undertaking a walk out the front door to go to the woodpile, we met ice pellets stinging our faces and ice underfoot causing hazardous slip-sliding. The crows and chickadees hid themselves in the woods and were soundless.

THE EARTH OF NATURE is our home; and the world of human societies is our home. We cannot take any action, personally or collectively, that does not affect our home the earth or our home the world. I think of the earth and its environment as home for us people as creatures within nature; and I think of the world as our geopolitical, economic, social, and cultural home. We belong to both the earth and the world and they to us. They are interwoven in our skein of life, bound together as one single life. On the earth we are beneficiaries, caregivers, and participating members of nature within the earth's whole—the planet itself, its land masses and waters, all the animals and plants that grow in the seas and on the lands, including us human animals. In the world we are both contributors to and recipients of patterns of cultures; nations and their governments; economies; institutions of families, education, and religions; ideologies and philosophies; domesticities; and all manner of arrangements of foodways, shelter, clothing, health, and human caregiving. I aspire to be a citizen of the world with simultaneous responsibility to nature's earth and people's world. Paradoxically, though, one can sometimes be the best world citizen by paying close attention to the local. The local and the global, like the earth and the world, are interlaced into a single skein. We must act locally, but it is to our peril to ignore national, regional, and worldwide matters.

I invite you, Jessica, to join me in being a citizen of the world and, also, to be as good a local citizen as is possible to be. For us together that means finding out all we can, learning together, from our vantage point of our acre near Hayward, Wisconsin, at the house we have named Coventry-in-the-Northwoods. Our centered beginning point here will take us back to our family homes in Red Wing and Minneapolis, our commitments in Wisconsin and Minnesota, the United States and United Nations. It circles us farther to all the cities and countries to which we travel or where we have any contacts, to all places in which our local, state, or federal governments act, or from which we ourselves or our people draw or contribute in any of our economic interactions like buying apples or shoes, electrical power, train tickets, oil, books, philodendron plants, or seed corn.

Quickly it becomes complicated when one declares she wants to be a citizen of the world! Is every human being on earth equally a citizen of the world with you and me? I want to say Yes, but then how does that require us to act in the *world*? As we live in the relative affluence of the American upper middle class, this comfortable lakeside cottage in the woods being a second home, a luxury in and of itself, what can we do about the poverty of some Americans who do not have enough money to pay for an adequate home, for basic food, for heat in the winter, or enough clothing or necessary health care for themselves? Or some people in rural areas who are migrant workers and sometimes have to live in crowded inadequate housing without sufficient water and sanitary facilities? What about refugees from war in their countries or from locations of natural disasters in our country or abroad where everything familiar or life supporting has been lost to them? People who sometimes have no homes at all and have to rely on charity organizations in countries foreign to them for makeshift shelters and minimal food and drinking water? Seeing each of these distressed people as a citizen of the world like us, what can we do for our shared world? Is life hopeless for many of the people of the world?

And what can we do for the *earth* from our one acre beside Callahan Lake in northwestern Wisconsin? I plant new indigenous trees and wildflowers every spring, but what good does that do in a country where some large-scale agricultural practice is remaking the biology of the fields in their owners' care—the farmers would say "which they own"—to support technologically redesigned or hybridized plants and seed they must buy annually instead of save seeds from their crops' last-season plants as farmers did in the past? And what about many farmers' use of fertilizers, pesticides, and insecticides for maximum single-crop production on large acreages, believing that this change of the earth's soil and the plants and animals of it is necessary for producing plenty of food for their markets and our consumption?

Or, what do we do about global warming in the face of the threat to the earth and humankind's very existence of the climate change verified in recent years by abundant scientific evidence as the doing at least in large part by human choices? The *Toronto Star* quoted an officer of the United Nations Environment Program in release of its Fourth Global Outlook report in October 2007 that "'humanity's very survival' is at stake."[1] Major causes of climate change include extensive deforestation for agricultural land use, for lumber and other industries' use of trees, and for expanded housing and building sites on the cutover ground; and, also, extreme overuse of fossil fuels of coal, oil, and gas and others of the earth's finite supply of reserve resources.

Deforestation and overuse of fossil fuels mean excessive amounts of carbon dioxide, methane, and nitrous oxide—"greenhouse gases"—are released into the atmosphere's air and water. The natural carbon cycle whereby carbon dioxide is gathered and stored within plant material—the trees—and used in production of their nutrients is broken in this process, as is the water cycle by which trees draw up ground water through their roots and release moisture into the atmosphere. Greenhouse gases are taken up by plants and animals from the air, water, and soil, and, in turn, people in the food chain in consumption of plant and animal materials as well as through breathing the polluted air and drinking the contaminated

1. Peter Gorrie, "Humanity's survival at stake: UN," *Toronto Star*, thestar.com, October 26, 2007. The report was further detailed in James Kanter, "U.N. Warns of Rapid Decay of Environment," *New York Times*, NYTimes.com, October 26, 2007.

water. Regions with fewer trees become drier with fewer sustaining water particles in the air and less rainfall to replenish lakes and streams, the atmosphere, and the earth's living creatures.

Considering these questions of the *world* and of the *earth* in such monumental and catastrophic terms does seem to make them overwhelming. Also, our identifying the contrast between our comfortable personal lifestyle in our family and the suffering and scarcity present in the daily lives of so many other people in our world could easily make our position seem to be facile or patronizing.

Still, I believe that people like us with the privileges of comfort in our lives, of adequate financial resources and access to leadership opportunities, education, and information must, by whatever name it is called, follow an imperative to act on what we have and what we know to improve the earth and the world for everyone. We must not isolate ourselves from the plights of other groups of people. Rather, we must act individually and collectively when it is possible on behalf of the earth's betterment, even if it comes at the expense of some of our personal desires and customary behaviors. For the problems on a scale much beyond our personal capacity to act, we must organize or join groups, lobby governments and industry, and support organizations both actively and financially that advocate the welfare of all people, the earth, and the world. Together, worldwide, we must "go green," that is, we must use environment-sustaining products and adopt practices in our homes, communities, and businesses that protect and clean our environment. Our state legislatures and Federal Congress must pass laws that require reversing the effects of depletions and poisons in the soil, water, and air and enable replacing the diminishing and contaminated resources. As members of the human community, we must participate in and advocate cleaning and restoring all the aspects of nature across the earth and then work to sustain clean air, water, land, and the whole of the earth's environment.

The notion of individualism runs counter to our need to address the stresses of our shared environment together as humankind. Although individual rights and opportunities are core values for democratic government and economic progress, extreme focus on the individual at the expense of social cohesion and shared public responsibility is immoral. We must parallel our effort for individual rights and opportunities with an equally fervent effort to include all of humankind in the benefits of clean, safe, and prosperous societies.

CRISES OF THE EARTH AND OF THE WORLD: OVERPOPULATION, OVERFARMING, AND OVERCONSUMPTION

In the United States and abroad, the first piece in the circle of damage to our environment and the world's well-being is *overpopulation*. With improved health care, cleaner water supplies and sanitation facilities, a more stable food supply, and cures for some formerly killer diseases along with vaccinations against the spread of others, the twentieth century saw the world's population grow exponentially. It increased from 1.65 billion people in 1900 to more than 6.5 billion people in 2000, a population explosion. The world population projection for 2050, if there is no change in the rate of growth, is nine billion people, or five times as many as there were in 1900. Yet, by then, at the current rate of use, land, water, food, and other resources will not support that population. This means we need to review and address worldwide all of our use of natural resources for agriculture, building construction, and all purposes of human consumption.

Yet very few people see the population itself as a critical problem. In many parts of the world no heed is given to what this portends. For example, the question of childbearing is fraught with many ideologies of individual choice, of state or religious control of family patterns of decision-making, and of the power of tradition. In some places, people continue unchecked childbearing out of the old pattern of fear of need for many children in families, offspring having been needed to carry out the families' work for securing their livelihood, and caring for the aging family members no longer able to work.

Although reliable birth-control methods and products have been available since the 1960s in highly industrialized countries like the United States and has slowed population growth, harmful arguments based on individualistic ideology permeate both political and religious discourse. There are "pro-choice" advocates of birth control and availability of abortion as "woman's right to choose" versus "pro-life" advocates of state and church control of decisions to give birth. Both sides of this narrowly focused dispute obscure the greater problem we face of global overpopulation. Even the claim, usually unstated but assumed, that birthgiving is a national issue is chauvinistic, for the implicit assertion that any state should decide who should have children is a claim of national ascendancy and an affront to world citizenship. The other extreme is total govern-

ment control of family-size choice. The "one-child" policy for families in enormously overpopulated China, for example, with punishment or forced abortion for couples attempting to produce more than one child, is an example of the collectivization opposite to the individualistic outlawing or endorsing birthgiving choices by states or other institutions on the premise of childbearing being wholly left to the individual.

Closely related to overpopulation, in fact, really, a part of the complex circle of too many people in the world to be sustained by the food and other resources of the earth, is what could be called *overfarming*. This is farming without reference to—and at the expense of—life-enhancing and life-sustaining trees and "natural" growth of grasses and other plants native to a locale, and without consideration of the insects and other animal life that sustain plant life, which, in turn sustains animals and humans. Overfarming along with overpopulation circles with what we might call *overconsumption*—people in industrialized countries eating and producing agriculturally animals and plants and derivatives from them far in excess of their human need for basic food and other of life's necessities. Rather, such people—people like us—work and travel and entertain themselves in patterns of consumption of foods, clothing, transportation, buildings, and goods and services far beyond their needs or their share of the world's per capita output. In fact, one of the arguments nations most often give for their delays in tackling global warming is that it would hurt their economy. Large-scale farmers and agribusiness leaders make the same argument on a private level: changes to more environmentally friendly agricultural practices would cause them to make less money. This claim may or may not be true in fact. Environmentally friendly agricultural and government policy and practices could become in the long run as economically viable as environmentally destructive ones.

We have a circle, then, a vicious circle, that encloses us as we act individually and collectively, that collectively impacts us individually, and individually limits us within our global collectivity. The circle is *overpopulation* circling with *overfarming* circling with *overconsumption*. All of these contribute to global warming and, also, to poverty and hunger in the world; and all of them must be changed literally to save the world. They need not be denied, only changed. People must continue to reproduce for future generations, farmers must provide food and other products, and human beings must have food and other resources for our survival. But our values about them all must change along with our allocation of quantities we produce and consume. Families, governments, and other human organizations must seek creative decision-making choices for fair and good lives in our future. This change must reach into every corner where we live.

For the earth and for the world, Jessica, for they are knotted inextricably—we must address the earth issues of climate change and of food. As people of the world and as participating individuals ourselves, we must see these issues as interwoven in all of human decision-making and must address directly in small and large actions the problems of *overpopulation*, *overfarming*, and *overcomsumption* as we learn about and make our choices about climate change, food, and agriculture.

CLIMATE CHANGE

After more than two decades of serious scientific warnings and scattered political crying in the wilderness about global warming from greenhouse gases endangering the very survival of the earth, the year 2007 was the year the deleterious human impact on climate change came into clear focus as a validated issue. The most symbolic act that called attention to climate change was the awarding of the 2007 Nobel Peace Prize to former U.S. Vice President Al Gore, long-time advocate for attention to reversal of climate change, and to the Intergovernmental Panel on Climate Change (IPCC), a United Nations–sponsored agency begun in 1988.

The day after the announcement of this Nobel Prize award, an e-mail message from New York Democratic Senator Charles Schumer popped up on computers all over the U.S. commending Al Gore and pointing out that when the two of them were together in Congress in the 1970s, Gore was prescient in his understanding of the need to address global warming. Even then, Gore had called on the U.S. government to pay attention to the damage being done to the earth through forms of pollution and carelessness about conservation. After Gore's defeat for the U.S. presidency in 2000, he devoted major time and effort to publicizing the urgency of reduction of human causes for temperature rises on the earth. He produced *An Inconvenient Truth*,[2] an Academy Award winning film with a companion book on global warming.

2. Al Gore, *An Inconvenient Truth: The Planetary Emergency of Global Warming and What We Can Do About It*. New York: Rodale, 2006.

The authoritative scientific counterpart group to Gore's public and political advocacy, the IPCC, which won the Nobel Peace Prize with Gore, is made up of representatives of all governments that are member states of the United Nations. It collects peer-reviewed scientific reports worldwide, has them vetted further by qualified scientists, and reports its assessments to the UN. The first report was in 1990; and there have been subsequent ones in 1995, 2001, and 2007.

By 2007, the IPCC reports gave compelling evidence of global warming and its consequences already severely affecting life on earth negatively. The IPCC argued in 2007 that it is 90 percent certain that human-made greenhouse gas emissions have caused weather behavior to fluctuate more dramatically than in past decades, there being more violent hurricanes and tsunamis, sporadic heavy rainfall, flooding and droughts, larger wildfires, greater regional temperature changes, and lessened snowfall best explained by increased earth temperatures. "Dead zones" in oceans and lakes resulting from pollutants like run-off fertilizers have caused the death of marine life. Warmer water temperatures result in coral reef decline in the oceans, threatening the habitat of some fish species, and causing the softening of shells of some crustaceans. (Remember scientist Eville Gorham's discovery when those little salmon embryos were put into increasingly warm water?) Polar ice caps and other glacial ice formations were melting at an increasingly rapid rate.

Deforestation and monoculture farming have brought the near extinction of some soil-inhabiting insect species and of animal and other plants dependent on forest habitat for survival. Also nearing extinction are many kinds of monkeys and apes, butterflies and other insects, owls and other birds, maybe even honeybees, insects vital to the pollination of food crop plants. Massive clearing of land for expanded farming, expansion of urban housing beyond cities and suburbs, and timber cutting has reduced the forests of the world; and soil change for industrialized farming has destroyed microorganisms and natural plants leaving much poorer soil less able to hold water and thus releasing excessive water vapor into the atmosphere, contributing still more to global warming.

The claim of the IPCC 2007 report is that "Warming of the climate system is unequivocal." The scientists argue in the report, "Global atmospheric concentrations of carbon dioxide, methane, and nitrous oxide have increased markedly as a result of human activities since 1750 and now exceed pre-industrial values." They predict serious consequences, even if efforts are made to reverse the effects of greenhouse gas emissions, and dire consequences if no change takes place. The earth will have hotter temperatures and sea levels will rise. There will be "frequent warm spells, heat waves and heavy rainfall" as well as a high likelihood of "increase in droughts, tropical cyclones and extreme high tides."[3]

After the 2007 Nobel Peace Prize recognizing attention to climate change, a surge in publicity about green, or environmentally protective, efforts already underway rose. Also, media, government, industrial, local and national citizen efforts to address climate change were highlighted and some citizens and institutions at all levels began to alter behaviors, laws, building and farming practices as well as starting or proposing a myriad of conservation efforts aimed at reducing greenhouse gas emissions and reversing global warming.

At last by 2008, some optimism was possible that attending to our environment is rising to the top of many people's list of concerns. Some neighborhoods, cities, and states have enacted laws and are adopting practices that take better care of our environment. As 2009 begins, the new U.S. president, Barack Obama, is undertaking initiatives on addressing global warming nationally and in world gatherings. This has been your mother's central advocacy issue for decades, Jessica, especially since earning her degree in environmental biology from Columbia University; and she is pleased that lots of people now are joining her and her cohort of environmentalists, including us.

FOOD AND AGRICULTURE

Equally hard to grasp as the climate change crisis for many people is the world's food crisis. There are too many people in the world to feed them the way most people in North America and Europe are accustomed to eating and farming. In many parts of the world, the conditions of lands and economies where natural or human-made occurrences of desertification, flooding, and soil depletion—most likely resulting from deforestation and human neglect, themselves related to climate change—inhibit adequate worldwide food production. These conditions, which contribute to poverty and want and even starvation, are further increased by totalitarian and war-making governments that do little to encourage ag-

3. "Intergovernmental Panel on Climate Change," *Wikipedia, the free encyclopedia*, on-line.

ricultural development and meaningful, sustainable farming practices for their people. Economically developed nations help the have-not nations in the form of food aid or monetary support, but often provide too little help in developing their own land use, their most effectively grown food crops, and the means to produce them, and the tools, equipment, start-up plants, and livestock most fitting for their circumstance. Too much foreign "aid" is in the form of leftover food products, seed stock, and equipment from the developed nations, most suitable for their own circumstance but less useful in places, topographies, weathers, and among peoples who are different from them.

There is excess of both consumption of foods and production of too few specific foods in the United States and other industrialized countries. In fact, nobody is yet addressing how an equitable worldwide distribution of foodstuffs and know-how for growing them well in many kinds of local conditions might look like.

Poet and farmer Wendell Berry has for decades written, lectured, and protested about what he thinks of as the failure of modern agriculture and of government policies supporting it. He writes of "taking proper care of our land" and of "the democratic distribution of usable property." He laments the extent of soil erosion, waste of water, and "toxic pollution from agricultural chemicals." He is distressed about the extensive losses of family farms and about the growth of "agribusiness" supported financially as well as legally by government policy.[4] Berry would prefer that all Americans, urban as well as rural, have "an intimate knowledge of the land" and know that care of the land, soil and water, plant and animal resources comes first, that replenishment be as significant as production, and that, at the end of the day, food be used only to feed the people. Food should be used not "as a weapon," as he accuses the U.S. government of doing in some of its foreign aid policies, or as an economic tool, as he believes some agribusinesses, including food processors and distributors, are manipulated by government policy to do.

Seeming to be prescient on the American problems of environmental protection and food, on the integral relationships among overuse of fossil fuels, human population growth, and the industrialization of food

---

4. Wendell Berry, *The Unsettling of American: Culture and Agriculture*. San Francisco: Sierra Club Books, 3rd ed., 1996, first published in 1977, p. vi.

production, Wendell Berry writes that we need to treat "the whole prob-lem of health in the soil, plant, animal and man as one great subject."[5]

Berry and like-minded others through efforts and books like his *The Unsettling of America: Culture and Agriculture* were the antecedents of the pay-attention-to-food part of the environmental movement in the late twentieth century. His work anticipated attention by the first years of the twenty-first century of growing and consuming foods grown locally, grown organically, or grown in tandem with watchful soil care. Berry's crying-in-the-wilderness poetic voice has at last been heard by farmers and consumers alike as we try to know and respect our land, as we try to become partners with the land in its preservation, restoration, and fruit-fulness. That's the task for you and me, Jessica, for all of humankind.

They have helped us know the earth and know the world. In a later chapter I will reflect on leaders and their ideas, as well as my own, about how we can love the earth and love the world.

5. Quoted in Michael Pollan, *The Omnivore's Dilemma*. New York: The Penguin Press, 2006, p. 145.

16

Moving from Knowledge to Wisdom

Out of the ground the Lord God made to grow every tree that is pleasant to the sight and good for food, the tree of life also in the midst of the
garden, and the tree of the knowledge of good and evil.

— Genesis 2:9

—Nature in Winter—This day was mud day. A sudden temperature rise
rapidly melted piles of snow so that car tracks on the road left deep puddles. I needed boots to wade through the mucky sand, soggy decaying
leaves, and water to get into the house. There were still mounds of snow
at places on our grounds, and it is too early for buds on the trees or for
sprouting plants, but I was glad for all the melting to provide moisture
that watered last summer's new little trees. It was a mess, though, to trek
about in.

AT THE END OF knowing, we seek wisdom. Wisdom is facts and figures, results and conclusions, and then more. Wisdom is not a feeling, not a thought, not even a collection of thoughts and feelings. Wisdom
is not simply understanding. It is not merely telling the truth. Wisdom is
not judgment, not arrival at understanding justice or loyalty or another
abstraction. Wisdom is neither scientific nor humanistic, neither poetry
nor mathematical reasoning, neither art nor equation.

Wisdom, instead, is perceiving the heart of the matter. Wisdom is
hearing or seeing or grasping and being transformed by what one hears
and sees and grasps and then communicating that transformation to others. Wisdom is being able to articulate the tough core of human under-

standing—at least for the moment. Wisdom comes from all the efforts and false starts, mistakes and paltry gains one makes when enlightenment dawns just beyond the exhaustion of the struggle to know. Wisdom is understanding that gives purpose and explanation to both science and poetry. Wisdom is beauty and truth and goodness codified and then decoded in a fiery flash of comprehension. Wisdom is a rainfall of waters of perception. Wisdom comes in gentleness that has prevailed beyond suffering to grasp acceptance of sure knowledge. Wisdom is born as serenity after hard labor, though it cries out instantly to be heard. Wisdom is receiving the wind from the treetops and imbibing its power.

And I do believe that wisdom is finally discernment, is finally the ability to discover the difference between right and wrong in its subtlety and in all the features of our lives.

Wisdom is necessarily the fruit of one person's work, but, achieved, it can be shared with all of humankind who can receive.

We have sought to learn by observing, by reading, and by listening. We have sought to know through science and through art and through combinations of science and art. We have looked at models in people's lives and at what people have made, written, and discovered in their productivity. We have looked at efforts to understand issues that our environment and our everyday lives present to us, and we have sought explanations on which we might act to make our own lives and those of the world's people better by our decision-making and action. There is one step more after learning, the quest for wisdom.

Wisdom is often associated with older people, and certainly many wise ones over the centuries have been old. Older people who have lived well become more secure in their identities and at the same time more open to new potential. They speak softly without need for argumentation and show by their words a lifetime of intense effort at gleaning from all the bits whirling around them clarity about what is good and true and right for their lives and the lives of others.

Wisdom refers to ethics, to decision-making, to choice. It is about the whole of life and the choices that make life bearable and full for the individual and for everyone. The old sometimes have learned on their way to wisdom both the questions and some of the answers about what is right from having experienced so much ambiguity, so much to-ing and fro-ing, so much of themselves at their worst—and at their best—and so many disappointments in human choices to harm and to hurt, to pollute, poison, and destroy—alongside knowing sheer joy in midday sunshine and in unexpected human acts of kindness, courage, and grace.

Still, not everyone who is wise is old, Jessica. Some old people can be fools, and sometimes children can be wise, as can young adults. The wise one is the one who can pierce to the heart of the matter and speak out boldly.

I invite you, Jessica, to join me in seeking to find wisdom.

An example of a person of wisdom I learned about from her publications early in my adulthood and appreciated greatly is Florida Scott-Maxwell (1883–1979). She was an old woman by the time she wrote the books that I read with such pleasure. When I was in my early twenties, I came across *Women and Sometimes Men* (1957); and it had a marvelous influence on me.

A Jungian psychoanalyst, having started her training with Carl Jung when she was fifty years old, Scott-Maxwell wrote *Women and Sometimes Men* in the 1950s after having published a previous Jungian-feminist work, *Toward Relationships,* in 1939. Scott-Maxwell's very gentle and kindly manifesto on the rights of women to have full personhood and social and economic rights and privileges equal to those of men spoke powerfully to my own sense of identity and my wishes for my future personal development. I read the book before the women's movement of the 1960s and 1970s and the popular feminist treatises of that time, and *Women and Sometimes Men* gave me my first real ah-ha understanding of my need for a feminist consciousness.

Much more significant later in my life to my gathering perspective on wisdom has been Scott-Maxwell's published "notebook" journal written in her eighties, *The Measure of My Days.* When I taught a course on "Women's Spirituality" in the early 1980s, I used *The Measure of My Days* as a textbook for several years; and Scott-Maxwell's is a book I return to now that I am in my sixties for reaffirmation of what I learned from her about wisdom.

The Measure of My Days may not even have been intended for publication. Scott-Maxwell calls it a "notebook" and it consists of jottings about her thoughts and musings in her largely private and solitary life. It is "personal." It is fragmentary. Yet, it records with rich clarity the accumulated force and serenity her thinking has given her. She writes of the knowledge of good and evil in every life, they being the two halves of the humanity of each human being, she believes. She writes in first person, writes of her coming to know the evil in herself, enabling her to also know the good in herself, and she believes similarly evil and good to be warring in all persons. In individual people; in social, political and international relations; in societies, and in nature there is no tranquility, but a continual combat of the aspects of evil and good present in each.[1]

She writes of the courage of individual initiative. "The opposition between the individual and the mass must be the very ground of evolution," she notes.[2] She comments that only the people who have dared to be individual have been able to "enlarge, to diversify" all through history. Such people of initiative are subject to great hate among common people, she surmises, for hatred is an easier response than change. It is much easier and far too frequent for people to go along, to be a part of the masses in deciding what to do, in living their lives. Yet, it is people with foresight and with courage who break out and lead to innovations for humankind.

She writes of matter-of-fact and satisfying conversations with her age peers about death. They see death as near upon them—"we cheerfully exchange the worst symptoms and our black dreads as well"[3]—but consider death as merely an enlargement of who they are at present. She likewise writes about views of an afterlife in a straightforward way, saying, "Personal immortality may not matter at all."[4] Mentioning God as a given in her experience—she equates God with life and uses Christian imagery and concepts readily in her notebook—she does not attribute life-taking to God, but sees the end of life as its beginning as coming from God. She writes of a life's individual end being a mystery. Yet, she sees no need for there to be more or another life. She writes, "In very truth, the old are almost free, and if it is another way of saying our lives are empty, well—there are days when emptiness is spacious and non-existence elevating."[5]

Her last word on death is, "My only fear about death is that it will not come soon enough."[6] Thus, it seems to me, the fact of death's coming and being the end of life for herself and each of us she has absorbed

1. Florida Scott-Maxwell, *The Measure of My Days*. New York: Penguin Books, 1979, first published by Alfred A. Knopf, Inc., 1968.

2. Scott-Maxwell, *Measure*, p. 25.

3. Scott-Maxwell, *Measure*, p. 31.

4. Scott-Maxwell, *Measure*, p. 39.

5. Scott-Maxwell, *Measure*, p. 119.

6. Scott-Maxwell, *Measure*, p. 75.

into herself as life-affirming; but pain and suffering, and, above all, loss of independence, that come with dying she hopes to avoid.

One of her life's issues has been "a wound that has ached in me all my life; the inferiority of women. It lamed me as a child."[7] She writes this in the context of rereading after fifty years Henry Adams's book *Mont-Saint-Michel and Chartres*, a book that I too have deeply appreciated. Adams's book touches her as he writes about the intense reverence for the Virgin Mary in the Middle Ages and the qualities attributed to Mary that the culture then came to value more profoundly in women of their own time and place. She continues her appreciative discussion of the book by moving the topic of women and men to her own time.

Women and men know each other, she believes, with men largely identified as public and dominating in the realm of work, and with women primarily private and supportive in the domestic arena. She writes that honest love between women and men might overcome this inequality, saying, "Yet when men and women truly love each other they project their greatest possibilities onto the loved one."[8] She does not reject domesticity as women's arena nor nurturance as a quality attached to women, nor does she reject public life and assertiveness as characteristic of men. Rather, in Jungian fashion of seeing complementary halves of feminine and masculine in each person, she argues that through loving understanding of one another, a man and a woman can come closer to realization of the wholeness of each one's self. Such wholeness is desirable for both women and men, she maintains.

She is surprised at greater passivity in herself in her eighties after great passion and drive in her seventies. She finds calm as she thinks her solitary thoughts, though the character of her thoughts have the same strength and conviction of her earlier life. She writes of her concern of the aftermath of the two world wars. She speaks of complacency she sees in society and a dearth of values promoted by parents to their children. She writes of dancing about on her clean kitchen floor as her kettle boils for tea, relishing the simple pleasures of ordinary life. She tells of watching a baby great-grandchild and knowing the perpetual care of motherhood, ruminating that a mother is ever hoping for her child to be exceptional,

7. Scott-Maxwell, *Measure*, p. 100.
8. Scott-Maxwell, *Measure*, p. 103.

"will somehow be a redeemer, . . . she is forever surprised and even faintly wronged that her sons and daughters are just people . . ."[9]

"I am ashamed to admit to myself that I am disappointed in humanity," she writes.[10] Still, she soldiers on, dancing alone in her kitchen to her teakettle's tune, honoring work and motherhood and life's comings and goings, waking recovered after a hospital stay and greeting the new morning, ruminating on balance in life, on aging, on love, on what makes one an "I," on the tension between good and evil, "fierce with reality."

This is Florida Scott-Maxwell's hard-earned life's lesson.

It is that passionate look at reality right in the nose that is wisdom, Jessica. It is easy to run away from it, to hide from it, to learn too little to recognize it, to try to wish it away, to argue for the sake of argument that it isn't scientific enough or not rational enough or not lyrical enough. It is easy to make excuses for it or to say it is not of the right ideology or not of the right school—at the height of my Women's Studies career Florida Scott-Maxwell was out of fashion because some feminist scholars were skeptical of Jungians—or not a member of the right crowd. All those excuses aside, the search for wisdom is the effort of giving it everything you have got to find out who you really are, what people are really all about, and what is really real. You will probably fail more than half the time. I certainly have. But the goal of transparent wholeness in your humanity is worth all the tries.

The Nobel-Prize winning poet, Wisława Szymborska, writes in her poem, "The Joy of Writing," words that are about an understanding that comes through the artistry of writing but could be about the arrival at wisdom:

> Is there a world
> Where I rule absolutely on fate? . . .
> The joy of writing
> The power of preserving.
> Revenge of the mortal hand.[11]

9. Scott-Maxwell, *Measure*, p. 17.

10. Scott-Maxwell, *Measure*, p. 78.

11. Wisława Szymborska, "The Joy of Writing," view with a grain of sand: Selected Poems. New York: Harcourt Brace & Co., A Harvest Original: 1993, trans. from Polish by Stanislaw Baranczak and Clare Cavanagh, p. 36.

Szymborska writes of the power resulting from the writer's exercise of her creativity as she imagines and writes of the world as she wants it to be. Let us similarly use the power of our own creativity, Jessica, to contribute wisely, in my conversation of the world as society and the earth as nature, to reshaping our world's environment of buildings and art and literature, schools and homes as grand and glorious and loving and our earth's environment as healthful and clean and beautiful as we can imagine it.

PART III

On Loving

Spring

. . . I have heard the lark and peewee and other birds already come to commence another year with us. Th[ese] were pleasant spring days, in which the winter of man's discontent was thawing as well as the earth, and the life that had lain torpid began to stretch itself.

—Henry David Thoreau, *Walden*

And faith, hope and love abide, these three;
and the greatest of these is love.

—I Corinthians 13:13

—Nature in Spring—Though nothing is budding yet, springtime is in the air. The falling rain on Sunday was a spring rain, soft and sweet-smelling; and the bright sun late in the afternoon that day and on the two sunny days since was springtime light of lengthening days.

17

Loving Yourself and Loving Other People

In those who harbor thoughts of blame and vengeance toward others,
hatred will never cease. In those who do not harbor blame and vengeance, hatred will surely cease. For hatred is never appeased by hatred.
Hatred is appeased by love. This is an eternal law.

—the *Dhammapade*, "the classic source of Buddhist ethics"
quoted in Diana Eck, *A New Religious America*

—Nature in Spring—The evening I arrived the lake was still frozen except for a few feet at the shore. The next day—when the temperature
reached seventy degrees—the ice cracked up into big patches and large
puddles were visible nearly to the middle of the lake. The next morning,
as the day warmed, it was as if I were watching the ice go out in front
of gently lapping waves. On the morning of the third day, the lake was
once again moving water, the ice gone.

Spring Song Haiku 1—It rained through the night
And all the fresh tree buds burst
With the morning light.

Spring Song Haiku 2—Up out of the soil
Came an earthworm multitude
Partaking of spring.

—Spring Holidays—Easter and Passover—Earlier I called Christmas
the Christian Love holiday. Perhaps I should have saved that name for
Easter, for Easter is the time Christians see the full meaning of their faith

opened up. It is the commemoration, as Christian theology articulates it, of the Resurrection of Christ, the overcoming of death when only two days earlier the disciples and loved ones of Jesus had experienced utter despair as they saw their leader reviled and humiliated in a public execution on a cross. Whether they interpret the reappearance after death of Jesus Christ literally as a physical reality or symbolically as a renewal of hope for living after the apparent finality of death, Christians base their faith on the meaning of Easter. Christian images of the Risen Christ and the Savior of the World point to hope as central to the faith and hope that is available to everyone, as they believe it to be. The Jesus who was born a child and celebrated at Christmas, as a man became the Christ, the One with God, who overcame the threat death poses for humankind, a victory that is celebrated at Easter. Thus, Christmas is the Christian Love holiday and Easter is the Christian holiday of Hope, perhaps the highest understanding of Love.

Christmas is also celebrated soon after the winter solstice (December 21 or 22), the time that ushers in winter; and Easter is celebrated at the beginning of spring, "the first Sunday after the first full moon after the 21st of March," the vernal equinox of March 20 or 21. Many other religions similarly have a holiday that begins with the approach of winter in December and another that welcomes spring in March or April. Contemporary pagans and WICCE members, for example, celebrate Yuletide in December, bringing in logs from out of doors and burning fires and candles as light against the deepening darkness that falls with winter. In the spring, they celebrate the greening of the earth on the vernal equinox by having open-air festival celebrations. They believe that these festive practices reach back to pagan events in prehistory.

Jews, too, face the winter with a celebration of lights and family gathering in their eight days of Hanukkah, which comes in their religious calendar on the twenty-fifth day of Kislev, a date that might occur in late November or any time in December, again a time around the onset of winter. Jews light candles in their homes each night for eight nights, lighting the first on the first night and increasing the number for each night. The holiday represents the rededication of the Temple and also stands for rededication of the home, so that the candles are sometime stood outside the door of the home or in windows showing light for the house.

Similarly, the major Jewish holiday of the year comes in the spring. Passover commemorates the Exodus of the Jews from bondage in Egypt and their salvation from destruction of their firstborn by the sign of a lamb's blood on the door signifying to the angel of death to exempt them, to "pass over" the households from the sacrifice of their firstborn sons. Passover comes on the fifteenth day of Nisan on the Hebrew calendar, which comes in March or April, similarly a springtime date. It is an event held in the home and is a time of the cleaning of homes by Jewish people and inviting their families and strangers to the ritual Seder meals at the Passover in celebration of their Jewish identity and of renewed life promised to them as a people in the original Passover.

When I was a graduate student, my friend Sharon Rubin and her husband, David, invited Wilson and me each year to their family Seder. Attending has been a happy memory held over my lifetime of Jewish inclusiveness in our friendship.

Sharon and David's Seder began, as most Seders do, with the call, "Why is this night different from all other nights?" And the answer comes: commemoration of deliverance of the Jews from slavery in Egypt, the Exodus. Their ritual meal of Seder in the Rubins' home followed the pattern of most Seders: the eating of unleavened matzo bread; the symbolic drinking of four cups of wine, with an additional cup set for the prophet Elijah, an expected guest at Seder; and the Seder plate of symbolic food, including bitter herbs representing the bitter experience of Jewish slavery, roasted meat standing for the sacrificed lamb offered at Temple, and a roasted egg, also suggesting the averted sacrifice of innocents on the original Passover. The ritual follows the book called the Haggadah, which many Jewish families, including Sharon and David, create or add to for themselves from the tradition. The evening includes the prescribed recounting of the liberating journey out of Egypt, a set of songs of praise, reading of passages from the Hebrew scriptures, and, often, as with Sharon and David, discussion of troublesome events in the contemporary world. After the food, the singing, the ritual, and the discussion, Seder ends with the cry, "Next year in Jerusalem!"

When I once visited Jerusalem with my Women's Interfaith Study group, I remembered Seder at Sharon Rubin's house; and for my sixtieth birthday, when Wilson sent out a request ahead of time to friends asking for poems or meaningful pieces of literature be sent to me, Sharon Rubin sent me a copy of her family Haggadah.

For Wilson's and my lifetime and in springtimes with our children and grandchildren, we have good memories of our spring Christian festival of Easter. Time and again Easter morning sees sunrise worship services on mountains or beaches or just anywhere out of doors, signifying the Risen Christ or the coming of new life with the Easter morning's arrival. Wilson and his brother Marshall always participated in sunrise services at their boyhood Methodist Church in Matthews, Missouri. As a child, as people often do, I got new clothes for Easter, made by my aunt 'Cile; and, Jessica, the year your mother was three, Aunt 'Cile made her and me little mother-daughter Easter suits of lightweight turquoise wool. We have pictures of us on the steps of our Cambridge, Massachusetts, house, dressed for church with our suits and white hats and white gloves. It wasn't much beyond three years old that your mother abandoned and would no longer wear dressy little white gloves and hats!

Easter brings for children and their families the fun of dyeing Easter eggs bright colors the day before and Easter-egg hunts with collecting the colorful eggs in baskets on Easter morning. Commerce has substituted chocolate eggs and chocolate bunnies for the boiled and colored hen eggs of tradition—tradition also has the story that the eggs are hidden for the children by the Easter bunny. However, while there is plenty of Easter chocolate around our house, we stick with the regular chicken eggs and the regular hunts. The year you were two, there was too much snow outside our Minnesota house for you to hunt eggs outdoors, so we hid the eggs in houseplants, art objects, and seat cushions in various rooms and you found them and put them in your basket. The last few years our neighborhood Harvest Bread bakery has made bunny-shaped bread loaves for Easter and I have bought them and distributed them to some of our family households and friends. One year Wilson and I learned to make Ukrainian Easter eggs, and we now have a small collection to display as Easter decoration.

Church services on Easter have banks of white Easter lilies in the chancel, sermons on life's renewal—or ministers' articulation of a theology of Resurrection—and rousing singing of "Hallelujah! Hallelujah!" and "Up from the grave He arose/ With a mighty triumph o'er His foes . . ."

These high holidays, with both their simple repeating practices and their major watershed meanings for the faithful, give children and grown-ups alike the familiarity of belonging. They translate into membership, community.

A FUSSY LINGUIST WROTE a column I once read on the misuse of the word "love," the confusion of it with "like." Love, he insisted, is the emotion reserved for people, while one "likes" desserts, colors, landscapes, or forms of dancing—things and experiences. I was taught this distinction as a young child working to become a perfectionist at grammar and language usage. In fact, the linguist's injunction could have come right out of my English-teacher mother's mouth. However, my adult persona bridles at being restricted in my claims of loving. I love the earth, my trees, the world, the morning sunlight. I love fresh peaches in August and pine needles blanketing the ground when the snow melts in the spring. I love the robins and chickadees, the goldfinches and sparrows, the ducks, geese, great blue herons, and loons we see at the cottage. I love the ocean—the Atlantic Ocean at Boca Raton, the Pacific at San Francisco—and the Mississippi River that runs between our Minneapolis home city and St. Paul. And I love Callahan Lake here at our Wisconsin cottage. I love ship travel and trains and airplanes, and I love my car. I love my Linden Hills neighborhood in Minneapolis, and I love Coventry-in-the-Northwoods, our house in the woods by the lake. Love is all these bound up together for me. Love is embracing and holding, holding onto for sustenance of life itself.

Loving people, though, still is primary. Loving all of nature and loving things that people have been able to make and to develop is an extension from our having learned first to love people. I love people, and near and dear people are called, appropriately, "loved ones." And I love many others whom I touch and who touch me. I love them the better for having loved my trees and sand and water. But I do love my trees and sand, rocks and water. Love for me can encircle all of nature with humankind.

And how better to think of love than the insight our word "lovemaking" suggests—the act of coming together sexually as male and female after mutual attraction toward the biological objective of reproduction, as do most plants and animals of the earth. But lovemaking does not stop with sex. It continues in nurturance and commitment, loyalty and patience, respect, tolerance, cooperation, forgiveness, and grace. Contemporary thinking has expanded our understanding of lovemaking to include caregiving and grace-filling along with sexual joy.

Loving other people and loving the earth and its creatures and its vegetation are central to being human, but first you must love yourself.

FIRST LOVE

Arrogance and self-importance are, of course, unseemly qualities for a person, Jessica. However, you must truly love yourself before you or someone else can fully love another person or others. Loving is a reciprocity, of course. You cannot really love yourself until you have known the love of another person or other people, and others cannot love you unless they know love in return.

Learning to love is being loved and giving back love.

I remember once when you were an infant only a few weeks old and I came for a visit. You were in your infant seat, which was set on the dining room table. Your eyes and face and body already knew how to respond when your mom or dad or a grandparent held you or got near you. As I spoke to you, leaning over you, your arms and legs wiggled with pleasure, your eyes shone, and you said, "Ah-yah-boo-go-gah!" I spoke back, you waited for me to finish, then said, "Ga-wah-ba-ba-ba-wah?" I laughed and spoke again, and again you waited politely—I do not lie: you already knew how to carry on a conversation: your dad heard us—and then you said very seriously, "Pa-bah-wah-yah-ma!" and we both laughed.

You began quite early to mirror both conversation and love, and soon you became very able on your own to express in language and affection your love for your people.

An infant's initiation into loving is by being loved. You reflect back what you experience; and when it is fully unrestricted loving that you know early, it is loving behavior that you mimic. Later, of course, a child must learn that she must sometimes sacrifice some wishes or desires of hers for the best interest of her own life or other people's lives or of her society. One must discipline oneself. But best interest does not cancel love, not withhold it, but magnifies love. Considering the best interests of all persons is an aspect of mature love.

As one grows in love, one learns to look beyond oneself alone and seek to understand what unselfish acts and choices are needed from a person to make herself, other people, and the world better. Having first learned to love oneself, one's love can go out and out and out, breaking through boundaries, as one knows respect of self and of others.

RESPECT, A WAY OF LOVING

Self-respect is essential, but when you genuinely understand respect, Jessica, you will know it is the first step of loving other people, another person, of loving at all. Respect may not be the full measure of love, but it comes first.

Respect is holding a loving attitude toward those you meet. It is asking yourself, How to I honor this person's core humanity? It is wondering, How do I disagree with this person or hold another stance from this person without insulting her or his dignity? How do I cherish this person even as I maintain difference with them?

The components of self-respect are a sure knowledge that one is truthful; a reliance on one's strengths, tolerance, and resilience; an inner core of self-understanding and confidence, yet an ability to change when facts and circumstance show different and better ways; and a feeling of well-being about who one is.

Respect is a level playing field for everyone. Respect gives the benefit of the doubt. Respect meets another person with an open mind. Respect honors every child, woman, and man as fully human. Respect hears another person out—though it also gently requires the other to hear oneself out, too. Respect is gracious. Respect is both firm and kind.

A big form of disrespect is a blast of uncontrolled anger aimed at a person.

ANGER CONTROL

For me one of the hardest tasks of moral responsibility is controlling my anger. My father had harsh anger, sometimes out-of-control anger, and he sometimes punished my brother and me unjustly when we were children because of what seemed to us was only that we had made him angry. I "stood up to him" as a child in a way my brother and my mother did not feel they could do; but the result for me, I think, has been that I took on some of his anger, his way of behaving, and it was damaging for me. I met "fire with fire," which may not have been good for my development, but probably helped defend and protect my self-confidence as a child. Sometimes I still have some anger toward him that I have not been able to let go. Although I think I have improved as I have matured, even now I sometimes lash out at people verbally or in writing if I am angry, when, instead, I need to think before I act, need to stop and count to ten, as some people advise, or need to stop, take a "time out," and ask just what made me so angry and what would be the best way to handle the situation and what would be the consequences, rather than just take the most immediate action.

"Hold your tongue" is a good piece of advice when you are angry.

Once in a while as a young child you scream at your mother or father when they don't allow you to get your way. I hope you and I both can learn to stop screeching anger and find more constructive ways to direct those negative feelings that make us want to scream or to write hostile words.

Nevertheless, there is good anger, righteous anger. When a person is truly wronged or sees an injustice done and is able to focus clearly and to direct the anger carefully at the wrongdoer in order to try to correct the situation, this is anger well expressed—good anger. It is quite different from "flying off the handle" in unfocused anger. The feeling one has after this kind of expression of direct and cogent anger is satisfaction rather than guilt or frustration, for even if the object of the directed anger makes no change, one senses having done the right thing. Sometimes, too, such focused, expressed anger can make significant change among people and in the world. For example, over the centuries some ethicists have argued for a "just war doctrine" by which a nation's public and aggressive action taken against a perceived wrongdoing enemy nation or people is affirmed as constructive expression of war-making by a nation's collective and justified anger. Many argue, for example, that World War II aggression against Hitler's Nazi Germany with Hitler's efforts to crush many nations and to annihilate some categories of people was "just war." Anger out of control, on the other hand, leaves the angry person guilty, the object of the anger puzzled or hurt or annoyed, and nothing is resolved. This applies equally to an individual showing anger and to a country going to war in an ill-advised self-aggrandizing national attack of hostility. Many of us feel that President George W. Bush's initiation and conduct of the war against Iraq was such misplaced international anger propagating an unjust war.

The responsible reply to anger of others, though, is forgiveness, even though it is easier to speak of forgiveness than to actually act and confer forgiveness.

FORGIVENESS

A man I know is dying. He did hurtful things to me in past years when we were colleagues, and I find myself thinking of those hurts and feeling anger against him rising within me. I remember a wise woman once telling me when I was agonizing over another relationship in which I felt misused, "You can forgive, though you never forget." Remembering this idea helped reduce my anger as I thought of my dying colleague's behaviors toward me. Why did he do those things? I wondered.

First I replied to myself angrily, "Because he was a puny little man with a microscopic little self-serving self!" And then I thought, "Yes, his ego was so small, perhaps bruised and hurt in some ways that he could not get beyond himself to think of what his behaviors were doing to other people, perhaps not even knowing how badly he was hurting me by his actions in our university setting."

"Well, it still hurts," I said back to myself, "but getting through that hurt made me tougher and stronger. And he *is* dying. This was all the life he had. Maybe he did all he could. Maybe protecting himself was all that he was capable of." And, as my anger lessened, I began to understand that this is how forgiveness comes about. Seeing his situation from his point of view and trying to enter into understanding as he would think and feel is the beginning of empathy.

It has not been so easy to forgive the members of the Ku Klux WoSt.

The day of what your granddad dubbed "the visit of the Ku Klux WoSt" (from an eavesdropping reported by then fifteen-year-old Natasha) was a watershed moment of my very life; and I felt broken and scarred from it for years to come. On a June day twenty-five years later, I realized that it was the anniversary of "the visit of the Ku Klux WoSt," and I felt quite sad and hurt. The words came to mind, "You can forgive, though you never forget," and I wondered if I had even been able to forgive them.

That Saturday in 1980 I was at home with a very serious strep infection. Wilson was in England taking a travel class to arts and architecture sites that, the autumn before, I had led the two of us in learning about at our leisure on our Cambridge sabbatical. Our close family friend, Tom Campbell, with whom we had been in England that fall with his wife, Donna, and daughter, Karen, was dying. Natasha at fifteen and Stiles at eleven were at home with me, doing the best they could to take care of their sick mother. In other words, my life was very complicated. Into this mix, my faculty women's support group from Women's Studies, of which I was chair, phoned and said they would like to come and bring breakfast to my home. That seemed lovely. Little did I know.

The women who came were five junior faculty members whom I regarded as close friends. I later learned that the sixth faculty woman, who was also a member of the group, had refused to come on learning what the group intended to do. That spring, with me as the leader, though I was on a nontenure-track and thus in a vulnerable position, we had won permanence in the University of Minnesota College of Liberal Arts for Women's Studies to be secured; and it appeared at that time the faculty and students wanted to carry me cheering down the mall on their shoulders like some celebrity football coach. In those early days Women's Studies was suspect, not popular, to say the least; and I was told that my calm, scholarly, and professional leadership style had won the day for us.

The Easter before, I had invited to dinner one of my faculty women's support group members and her husband, hoping for shared friendships among us as couples. The preceding autumn Tom Campbell and his family had been in England when we were, and we had enjoyed a lot of special time together, including the moment when Wilson and Donna Campbell were raving on about how marvelous it was to be in England and Tom and I looked across the table at each other knowingly and said to each other: "Where had you rather be?" "Yes, at my administrative desk in Minnesota!" "Me, too!"

The next June when both Tom and I were back at our administrative desks, Tom learned he had terminal cancer and I had to fight for the survival and establishment of the academic program I had helped create on our campus and nationwide, but we were both much happier to be in Minnesota than we had been that year in England.

Then came the June morning, after the successful resolution of the permanence fight for Women's Studies in our university, that my Women's Studies support group members came to our home and did their damage to my psyche. They did bring breakfast rolls. Natasha took her younger brother, Stiles, downstairs to watch television in the lower level family room, while we women sat in the big living room above; but Natasha listened to what went on; and, when her dad came home, she, not I, told him what had happened; and he, a former civil rights movement activist, privately named the group the "Ku Klux WoSt." That name has stuck in our household for twenty-five years, and their visit was a catalytic moment for my career and for my life.

At the "breakfast" they questioned the stability of my mental health and even questioned whether I really had strep. They condemned me for being concerned that my nontenure-track position be turned into a tenure-track one on the strength of Women's Studies having become permanent, and they told me I should resign as chair. Because I thought we were faithful friends and I had so recently been their leader in our very successful effort, I was flabbergasted. I declined to resign the chair.

After that day, my whole life turned into a nightmare that lasted several years. The job I had initially loved and poured all my energy and enthusiasm into turned into an internal Women's Studies fight that was literally a battle for my professional existence. When Tom Campbell died in August, I broke down sobbing at his funeral, which caused a lot of fuss about what on earth was wrong with me.

I felt so humiliated and distressed by that confrontation with my faculty women's group that I did not tell anyone, not even your granddad when he came home from England. I did not tell other faculty members in Women's Studies or the university, not anyone, for several weeks. The feeling I had was the filthy one that I now realize is accepting victimization, the same feeling I had experienced alone in the New York subway system when I was a young college student going to meet my boyfriend at the time and a hairy young man suddenly appeared and exposed himself to me in the underground stairwell. I ran up the stairs and out onto the street and soon found my waiting boyfriend, but I did not tell him what had happened, did not ever tell him. I felt too ashamed, too degraded, as if it were my fault, as if I had done something untoward, when in fact I had experienced abuse.

Your mother, just as strong at fifteen as she is now, told her father when he came home; and another more senior woman in the leadership of Women's Studies and in the university administration had gotten word of what had happened in some way and called me to come and talk with her about it. She and other women and men faculty offered to me then, and continued to provide, rock-solid support for my getting on with my work and with my life.

In Women's Studies that fall, the woman I had invited to Easter dinner resigned from the faculty and went back to her home department, refusing to participate in Women's Studies "until Gayle Graham Yates is no longer chair." A senior faculty woman with tenure was appointed to preside over the meetings of Women's Studies, though I was still chair; and at one meeting a year later a young philosopher, whose job I had helped secure for her only the year before, made a motion that I be removed from the chair. It was turned down with only three votes favoring it, but I had to sit through the outrageous debate over my fate in office.

After another year and my having been restored to full authority of my office, I resigned the chair and soon asked that my appointment be moved home to American Studies.

The faculty woman I had liked very much who had resigned from Women's Studies on my account and who was a Protestant like us did not ever again have a meaningful conversation with me or participate favorably in any University business in which I had a part. In fact, she went on for the rest of her career taking actions that opposed my professional progress. One of the other members of the group, who happened to be Jewish, was elected to succeed me as chair. Though all of us were junior, these two were tenured and thus had the most institutional advantage. A second member who was Jewish came to me the next fall, on a day I later realized was Rosh Hashanah, the Jewish New Year and the first of the Ten Days of Repentance, and told me that I had misunderstood what the women's group had meant by their visit. She told me she felt shame about that day, but she also said, "You understand, don't you, that we can never be friends again?" I didn't understand that at all, for, if she felt shame and was apologizing, I could not see why reconciliation of our friendship, which mattered a great deal to me, was not a possibility, so she too was perpetually in the "opponents" camp. The woman who had chosen not to come to my house told me much later that she had not wanted any part of what the women's group members were going to do, but she didn't want to talk about it further or to take the questions the other women faculty members raised into a public forum.

Was I able to forgive them? Just a little bit, but they continued to get positions and opportunities that I would have enjoyed, too, and they had a part in my not getting to hold offices or have experiences that would have been appropriate ones for me. I had to radically reorient my life at my workplace, and it was a huge victory that I simply survived and got on with my professional life in a dignified and productive way. I learned how difficult it is to mix friendship and work, but I did learn those boundaries, and I enjoyed the fast friendship and respect of several other faculty members, both women and men, with whom I worked. I learned to live with the truism that life goes on.

But did I forgive them? Well, I have worked at it. And later, when some more bad things happened to me, it wasn't as hard as before to try to understand. When two of my former PhD students of whom I was quite fond and who were working with me on editing a book sabotaged our contract and destroyed the work we had done, I could be sad at the loss and work on forgiving them but yet know that we would not be friends again. However, I could absorb the disappointment into myself and say of them, forgivingly, that they needed to be working on their own career priorities and couldn't allow this book to be a part of them.

So, what is my advice on forgiveness, Jessica? Forgiveness is a worthy goal when you have been hurt or damaged. Try to forgive. Do the best you can.

Love is the primary expression of being human. Its converse, hate, is always nipping at our heels. Don't let it bite. Forgive, as best you can. Control your anger, as best you can. Respect yourself, other people, and the world. Love is possible. You already know it well. I love you.

18

Features of Love

Overhead the stars stretch to the horizon, dotting the blue-black sky like
the delicate speckles on the loon's side.
And then it comes again—the [loon] call known as the wail . . . Heard
for the first time, it isn't neatly called by any name. It is a sensation
up the spine, a chill to the skin, a creator of that little gap in the mind
through which one sees eternity.
. . . you are never the same again once you have heard a loon.

—Joan Dunning, *The Loon: Voice of the Wilderness*

—Nature in Spring—Sleepless after midnight last night in the thick
darkness, I heard loons wailing and yodeling wild mournful trills from
the lake below. The loons are back! I smiled into my pillow in my dark
bedroom at the springtime reassurance of the loon sounds coming
from our northern lake. Peace settled over me as I listened to the loons'
woodsy lakeside bedtime song.

This morning I saw a single loon swimming alone a few yards
from the shore. Perhaps it was a male just back at our lake from his
wintering on seashore open water. Perhaps he was swimming beside
the shoreline in search of his territory and a nesting place in preparation for his mate's return to Callahan Lake.

Ducks fly down to the lake and swim about, joyful they seem,
matching my springtime mood.

And then I look up and the bald eagles fly overhead emitting their
cawlike screech.

Expressions of love are manyfold. The ones closest to my heart are grace, courage, and integrity.

GRACE

Grace is the word that for me most encapsulates love. I pay a person a high compliment if I call him or her graceful. While graceful can mean simply elegant or beautiful in one's walk, manner, or conversation, I use it more comprehensively to mean love-filled, generous, lovely of spirit.

Gracious means exhibiting grace. We speak of having a gracious host or hostess, meaning they thought of little kindnesses, welcoming words, and attention to our tastes and personal needs for us as guests, as well as providing delicious food, a beautiful table, or clean and fragrant sheets on their guest-bed for us, or a warm fire in the fireplace and our favorite hot drink in the sweetness of a winter's night gathering in their home. I think of my 95-year-old friend, Martha Ray, mother of my now-deceased college roommate and lifelong friend of the same name. She is perpetually the gracious hostess when I visit her. The food we eat in her breakfast room is memorable, the bedroom in which I sleep with the wonderful antique furniture that was her daughter's is beautifully prepared with a stack of pillows for me, our conversation is always delightful. Once in a political season, she, a Republican, knowing I am a Democrat, said to me very pleasantly, "I suspect we are on different sides, so let's just not talk about this election."

The qualities of grace are loveliness, kindness, sweetness, charm, agreeableness, joyfulness, shared pleasure. A gracious person puts another person at ease, gives clear attention to what the other person says or wants or needs, is delightful to be with, but does not sacrifice form for fairness, does not offer charm with emptiness.

Widespread use of the word grace comes from its religious meaning. Although I use it in a personal and social form, it first came into our vocabulary as a religious reference. For many Christians, divine grace means that God is available to humankind, and to individual persons, without restrictions, without reference to deeds or behavior of the person. That is, within the grace of God, the human is free from the constraints of human foibles, in theological language, freed from sin, inherent in human nature, by grace, the infused love of God. One Roman Catholic view is that grace is God's life by which people are able to become renewed, to receive salvation. This view confirms that creation comes from God, life comes from God, and salvation comes from God—creation, life, and salvation, the components of grace.

"Amazing Grace" is a nineteenth-century evangelical religious song with a mournful minor melody often sung at funerals that gives one conservative view of grace. It goes, "Amazing grace, how sweet the sound/ That saved a wretch like me./ I once was lost/ But now am found/ Was blind, but now I see." My worldview decries calling myself or other persons "a wretch," for I have a much higher regard for human nature than to see it in wretchedness—inherently sinful. However, grace that recovers the lost and gives vision to the formerly blind is a welcome understanding for me.

A biblical story that illustrates grace is Jesus's Parable of the Prodigal Son, in Luke 15:11–21. A second son asks his father for his inheritance and leaves home, squandering his resources as he lives a profligate life in a foreign place until he has lost everything, including his dignity, and has to feed pigs for a living. He returns home chastened. His father, though his first son has stayed home and been faithful in the work of the family, welcomes his returning prodigal son fully with lavish feasting and rejoicing. When the first son complains that he has been dependably at home, the father rebukes him, saying that the son who had been lost has returned, the son who had been dead now lives again.

Whether or not one subscribes to a specific religious view of grace, the word that entered our vocabulary from religious history gives us meaning for personal grace, for acts of graciousness. Grace is life infused with love. Grace carries generosity, empathy, and freedom. Grace is the freedom to be oneself—as the 1972 Marlo Thomas children's song would have it, "Free to be you and me." Grace is good manners on a continuum with good faith. Grace is fair-mindedness and kindness, joyousness, and loveliness.

There is grace in loving lives and then there is courage.

COURAGE

After you and your granddad had capsized the canoe one day the summer you were four and you both got back to the house safely, but wet and cold, Wilson said, as you sat hugged in your mother's arms wrapped in dry, warm towels and blankets, "Jessica was very brave!" and you replied, "But Granddad was even braver!"

It turned out that it had taken both of you, four-year-old you and 67-year-old Granddad, to manage to avoid disaster from your accident. Wilson tells us that he was frightened when he came up out of the water because he could not see you. Because the canoe was upside down, he was afraid you were trapped under it; but, instead, you were floating face up just a short distance from the canoe, your life jacket your parents had provided for you and had made sure you wore had done its job. You called to him, "Over here, Granddad!" and he swam over and took you in his arms. He had to think fast, and he is very good at calm, deliberate decision-making in a crisis. He thought he could stand on his tiptoes on a little knoll he felt on the bottom of the lake near the upside-down canoe, but he had on his boots and heavy jacket under his life preserver, so he had to get rid of the boots (Why on earth did he wear heavy boots out on the canoe? we thought but did not say aloud) and try to right the canoe while holding onto you. With your arms around his neck, he managed to get the canoe right side up but there was still the problem that it was filled with water, its gunwale level with the lake surface. He decided to put you into the canoe on the seat so he could tilt the boat and get out some of the water and dip more out with your red bucket, which was still in the canoe. "You will have to be brave," he told you. "But I am scared, Granddad!" you replied, and you were crying. "I am a little bit scared, too," he said, "but we can be both scared and brave."

"Look!" you said, "Our paddle is getting away!" so he had to swim off a little distance to get the paddle, which he had not seen floating off. He gave the paddle to you to hold in the canoe. Then, with you in the boat and holding onto him, he tilted the boat to get rid of some water and he dipped out a lot more of it. After that, he had to manage to take off those heavy boots under water. "I'm cold, Granddad!" you told him, and he noticed that your lips were blue, so he wrapped you in the sopping-wet beach towel you had on board but that did not seem to help much.

"If there were angels, we could certainly use one now!" you told him.

Very soon the bald eagle that lives on an island in our lake was circling above you, much closer that Wilson had seen it before. The eagle landed on a treetop very near you, and he called your attention to it, believing that it was eyeing you. You talked about the eagle and its watchfulness, and said to each other that it was watching over you. Then, Wilson told you that he was going to try to swim to shore towing the canoe. He said you might help by talking to him. So, you talked away and he swam, pulling you and the boat to safety. "We made it!" he told you. "No, we haven't," you replied, "We aren't home yet!"

At our dock, after he had been able to paddle the canoe the rest of the way home, you asked your granddad to let you run to the house by yourself to "go tell them."

"We fell in the lake," you told your mother when she met you at the door, squelching her alarm at seeing you wet, "but I was very brave."

Bravery requires preparation, paying attention, quick thinking, self-confidence, and support. People can be brave and still have outcomes that are hurtful or even tragic; but the best chance of success at facing difficult situations is to have all the components of bravery.

Foolhardiness is the opposite of bravery, as Aristotle told us. It is foolhardy to take unnecessary risks, to go into situations unprepared, to go into situations one does not understand, to overestimate one's abilities and skills and plunge into actions for which one is not ready. It is foolhardy to think only of oneself and one's personal gains. It is foolhardy to be unrealistic about the risk one is taking and dishonest with oneself and others about how much one knows and understands what you are doing.

Both you and your Granddad were able to be brave during your crisis after your canoe accident because you both had all the component characteristics for bravery.

You were prepared by wearing your life jackets. Granddad was also prepared by knowing how to swim.

You both paid attention to what needed to be done. Wilson recognized the canoe needed to be righted and the water bailed out. You observed the paddle float away and needed retrieving. Your Granddad saw the eagle and suggested it was a good omen for you. It also gave you something to think about and pay attention to beyond your difficulty in the water.

You both acknowledged your feelings that you were afraid—it was okay for you to cry, but you did not panic—and that you both wanted to be brave. And, being the adult, your Granddad took charge in an appropriate manner, reassuring you in a way that he might not have felt and asking you to help in a way that he knew you could: talk to him while he swam towing the canoe.

The two of you believed in each other to make it home safely, and you encouraged each other with humor—your angel comment—and observations and simple conversation.

You both knew you had not only each other's emotional support but also the support of those of us back at the house. And who knows? Maybe the universe watched over you in the eagle's eye.

This incident from that summer at the lake, one we don't want to repeat, taught us all a great deal about bravery, about courage.

INTEGRITY

Courage and grace bond in integrity as they constitute love. One's integrity is one's wholeness, honesty, and surety. Love is manifest with courage, grace, and integrity together.

Integrity, in perhaps an unusual way, is illustrated for me by the well-known twelfth-century true love story of Abelard and Heloise, based on their letters to one another. As with many a significant historical tale, figure, art work, or poem, some of the intrigue of this story is the various ways, even conflicting ways, it can be interpreted over time.

I read the letters of Abelard and Heloise, three composed by Heloise and four by Abelard, and wrote a short play based on them when I was a student at Boston University in 1963. My professor, Ruth Winfield Love—"Lady Love"—produced and directed a performance of my play at Boston University that winter. Most recently, I was reminded of Abelard and Heloise when reading the excellent book by Thomas Cahill, *Mysteries of the Middle Ages: The Rise of Feminism, Science, and Art from the Cults of Catholic Europe*.[1] Cahill devotes a section to Peter Abelard's work and thought, to Abelard and Heloise's letters and relationship, and to an interpretation of them and their romance after the intellectual effects of new ideas from contemporary feminism.

Peter Abelard (1079–1142) was a brilliant medieval Parisian philosopher and teacher—young, handsome, and extremely popular. Born to a noble family in Brittany, he arrived in lively and cosmopolitan Paris as a student in his twenties, soon set up a Left Bank school that would eventually form the groundwork for the University of Paris, and in his early thirties was appointed Professor of Logic and Canon in the presti-

---

1.   Thomas Cahill, *Mysteries of the Middle Ages: The Rise of Feminism, Science, and Art from the Cults of Catholic Europe*. New York: Doubleday, 2006, pp. 196–206.

gious school of the Cathedral of Notre Dame. Students flocked to him. He became the most celebrated thinker of his time, developing, in contrast to the prevailing Scholastic and Platonic idealistic notions of the era, an Aristotelian-style endorsement of doubt as the first step to reason and an affirmation of the prime reality of objects, things, and material substance also in contrast with the priority of ideas or the handed-down tenets of the Church. Most importantly in twelfth-century Paris, this called into question the authority of Church doctrine, absolutistic or "received" as it was, and suggested that rational argument must preface acceptance of a doctrine, or, indeed, provide the basis for ethics. He thus argued, in an Aristotelian manner new for Middle Ages Europe, that doubt must be raised and rational argument provided to overcome it before behavior can be accepted ethically or understanding be recognized philosophically. His book *Sic et Non* or *Yes and No*, for which he was famous, is a compilation of 158 passages from Church Fathers and Christian doctrine he subjects to the logic of apparent contradiction without resolving the theological and logical questions he poses.

Into this dazzling philosopher's life appears the comely and erudite teenager Heloise. Heloise was the niece and ward of Canon Fulbert of Notre Dame, and her uncle had seen to her being well educated. Taken with her as with no woman before, Abelard gained her uncle's permission to be her tutor, then, claiming he needed easier access to her to oversee her studies, gained residence in Fulbert's home.

As Abelard taught Heloise, their relationship moved from tutorial to romantic; and, when Abelard was thirty-seven and Heloise was nineteen, they became lovers. Soon she became pregnant. On learning this, Abelard sent her to his sister in Brittany to bear the child, a son she named Astrolabe. Abelard went to her, pledging to marry her, but she refused, saying his work and advancement in the Church (which, though he was not ordained, had control of academic life as well as clerical life). They agreed to live separately. Unable to be without her, however, he confessed their love to her uncle, went for her, and they married in secret. Abelard brought her back to Paris and set her up in a convent in Argenteuil. They had clandestine meetings, and he decided to admit to Fulbert that they were married.

Though the uncle seemed agreeable when told of their marriage, Fulbert was enraged when he learned of Heloise's residence in Argenteuil, believing Abelard to have abandoned her. In the middle of one night when

Abelard was sleeping, some servants, believed to be Fulbert's, slipped into Abelard's room and castrated him.

Abelard's catastrophe was instantly known throughout Paris, and his students gathered at his doorway in loud protest. Abelard, however, was suffering too deeply from the bloody violence done him as well as from humiliation to see anyone, so he resolved to leave Paris for a monastery. The men who attacked him were caught and treated in the same fashion they had treated Abelard, though Fulbert was not ever charged with the crime.

Thus, Abelard left Paris to become a monk, but not before seeing that Heloise became a nun and was taken care of in a convent where she could rise to leadership. Later, after students followed him and his controversial reputation led to book burning, Abelard moved still farther away, but established Heloise in a convent called the Paraclete, which he had founded and given to her and her nuns.

Abelard and Heloise continued their monastic life for the remainder of their lives, and we would know none of their story save for the letters written much later recounting their great love, its tragic end, the striking brilliance of each of their minds, and, in Heloise's case, her unrepentance over her love for him being central in her life.

About ten years after their separation, Heloise somehow gained access to a letter from Abelard to a friend of his who was in some kind of misery and Abelard seemed to have wanted to comfort him by telling of his own woes. In his autobiographical letter, he writes of meeting Heloise:

> There was in Paris a young creature (ah, Philintus!) formed in a prodigality of nature to show mankind a finished composition; dear Heloise, . . . Her wit and beauty would have stirred the dullest and most insensible heart, and her education was equally admirable. Heloise was the mistress of the most polite arts. You may easily imagine that this did not a little help to captivate me: I saw her, I loved her, I resolved to make her love me.[2]

His letter and hers that follow recount their amazing love story and its tragic consequence. As mature and separated lovers, they seem to have

---

2. *The Love Letters of Abelard and Heloise* [1901] at sacredtexts.com. Translator anonymous, edited by Israel Gollancz and Honnor Morten.

contrasting views on how they conduct their current lives, but they remember together the shared life and love they had.

One of the remarkable features of their relationship is Heloise's insistence that she not marry him. He writes that she argued in all possible ways "to divert me from marriage—that it was a bond always fatal to a philosopher; that the cries of children and the cares of a family were utterly inconsistent with the tranquility and application which study require. She quoted me all that was written on the subject by Theophrastus, Cicero, and, above all, insisted on the unfortunate Socrates, who quitted life with joy because by that means he left Xanthippe."[3]

He reports that Heloise even had his sister Lucilla, with whom she is staying after the birth of their child, try to argue with him, saying, "Can you be sure marriage will not be the tomb of her love?"[4]

Their secret marriage—or, apparently, the unorthodox lifestyle they adopted of living separately, she in a religious house—still brought about the disaster of his castration—the "loss of his manhood," as he expressed it.

Heloise, in writing to him after receiving the letter, acknowledges following his plan of her becoming a nun, is still and forever the lover writing to her beloved. She writes, "Irresolute as I am I still love you, . . . I have renounced life, and stript myself of everything, but I find I neither have nor can renounce my Abelard. Though I have lost my lover I still preserve my love."[5]

As I wrote earlier, I use this story to illustrate integrity. Yet, I must acknowledge other interpretations of this set of love letters.

The editors of the 1901 edition of the letters, now available on the Internet, write:

> And Abelard, the great leader and logician, his treatises are forgotten, his fame as a philosopher is dead—only his love letters live.

> And Heloise, the beautiful and the learned, who stands second to Sappho, is known merely as an example of the passionate devotion of woman.

3. *Letters*, p. 14.
4. *Letters*, p. 16.
5. *Letters*, p. 40.

> So, they remain to us, the typical lovers; he with man's mania to
> master, she with woman's one desire to submit.[6]

In 1901, the lovers Abelard and Heloise were seen as typical gender-role
stereotypes, he masterful, she submissive, even though they are both intellectually brilliant and capable writers.

In 2006, by contrast, Thomas Cahill writes of them, "Here in the
second decade of the twelfth century we meet a couple whose sensibility is as modern as our own, as rational as the wryest critic writing in
The New York Review of Books, as flagrant as the lovers in a buzz-worthy
contemporary novel. Little if anything separates us from them."[7]

And what does the century's separation have to say of these interpretations? In the turn-of-the-twentieth-century version, traditional gender-
role stereotypes hold. By the time Cahill writes, new feminist scholarship
and social activism had changed our understanding of women and the
social behaviors of men and women, along with our very different understanding of the role of sexuality in human lives. Cahill's treatment of
Abelard and Heloise took advantage of this new knowledge and interprets
the couple very differently.

Cahill shows the advances in the Middle Ages of appreciation of the
Virgin Mary in the Church, even her centrality to their faith for some
people of "the cult of the Virgin." This leads to larger respect and honor
for all women, even for women in traditional women's roles. But, in
Cahill's presentation of Heloise (and, indeed, what I read for myself in
the *Letters*), he writes of the independence, the personal authority, and
the ability to make choices that were Heloise's characteristics. It is hard
for him to write of a submissive woman when he reads her assertions that
her first love is Abelard, not the Church, not even God to whom her work
as a nun is devoted. Cahill's Heloise is a full-blooded decision-making
woman—like a "modern" woman. Yet he goes on to write of the harsh
treatment the couple received as having exact consistency with the times
in which they lived.

And why do I see the story of Abelard and Heloise as one of integrity?
Because, however interpreted, Abelard and Heloise were authentic human
beings; their lives and longings and resolutions to their all-too-human
travail are examples of lives of wholeness, *whole-some-ness*. The specifics

6. H.M. [Honnor Morten], "Introduction," *Letters*, p. ii.

7. Cahill, *Mysteries*, p. 200.

of their sensational love story, perhaps not as unusual for the Middle Ages as we moderns have claimed them to be, are details of a coupling of equals, a pairing of two people who genuinely cared about each other and cared *for* each other. Heloise, though eighteen years younger than Abelard and not his peer in public life and acclaim, as a woman could not have been in the 1100s, had nevertheless equivalent values, intellect, and insights to those of her beloved. Although beauty is not supposed to count as much as inner strengths in evaluating persons, it has been written repeatedly that both Abelard and Heloise were very, very handsome. They must have indeed been a gorgeous couple. Add to that the passion they articulate in their letters and we have rare loveliness in their equality.

In particular, they seem to have cared at least as much about the other as the self. Although Heloise's declaring that she prefers to be Abelard's "whore" to his wife is titillating even a millennium later, her intention can be interpreted wholesomely even in her own words that she cares more about his success in his career, about his accomplishment, because his advancement is tied to the Church and would require celibacy.

When the worst comes, as Abelard writes, "in short, without losing my life, I lost my manhood,"[8] he sees to Heloise's well-being, as well as his own, making possible her being established in a convent. Later, when each of them must go to other religious sites, he pays attention to her needs again, providing her a place in a monastic setting he has founded where she can rise to be abbess, a testament to her high level of ability and skill and its recognition by him. Both actions bespeak the character of the two people.

Even the tone and depth of the letters themselves tell of the integrity of the two. Both are candid and serious about the sexual pleasure and companionable delight they found with one another. Both are excellent writers so that their intellectual depth and wise and candid reasoning appear in the texts of their story.

Therefore, as I see it, the integrity of Abelard and Heloise is manifest in the authenticity of their care for one another, the ardor of their love and its expression, and their faithfulness to who they are as persons, even as they are severely tested in crisis.

Integrity is love. Courage is love. Grace is love.

---

8. Abelard, *Letters*, p. 16.

19

Family Love

I love tulips better than any other spring flower; they are the
embodiment of alert cheerfulness and tidy grace, and next to a
hyacinth look like a wholesome, freshly tubbed young girl beside a
stout lady whose every movement weighs down the air with patchouli.
Their faint, delicate scene is refinement itself; and is there anything
in the world more charming than the sprightly way they hold up
their little faces to the sun?

—Elizabeth von Arnim, *Elizabeth and Her German Garden*

—Nature in Spring—The autumn before you were born, Jessica, when
your mother was expecting you, she did her first flower gardening at
your dad's and her first house. One late October day, she asked me to
come over with my tulip-planting drill and help her plant her tulip and
daffodil bulbs. She wanted them in before the ground froze and it would
be too late to plant them for the next spring's sprouting and blooming.
We happily planted the bulbs and left them to rest through the winter.

Early April in Minneapolis is often still too cold for tulips to show
up; but, by some weather marvel, the April you were born was warm
enough for tulip leaves to unfurl while your mother was in the hospital giving birth to you, and when your parents brought you home for
the first time, wrapped in your green flannel blanket, you were greeted
from the sunny bed beside the garage door with bright blossoms of your
mother's very first tulips.

Our family has many similarities to other American families. You and your twin brothers David and Justin are a family with your mother, Natasha Yates, and your father, Ian Scheerer. Our extended Yates family includes your family; your Yates grandparents, who are your granddad and me, Gigi to you grandchildren; and your Uncle Stiles and cousin Sage. Stiles and Sage are a family, for, after the divorce, Sage has two single-parent families, the second with her mother, Tina, with whom she lives half her time along with half her time with your Uncle Stiles. You are privileged to have another extended family of Scheerers, your dad's side of the family.

I believe that life begins with relationship, and the crux of relationship is love. Ideally, a baby is born into a relationship of love, or she or he might be adopted into a relationship of love, or she might find a family in which love claims her as an older child or even as a teenager if she or he has had the misfortune of missing out on deep family love earlier in life.

By this claim, I mean to be sidestepping the religious-biological arguments against abortion that assert that life begins at conception or that the beginning of life is at the time of fetal viability. Life begins in relationship, I contend, thus, after birth. I believe that a baby is entitled to be loved from its very earliest consciousness; thus, I claim that life begins—and a family originates—in the first moments a parent or caregiver holds a baby person in their arms, looks into its eyes, and glows with love for it.

Your mother's birth was a high and holy moment in my life as her mother. In a hospital in Stoneham, Massachusetts, on a gorgeous, golden October afternoon, elated with excitement, but also experiencing the hard, sharp pain of labor, your granddad and I were together in the delivery room for her bold appearance. Laid on my abdomen for our first contact, she cried real tears (not usual until two months old or so)—precocious Natasha, as she always proved to be; and both Wilson and I loved her intensely in that moment we first touched her, our newborn child, our new family member.

Poet Robert Frost's line "Home is the place where/when you have to go there,/they have to take you in"[1] is about family. You can't disown family—oh, some people do, and it is hideously painful; but in most cases, however troubled and sordid a person's life turns out, family is family, and family members do what they can for one another. Visit family members

---

1. "The Death of the Hired Man," *Complete Poems of Robert Frost*. New York: Henry Holt and Co., 1959, p. 53.

in jail, try to get medicine for very sick members, try to get children to school and problem teenagers and adults into programs that help rescue troubled people from their problems, try to earn a living for them.

Our family has been especially fortunate in our adults having good jobs and incomes, good education and career preparation, good supporting social services and government organizations. Along with love, education, income, and social support are necessary for the survival of families. Both Wilson and I have been professors, Natasha and Stiles MA-degree-holding teachers, and Ian a banker with a law degree. Our jobs, in which we have found satisfaction and earned good income, contribute both to our personal and family well-being and to our economic security and community standing as a family.

Yet, as the Apostle says, "the greatest of these is love."

Very early, children show love when secure in love. Once when your mother, Natasha, was not yet three and I was crying because I had thrown two sterling silver spoons in the trash, she touched me and said, "Mommy, put your head on my shoulder. You can cry on me!"

Later, when Wilson and I were irate with Natasha about some early teenage offense and the three of us were arguing mightily in the living room, four-years-younger and quieter Stiles came into the room and gave us a wooden cross he had been downstairs nailing together on which he had painted the words, "To love is to listen." Silence fell. "To love is to listen" became a kind of family motto for us. Sometime later, Natasha and Stiles baked a cake together and wrote on the frosting in icing letters, "To love is to listen."

Nobody is perfect, but in a loving family we can remind each other how we need to treat one another with love.

When I was a little girl, my mother was my beloved. Her smiling face must be my first memory, for it is what I think of when I try to think back to my earliest time. I remember her beautiful smile with her warm brown eyes, her graying naturally wavy hair, and her perfect white teeth. One of the first things I remember her teaching my brother Merrell and me was how to brush our teeth. We used Ipana toothpaste and fresh new toothbrushes, and she talked to us about how we needed to keep our teeth healthy, as she had done as a child in her poor rural family when she made toothbrushes out of the soft bristles of twigs from sweetgum trees. Because her smile was so rewarding, we made every effort to do as she taught, believing her beautiful teeth were toothbrushing's result.

I thought my mother was very beautiful. She was clever and smart—she could answer all of my questions with satisfactory answers—and she was very religious, though private about her devotion, in contrast with raucous piety in some of the surrounding country churches. She had lovely manners, good taste, and she was my world's reigning authority on grammar and English language usage.

My mother was a teacher. From my infancy, she took the big yellow school bus with the pupils and rode to Wayne County's Central High School where she taught English. Merrell and I stayed home with our paternal aunts Bessie and 'Cile who lived in a small house across the driveway from ours, and they loved us too. We said we had a "real mother, a first mother, and a second mother." Aunt Bessie did most of the cooking for both our households. Aunt 'Cile sewed, making all my clothes and embroidered pillowcases, crocheted doilies, and other home items; and in winter months she and Aunt Bessie quilted marvelous thick, warm, and wondrously patterned quilts, every stitch by hand. Aunt Bessie would make cookies for Merrell and me—sugar cookies, gingerbread cookies, peanut butter cookies, and oatmeal cookies, along with pies and cakes, chicken-and-dumplings, salmon croquets, fried chicken, smothered steak, black-eyed peas, and cornbread for the family, everything home-made, made from scratch. She would cook squirrels and wild turkeys when the hunting men and boys killed them, and once Merrell killed a possum and persuaded her to cook it, though there weren't many takers for eating it—possum is very fat and wild tasting.

Although Mother was at school when we were very young, and then afternoons and weekends after we went to school ourselves, my brother and I ran free all through the woods and around "the place"—the farm and forest land my father had inherited from his father, and his father from my great-grandfather before him. The eldest Graham man had homesteaded that land in Wayne County, Mississippi, not many years after coming to America from Ireland in 1850 with his new bride, Margaret. My father farmed the land, raised some cattle, hogs, and chickens on it, and tended to its woods; and my brother and I loved it. Merrell and I knew the bliss of childhood on our land as in no other place. We ran after each other through the woods playing hide-and-seek, cops and robbers, cowboys and Indians, or just darting about in and among the trees. We ran our toy trucks in the good earth. We pulled our wagon over the rutted farm roads and through the mud puddles in them on "the place," and we dug water-and-black-dirt oil wells under the chinaberry trees. We ran around barefoot outdoors in the rain, and we laughed at the downpour when showers soaked us among Daddy's pine trees "up on the hill" on our land.

It was the land, our parents, and our aunts that gave Merrell and me the security that was family as we grew up. It was our mother who taught us grace and integrity and gave us confidence and hope. It was the land that gave us freedom.

Mother was a complicated person. College educated but living in a rural community and a family of local people who by and large had never left the county or had advanced education, she felt a person apart in many ways and communicated this "difference" to her children. Constructively, it translated for us into the drive to become well educated and well informed, to go to college, and to aspire to a professional occupation. As a girl, I was to be educated as well as my brother, though it was "in case you ever need to make your own living" rather than for the intrinsic value of education. And this reflected a bitterness on my mother's part, for she felt compelled to teach school to earn enough income for the family, since my father's farm income was meager beyond the essentials he provided of milk and butter and beef, pork, lard, and sausages, eggs, chickens, vegetables, corn, and sugar cane for our table, feed for his animals, lumber from his trees, fish from his pond and the creek and river, and spring sweet strawberries and summer ripe tomatoes and watermelons he grew. Mother's ideal for herself seemed to have been a middle-class housewife and stay-at-home mom; but her particular marriage and our family situation did not allow that. Her bitterness was the negative side of Mother's being "different."

Mother was articulate and loving. She was more directly expressive of feeling than most of the other adults surrounding us, though in their context, of course, our father's taciturn growing of food, Aunt Bessie's cookie-baking, and Aunt 'Cile's sewing were their ways of providing love, just as Mother's love was expressed in words. Mother would say, "You can do anything you want to do if you try hard enough." Although not exactly true on the face of it, she inspired confidence in her young children.

She told us that she loved us, though she was not willing to brag about us or let us seem to stand out from others in public. When I was a teenager and state vice-president and then president of the Mississippi Future Homemakers of America, she and my father would drive me to all the meetings where I was to preside or speak; but, when other adults said to her, "You must be so very proud of your daughter," she would say, "No more than you are proud of yours." Oh, to have heard my mother say, then, or even to this day, "I am so very proud of you." But she couldn't do it.

Mother was extremely loyal to her parents, brothers, and sister. They had been very poor and rural, what an outsider might call "backwoods," and the parents and older two of the seven children were minimally educated, or not at all. My grandfather died when I was an infant and grandmother when I was seven, so I did not know him and barely remember her. She was a little old woman who wore a headscarf wrapped around her hair all the time and baked what she called "teacakes" for me, as I remember her. I also remember her clean-swept and thickly shaded dirt yard with large and fragrant gardenia bushes growing in it. My mother's brother Luther, the third oldest, got himself off to college, worked his way through all the way to a PhD, and got all the younger siblings into college behind him, including my mother, the youngest child. It was Luther, of course, whom my mother adored, practically idolized all of her adult life, but she was very attentive to her brothers and sister who lived in the county, as well as to the two other brothers who lived farther afield in Mississippi. (Luther, ironically, though the innovator and giant of this family, went off to California and became a professor of agronomy at the University of California at Davis and seldom came home again, though Mother kept in touch with him with letters. We never did meet his wife and sons.)

Mother's loyalty and attention to her family provided a model, albeit an unconscious one, to my brother and me for what family loyalty looked like. And, of course, family loyalty was equally present in our Hiwannee community where we grew up, there being lots of Grahams living there in addition to our "place" being the "home place" for the extended family and for holiday family gatherings. This was not spoken aloud. It just was. When I was ten and when Aunt 'Cile's fiftieth birthday was approaching, I wrote post cards to all her brothers and sisters, nieces and nephews inviting them to come to us on the Sunday that was her birthday. I asked each to bring food for a noontime dinner-on-the-ground at "the old place," the site of the original house where their grandparents had first lived, by that time just a clearing in the woods. My parents, Merrell, and Aunt Bessie were, of course, my confederates; and Daddy and Merrell put up big tables on sawhorses under the huge oak trees that had once shaded the old house and cleared the farm road to enable cars to drive back there on our land. Every one of the relatives came, right down to the youngest great-niece. Aunt 'Cile was very happily surprised, and everyone had a good time.

The family in which I grew up did the best they could to prepare me for adult life, first my mother, then all our other relatives with our relationship to that land. When I became older, with my prematurely graying, naturally wavy hair, and facial features—along, no doubt, with my educated persona—people would say I looked like my mother. I resisted this for a while—until I took a close look in the mirror. Whatever I think about it, yes, I do look like my mother.

And your mother, Jessica? I think your mother has been the best mother yet. I have thought all along she looked more like her dad, but, sometimes when I look at Natasha now in her forties with her wavy, prematurely graying hair and ready smile, she looks like my mother. Mother to mother to mother. It is a compliment to us all. I see my mother in my own face. I see my mother in your mother, my mother in my daughter; my mother, myself, my daughter; my beloved, beloved daughter, your mother.

20

Romantic Love

The flowers appear on the earth; the time of the singing of birds is come,
and the voice of the turtledove is heard in the land;
The fig tree putteth forth her green figs, and the vines with the tender
grape give a good smell. Arise, my love, my fair one, and come away.

—*The Bible,* King James Version, Song of Solomon 2: 12–13

—**Nature in Spring—Oh, a crocus! A robin! Another robin! Sparrows
copulate in the tree outside my window!**

**I saw a ragged row of thirty or more ducks flying overhead, quack-
ing away, when I was outside watering the barely budding trees.**

**Out for a walk, I saw a bird in flight with a nestmaking twig in its
beak!**

ROMANTIC LOVE IS WHAT many people think of first when the topic
of love comes up. "I love you" on St. Valentine's Day is usually said
to one's romantic beloved, one's loving partner, one's spouse, "girlfriend,"
or "boyfriend." Red heart-shaped cards and romantic dinners, boxes of
candy, and bouquets of red roses fly on Valentine's Day—my florist sister-
in-law says that more bouquets of red roses are sent at Valentine's than
any other flowers at any other time. Although there are also children's
exchanges of Valentine cards and Valentines for teachers and parents and
friends, the cards suggest the kinship there is among all kinds of love.
Romantic love is foremost. It is the love that leads to long-term or lifetime
relationships, to marriage, to partnerships. It starts in a surging thrill of

body and soul in sight or thought of the beloved and leads a couple to who-knows-where.

WOMEN MARRYING WOMEN AND MEN MARRYING MEN

Out of the blue one summer day in our cottage living room, you asked me, "Did you know that boys can marry each other?"

I collected my thoughts and answered simply, "Yes."

The summer that you were five was a year of much ado in our country over gay marriage. In Massachusetts, in New York, and in California various public officials or public bodies had endorsed marriage between same-sex couples and weddings were performed for some gay couples. However, this was in the context of a raging national debate on the ethical correctness of gay marriage, pointing back to the judgment from some conservative corners that homosexual people were behaving wrongly. Whereas contractual and benefits rights for same-sex partners were in place in some locations, many gay and lesbian people and their supporters thought full equality for same-sex loving partners could only be gained through the same legal practice and ceremony that gives full public recognition to heterosexual unions—marriage. Thus, national political organizations, religious bodies, and government units debated the rights of gays to marry. Within the year the first publicly gay bishop was approved in the Episcopal Church, and this proved contentious within that denomination and within some other religious bodies.

In your home, clearly, this is a nonissue. The simple answer is Yes, Hallelujah! Your mom and dad get top marks on parenting! The complications and social and political fusses can come later. Right now, for a small child, the simple answer is Yes.

Once at my university the professor who taught women's biology ignited the emotions of a class by declaring, "Of course, being a lesbian is okay! Every species has a variety that doesn't breed!" Some of the subtlety was missing, apparently, according to her students. I have a friend who is a lesbian and who bore a child. Her son's devoted co-parents are a couple of gay men. I have never asked who the biological father of the child is and it doesn't matter. And then there are the situations of in vitro fertilization and of surrogate pregnancy and, indeed, of adoptive parenting where "breeding" is not the point. So what is? One of my colleagues who had a conventional nuclear family life during his children's growing up time, when his son told him he was gay said simply, "Well, love is love." The point is love. That's it.

Yes, love is love. And whom do we know and care about personally whose love is gay? There are Sue and Carolyn, Sue who was your mother and Stiles's babysitter when she was a student and who has kept me enlightened on what friendship is all these decades of our shared good friendship. When Carolyn, became Sue's partner, I asked her how she wanted me to treat them, and Carolyn replied emphatically, "Treat us just like you would treat any other couple!" Then there are B.J., your Uncle Stiles's godfather and namesake whom we all adore, and his partner, Steve. And there is Tom, who was best man in your parents' wedding.

When Sue and Carolyn had been a couple for ten years in the summer of 2006, they had the most gorgeous service of commitment for their relationship I have ever seen. It was held in the beautiful Bigelow Chapel, which we all love; their pastor conducted the service and their families and friends came, all of us to bless this relationship of Sue and Carolyn that we so cherish.

In October 2008, after California Supreme Court action had legalized gay marriage, B.J. and Steve were married in the tranquil and luxuriant garden, the AIDS Grove in San Francisco's Golden Gate Park. Wilson and I attended. It had rained the night before, threatening the prospect of the outdoor nuptials, but the wedding morning came dry and clear for the San Francisco trolley cars to take us eighty guests to the park. A brass trio played wondrously, the flowers for the ceremony were splendid, and everything was perfect for this elegant and profound gathering. Assemblyman Mark Leno performed the ceremony and when he pronounced B.J. and Steve lawfully spouses, there was hardly a dry eye among the numerous couples of men holding hands with one another or the smattering of us nongays in the wedding party.

"Love is love" is not a simple point. I am hopeful, though, that its understanding improves in the near future years to the point that gay marriage is just one form—a common form—of establishing a family. When your granddad and I were growing up, we scarcely knew what being gay meant, scarcely knew gay people, or, rather, we did not know that some of the people whom we knew and loved were gay, nor did they themselves, in some cases. Now we know. Love is love.

BRIDE AND GROOM, MOM AND DAD

Gay marriage is good in our family's book of protocol and ethics, and heterosexual marriage is good, too. Traditional values more circumscribed than ours insist that marriage between a man and a woman is for the singular purpose of having children. Although birthgiving and parenting between a couple within a marriage is a good value, our family values expand to include coupling for companionship and pleasure, nurturing children in families of several organizational patterns like single-parent adoption, along with married couples of all varieties, and unmarried people with commitments to one another and the child.

In the family into which you were born, your parents' marriage has been very special.

Your mom and dad's wedding was a watershed moment of joy in our family. Natasha had been choosy about finding a husband, but when your dad appeared in her life, he was the one. It took him longer to figure this out than it had taken her; so on the morning of her thirty-fourth birthday, after she had been telling both him and me that she needed a new electric teakettle, and after he had apparently told her repeatedly he had a birthday gift for her that she really wanted—in her mind translating to an engagement ring— when he gave her an electric teakettle, she thanked him and then asked him to marry her.

The two of them along with Stiles had brunch with us later that morning, and I gave her the second electric teakettle birthday gift. Then, we turned our brunch at the Calhoun Beach Club into a champagne engagement celebration. That night, Natasha phoned me: "Mom, do you think you could get the Weisman Art Museum for our wedding?" Could I ever?! I was thrilled. I was going to get to be the mother-of-the-bride in "my museum"! Their wedding day allowed us all the preparation and planning, all the beauty and delight of a season of family pleasure.

Your granddad helped her shop for her wedding dress—the two of them had shopped together often in the past. Not me. I hate shopping. I order things from catalogues or run out to a store and pick up the first thing that halfway decently fits my need. Wilson and Natasha relish shopping. They go to many stores, look over all the possibilities, and consider what works for their taste. They did the same for piano recital dresses and other festive clothing when Natasha was a child. After much looking, they found the perfect wedding dress. They invited me to come to the bridal shop at Dayton's, Minneapolis's premier department store, to see the chosen dress after everything was decided—and to bring my credit card.

On the morning of the wedding, Stiles and Tina had a surprise breakfast at our house for just our family, and Natasha brought me a cross-stitched piece she had made for me to hang above the back doorway, saying "Feed the birds!" and with it a card on which she had written, "I appreciate you." I got the same kind of recognition when others asked the bride and groom who helped make the wedding happen. "My/Natasha's mother!" the couple would chorus together. I was deeply pleased.

Stiles was his sister's only attendant in the wedding, her "brides-knight." He also escorted me down the aisle just before the ceremony began and gave me a hug as he seated me beside his grandfather, Dad, on the bride's side of the aisle we had made of chairs in the museum's permanent collection gallery. With no flowers decorating the space, only the art that was there already, two favorite pieces of sculpture flanked the wedding party. On one side was David Smith's sculpture "Star Cage" in abstract metal with tiny little blue specks of paint on it, scientist Natasha's favorite piece in the museum. On the other side was Barbara Hepworth's abstract wooden pair of figures, merged somewhat, which we all like, but Ian and his family enjoy in particular because they have relatives in Cornwall where Barbara Hepworth lived and worked.

Natasha and Ian spoke their vows. They emerged triumphant from one gallery space into another, married, to greet their 150 guests. Our wedding dinner just at sunset in the west-facing riverview gallery was lovely. With colorful sunset radiance in the purple dusk brushing red and golden beams on the flowing Mississippi River below us, we made toasts and offered well-wishes, danced, laughed, and wept a few tears; and there your mom and dad were, newly wed. They were ready to start their life together, surrounded by their relatives and many good friends.

The dream event that was their wedding solidified into care and concern and deeper loving as they made their home together, first in Minneapolis where you and your brothers were born, then in Red Wing where your family continues to flourish ten years later in your Mississippi River town.

Those two teakettles worked.

EROTIC LOVE

Nobel Prize-winning novelist Toni Morrison wrote in her novel *Tar Baby*, "But soldier ants do not have time for dreaming. They are women and have much to do. Still it would be hard. So very hard to forget the man who fucked like a star."[1]

Your granddad, Jessica, is the sexiest man alive. Unlike Morrison's character, Jadine, in *Tar Baby*, I have chosen not to forget him.

And my opinion is the only one that matters about his suitability for sexual congress. Ours has been a good life together for almost half a century, and erotic love has been an encompassing dimension of our long-lived romance.

Kissing one's beloved ever-so-gently and touching oh-so-slightly are erotic, sometimes as much so as full-fledged sexual connection, if the kiss and touch are with your one-and-only. A hug that lasts for quite some time or a kiss that goes on and on can be increasingly erotic. A fire of passion that burns through body and soul is intensified eroticism, as one yields to the physical, sensual joy of loving. Moving one's hands over the whole body of one's beloved, gently, firmly, and purposefully, can be wonderfully erotic. Loving physical exploration by the one lover of the other lover of all the creases and cavities, all the bits and pieces of the other is shiveringly, shimmeringly erotic. Orgasm is fun, too, though it is not all there is, for, alas, orgasm means it's over; and the prelude, prologue, and prolegomena are just as exciting as the crescendo that brings the finish.

Now the only erotic sensations are not always within the confines of love. Here comes the sticky part. Even thinking about the pleasure of another's body is erotic. I get a tingling in my twat just seeing a gorgeous man on the scaffolding of a construction crew—not just any man, mind you, but a gorgeous one that suits my fancy. A woman can also experience genital sexual excitement, just as a man or boy can get an erect penis from seeing certain art work, hearing certain music, or watching theater or movie scenes. You had some inkling of this reality when, after you and I had one night watched the old movie *Casablanca* together when you were eight and we were reporting this fact to your parents somewhat guiltily, you said, "But I covered my eyes in the kissing scenes!"

Here is where the questions of ethics come in, the points of mature decision-making, every young person's dilemma and society's sometimes

1. Toni Morrison, *Tar Baby*. Random House, 1981, p. 292.

confusing contradictions about what is and is not sexually appropriate—indeed many people's lifelong difficulties about how to choose and how to behave sexually. Sexuality is simply the erotic part of our being human, the sexual part that arouses our feelings and gets our full attention. The erotic is neither good nor bad in itself. It simply is part of our being human.

When your granddad and I participated in workshops of the University of Minnesota Program in Human Sexuality, an insightful young woman on the staff would introduce this paradox of our sexual feeling and our society's conflicting message to young people about it this way: "You are told 'Sex is beautiful! Sex is wonderful! Sex is sacred!' then, 'Don't do it! Sex is dirty! Sex is shameful! Save yourself!'"

The paradox she expressed highlights the core contradiction about sex in American culture now and over the past several decades. The cultural norm of no-sex-before-marriage has relaxed since the 1960s, but the quandary about what to do about sex for young people continues. For ages before 1960, sex-only-after-marriage stood as a goal rather than a rule, for there were obvious exceptions like heartbreaking teen pregnancies with young mothers giving up babies for adoption, alleged six-month pregnancies within new marriages, backroom abortions before they were legal, and lifelong damage to unmarried individuals from sexually transmitted diseases.

There is more information about matters of sex available now, Jessica, as you become a teenager and an adult, and our society is more open-minded about teenagers experiencing sex, unmarried couples living together, sexual choices that are gay and lesbian, and other changes from the old rule. Only sex inside marriage and after marriage is a heavy norm in some communities. Even with that no longer being widely agreed upon, it is very hard, I think, for a young person to make informed and intelligent decisions about sex. Something so charged as sex offers many pitfalls and illusions as you face specific sexual encounters, choices, and situations. It would be much easier to have some rules.

So, I am going to give you a rule. It still needs some qualifications, some information, insights, and judgment; but on the face of it, it is simple.

Have sex only within a fully loving relationship. Make love only when the two of you are certain you are in love.

Erotic behavior is wrong only when one of us acts sexually abusively toward another person on the basis of our erotic feelings. Making love, sexual love, erotic love is a choice; and it can be a devastatingly hurtful choice, an all-too-casual choice, a reckless devil-may-care choice, a testing-the-waters choice, a choice of quick affirmation of caring for one's beloved, or a choice for a deep and abiding moment of renewal of a pair of people's love in their ecstatic coupling.

Erotic love in contrast with mere eroticism is lovemaking with the partner one loves deeply. Erotic love is mutually desired and mutually enjoyed sexual engagement between a pair of mature, consenting, and eager people.

I encourage you to wait until you are quite sure that you love the person with whom you are about to have sex before you make love.

I encourage you to be very thoughtful ahead of time about deciding to have sex and to be very feisty in opposition to someone who proposes sex with you or tries to insinuate sex upon you against your will.

I encourage you to know as much as you can about the consequences of sexual activity in contracting HIV-AIDS or other sexually transmitted diseases and of becoming pregnant and to take precautions against either by using birth control devices or other protection. If you will possibly have sex on a given day or night, carry condoms in your purse.

I encourage you to explore the full range of your feelings, to talk about your feelings and your sexuality fully and freely with a few people you trust very much (like your grandmother), and to think ahead about why you would want to say No and why you would want to say Yes to sexual experience.

And, when the time comes and you are ready and you know this is the right choice, give yourself to erotic love with your beloved with the full grace and glory of your magnificent womanhood.

If somewhere along the way, you mess up, it is okay. Sexual messing up is one of the most common mistakes of being human. Just try not to.

Do the best you can to follow my rule: make love only when the two of you are fully in love.

To you my beloved first granddaughter, daughter of my daughter, I offer you my example in erotic love. For nearly fifty years, your granddad and I have loved one another. Let our model be yours. Our erotic love has been fully satisfying. May yours be the same over your lifetime.

21

Friendship

> "Chloe liked Olivia," I read. And then it struck me how immense a change there was. Chloe liked Olivia perhaps for the first time in litera-ture . . . And I tried to remember any case in the course of my reading where two women are represented as friends.
>
> —Virginia Woolf, *A Room of One's Own*

—Nature in Spring—Walking about our grounds at Coventry-in-the-Northwoods on the spongy, wet mulch, I saw masses of false lily-of-the-valley in the pine woods. I saw starflowers on the edge of another woodsy place and stalky yellow wild mustard and yellow flowering dan-delions spread around our property. On the drive into town, near the roadways under hardwood trees, I saw many big white trilliums, per-haps my favorite of these Northwoods wildflowers.

FRIENDSHIP IS A VERY precious form of love and includes the excite-ment and delight of other loves like family love and romantic love. Like other forms of love, too, it can be corrupted or lost, damaged or hurt, leading to separation and disappointment. Sometimes, though, lost friendship is less dramatic, is but a gradual withdrawal or decline of at-tention. Friendship can be momentary and short, even a single occasion of enjoyable connection and pleasure in one another's company for a shared task, for fun, or for a serious project, and then end at that point. Or friendship can be established and endure for the duration of one kind of experience—say, during a period of schooling together—and then end without much thought about it when that particular experience has passed. Or it can last a lifetime. Lasting friendship needs to be nurtured, cared for, and continually cultivated. One needs to be intentional about being a friend.

Friendship is very important to me and I work at maintaining a number of friendships by correspondence, meeting for times together, phone calls, or gifts and other offerings of support. Some friendships are my own alone. With some couples or individuals your granddad and I have shared friendships. Some friends and I are members of groups where friendship is a dimension of the group being together.

My friends are of course men as well as women, but some of my deepest friendships are with women.

WOMEN FRIENDS

I have a small group of people, most of them women, I think of as my "best friends." What makes us friends? First, of course, we care about one another very deeply. Usually we share values and crucial approaches to life. Often we have shared pivotal experiences in our lives. For several of us, after many years of friendship, even though our lives have become quite different, we remain loyal friends. Conversely, we sometimes meet someone new and click in such a way that we feel our friendship has already lasted a long time.

Martha, known by her middle name Adrienne as an adult, was my college roommate at Millsaps College, starting in 1957. In recent years, we frequently met at her mother's house in Meridian, Mississippi, and she let me use her sister's room and share her elegant ninety-plus-year-old mother. Just before Christmas last year, I got a phone call from the police in Martha's town saying she had been found dead and mine was the last phone number called on her cell phone. I may have been the first person who learned of her death. I quickly saw to it that her brother and her sons were contacted, and I personally got in touch with her mother. I phoned her several times and talked with and listened to that beloved sorrowing older woman. I sent flowers and presents and letters and grieved with her family, especially her mother, over our loss at the Christmas holiday time that came so soon. Again, we phoned one another and mourned at her February birthday time, and on all the special days that followed through the year that reminded us of our love for her and our loss.

Maggie and I met in 1962 when we lived in the same building in Boston and went through our first pregnancies, childbirths, and early mothering times together. These many decades later I go most years for a week or a month break from Minnesota winter to her home in Florida. Katie and I also lived in Boston in our years of young adulthood and learned to practice gourmet cooking and lavish entertaining on minuscule budgets with a group of friends—graduate students, beginning social workers, and psychologists, all financially poor but rich in imagination and hopes for our future. I served as the twenty-eight-year-old honorary "mother-of-the-bride" for Katie and her Thom's wedding; and last fall when Thom died suddenly almost forty years later, I was among the people Katie herself phoned.

Mary, Bobbie, and I shared an office in graduate school at the University of Minnesota in a program where Jean was a young assistant professor in the late 1960s and we four became fast friends. We told each other our anxiety dreams about failing our preliminary examinations—in a dream, one of us jumped into an empty swimming pool at the behest of our PhD advisor: it is revelatory of our shared anxiety that I don't remember which one of us had that dream. On the afternoon of my prelims, Mary even took me shopping, an activity I loathe, though I wanted her company—and she had a bottle of champagne (illegal on the university campus) stashed in her desk drawer for when the ordeal was over. Once we had a series of Sad Ladies Lunches when things weren't going our way. Betty Ann, older than we were, was our graduate school friend, too. She bought special gifts and sent postcards when she traveled to England; and later in life, after retirement, she took a book-binding course and made books out of note cards and postcards we had sent her over the years.

Geneva, Virginia Gray, and Shirley were among my early University faculty women colleagues. Geneva chaired African-American Studies, was from a family of black leaders in New Orleans, a Methodist like Wilson and me, a musician, and a no-nonsense civil rights and equality for all advocate—that meant women, black people, and all other sorts of people. At her two-hour funeral at Hennepin Avenue United Methodist Church, it seemed that every black musician in the Twin Cities performed.

Virginia Gray was a political scientist, still is. She taught a course on "The Political Behavior of Women" in the early days of Women's Studies and used my first book, *What Women Want*, in her class. She served on the Women's Studies governance group. I sent her flowers when her husband left her. And, years later when I visit her in Chapel Hill, where she now teaches at the University of North Carolina, we still care together about politics and government and women's issues; but we also talk about good food, our adult children, their weddings, and our grandchildren.

Shirley was one of the leaders of the Women's Studies group that hired me at the University of Minnesota. She held an administrative office and offered us all insights into university governance along with her keen wit, common sense, and highly intelligent judgments. She moved to Oregon after some years, suffered through the death of her beloved husband, Jack, and could even inject humor into her sober account of getting through his last months, saying, "I learned to live without sleep." Not long ago she hosted me for an incredible week of travel companionship in Oregon with days and overnights, dinners and breakfasts across much that Oregon has to offer—the coast, sea lions and aquarium visiting, the mountains and a snowy September failed attempt to see Crater Lake, university campuses, a winery and its vineyard, restaurants, a farmer's market, and a craft market.

Marilyn was a part of my women's leadership breakfast club in recent years; we went on a women's interfaith study trip to Israel together; and she invited me to join her book group. Sue, whom I wrote of earlier with her partner, Carolyn, became my friend after being my student in the early 1970s. She was your granddad's student and friend, as well. She had then, and has now, the same fervor I have about women's and social justice issues. In our early years, she and I were supportive of each other when the other was needful and many people around us did not understand what we were about as feminists. As your mom's and Stiles's babysitter when they were young children, she was close to us as a family.

Jill, Virginia Watkinson, and Carolyn welcomed us to the neighborhood on Mulberry Close when we first went to live in Cambridge, England, in 1973 and each had children near our children's age. Carolyn taught me how to swear in British English—she really meant to be telling me how not to swear, but the lesson stuck backward, so every time I say "bloody hell" I think of Carolyn.

Jill had us to parties for her don-husband's Cambridge college members, and Virginia taught us about Guy Fawkes Night and other British holidays, and she invited our family to dinner on Christmas Day. Thirty years later we still exchange Christmas presents; and, when your cousin Sage was expected and your uncle Stiles wanted a quilt with a "Curious

George" theme, Carolyn, an extraordinary quiltmaker, designed and made a quilt that arrived the day before Sage was born. At the time of another of our sabbatical stays in England after our children were grown, Carolyn came over to our house early one morning on her bicycle to bring homemade jam for Natasha to eat on her breakfast scones on the day your mother was arriving for a visit. When Wilson and I, Stiles, and Sage went to England together when Sage was five, Stiles packed the "Curious George" quilt Carolyn had made in Sage's backpack and brought it with us to dinner in our hotel restaurant to show Carolyn and Keith, Virginia, and Stephen as we had dinner together.

Jill now lives near London and takes us to theater events we would not easily know about when we are in London, and once she got a new membership in the Tate Modern just so she could take us there in the early evening to see the lights on St. Paul's Cathedral across the Thames from the members' dining room. The last time we were in England, accompanied by Stiles and Sage, we spent a weekend in her and Peter's home in Hitchin and watched the Wimbledon women's finals tennis match on TV with them, consuming traditional Wimbledon strawberries and cream and champagne together.

Virginia still writes marvelous letters with sardonic commentary on English life; and, she, a librarian by occupation, sends book recommendations to me on a regular basis. It was she who sent a clipping about the upcoming publication of the first of the marvelous mystery novels set in Botswana, your mother's Peace-Corps-Volunteer country, *The Number One Ladies' Detective Agency* series, letting us know before most other Americans about these soon-to-be international bestsellers.

All these women have remained my friends over the years since our initial meetings, and I think of them with much gladness and affection. These friendships and more I have nurtured over the years, and my friends have nurtured me. I deeply treasure friendship. Stories of friendship, or images of it, provide its definition. Friendship is being engaged deeply in your friend's life. It is understanding what matters to the other person, maybe without even putting it into words. It is allowing one's friend to be herself or himself, as is, without judgment. Friendship is acceptance. It is faith in each other. It is loyalty. Friendship is the dearest of bonds.

22

Loving the Earth and Loving the World

> There is much confusion between land and country. Land is the
> place where corn, gullies and mortgages grow. Country is the
> personality of land, the collective harmony of its soil, life, and weather. . . .
> Poor land may be rich country, and vice versa. . . .
> I know, for example, a certain lakeshore, a cool austerity of pines and
> wave-washed sand. . . . [and] a headland, behind which a sudden
> roistering of loons reveals the presence of a hidden bay.
>
> —Aldo Leopold, *A Sand County Almanac*

—Nature in Spring—This morning while lying on the couch propped
up on pillows and looking out the window at the trees "doing nothing,"
I noticed that the small white pine we planted last spring under the
others to make the woods fuller had a tuft of new growth atop it. "This
is delight," I thought. "I know the feeling of delight, sheer delight in the
growing tree, joy!"

Lying back on my couch pillows, occasionally sipping from my
cup of tea, I observed with equal pleasure the other greenery that was
framed by my north windows—a large white pine with branches visible
from the top to the bottom of my window view on the left; several feet
behind it the tall, thin, white trunks of two birches that reach high out
of my view; and to the right, our chokecherry tree mingling branches
with the white pine in the center, branches still covered with the husks
of flowers just faded, the tree visible from bottom to top of fully half
of what I can see through the framed glass. "*Everything* is growing," I
thought, and I tried mentally to measure the budding extensions on the

large white pine's branches: four inches? six inches? one or two of them maybe eight inches?

To lie here and enjoy the foliage and new growth of three kinds of trees I have been caring for was enough for happiness.

Still reclining on the couch, I wrote some letters, had breakfast and later "elevenses" and then finally went to the bedroom and got dressed to walk out to the mailbox with my letters. As soon as I came back to the house, though, I propped myself back up on the couch pillows and joyfully surveyed the trees around the cottage whose world I share.

IN THE PART II section of this book, "On Learning," in Chapter 15, I wrote of knowing the earth and knowing the world as part of what we must learn as we seek to take ethical responsibility in our lives. In this part, "On Loving," I move the focus from our efforts to know the world and to know the earth to consideration of what we might do to love the world and to love the earth. My framework extends from loving individual people with many types of love to loving communities and nation. Now I turn to loving the earth, as I defined the earth before as all of nature, and loving the world, as I designated it before to cover peoples and society. I will address loving the earth and loving the world with two topics I began discussing under learning the earth and learning the world, climate change and food and agriculture.

ON CLIMATE CHANGE

Once again, on climate change we can start with the local. That is not enough by far, but it still is a place to start. In our Minneapolis neighborhood, Linden Hills, there is an initiative for going green, which includes an effort to develop solar heat for homes, as well as to buy local products so that food and goods will not have to be transported great distances, to buy environmentally friendly products for our homes and businesses, and even a small electric car being for sale in the neighborhood at our co-op store. Solar heat, electrically powered vehicles, and using primarily local foods and goods would reduce the need for greenhouse-gas-emitting fuel, and fuel for vehicles both for personal use and for transporting goods and foods. What individual people, families, and households can do can be fostered at the neighborhood level.

There is now talk quite popularly of measuring one's "carbon foot-print" and published lists of ways one can contribute as a person or family toward zero-use of carbon, which would ultimately lead to a small part in reversing the emissions of greenhouse gases. Alas, I went on-line and took a carbon-footprint test and found myself to be an "average American." Not good. My share of carbon emissions is about three times what it should be. What must I do? Stay out of airplanes? Not drive my own car? Eat less meat, nonlocal, and out-of-season foods? Reduce electricity use for appliances and lighting, gas use for heating? Hard. Bodes serious lifestyle changes. (What I do right is plant trees!)

At the public level, there are beginning to be good-faith efforts to limit industrial pollution; agribusiness changes to eliminate contributions to greenhouse gas emissions by such measures as storage of gases, more precise measurement of water and fertilizers used on crops, alongside efforts to replace fossil fuels with wind-powered and solar-powered fuels and fuels made of grasses and corn. Changes are being made in airplanes, cars, trucks, and other vehicles for most efficient fuel use of alternative fuels made from plants like grasses or sugarcane or conversion to electrical power for some or all of their source of energy and with the generation of electrical power being done by solar, wind, and even nuclear sources. Legal limitations need to be made by governments; voluntary changes by businesses big and small; and design, development and research changes by scientists, farmers, and inventors. We citizens can work toward these changes by our actions as consumers—buy hybrid cars, travel less, buy green products—and by the public stands we take and the government officials we support. We can be constantly mindful that our own actions speak for ideas we believe in and for public goals we espouse.

Members of our family were engaged in homely versions of environmental protection before 2007, but it was a 2007 morning when I was in your home in Red Wing for breakfast and you said spontaneously, "I know how to save water in the family," and then you quickly named some ways: "take fewer showers, don't water the lawn, don't use bottled water, wash clothes in cold water, drink less tea and coffee . . ." And where did you learn that? "I read it in my children's *National Geographic*," you replied.[1]

I was reminded of your brother Justin being sent to the bathroom with me when he was about three and told to "show Gigi how you wash

1. David George Gordon, "The Green List," *National Geographic Kids Magazine*, November 2007; Issue no. 375, p. 10.

your hands." Taking it to mean that I didn't know how to wash my hands, he went about it very seriously. He turned on the faucet and wet his hands. Then he turned the water off. "No waste!" he explained. Then, continuing to show me, he rubbed soap on both hands and lathered them thoroughly right up around his wrists before saying, "Mo' water," and turning the water back on just long enough to rinse off the soap. "See?" he concluded.

Our attention has been clearly called to the issue of global warming and the devastation it might bring if we don't act and act quickly to reverse the dire consequences it portends. I hope that the effects of Al Gore's *An Inconvenient Truth* and all the efforts of scientists and government officials like those in the Intergovernmental Panel on Climate Change (IPCC) will dramatically curtail, stop, or "recycle" the emissions of greenhouse gases; stop or slow deforestation with creative farmland and housing construction planning; conserve and clean our worldwide water supply; and limit or cease other contributions to global warming. I hope these labors replicate on a grand scale what happened in the aftermath of the publication in 1962 of Rachel Carson's *Silent Spring*.[2]

Rachel Carson was a very careful scientist, a marine biologist, and a former employee of the U.S. Fish and Wildlife Service. She was serious about her advocacy for change in her book based on her opposition to use of pesticides like DDT in agriculture and her demonstration of their poisoning effects on animals, the water supply, and people; but, like any writer, her success depended on her readership and actions that might be taken by some of those readers and their exercise of power.

Fortunate for her mission and for all of us, her resultant beneficiaries, the public outcry *Silent Spring* raised led to the banning of DDT and other pesticides and to important changes in laws that controlled the use of toxic chemicals in the environment.

Rachel Carson had already published previously when she began writing *Silent Spring* after receiving a letter from a woman in Massachusetts telling her that DDT was killing birds. In her book, Carson carefully documented the deleterious effects of pesticides on birds, fish, streams, shellfish, grasses, insects, and other animals. Her writing is powerful. She speaks of "robin mortality," of insect mutations, of the bobwhite quail being "all but eliminated."[3] She tells of "all the little tree birds" along with

2. Rachel Carson, *Silent Spring*, introduction by Vice President Al Gore. Boston: Houghton Mifflin Company, 1994 reissue, first published in 1962.

3. Carson, p. 167.

"livestock, poultry, and household pets" lost at a pesticide-treated farm. Describing the science rather fully, she shows how insecticides contribute to cancer in human beings.

The book might have gone nowhere had there not been considerable public attention paid to it, led by President John F. Kennedy after he heard about it. President Kennedy appointed a panel to examine Carson's conclusions in *Silent Spring*, and members of Congress soon acted to curtail the use of such chemical spraying. In his Introduction to a 1994 edition of the book, Vice President Al Gore wrote that "[t]he publication of *Silent Spring* can properly be seen as the beginning of the modern environmental movement."[4]

Just as the book eventually led to laws banning the use of the pesticide DDT, it also brought far greater attention of public leaders and citizens alike to the harm that could be done by the use of chemicals in agriculture.

There are now several efforts in our public domain to reverse or to control global warming, not least of which is President Barack Obama's charge to his new government to develop policies and programs for green energy sources and to combat the waste and harm in deforestation, wildlife habitat destruction, and air, water, and soil pollution. Many creative scientists are conducting projects to develop alternative fuel sources. Two examples at our University of Minnesota are biologist Clarence Lehman's work on both soil conservation and possible fuel production from prairie grasses, and chemical engineering professor Lanny Schmidt's efforts to isolate hydrogen effectively to be used as a clean and practical source of fuel. Architects and builders are at work on sustainable, environmentally friendly new buildings and adaptations of old ones. An example we saw in San Francisco is the new science museum in Golden Gate Park by architect Renzo Piano. Built from recycled or energy-conserving materials, the sustainable California Academy of Sciences building has a "living roof" covered almost entirely with plant materials interspersed with solar-power collecting panels. The prize-winning, impressively green building houses a planetarium, a rain forest, and an aquarium.

---

4. Vice President Al Gore, "Introduction," Rachel Carson, *Silent Spring*. Boston, New York: Houghton Mifflin Co., 1994, p. xviii.

ON FOOD AND AGRICULTURE

Closely related to climate change and our need to address it and correct its global impact is the issue of food and agriculture and what we need to do to feed ourselves and the people of the planet more responsibly. Enter, in the midst of our current excess and our beginning arguments for change in the way we view and use foods, journalist and science writer Michael Pollan.

Pollan, now a journalism professor at the University of California at Berkeley, previously lived on the East Coast. He calls himself a gardener foremost, and among his earlier works is a charming and sensible book, *Second Nature: A Gardener's Education* (1991). He gained wider recognition as a powerful naturalist voice with the best-selling *The Botany of Desire* (2001) and then flew onto the bestseller lists and stayed there in 2006 with *The Omnivore's Dilemma*.

Pollan took "a plant's eye-view" in *The Botany of Desire*, as he wrote about the coevolution of apple, tulip, marijuana, and potato plants with people. He showed much research to buttress his point that the plants adapted themselves to people's use of them and to people's movement around locations to distribute the plants, and that the most fit plants survive their evolution in tandem with people. Pollan uses as examples Johnny Appleseed's spreading apples on his journeys in frontier America as a way the apple spread across the United States, and "tulipmania" in seventeenth-century Amsterdam as the way tulips remained a competitive domestic plant alongside the people who grew them.

In *The Omnivore's Dilemma*, Pollan further developed his notion of coevolution of plants with people. His considerable writing skill plus imagination and keen intelligence present the research he did as both a working participant on sites and a gatherer of information sources. The focus of this major work was to support conclusions in another direction from his earlier work—that of Americans' relationship to foods. In *The Omnivore's Dilemma*, Pollan takes the reader through four contrasting sources of dinners available to the American's table. They are industrialized agriculture, by far the largest source; organic food on a wholly self-sustaining farm; another he calls "big organic"; and the hunter-gatherer.[5]

Pollan starts with the premise that food is people's closest connection to nature in our time, for our food all goes from its origin in plants "pho-

---

5. Michael Pollan, *The Omnivore's Dilemma*. New York: The Penguin Press, 2006.

tosynthesizing calories in the sun" all the way to the meal on the dinner table. He argues that all the food chains he discusses—the industrial, the organic ("big organic" and the self-contained farm he puts in one chain), and the hunter-gatherer—"do the same thing: link us, through what we eat, to the fertility of the earth and the energy of the sun."[6]

For the three food chains and the four dinners at their end, in sections titled "Industrial: Corn," "Pastoral: Grass," and "Personal: the Forest," Pollan traces each food item from its origin in plants on the farm or food source, its development and production, its harvesting and processing, its lines of distribution to its preparation site, the making of the ingredients, and finally, the combining, preparing, or cooking to put together and serve the meal.

The book has three layers: first, storytelling of how the author went about learning the sources and the journeys of the foodstuffs going into each meal; second, information about the practices and products that went into producing and distributing the food; and, last, judgments about the harm done to people, the animals, the plants, the soil, and the earth by some of these practices and products. A part of the book's appeal is the author's voice, always wise, kindly, and gentle, even as he delivers harsh judgments of nearly every phase of the food industry. He describes and judges everything from agribusiness to factory preparation, packaging and freezing of food to be sold at supermarkets and fast-food restaurants and the fact of foods traveling hundreds of miles at great expense financially and environmentally.

Derived from the industrialized food chain, the first meal is a fast-food restaurant hamburger dinner. The largest plant source is corn—the beef having been fed corn, the soft drinks, ketchup, salad dressing, even bread and cheese having corn derivatives in them. Pollan points out that more than a fourth of the 45,000 items in the average supermarket have corn in them—everything from "modified or unmodified starch, glucose syrup, lecithin and dextrose, lactic acid . . . coffee whitener, Cheese Whiz, canned fruit" and the ubiquitous high-fructose corn syrup, which now rivals sugar as a sweetener. Pollan shows from his firsthand view at a feed lot how cattle, hogs, and chickens are penned and fed corn to fatten them quicker and move them to market faster; but the process is providing less healthy animals. To raise corn, many farmers, along with using greatly

6. Pollan, *Dilemma*, 7.

hybridized seeds, use carefully prepared chemical fertilizers that rely on petroleum-based nitrogen rather than the natural ingredients in the soil or ingredients like the humus from plants or animal manure. Thus, he says, we have "allowed the food chain to turn from the logic of biology and embrace the logic of industry. Instead of eating exclusively from the sun, humanity now began to sip petroleum."[7]

The second and third meals come from organic farming. The meal he describes in almost utopian terms, beginning with the chapter he titles "All Flesh Is Grass," is the one he is eventually served at Joel Salatin's Polyface Farm in Virginia, where he works as a farm hand to learn how the fully sustainable, self-contained organic farm of a few hundred un-promising acres works. The only label Joel Salatin is willing to accept is "grass farmer." His animals eat the grass he grows—pigs, cattle, and chickens alike. Salatin has portable fences and a chicken coop, which he moves around to different sections of his acreage for the animals to feed and then leave behind their manure. He cuts grass and dries it for hay to feed the cattle in the winter; and at animal slaughter time, he saves the blood and entrails in a compost pile to serve as further fertilizer. He also maintains a forest as an important feature of the farm.

Besides animals for reproduction, for eggs and milk and meat, Polyface Farm grows vegetables, tomatoes, sweet corn, and berries—nearly all the food needed for the farm family to eat and some to sell. However, the food is only sold locally and is not available to send away.

The food Pollan ate at Polyface Farm included farm-fresh broccoli, sweet corn, chicken, and daily deviled eggs that were among the best he had ever eaten.

Pollan prepared the "big organic" meal with foods from his local Whole Foods store. He did not excoriate large supermarket-style organic food marketing, for he thinks growing and making available food grown without pesticides or artificial fertilizers is a good thing and a step in the right direction. Nevertheless, he points out that some of the limitations of large scale that is a problem for industrialized agriculture are still pres-ent. As he describes purchasing lettuce at his local Whole Foods store, he points out that large corporate organic farms produce much of the food sold across the country as organic; for example, Earthbound Farm in California grows 80 percent of American's organic lettuce. The farms

7. Pollan, *Dilemma*, 45.

that supply organic food stores are an average of 1,500 miles away from the store, he says, making the cost in fuel and thus the cost in carbon emissions expensive. Pollan writes, "The food industry burns nearly a fifth of all the petroleum consumed in the United States (about as much as automobiles do). Today it takes between seven and ten calories of fossil fuel energy to deliver one calorie of food energy to the American plate."[8]

The final meal—that of the hunter-gatherer—is fun for Pollan, but it requires months to get ready with assistance from a friendly hunter willing to coach him, from a winemaker, and from an expert mushroom hunter. He made his own bread, used vegetables from his garden, and learned to gather yeast from the air. The biggest challenge was the hunt in northern California for the wild pig. Still, he did it.

With his hunter friend Angelo, Pollan was able to shoot the pig on his second try. Immediately, he felt shame about taking the life of an animal, and wondered if maybe Angelo's shot had not been the one that actually downed the pig; but, no, Angelo assured him that it was his kill. There in the woods Angelo dressed the pig for him, and he began to reconcile with the drama of food that he was enacting. The pig's blood flowed among the acorns on the ground under an oak tree, and Pollan could imagine the pig having rooted for its food among the acorns, thus having been sustained by the oak-photosynthesizing energy that had fed the acorns that would now mix with the pig's blood on the forest floor to make new nutrients for the trees and other plants and the animals that would follow. He writes, "Sun-soil-oak-pig-human: There it was, one of the food chains that have sustained life on earth for a million years made visible in a single frame, one uncluttered and most beautiful example of what it is."[9]

To the end, Pollan continues his very serious message with a tone that is almost lighthearted. Still, he doesn't stray from it and reminds his reader periodically what he means most deeply, "[W]e know that civilizations that abuse their soil eventually collapse."[10]

After *The Omnivore's Dilemma* won numerous prizes and became considered a watershed work, Pollan followed it with the publication of *In Defense of Food: An Eater's Manifesto*, which rose immediately to the top of the best-seller lists in January 2008. In this book, Pollan turns to giving

---

8. Pollan, *Dilemma*, p. 183.

9. Pollan, *Dilemma*, p. 363.

10. Pollan, *Dilemma*, p. 151.

direct advice about food. Sloganlike, his message is encapsulated on the cover, "Eat food. Not too much. Mostly plants."[11]

Taking Pollan's sensible advice personally and in our homes, organizing ourselves into advocacy groups, or using our influence to support responsible farming and responsible relationships to food—aka, eating—are ways out of the helplessness some feel about our food habits contributing to the destruction of the earth.

Eat your spinach. Eat slowly. Enjoy every bite. Know your farmer, your farmer's market, and your storekeeper. Let your food budget do your talking.

We can do it, Jessica! We can make a difference.

---

11. Michael Pollan, *In Defense of Food: An Eater's Manifesto*. New York: The Penguin Press, 2008, cover.

PART IV

On Hoping

Summer

the lake sits silent
the loon wails to the moon
up above
howling
a wolf calls out to its pack
it is dinner time
in the dark murky waters
the fish say goodnight

—Nathaniel Danforth, 8 years old, 2005

—Nature in Summer—For a couple of hours today it rained a gentle rain, and it was chilly. The rain now has stopped, and the lake's surface ripples with a silvery slate-gray. As I write in the early evening, sunshine appears from the west through the fresh new green leaves of the trees. Drops of rain glisten silver on the white pine's needles, summertime tiny tree ornaments on every needle.

Stop the presses: there is the eagle! The bald eagle that lives on the island near our cottage just flew over! That magnificent bird with its huge black wingspan and its white, white head soared just beyond my topmost window! It appeared almost to float in its leisurely flight above the tops of the trees! It flew toward its nest in the highest part of a tree on the island where it and its mate seem to have hatched and raised their young every year that we have come here. I have just written your brother David, who particularly likes eagles, a postcard with a bald eagle pictured on it, telling him that I hope we can see the eagle when he comes up here next time! Just this moment it seems it came to visit me!

23

Light and Love

Whatever peace I know rests in the natural world,
in feeling myself a part of it, even in a small way.

—May Sarton, *Journal of a Solitude*

—Nature in Summer—The birds in our woods and on the water are a
joy to see and hear. This week I saw a great blue heron soaring low, a
pair of mallard ducks flying and quacking, robins hopping about on
the ground, and hummingbirds fluttering among red flowers. A pair of
loons played out in the middle of the lake for a long time one afternoon
and at night sang their loon calls in the distant darkness.

—Summer Holidays: Memorial Day, Fourth of July, and Labor Day—
Summer is bracketed in the United States by Memorial Day on the last
Monday in May and Labor Day on the first Monday in September. In
the middle of summer is Independence Day, known commonly by its
date, the Fourth of July. All are civic holidays, none begun in religion or
suggesting religious reverence, though civic respectfulness and honor
due them have kinship with religious devotion. These holidays all have
sanctity about them, a presence of spirituality. They are days of collectively honoring significant past events and leaders of our country that
have been pivotal in forming and continuing our national life.

The calendar we follow is called the Gregorian calendar from its
origin, but it is "the calendar" in most of our minds. On the calendar
and in our English language, holidays originally were "holy days," days
set aside in the Christian year as feast days and days annually honor-

ing high moments or important people of Christianity. For example, Christmas was "Christ's mass" or the service and feast honoring the birth of Christ; and there are many saints' days not now so regularly honored such as the Feast of St. Joseph on March 19 and the Feast of the Conversion of St. Paul on January 25. Today most calendars in most countries have a mix of holidays religious in origin and civil ones, which are designated by each nation's government. Our summer holidays of Memorial Day, the Fourth of July, and Labor Day were set by the U.S. federal government. Because they come in summertime, besides their being national days of celebration, they are also especially days of rest or days of family time, of picnicking and being out of doors and enjoying warm weather.

Memorial Day is one of four federal holidays that now come on Monday—the birthday of Martin Luther King, Jr. on the third Monday in January, Memorial Day on the last Monday in May, Labor Day on the first Monday in September, and Columbus Day on the second Monday in October. They were made Monday holidays by a 1968 law so that federal government employees could have three-day weekends with most federal offices like post offices, courts, and government service buildings being closed. Though the law does not require that businesses and state and city offices also be closed, many of them are, so the holidays can serve as "long weekends" for families, workers, schoolchildren, and most employed people.

Predominantly in our awareness, the Memorial Day holiday weekend signals the beginning of summer even though the summer solstice according to astronomy is not until June 21. Spring flowers and spring rainfall have come in April and May and gone by late June, and the weather has warmed since the vernal equinox of March 21. Soon school will be out for students of all ages, and the time to wear shirtsleeves and sandals outdoors in the summery warmth has come. People sometimes go "up north" to lake and river places for the beginning of the boating and swimming season. People who stay in their cities and towns picnic in parks or in their backyard gardens, happy to celebrate summertime.

Many countries have some kind of day like our Memorial Day on which they recognize their war dead. In our country, Memorial Day was established at the end of the Civil War. In the South citizens in some places had a "Decoration Day" in the spring at which time people tended the graves of their dead; and in 1866 in Waterloo, New York, some prominent citizens began an event to honor the Union dead of their town and urged its adoption nationwide. Although some Southerners were reluctant to honor the Union dead after their recent Confederate defeat, a ceremony in Columbus, Mississippi paid tribute to both Union and Confederate soldiers who had died. In 1868, General John A. Logan, who was commander-in-chief of a veterans' organization and one of the instigators of the Waterloo, New York, event, issued a proclamation that Decoration Day be observed nationwide by putting flowers, flags, or other items showing respect on the tombs and gravesites of the fallen soldiers. In 1882, the name Memorial Day was first used, and gradually over time the day came to be one of honoring all the nation's war dead and even in some communities all the people buried in their cemeteries.

In our era, there are sometimes military memorial services and, especially in military cemeteries, graves are dressed with flags and flowers on Memorial Day. For most people, however, the somber aspect of the day of honoring war dead has lessened considerably. This day—and long weekend—has become one of rest and renewal for everyone, though it is a time of national pause and recognition. It is also the marking of the beginning of summer on the schedules of communities and families.

The Fourth of July comes in midsummer. It is celebrated with fireworks and parades and outdoor concerts. Brass bands play patriotic songs on bandstands decorated with red, white, and blue bunting. Sometimes under banners of stars and stripes, in public community programs, we show patriotic allegiance by singing fervently "My Country 'Tis of Thee," "God Bless America," "This Land Is Your Land," and the national anthem, "The Star-Spangled Banner." These programs are followed by picnics. When I was a child, the watermelons my father had grown were ripe by the Fourth of July. Cold watermelon, fresh peaches, potato salad, and cold fried chicken go together for Fourth of July picnics in my memory.

The Fourth of July is the birthday of the United States of America.

On this date in 1776 the Declaration of Independence, the document written by Thomas Jefferson, was signed by the thirteen colonies' delegates to the Continental Congress. The colonies were to make up the United States of America, the new country that proclaimed to be free from the governance and control of the king and crown of Great Britain. Stating, "We hold these truths to be self-evident, that all men are created equal . . . ," the signers of the declaration introduced their new nation and the notion of democracy on which governments act, "deriving their just powers from the consent of the governed."

With the Declaration of Independence thus proclaiming on July 4, 1776, the advent of our new nation, the celebrations began of Independence Day.

When your mother and Stiles were children and we lived in suburban New Brighton, Minnesota, there was a program beside a pond in the town park each Fourth of July. Finally at dark—which in northern Minnesota comes well after nine o'clock—some New Brighton citizens would set off fireworks, and what a grand display it would be: bursting balls of yellow light, one after another, Roman candles shooting off trails of sparks, flashes of flying red fireballs followed by blue ones, followed again by booms and varooms and more blazing shapes of lights in the sky that reflected upward from the pond. In New York City, there is usually a fireworks display over the East River on July Fourth; and in our city of Minneapolis there has often been one over the Mississippi River. These are repeated in countless cities and towns and over countless bodies of water all over America.

Labor Day brings the end of summer, even though the weather may be hot for a while longer and the date of the autumnal equinox is about three weeks later on September 21. It too is a picnic-time; and for those people in Wisconsin, Minnesota, and Michigan who have summer homes "up north," Labor Day weekend is closing-up time, just as Memorial Day weekend is opening time.

Most schools across the country start back in session on the day after Labor Day, and businesses and stores get down to autumn and winter preparations after Labor Day.

Labor Day in the United States began in 1882 when the Central Labor Union pressed for a day off for workers and it was passed into law by Congress as a federal holiday in 1894. It has been marked by parades of labor union members and festive gatherings for workers and their families in many American cities over the years. The emphasis for the holiday has continued to be on working people down to the present; but, like Memorial Day, Labor Day, with its three-day weekend, has become a generalized national holiday for everyone. It is a free day, a day for pause, for rest, and for enjoyment of time on one's own, with families, friends, or neighbors.

Labor Day also signals that the leisure time, inactivity, and warmth of summer are about over. It is time now to get back to the serious business of living, working, and going to school.

I CAPITALIZE LIGHT AND Love. These singular words provide images for what I believe can stand for provision of humankind's basic needs. They encompass the sacred or spiritual (Love) and the material or physical (Light). I use these words metaphorically, but somewhat literally as well. Light and Love are the sources of power, of empowerment, of attainments of power. They demonstrate the recognition of the potency of power, of powering flashes of both insight and energy for forces of change along with the literal energy for maintenance of life.

Trees grow toward the light. The ebbs and flows of ocean waters follow the pull of force by the heavens' lights. The loons return to the lake in the spring and start their autumn flight back to their overwintering seas from signals of light lengthening and shortening the days. People look to light for warmth and brightness for their very lives.

Love gives the spiritual version of Light. Love provides the tenderness that gives care of trees and ocean waters, the loons' environment, the clarity and cleanliness of the air beneath the sky, and human compassion and comprehension. Love is the generating force that enables human procreation. Love gives care for babies and children, adults, friends, family members, and strangers. The possibility of Love in the universe sustains creation, creativity, and regeneration. Love makes webs of goodness, of cooperation, of shared strength among neighbors, nations, and families. Love also embraces human energy and connects it with that of the plants and trees, the seas and rivers and lakes, the birds and animals and other wildlife the world over. Love finds ways to sustain, to replenish, to repair, to care, and to grow.

Light is the core power and central defining property of the natural world.

Love similarly is the primary power and the defining attribute of the nonmaterial world.

The reverse sides of Light and Love can kill, maim, deform, and deny. The absence of light withdraws the giving of life; distorted light in the form of gunfire and bombs destroys. Light manipulated by people can be put to creative and constructive use or can be wholly ruinous. Similarly love abased can wreak destruction, just as manifest love can create major good. Love can empower life, but love gone astray can hurt dreadfully. Willful manipulation of love, self-centered love, self-aggrandizing love by person or nation can inflict havoc and take lives. Literally, this is not even love, but let's call it love's opposite for the sake of argument. Effectively channeled love through people's gathering and cooperating can bring peace, tranquility, harmony; but love's opposite brings on mistrust, diminishment, pain, abuses, ruin, drought and famine, war, and annihilation.

Many religions and nations celebrate high moments with light.

In India, Hindus, Sikhs, and Jains all celebrate a Festival of Lights called Diwali. It is a five-day festival widely held across the country. It comes at a time in the Hindu calendar that corresponds with an October or November five-day period in the calendar we follow in the United States. Diwali originated as a celebration of a new economic beginning at the end of the monsoon season in India. The primary focus is the lighting in homes and gathering places of many kinds of lights and lamps, particularly earthen lamps. Diwali commemorates the victory of good over evil and celebrates the possibility of hope for humankind in the future. For Hindus this is a special time to worship three of its deities. One is Lord Ganesha, the elephant-headed god of beginnings and of obstacles, the patron of the arts, of intellect and wisdom, sometimes seen as the leading deity. The second is Lakshmi, the goddess of wealth, light, wisdom, of maternity and kindness to children, the foundress of the earth, whose image is the lotus flower. The third is Lord Mahavara, one who attained enlightenment. Jains as well honor Lord Mahavara at this time.

Across India and worldwide among Indian expatriates or people of Indian ancestry, Diwali is celebrated today with lights, and the cultural aspects of the festival are observed and enjoyed. The central lighted lamp of Diwali in the holiday symbolizes an enlightened mind. People often have new clothes for Diwali, signifying a new start, a freshness of a new time; and Indian businesspeople see it as the beginning of a new year. Firecrackers are lighted in celebration of the Festival of Lights.

In Christianity, the image of Light is often used for Christ as in "Christ is the Light of the world." Candle lighting and other illumination are common in church services, and lights are often prominent in celebrating Christian holidays such as Christmas.

In Judaism, too, lights figure significantly. One of the Jewish people's long-lived symbols is the menorah, a seven-branched candelabrum in the temple, which bears an eternal flame. This flame stands for Israel, the land

and the heart's home of the Jewish people; and the light of the flame is believed to have spiritual power, to bring peace, reconciliation, and non-violence. At Hanukkah, the menorah has nine branches, commemorating the miracle of a day's portion of oil lasting eight days.

In all these religions, light symbolizes the deeper enlightenment and peaceful understanding members have of their core Light of the holy.

Light carries similar religion-like cohesion in some civic celebrations. The Fourth of July—American Independence Day—with its fireworks displays reminds one of a religious celebration. New Year's Day is sometimes celebrated with fireworks, also. In the millennium year 2000, we were able to watch televised displays roll across much of the world as the New Year turned in many countries and cities, including Australia, South Africa, India, Paris, London, and New York.

Transmission of this sense of security in holy light takes place in families, communities, and nations in the form of love. Those who are religiously engaged sometimes symbolize Love-with-a-capital-L as deity and therefore as the focus or personification of their religions. Others see the ethical core that emanates from human love as their source for guidance for their lives. Either way, people need love as much as we need light for our survival.

In my own life, I was brought up in a community of faithful Christians and am still a member of Christian families and friendship groups. I am a "cultural Christian" or "member of the Christian tradition." At this time of my life, though, my personal vision of Light and Love is what I need of prayer, creed, doctrine, systematic religious thought, or activist manifesto. I enjoy learning about the commitments and values of people who are Hindu, Buddhist, Native American, Jewish, Muslim, Wiccan, and members of other communities and traditions that provide centering and religious meaning for people, as well as those of Christians in all three major branches of Christianity—Catholicism, Orthodoxy, and Protestantism.

I love participating in the holidays and celebrations and observances of my Protestant Christianity. They are my own, and I believe that members of other faith communities have the same kind of joy and satisfaction in their parallel holidays and observances. I delight in being a guest at religious events of any religion. I seek to be respectful of my loved ones who draw deep meaning from taking Communion and keeping a daily faithfulness within their Christianity. This is the tradition in which I spent my childhood and youth and that made an enormous difference in my life in the leadership opportunities the Methodist Church gave me as a teenager and young adult. So Protestant Christianity, Methodism in particular, is my "faith community" if no longer a part of my everyday life.

In the later years of my university teaching, I become engaged in scholarship and classroom experience around contemporary American religions, and this academic work gave me meaning and value for my personal spiritual life as well as my intellectual life. I came to honor the principle that Light and Love are dominating references and images for most of the religions in the world, and they came to fill my life with meaning and understanding in places that had been empty for some years.

Above all, along with my scholarly search for meaning in religions, I have found enormous spiritual satisfaction in nature. I find joy in the light on the water of the lake, thousands of different sprinkles of light at one time, a tranquil silver-slate shimmering surface at another, washing beams of orange sunset on some evenings, always moving light on water, always shining changes on the watery surface. I find satisfaction in the stars on a clear night, in the wisps of moonlight on some cloudy nights, and in the full moon seen twice on some moonlit nights, once in the sky and again in liquid light on the lake below. I find personal peace in the wind that blows cool and warm, hot, cold and frigid among the trees' limbs and branches.

I also delight in language, in writing well, in finding words that convey exact meaning and also that express understanding and compassion for those who read what I write or with whom I speak.

I find my challenge for my destiny to help keep the waters and the air, the trees and the grounds on which they grow healthy and clean and available to my loved ones and all the people of the earth today and in the future. My use of words, my writing, may be my best effort to fulfill what I want to do in my life for helpfulness both with nature and with people.

Love of the earth is one with the religions of the world. The presence of both Light and Love in the world and our lives gives us nourishment, strength, and endurance to live as we must to bring safety, peace, and health to the earth and to all among us. This is the challenge I offer to you, too, Jessica. Already as a little girl you enjoy nature and you write very well. You share with me and with other members of our family meanings that sustain us.

Love the earth with me. Write about what you love.

Go also to your family's Presbyterian Church for its offering of a path of Christian faith to you as a child, Jessica. Revel in your community of faith. It is not a contradiction also to revel in nature and its earth alongside your choice of your particular institutional religion. Love the earth with all your might and influence and action. Love the trees and wildflowers, all the plants and animals, the air and the waters upon all the earth. May both Light and Love be your guides.

24

Taking Responsibility

No matter how old a mother is . . . [s]he never outgrows the burden of love, and to the end she carries the weight of hope for those she bore.

—Florida Scott-Maxwell, *The Measure of My Days*

—Nature in Summer—The weather has been nice here much of the time this summer, but today was extraordinary: the real beginning of summer—sunny, hot-but-not-too-hot, a slight breeze, birds singing. I took my breakfast to the dock and for a while watched dragonflies and saw the turtle that seems to live here swimming about. Then a pair of loons appeared, very close, and entertained me for several minutes, once being on one side of our fallen pine tree in the lake, then diving and coming up on the other side of it.

I have delighted in the summer wildflowers in the grass here, common daisies or ox-eyed daisies; orange hawkweed, also known as Devil's Paintbrush; and red clover. I enjoyed seeing them as I did hours of yard work with great sweaty pleasure, watering my little trees and clearing trash plants—poison ivy, blackberry vines, thistles—from our cottage grounds.

WITHOUT ANY QUESTION, THE most horrible moment of my life was the November afternoon at my office when I answered the phone and your mother said, "Mom, the doctor says I have cancer. Can you come over?"

I went straightaway, of course. Natasha was alone at home with you and your brothers, small infants, and she was crying, but she did not want to frighten you. I got there as soon as I could to listen to her and to help her occupy you. Soon your dad was home, and he did exactly the right thing: he went to the couch where she was sitting and wordlessly put his arms around her. The next day when her brother Stiles came he did the same thing: walked in through the door, sat down beside her on the couch and put his arms around her.

She, and with her all our family, had already had a nightmarish few months. With you just turning two years old, she learned that her welcome pregnancy with your twin brothers was high risk with a disorder called Twin-to-Twin-Transfusion Syndrome; and she was put on bedrest, necessitating your going to daycare during your dad's hours of work at the bank. This was not the way she had planned it. In her late thirties, a late time for mothers of newborns, she had intended to stay home with her children your first years; and she and your dad had agreed to that as a plan for your family. Instead, your dad had to pack a cooler with lunch and drinks to put beside her in her upstairs bedroom, get you dressed and take you to your all-day nursery school on his way to the bank each morning. Although your nursery school was a very good experience for you, your mother's frustration at being on bedrest was a tremendous grief for her. She felt she was missing out on what she had long looked forward to doing.

Yet, as she always is around matters of health, your mother was very tuned in, well informed, and very much in charge when "something not quite right" in June announced David and Justin's impending premature arrival. She got herself to the hospital where her perinatologist rushed her into surgery for a Caesarian section and David was born first, weighing one pound and ten ounces, and Justin born a few minutes later weighing two pounds and ten ounces.

Both your mother and your father showed incredible strength, faithfulness, and love over the coming summer weeks while the boys were in neonatal intensive care, had illnesses and infections—David had surgeries—and your parents went daily to the hospital to visit them. Everyone in your family had illnesses that summer. Both your mother and tiny David had emergency room visits and hospital stays. Even your normally robust dad, Ian, came down with something.

At last in September when your brothers came home for good, both weighing in like healthy newborns, and in October when our whole family came to Coventry-in-the-Northwoods to celebrate Natasha's thirty-ninth birthday, we finally breathed easily. After such a long time, the difficulties were behind us—we thought.

Then came that life-transforming November afternoon and breast cancer.

Natasha did what she does in life's crisis situations. She gathered all the information she could, she went to doctors and pressed for under-standing as well as plans for treatment, she urged our family members to go on with our lives as we had planned them, she accepted or declined people's offers of help, and she wept. She wept for the loss of time with you three babies she knew would be the case. (I can just hear you saying, "I wasn't a baby! I was two years old!" But in her heart you were her baby girl.) She wept for the normality she had hoped for in her being a wholly available mother. She wept for the fears placed in herself, Ian, and all our family by the scare of that word: cancer. She wept for the unknowns about treatment and reactions and recovery periods. But, not once, not once, did she weep for herself, not once was there a shred of self-pity or selfish-ness in her weeping. Rather, she braced herself, raised herself to her full five feet two inches, and attacked that cancer head-on. She went to work on solving the problem.

You see, it was not her life alone she was fighting for, but for you, David, Justin, and Ian. She was scared about having the disease, all right, and she wanted to be well; but her reason for battling with everything in her being to overcome that cancer was for her family.

I have always been very proud of my daughter, but in those weeks and months of her fighting cancer, I saw a form of courage, a strength of character and determination that amazed me. Now she was in a realm of courageous action, of self-control, of strength and grace and generos-ity that was entirely her own and she seemed to transcend all that had been before in her life and focus her total energy and her being on getting well.

The key to Natasha's strength and endurance for that difficult time— and possibly of her recovery itself—was her taking responsibility for herself. At the heart of Natasha's resolution of the trauma of her illness was her decision from the start to take responsibility, not to let things happen to her, not to depend on someone else whether it be doctors or other experts or her husband or her parents or other loved ones—oh, she welcomed our support, every one—but to be in charge of what was happening in her life herself was her firm and resolute focus as she set out to get well. Hers was courage of the first order.

She chose a surgeon and an oncologist, she got a second opinion about her diagnosis, she set the date for surgery and a plan of treatment—four rounds of chemotherapy three weeks apart starting three weeks after the surgery, followed by eight weeks of radiation treatment. She decided to have a lumpectomy rather than a mastectomy. On the morning of her surgery, according to your mom's requests, your grandmother Scheerer, whom you call Nana, and I, Gigi to you, were at your house early to take care of the children, she to look after the boys while I took you to nursery school. Your dad had taken Natasha to the hospital before anyone else was awake, and both your grandfathers, Grandpa Scheerer and Granddad Yates, joined them at the hospital. That evening when she came home from the surgery, she even sat up at the dinner table and told funny stories in the children's voices. In utero, as Baby # 1, she said, David, who is smaller and got less nourishment through the faulty umbilicus, said to Justin, who got more nourishment and had torticollis with a somewhat pointed head, "Hey, Baby # 2, you just get all that blood and food! I will show you! I will just sit on your head and make it pointy!" Soon, though, she had to go upstairs to bed.

Not long after the surgery, you took your two-year-old self up to her bedroom, taking with you your little plastic fork and spoon. "Show me your breast with the lump," you requested. Not wanting to alarm you with the bandages and drain tubes, she showed you her healthy breast. Very gently, you went to work with your plastic instruments, saying, "I will be the doctor. I will scoop that lump out of you. There! It is gone." And then you got up and walked toward the door. Pausing at the door, you turned and asked, "Do you want the door open or closed?" then answered yourself, "Closed. Because you are resting." And you walked out and down the stairs.

Along with you, all our family members and many of our family friends, your neighbors, work friends of your dad's, teacher friends of your mom's, and people from your church did many helpful and lovely things for Natasha and your family. Bouquets of flowers were delivered by florists or by their givers. A little boy across the street and his mom came with a rose. Vases of blooms came and kept coming. Some lovely gifts like jewelry or Godiva chocolates or restaurant gift certificates arrived. Couples from your church signed on a rota to bring food, as they had already done over the summer when David and Justin were in the hospital. Our friends Sue and Carolyn brought home-cooked dinners to you every week for an entire year. When Natasha finally agreed that she could use some help in addition to your grandparents and other relatives for child care and household chores, she allowed me to coordinate the names and schedules of a number of people, women in particular, and some who were grandmothers or grandmother-hopefuls who enjoyed babies, to come and care for you children, buy groceries or do household jobs, or do needed tasks that occurred to Natasha, Ian, or me.

Natasha suffered more than her doctors thought she might around each of the steps of her treatment. She was particularly cross when the first treatment came just before Christmas and, though she had been assured by the doctors that the chemotherapy would not affect her adversely, she was very sick and unable to participate in family Christmas events. Each year in that period of time we had a progressive dinner on the night before Christmas Eve, with hors d'oeuvres at Stiles and Tina's house, then the main meal at your house, and I provided dessert. That evening, when your great-uncle Marshall and Mary-Ellen and cousin Michael had just arrived, though she insisted that we come on to your home and Ian made a marvelous curried turkey dinner, she was unable even to leave her bed. And at our dinner on Christmas Day, she was able to be there, but just barely. Photographs show her rather pasty-faced as she sits on the couch holding her two small red-suited baby boys.

Subsequent chemo sessions and their aftermath were not quite as bad, but still debilitating for her. She dealt with her hair coming out by going to the hairdresser and getting a buzz cut before it started; and then she got hats, but not a wig, to deal with it. She often went with her head uncovered, but had to wear a hat outside for it was winter. Her hats were very dramatic and beautiful, and she wore them with flair. It was about that time that she wrote a children's book, "My Mom Had Cancer," quite a marvelous book that I hope she still will be able to publish. It is written in the voice of a young girl and covers the sequence of events that the family goes through as they deal with breast cancer, much like you and she and our family experienced it.

Natasha also took advantage of several kinds of services for cancer patients—a support group, classes of special interest to recovering people, extras like massage and foot reflexology to make her feel better. In this period of time she also began to write poetry and later published a poem about her and your family's experience with cancer in a volunteer organization's publication.

Radiation treatment was not as difficult for her as chemo had been, but it came to be very tiring. When it sapped her energy, it was frustrating for her to have to turn to family and friends for more assistance just for her to be able to get some rest. Still, she had become graceful about accepting help and vowed to "give back," when she was well, in the form of help for other people.

By May all her treatments were over, and her oncologist told her she was "cured." She celebrated by enrolling your whole family to participate in the Susan G. Koman March against Breast Cancer on Mother's Day. Pictures from that day are priceless. It was raining, but there you are, the five of you, huddled under umbrellas, each of you with a colorful pink and green scarf and pink t-shirts from the march organizers, David and Justin with puzzled looks on their faces as they sit in their double stroller, and you with your indomitable smile of a new three-year-old. The victorious family making your statement: we have beat cancer, and we march for others to join us in conquering it, too.

Your mom was prepared to take responsibility for her health even in the dire circumstance of having cancer, that life-threatening disease, for she had developed a mindset, an attitude, an approach to life that caused her to think immediately of finding out about and doing what would restore, enhance, and preserve her good health. Such an attitude or mindset is what Aristotle called becoming "habituated" or forming a habit of constructive planning and action to immediately address a problem.

Such a similar positive habit of taking responsibility is what I developed in my feminism in the 1970s, enabling me to speak or act without delay in all situations where sexism, anti-woman words or behavior, or demeaning women and girls take place. Although I may now be more polite than I was in my feisty early years, I nevertheless automatically call the hand of a person saying women can't be lawyers or police officers or handle money effectively or anything else that makes women in general secondary or inferior to men or circumscribed by gender. Indeed, I respond with similar informed indignation if I hear that men can't be good child care providers, cooks, or household managers, or any of the other gender-role labels that were traditionally assigned to women. Of course, some individual women or men can't do certain things very well at all; but the point of addressing sexism is to raise the awareness that women and men can behave in relationships, can function in occupations, and can perform tasks in many ways similarly to each other. There is much yet to be learned about the biology and behavior of women and of men, but the feminism of which I have been a part has opened the way for more research by experts and greater flexibility by everyone in interpreting the particulars of social gender behavior.

Likewise, for me feminist attention to language has been a major cause. It still surprises me that women as well as men say that "women are included in" the generic use of "man." My experience and the linguistic history I have studied tell me that just isn't so. I did an English language research project on the history of the words for "woman" in a linguistics class long ago. It highlights the fact that inherent cultural biases are present from the start in language and they continue in sometimes surprising ways as cultures and their languages change over time. I learned that the word "hussy" in Old English originally just meant woman. It came from the word "hus" that meant "house" and the "hussy" was simply the woman of the house. The word "husband" gradually evolved to refer to the man attached to or "bound to" the "hussy" or "hus-band"! The development of the word "woman" has a surprising history, as well, for the word for "man" existed first and the word "wif" was a parallel word for "woman," then their marriage yielded "wifman" or "woman."

Not everyone is going to learn the history of our language or even the history of specific words, but I am set on automatic pilot to remind people in my presence, to use in my writing and my own conversation, and to teach those around me with whom I have influence that respectful, carefully understood gender-inclusive language usage is normative, is the way it ought to be. It is my "habituated" practice in both use and advocacy of language practices, of behaviors, and of generating opportunities in which I have a part to include women and men, girls and boys on an equal basis, to think of righting the wrongs of sexism at all times. It is my mindset or attitude or ingrained habit of mind.

Similarly, your granddad and I have an antiracist attitude or mindset. We were both civil rights movement activists at the turn of the 1960s. One of the stories of pride in our family is that Wilson was the first white student who went to jail for a night in the early days of the Nashville civil rights struggle. Recently there was an NBC News video made of former civil rights leaders in which the footage was replayed of him carrying a placard supporting desegregation, a placard handed to him by leader John

Lewis, now a member of Congress from Atlanta. In the next frame, Wilson is being hit on the back of the head by a white heckler and is seen falling, falling, falling to the ground and both of them shown being arrested after that. There was also a newspaper story in the Nashville *Tennessean* the next day after Wilson and the heckler were arrested. It showed a series of pictures spread across the top of the front page of Wilson's fall after being hit. He spent the night in jail and says it was scary as some of the white jailed men circled him saying, "You the nigger lover? Nigger lover?" but one man in the cell came to his rescue and stopped them from hurting him.

Wilson's jail experience and much publicity about it are very minor compared to the suffering of many other people, including even the deaths of some people in the struggles of the civil rights movement. However, that effort for Wilson galvanized his antiracist beliefs and his lifelong actions on them. Similarly, my participation as a Mississippi college student in an interracial seminar with students at predominantly black Tougaloo College and some from my then-all-white Millsaps College, when even our gathering as blacks and whites was against state law, established for me and other students our course for the rest of our lives as both antiracists and activists on behalf of civil rights. We learned this had to mean equal treatment of members of all races, not only under the law, but also in social and personal behaviors and advocacy. Respecting and honoring all people without discrimination became a mindset, an automatic behavior, an integral part of our lives as persons and as a family. Both Wilson and I learned we must take responsibility for our society in a reflexive way without having to think through "what might be right" in any given situation when the question had to do with race or respectfulness of persons from whatever background.

This mindset or attitude or habit of mind was what your mother had developed that made it possible for her to take responsibility for her own health when confronted with cancer. She didn't know what the outcome would be. She didn't know how she would be able to manage the many parts of her life that she wanted to continue to be in charge of. She didn't yet know many of the particulars of what was needed to combat cancer in terms of medical care, financial coverage, family, and childcare. What she did know was how to take responsibility for herself. And she proceeded with great skill, intelligence, compassion, and even at times humor. It was all our good fortune that she was cured of cancer and that she is happily alive and well in Red Wing caring for her family just as she dreamed of doing, living in a marvelous old Victorian house surrounded by lots of friends and supportive townspeople as she serves as an advocate for the environment's protection and for your town's well-being, as well as your family's. There was, of course, risk and uncertainty about whether she would recover and what the outcome would be; and, though Natasha had an enormous support system of family and friends and medical professionals, without a doubt the primary reason for your mother's restoration to good health was her taking responsibility for herself. It took great courage, which she found within herself to use.

"Courage" is the title poet Anne Sexton gives to her poem on the subject. She is able to treat it whimsically. Even though courage is such a strong, even fierce emotion, she is able to treat it gently. Her poem reminds me of the soft and gentle strength of your mother's courage when she faced cancer. Sexton writes:

> Next, my kinsman, you powdered your sorrow,
> you gave it a backrub
> and then you covered it with a blanket.[1]

Sexton's image expresses to me precisely the paradoxical attitudes and actions your mother took to lead her to her life's renewal. We are ever-so-happy that her taking responsibility has given us all the good life we have now with her.

1. Anne Sexton, "Courage," *Good Poems*, Garrison Keillor, ed., p. 214.

25

Living Well

> [Hope] sticks to the wings of green angels
> that sail from the tops of maples.
>
> —Lisel Mueller, "Hope," *Good Poems*

—Nature in Summer—Rioting colors of zinnias, geraniums, purple asters, dahlias, yellow and white daisies, phlox, impatiens, day lilies, and all manner of summer flowers; tomatoes ripening on the vine, green beans and zucchini and cucumbers and melons ready to gather and fill baskets to overflowing; foliage growing wild all over everywhere; hot afternoons melding into cooler evenings with late night sunsets; swims in the lake with children, safe and happy, jumping and laughing and calling out to one another; and canoe rides in warm dusk hours with peace among us. This is summer of our dreams. This is summer of our here-and-now.

. . . in the darkness right now, I hear a veritable chorus of loons out on the lake so late at night.

I WOULD NOT HAVE imagined earlier in my life that I would think living well so simple. Digging in the earth to plant trees. Hugging my twin grandsons in one rocking embrace. Writing postcards of encouragement to presidential candidates, environmentalists, and my beloved. It all started with learning about trees, with "seeing" trees as if for the first time.

LEARNING ABOUT TREES

Though we don't have any linden trees at Coventry-in-the-Northwoods—apparently they don't grow this far north—my life is full of linden tree memories, of linden trees in early summer perfuming my walks, of linden trees being the marker of a manner and time I became more attuned to the particularities of trees and their names. Our neighborhood in Minneapolis is called Linden Hills; and though my friend Bobbie and I once long ago took a Tree Trek class from a horticulturist of the Minneapolis Parks Department, and we learned about the local tree called basswood, I don't remember linden being mentioned. When I taught in Berlin, my classroom and office were on Unter den Linden Strasse (the street under the lindens) along with the other main university and government buildings and the famous Brandenburg Gate. There linden trees were German, and the rows of beautiful trees on the meridian of the vast, busy urban street leading up to the towering Brandenburg Gate were lindens.

In England I walked on the footpaths of the greens, as their urban parks are called, under the "lime trees" in June and wondered at their leafing and budding and the opening of their tiny blossoms with surrounding fragrance. As an American, I thought them strangely unlike the familiar citrus fruit tree producing tangy lime fruits, but took the Brits' word for the trees' name, not once thinking "linden." It took living in each of the three countries more than once and doing serious-minded research to sort out the linden trees. Not ever a botanist or even a very well-informed or educated naturalist, if a wannabe, I had to make associations and then some and finally "look it up" to make sense out of those wonderful trees.

It was on a later stay in England in early summer, when walking under the fragrant trees with bees buzzing around their hanging clusters of small flowers, that I had the Eureka! moment. Those trees smell a lot like linden trees! Those trees look a lot like linden trees! And I went to the library and reference books, which told all. What the British call lime and what the Germans and North Americans call linden are the same tree; and, alternatively, the tree is sometimes called basswood in the United States. All these names are for linguistic-historical reasons because "linden" comes from the German root "Lind" and from "linde" or "linne" in Anglo-Saxon, agreed upon in modern times as "linden." "Basswood" moreover is taken from the word for the inner bark of the tree, "bast."

Thus, these German, English, and North American trees are the same, even being named from the same linguistic roots.

It is tempting to make a parable of ignorance and competence of this experience of mine. Even so, mere love of the trees, enjoyment of their beauty, and simple delight in their scent were too little for my learning. It mattered to have a name by which to know them as a family and to know them more deeply tree-by-tree as who they are in all these places I have called home—Germany, England, Linden Hills in Minneapolis: homes of my heart, homes to my trees, homes to my using my nose, my vision, and eventually, my understanding.

The linden trees were the beginning.

WORKING WITH TREES

After several years of owning our cottage and acre of land on Callahan Lake in Wisconsin, I moved closer to my dream of making this place my cultivated wild arboretum that I want it to be. I have planted new trees each spring and I have thoroughly enjoyed caring for them. In planting trees, I am doing what I want to do most deeply, both materially and spiritually, to make the world a better place. This is my way of taking responsibility.

Last year I became acquainted with "restoration landscaper" Paul Hlina. Paul works wholly with native plants he grows from seed, and he helped us design our space and plant new trees and shrubs and wildflowers that have grown in this area for many generations. Last summer Paul helped us take nannyberry plants we had planted ourselves and move them to better soil and location for them. He brought some tamarack trees and put them down near the lakeshore. On the east side of our property, he provided a good-sized plum tree, replacing the tiny ones I couldn't get to grow over four years of their just standing there. Nearby he put a bed of pearly everlasting wildflowers surrounded with a mulch of straw. I had fun showing you four grandchildren the little ancient native plants topped with a small pearly blossom that Paul says will stay in bloom until November. On the west and east sides of the house in the woods are new pagoda dogwood, sumac, snowberry, bush honeysuckle, and hazelnut trees. Near the screened porch with our three good-sized sugar maples that have been there five years are two new yellow birches. In sunny spots on each side of the driveway near the front of our land are new plantings of ninebark, sand cherries, white pines, red pines, white spruce, service-berry, snowberry, and chokecherry. Near the door and the deck on the west side of our house is now another straw-mulched bed of anise hyssop, lance-leafed coreopsis, black-eyed Susan, butterfly weed, button blazing-star, sky-blue aster, and bergamot/bee balm. I do feel wonderful about doing my part for our environment with my trees. I know it is only a tiny, tiny part but it is something I can do. My restoration trees. When I was with my friend Jean Ward, who grew up in northern Minnesota parallel in climate and soil to our Wisconsin location, and told her about the plants, she exclaimed, "Oh, my grandmother had those!" And so it is that I want you and Sage, Justin and David to be able to say many years from now, when recognizing these trees and shrubs and wildflowers, "My grandmother had those, and she loved them."

ON LIVING WELL

If learning to plant trees and to identify more and more tree species is a new part of these my "ripening" years, the tree can also be an image for many of my renewed or recently acquired interests and aspirations. It grows as both a beautiful and an essential part of nature with its full root system, its tall and sturdy trunk, and branching, leafy limbs spreading a canopy over the earth beneath it. Its vital role in the earth's ecosystem includes drawing up water from the earth through its roots, absorbing carbon dioxide from the atmosphere, photosynthesizing sunlight through its leaves into nutrients, sending out from its leaves vapor with its critical oxygen to the atmosphere, all processes important to life itself on our planet.

The image of the tree, articulated in its biology, gives us an ethical understanding of the interrelation of all of life: the condensation of issues into patterns of relationship whether biological, individually human, or social. The tree image suggests from the biological to the social that the bark is the skin that surrounds and protects. The roots below and the leaves above signify the tree's integral connections, and thereby all of ours, with other parts of life. The trunk shows substance, strength, and stability. The giving and taking of water, sunlight, carbon dioxide, and oxygen stand for creativity and creation out of available materials transformed. And its seeds are the crucible of its reproduction.

For me, then, and for my suggestion to you, Jessica, the tree can stand for creative writing and the other arts—our taking a human ability and its development and turning words, ideas, and objects into poetry, fiction, sculpture, and paintings, dance, architecture, physics and biology interpretations, philosophical viewpoints, and political theories and explanations. The tree can stand for a model of our search for solutions to our world's problems of global warming, overpopulation, overconsumption, overfarming, and abuses of the land, foodstuffs, the waters, and the air. The tree can stand for forms of resolution of our social needs to address poverty, injustices, and war-making conflicts in our world. And the tree's seeds are ever with us telling of opportunities to begin again, to grow, and to change. The tree is a wonderful image, as well as a reality of delight and of sustenance.

In these years of my sixties, I find satisfaction in both the continuities comparing my early life with late adulthood and the contrasts between my childhood and youth and my late life. The freedom I felt on the land in my childhood Mississippi was directly related to my desire to have, live in, and enjoy our Wisconsin cottage in the woods, even though the years between childhood and late life I have spent becoming a fully urban, well-traveled, cosmopolitan, and professional person who might seem to be far removed from the country person I was born as on the farm. My tree image is a very powerful symbol for who I have always been along with who I am and who I want to continue to be. All the intervening years between when I was a child and now when I am in my sixties, there might seem to have been a total disconnect as I learned city ways, cold weather clothing, international lifestyles, air travel and trains in Europe in contrast with my rural Mississippi upbringing. Yet, that is not finally the case.

After years of not even thinking about it, I remember the oak tree in our front yard at our house on the farm. It was already good-sized when I was a child, and its story was told and retold with pleasure in our family. The fact is that when my father went to the 1934 World's Fair in Chicago with his Illinois cousins, a very rare and unusual trip for him, he picked up an acorn and brought it home, planted it, and it grew into this fine tree. My father had planted trees. Earlier, I did not identify with him at all in this endeavor, and it was my brother who became a forestry major in college and planted trees professionally. Yet, the resonance, the familiarity, my personal history with tree planting occurs to me now, decades later, and makes a kind of continuity in my life of a heritage that I can claim.

Living well has many parts. It requires finding models for one's life—role models in persons or models of exhibited values or literary, philosophical, or religious visions of life worth living. I recommend Aristotle's *Ethics* and Broker's Ojibway narrative *Night Flying Woman* as written works that have given my students and me ways to understand how to live. I also recommend to you, Jessica, essays and fiction by Eudora Welty, art works by Georgia O'Keeffe and George Morrison, architecture by Frank Gehry and by John Cook and Joan Sorano, and science like that done by Eville Gorham.

Living well is planting trees, and, also, is playing croquet with small boys.

Living well is finding richness is silence and solitude.

Living well is enjoying laughter in the company of family and friends.

Living well is honing your skills at reading, observing, and listening.

Living well is reading books—book after book after book.

Living well is paying attention.

Living well is seeking the best possible education—all your life long.

Living well is taking prudent care of your money, budgeting wisely for yourself, but giving generously where there are needs for gifts.

Living well is having the resourcefulness to change directions when going the way you are turns wrongheaded.

Living well is cultivating "doing nothing" to perfection.

Living well is being a good sport, win or lose.

Living well is showing true and honest empathy.

Living well is being a friend and a good family member.

Living well is showing sympathy at death or pain or loss and sending flowers when someone you know or love needs them. Or, "just because" you like to send flowers. Picking flowers from your garden and taking them to someone is even better.

Living well is growing your own garden.

Living well is experiencing and giving sexual joy.

Living well is loving well, in other words.

Living well is being public-spirited.

Living well is practicing good citizenship in your community, nation, and world.

Living well is doing the work that thrills you and helps make people, a place, or a situation better for your having done it. Or, if you have to do work that seems monotonous, routine, and mundane, use your creativity to transform your work into effort that is exciting, useful, and beautiful.

Living well is finding your spiritual depth.

Living well is taking responsibility in your family, your community, and your world.

Living well is caring for and conserving all that you touch of the earth and its resources, mindful of your children and their children and theirs.

Living well is letting yourself be who you yourself truly are.

26

Hopefulness

Hope is that thing inside us that insists, despite all evidence to
the contrary, that something better awaits us if we have the courage to
reach for it, and to work for it, and to fight for it.

—Barack Obama

—Nature in Summer—Today, still in August, walking down the road
past the big maple tree on my way to the Chief River, I was startled
to see some leaves at the end of a few branches already changed from
green to autumnal orange. Late August heralds of autumn in the Upper
Midwest, like cool-blowing winds, early turning leaves, and an earthy
fragrance anticipating chill in the air, always surprise my Mississippi-
bred consciousness where autumn weather delays coming until
November. Falling leaves and frosty mornings will be here soon. For
professors, teachers, and schoolchildren, this is the beginning of a new
year. With new backpacks, notebooks, pencils, and erasers, everyone
will go off full of hope to their schools and their desks. Our hopes rise
for a new beginning, for new promise for ourselves, our classrooms, and
our world. Even governments and businesses after summer vacations
start back along with the schoolchildren in September. Hope comes
with the newness of September's changing colors, earlier sunsets, and
invigorating breeze.

THE FIRST DAY OF school, not January first, has been the real beginning of the new year for me all my life. Those years I was a school-
child, a college and university student, and all the years I was a professor,

the new start came each September, still summertime, though with just a hint of fall, when I would go out every morning dressed in my new school clothes with my book bag and be off to new classes with fresh subjects and an uncharted start.

The start of school is the real new beginning for anyone whose life has been on a school year schedule, even a retired professor like me. And with the new year rises new hope.

President Barack Obama used the theme of hope in his campaigns for both the Democratic nomination for office and for the presidency itself. Indeed, his autobiographical work about his entrance into national public life is titled *The Audacity of Hope.* In his speech at the time of winning the Iowa caucuses in January of election year 2008, he said, "For many months, we've been teased, even derided for talking about hope. . . . Hope is that thing inside us that insists, despite all evidence to the contrary, that something better awaits us if we have the courage to reach for it, and to work for it, and to fight for it."[1]

The Obama campaign gave millions of Americans, indeed, people around the world, new hope for a better, socially egalitarian, and fair and just society and government in the United States; and his landslide victory in the 2008 presidential election gave jubilant expression to that hope as he moved toward governing. Our nation and the world anticipated his presidency with unprecedented joyfulness about what can be done worldwide. His inauguration as president of the United States on January 20, 2009 ceremonially encapsulated his and the American people's new surge of confidence that hope is available to us in our political future.

Similarly in literature, Emily Dickinson articulates the same yearning in her poem "Hope." The poet uses the metaphor of a bird for full presentation of an understanding of hope. Amazingly, she uses neither the word "bird" at first, nor a name for any particular kind of bird, as she develops this metaphor. Starting

> "Hope" is a thing with feathers—
> That perches in the soul—

the poet concretizes with the characteristic "feathers" and the behavioral verb "perches" a bird made vivid in our imagination as the poem jux-

---

1. Barack Obama, Iowa Democratic caucuses victory speech, 3 January 2008, quoted in the San Francisco *Chronicle*, Special Election Edition, "The World Read All About It," 9 November 2008, p. U3.

taposes the abstract feeling, hope, in its abstract location, the soul. The reader, this reader anyway, feels a quickening of reality of what can come inside oneself, the self, or familiar "soul" as Dickinson names it, of that yearned for hope promised by the "thing with feathers" metaphorically perched within.

The poem continues with the song—the "tune" without words—being sung perpetually and through all kinds of weathers—the "gale," the "storm," and in "the chillest land" or on "the strangest sea"—providing warmth to the hearer. "Yet," she tells us, the singing bird asks nothing in return for the continuous song, "never . . . a crumb."

These uses of the language of hope provide handles of promise for us to grasp. The first is my own feeling of welled-up hope as expressive of the new beginning each new school year offers. The second is President Obama's public and political message of hope as foundation for a new course for government. The third is Emily Dickinson's interior and poetic expression of hope as sustaining and containing solace for the soul.

From my own and many others' first-day-of-school experience of hopefulness, from the image and the emotion provided for hope politically by President Barack Obama, and for the literary expression of the meaning of hope, I find these various ways to grasp hope, this "thing with feathers," and pass it along to you, Jessica, as a fundamental in our way of life. It is an approach to life, it is an aspiration toward goodness, it is a motive for kindness, it is a satisfaction that lights our dark of night.

We learn of hope that hope takes risks. Hope embodied bears courage, perseverance, grace, and strength.

Hope in our hearts sings our song.

Hope in our minds gives form to our future.

Hope converges with our love to build community, neighborhood, coalition, and nation.

Hope at our fingertips develops our skills and our attitudes.

Hope we find in the book, on the path, and in the treetops gives us guidance.

Hope takes us over the finish line.

Or, if we fall back, hope promises another chance another time and companionship on the journey.

Jessica, this is my offering to you. Hope. Let hope ever be with you. Let hope "perch" inside you like Emily Dickinson's singer of its "tune," whatever the weather outside your window or in your soul. Let hope lead you, let hope be your light, let hope shape your love.

Live, Jessica, ever in hopefulness.

Epigraph Sources

Front matter—epigraph for book—Michael Pollan, *The Botany of Desire*. New York: Random House, 2002, pp. 109–110.

Section 1—Erazim Kohak, from *The Embers and the Stars*, quoted in *The Wonders of Solitude*, edited by Dale Salwak. Novato, CA: New World Library, 1998, p. 78.

Chapter 1—Nikos Kazantzakis, *Report to Greco*, quoted in *The Wonders of Solitude*, edited by Dale Salwak. Novato, CA: New World Library, 1988, p. 80.

Chapter 2—Joan Chittister, *Illuminated Life: Monastic Wisdom for Seekers of Light*. Maryknoll, New York: Orbis Books, 2000, p. 84.

Chapter 3—*Bible*, King James Version, Genesis 1:11.

Chapter 4—Michael Pollan, *Second Nature: A Gardener's Education*. Grove Press, 2003, p. 18.

Chapter 5—George Morrison, quoted in "The Art of George Morrison and Allan Houser" by Gregory Schaff, *Native Peoples Magazine*, 1 Sept. 2004. Found on-line at www.nativepeoples.com.

Chapter 6—Henry Beston, *The Outermost House*. New York: An Owl Book, Henry Holt and Co., 1992, p. xxxv. First published by Doubleday, 1928.

Chapter 7—Emily Dickinson, "Poem 254," *The Poems of Emily Dickinson*, edited by Thomas H. Johnson. Cambridge: The Belknap Press of Harvard Univ., 1951, Vol. 1, pp. 182–183.

Part 11—Wallace Stevens, "The Snow Man," *The Palm at the End of the Mind: Selected Poems and a Play*, Holly Stevens, ed. New York: Vintage Books, 1972, p. 54. Poem first published in 1921.

Chapter 8—Alexander McCall Smith, *The Sunday Philosophy Club*. New York: Pantheon Books, 2001, p. 140.

Chapter 9—Verlyn Klinkerborg, "Donald Hall, Poet Laureate." *New York Times*, June 15, 2006, p. A22.

Chapter 10—Henry Beston, *The Outermost House*. New York: An Owl Book, Henry Holt and Co., 1992, p. 217. First published in 1928.

Chapter 11—Leo Tolstoy, from *A Calendar of Wisdom*, quoted in Sonny Brewer, *The Poet of Tolstoy Park*. New York: Ballantine Books, p. 218.

Chapter 12—Henry Beston, *The Outermost House*. New York: An Owl Book, Henry Holt and Co., 1992, p. xv. First published in 1928.

Chapter 13—Ben Shahn, quoted in *Masters of Modern Art*. New York, The Museum of Modern Art, distributed by Doubleday and Co., 1958, p. 162.

Chapter 14—Emily Dickinson, "Poem 1129," *The Poems of Emily Dickinson*, edited by Thomas H. Johnson. Cambridge: The Belknap Press, Vol. ii, p. 972.

Chapter 15—Wisława Szymborska, "View with a Grain of Sand," *view with a grain of sand: Selected Poems*. New York: Harcourt Brace & Co., A Harvest Original: 1993, translated from Polish by Stanislaw Baranczak and Clare Cavanagh, p. 136.

Chapter 16—*Bible*, King James Version, Genesis 2:9.

Part iii—Henry David Thoreau, *Walden*. Boston and London: Shambhala, One Hundred Fiftieth Anniversary Edition, 2004, pp. 33–34.
Also, the *Bible*, King James Version, 1 Corinthians 13:13.

Chapter 17—The Dhammapade, "the classic source of Buddhist ethics," as quoted in Diana Eck, *A New Religious America*. San Francisco: HarperSanFrancisco, 1997, p. 130.

Chapter 18—Joan Dunning, *The Loon: Voice of the Wilderness*. Boston: Houghton Mifflin, 1985, p. 16.

Chapter 19—Elizabeth von Armin, *Elizabeth and Her German Garden*. London: Virago, 1985, pp. 71–72. Originally published in 1898.

Chapter 20—*Bible*, King James Version, Song of Solomon 2: 12–13.

Chapter 21—Virginia Woolf, *A Room of One's Own*. New York: Harcourt, Brace, and World, 1956, p. 86. First published in 1929.

Chapter 22—Aldo Leopold, *A Sand County Almanac*. New York: Ballantine Books, 1970, pp. 177–178.

Part IV—Poem "the lake sits silent" by Nathaniel Danforth, 8 years old, 2005.

Chapter 23—May Sarton, *Journal of a Solitude.* New York: W.W. Norton and Co., 1992, p. 16.

Chapter 24—Florida Scott-Maxwell, *The Measure of My Days.* New York: Penguin Books, 1979, pp. 16–17. First published in 1968.

Chapter 25—Lisel Mueller, "Hope," *Good Poems*, Garrison Keillor, ed. (New York: Viking Penguin, 2002), p. 224.

Chapter 26—Barack Obama, Iowa Democratic caucuses victory speech, 3 January 2008, quoted in the San Francisco *Chronicle*, Special Election Edition, "The World Read All About It," 9 November 2008, p. U3.

W9-CGS-456

OECD
ECONOMIC SURVEYS

DOCUMENTS OFFICIELS

JUL 1 8 1988

GOVERNMENT
PUBLICATIONS

UNITED STATES

ORGANISATION FOR ECONOMIC CO-OPERATION AND DEVELOPMENT

Pursuant to article 1 of the Convention signed in Paris on 14th December, 1960, and which came into force on 30th September, 1961, the Organisation for Economic Co-operation and Development (OECD) shall promote policies designed:

- to achieve the highest sustainable economic growth and employment and a rising standard of living in Member countries, while maintaining financial stability, and thus to contribute to the development of the world economy;
- to contribute to sound economic expansion in Member as well as non-member countries in the process of economic development; and
- to contribute to the expansion of world trade on a multilateral, non-discriminatory basis in accordance with international obligations.

The original Member countries of the OECD are Austria, Belgium, Canada, Denmark, France, the Federal Republic of Germany, Greece, Iceland, Ireland, Italy, Luxembourg, the Netherlands, Norway, Portugal, Spain, Sweden, Switzerland, Turkey, the United Kingdom and the United States. The following countries became Members subsequently through accession at the dates indicated hereafter: Japan (28th April, 1964), Finland (28th January, 1969), Australia (7th June, 1971) and New Zealand (29th May, 1973).

The Socialist Federal Republic of Yugoslavia takes part in some of the work of the OECD (agreement of 28th October, 1961).

Publié également en français.

Contents

Tables

Text

4

Diagrams

5

BASIC STATISTICS OF THE UNITED STATES

THE LAND

Area continental United States plus Hawaï and Alaska (thous. sq. km)	9 363	Population of major cities, including their metropolitan areas (1.7.1985 estimates):	
		New York	8 466 000
		Los Angeles-Long Beach	8 109 000
		Chicago	6 177 000

THE PEOPLE

Population, 1987	243 773 000	Civilian labour force 1987	119 849 500
No. of inhabitants per sq. km	26	of which:	
Population, annual net natural increase		Employed in agriculture	3 022 500
(average 1978-1987)	21 188 000	Unemployed	7 410 167
Annual net natural increase, per cent,		Net migration (annual average 1978-1985)	629 000
1978-1987	0.95		

PRODUCTION

Gross national product in 1987 (billions of US $)	4 488.5	Origin of national income in 1986 (per cent of national income[1]):	
GNP per head in 1987 (US $)	18 413		
Gross fixed capital formation:		Agriculture, forestry and fishing	2.4
Per cent of GNP in 1987	16.0	Manufacturing	20.0
Per head in 1987 (US $)	2 940	Construction and mining	6.5
		Government and government enterprises	14.5
		Other	56.6

THE GOVERNMENT

Government purchases of goods and services 1987 (per cent of GNP)	20.6	Composition of the 99th Congress:		
			House of Representatives	Senate
Revenue of Federal, state and local governments, 1987 (per cent of GNP)	34.7			
Federal Government debt as per cent of receipts from the public, 1987	222.1	Democrats	253	47
		Republicans	182	53
		Independents	–	–
		Undecided	–	–
		Total	435	100

FOREIGN TRADE

Exports:		*Imports:*	
Exports of goods and services as per cent of GNP in 1987	9.5	Imports of goods and services as per cent of GNP in 1987	12.2
Main exports 1987 (per cent of merchandise exports):		Main imports 1987 (per cent of merchandise imports):	
Machinery	28.5	Food, feeds and beverages	6.0
Transport equipment	16.0	Industrial supplies and materials	26.3
Food and live animals	7.9	Capital goods (excl. cars)	21.1
Crude materials (inedible)	8.4	Automobile vehicles and parts	20.8
Chemicals	10.8	Consumer goods (non-food)	21.1
Manufactured goods	7.0	All other	4.7
All other	21.4		

1. Without capital consumption adjustment.
Note: An international comparison of certain basic statistics is given in an annex table.

This Survey is based on the Secretariat's study prepared for the annual review of the United States by the Economic and Development Review Committee on 22nd February 1988.

•

After revisions in the light of discussions during the review, final approval of the Survey for publication was given by the Committee on 20th April 1988.

•

The previous survey of the United States was issued in November 1986.

Introduction

Trends in the real economy in 1987 stand in marked contrast to developments in the financial sphere. On the real side, growth remained relatively strong, employment rose steadily and unemployment continued to decline. The expansion of the economy became more balanced, with real net exports progressively taking over from domestic demand as a source of growth. Despite substantial gains in production and employment, underlying inflation remained moderate. On the financial side, however, there was a further deterioration in the already-large imbalance between domestic saving and investment, a trend resulting from the persistence of a large Federal deficit and a fall in household saving. The accounting counterpart was found in a widening current external deficit to a record level of $161 billion in 1987. In a context of rapidly rising external indebtedness, it became more difficult to attract private foreign capital inflows at existing interest and exchange rate levels. The dollar came under strong downward pressure at times, and there was large-scale official intervention.

Following the stock market crisis, the short-term outlook for the U.S. economy remains uncertain, though prospects for an improvement of the current external balance would seem to have increased as domestic demand growth is generally expected to slow. Household saving should rise and the Federal budget deficit stabilise as a result of the agreement reached between Congress and the Administration. A continuing improvement in trade volumes, eventually showing up in a decline in the nominal current account deficit, could help support the dollar, giving policymakers more time for a medium-term solution to the problem of imbalances. However, there are, as always, risks attaching to the outlook. Domestic demand could weaken too much, leading to a recession. On the other hand, domestic demand could remain too strong, delaying the improvement in the trade deficit and increasing the inflationary danger. The U.S. economy remains therefore faced with the task of unwinding domestic and external imbalances, while sustaining non-inflationary growth.

After briefly reviewing trends in the domestic economy in Part I, the factors behind the persistent current account deficit are analysed in Part II. Monetary, exchange rate and fiscal policies are dealt with in Part III. Part IV presents the short-term outlook for the economy and discusses medium-term issues involved in unwinding the external imbalance. Developments in U.S. financial markets over the last few years, which have become particularly relevant in view of the recent stock market crisis, provide the focus of Part V. Finally, policy conclusions are presented in Part VI.

I. The domestic economy

The economy in 1987

Activity remained unexpectedly strong in 1987. Real GNP grew 4 per cent in the year to the fourth quarter, implying an average growth for the year as a whole of nearly 3 per cent, the same as in 1986. The pattern of growth changed substantially (Diagram 1). In spite of a large increase in inventories, total domestic demand growth slowed down, reflecting a weakening in consumption and residential investment. For the first time since 1980, real net exports made a sustained, positive contribution to GNP growth. Employment rose briskly and the unemployment rate fell a full percentage point. Measured inflation rose somewhat in 1987 as a result of a rebound in oil prices and higher import prices. Although underlying inflation remained relatively subdued, at times during the year inflation expectations appeared to flare up. In spite of the adjustment in the real trade balance, the nominal trade balance deteriorated further, as the terms of trade worsened in the wake of earlier dollar depreciation. In a context of widening international imbalances, an apparent deadlock between the Administration and Congress over the FY 1988 budget and rising interest rates, the stock market suffered a sharp decline in mid-October.

Demand components

The main elements of strength in 1987 were real net exports, business fixed investment and inventories. The real trade deficit narrowed substantially, contributing 0.3 percentage points to GNP growth. Following four years of virtual stagnation, export volumes (goods and services) rose by around 13 per cent in 1987, with the volume of manufactured exports enjoying a 16 per cent increase. Import growth, while lower than in 1986, remained nonetheless relatively rapid (around 7 per cent on average for the year). Improved real trade performance impacted positively on the manufacturing sector. Manufacturing output and productivity growth were both

11

Diagram 1. **REAL GNP, DOMESTIC DEMAND AND NET EXPORTS**

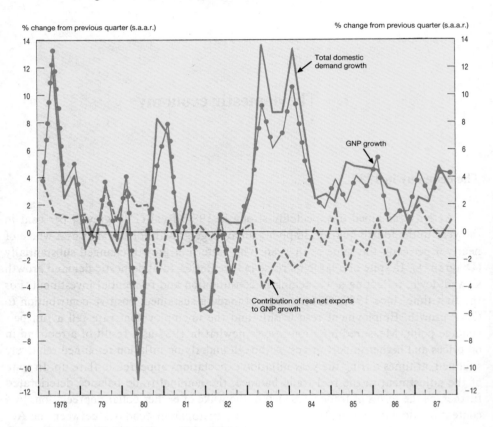

% change from previous quarter (s.a.a.r.)   % change from previous quarter (s.a.a.r.)

Source: Department of Commerce, *Survey of Current Business.*

strong as capacity utilisation returned to its 1984 peak (Table 1 and Diagram 2). The increase in manufacturing output accounted for more than one-third of the rise in real GNP and the major part of the productivity improvement.

The recovery in the manufacturing sector partly explains the rebound in business fixed investment from mid-1987, following two years of relative weakness (Table 2 and Diagram 3). Investment in petroleum processing and oil extraction steadied after its 1986 fall, while construction activity, which had been adversely affected by the higher effective tax rate on rental property investment contained in the Tax Reform

12

Diagram 2. **THE RECOVERY IN MANUFACTURING**

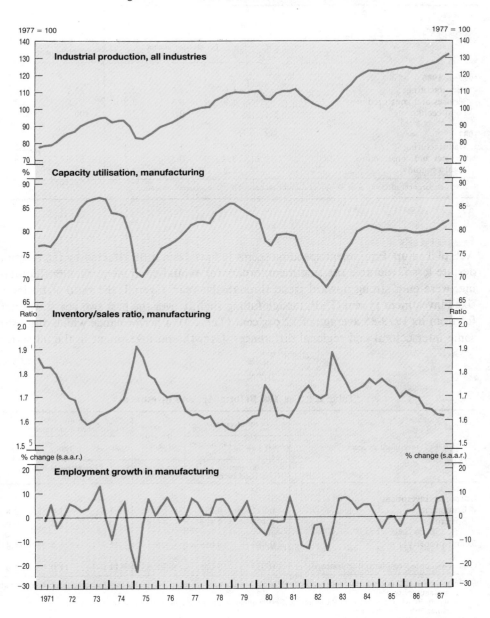

Source: Council of Economic Advisors, *Economic Trends.*

13

Table 1. **The sources of GNP growth**

	Employment	Output per employee	GNP	Contribution to GNP growth	Share of GNP
	Per cent per annum (year-on-year)			Per cent	
1979 to 1986					
Manufacturing	−1.5	3.7	2.2	22.1	21.8
Services and construction	1.9	0.3	2.2	77.9	78.2
Total economy	1.5	0.7	2.2	100	100
1987					
Manufacturing	0.6	3.7	4.3	32.4	22.2
Services and construction	3.0	−0.5	2.5	67.6	77.8
Total economy	2.6	0.3	2.9	100	100

Source: Department of Commerce; *Survey of Current Business;* OECD Secretariat estimates.

Act, picked up. Equipment spending seems to have been little affected by the reform, despite less favourable tax treatment; orders for capital equipment, though fluctuating, were on a strong upward trend through the year. Overall, the ratio of business fixed investment to real GNP, though falling slightly over the past two years, was not far from its 1979-85 average of 12 per cent (Table 3), a performance which disguises some intersectoral and regional differences. Growth and investment in the oil states

Table 2. **The Tax Reform Act and investment**

Investment category	Cost of capital		Change in the cost of capital	Growth rate of investment (volume)[1]		
	1981 Law	Tax Reform Act		1981-1985	1986	1987
	Proportion of purchase price		%	Percentage change per annum		
Corporate investment[2]						
Equipment	0.211	0.233	10.4	5.8	2.9	2.8
Structures	0.126	0.125	−0.8	0.6	−12.8	−4.6
Rental property[3]	0.086	0.099	15.1	15.3	−6.5	−24.4
Owner-occupied residential investment[4]	0.035	0.045	28.6	11.0	11.0	−3.0

1. Investment at 1982 prices for corporate sector; single family housing starts for owner-occupied investment; multi-family housing starts for rental property.
2. Assuming 30 per cent leverage: in the average U.S. firm about 70 per cent of its borrowing is equity-financed.
3. Assuming 70 per cent leverage.
4. Average marginal tax bracket.
Source: Department of Commerce and OECD Secretariat estimates.

Table 3. **Domestic and foreign saving**

Percentage of GNP

	1979	1984	1985	1986	1987	Change 1979-1987
Gross private saving	**17.8**	**18.4**	**16.6**	**16.1**	**15.0**	**− 2.8**
General government balance	0.5	− 2.9	− 3.3	− 3.5	− 2.4	− 2.9
of which:						
Federal budget balance	− 0.6	− 4.6	− 4.9	− 4.5	− 3.4	− 2.8
Gross domestic saving	**18.3**	**15.5**	**13.3**	**12.6**	**12.6**	**− 5.7**
Gross private investment	18.1	17.9	16.0	15.8	16.0	− 2.1
Domestic surplus/deficit	**0.2**	**− 2.4**	**− 2.6**	**− 3.2**	**− 3.4**	**− 3.6**
Net foreign saving[1]	**0.0**	**2.8**	**2.9**	**3.4**	**3.5**	**− 3.5**
Memorandum items:						
Household saving ratio						
(Per cent of disposable income)	6.8	6.1	4.5	4.3	3.8	− 3.3
Real business fixed investment, gross	12.2	12.1	12.6	12.0	11.7	− 0.5

1. Equal to external current account with the opposite sign. Net domestic dis-savings is equal to net foreign saving plus errors and omissions.
Source: Department of Commerce, *Survey of Current Business.*

and the agricultural mid-west have lagged behind, whereas activity and capital spending in New England have been booming.

Changes in inventories were a major contributor to growth in 1987. Inventory accumulation accounted for around one half of the total increase in real GNP in the year to the fourth quarter and for nearly one-third of the average growth for the year. The inventory build-up was particularly large in the fourth quarter, as production continued to expand strongly in spite of the weakening in consumer spending and non-residential fixed investment. Nevertheless, inventory-to-sales ratios at end-year did not suggest a widespread overhang of undesired stocks: excess accumulation seemed to be confined to certain segments of the retail market, such as cars, appliances and clothing.

Personal consumption expenditure grew relatively fast in the middle quarters of 1987, but fell significantly in the fourth quarter in the aftermath of the stock market crisis. Overall, the growth in real consumer spending decelerated substantially in 1987, falling to 1.9 per cent on average for the year and coming almost to a standstill throughout the year. Nonetheless, private consumption expanded faster than real disposable incomes, which were depressed by the faster rise in consumer prices and

Diagram 3. **FIXED INVESTMENT**

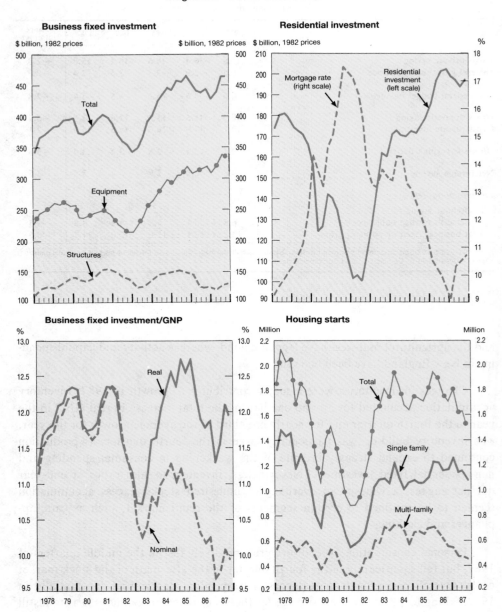

Business fixed investment

$ billion, 1982 prices $ billion, 1982 prices

Total

Equipment

Structures

Residential investment

$ billion, 1982 prices   %

Mortgage rate
(right scale)

Residential
investment
(left scale)

Business fixed investment/GNP

%   %

Real

Nominal

1978 79 80 81 82 83 84 85 86 87

Housing starts

Million   Million

Total

Single family

Multi-family

1978 79 80 81 82 83 84 85 86 87

Source: Department of Commerce, *Survey of Current Business.*

16

Table 4. **Accounting for growth in private consumption**[1]

Growth rates, per cent per annum

	Real consumption growth	Due to			
		Employment growth	Real income growth	Tax changes	Saving ratio
1981 Q4 - 1985 Q4	4.2	1.1	1.9	0.3	0.9
1985 Q4 - 1986 Q4	4.1	2.3	1.4	− 0.2	0.6
1986 Q4 - 1987 Q4	0.7	2.7	− 0.4	− 0.3	− 1.3
1981 Q4 - 1987 Q4	3.6	1.6	1.4	0.1	0.5

1. Calculated as:
    $c = e + (y - e) + (y^d - y) \pm (c - y^d)$,
    where c = the growth in real consumption; y = growth of real personal income; y^d = growth of real disposable income; e = growth of civilian employment.
    Source: OECD Secretariat estimates.

higher tax payments (Table 4). A declining household saving ratio has been a marked feature of the last four years: it halved, from 6 to 3 per cent, between the end of 1984 and the middle quarters of 1987, before recovering somewhat in the fourth quarter. The wealth gains implied by the rising stock market up to October were probably a major factor behind this development (see Annex I), although financial incentives offered by auto companies have also contributed to increased consumer expenditures. The ratio of household debt to disposable income continued to rise in 1987, even though tax deductibility on consumer debt interest payments was being phased out in accordance with the Tax Reform Act. Some of the substantial increase in mortgage debt seems to have been used to finance consumption, as many households switched from consumer credit to home-equity loans.

The Federal deficit averaged just under 5 per cent of GNP between 1982 and 1986 (Table 3). Allowing for the state and local surplus, the general government deficit was 3 to 3½ per cent of GNP in this period, a figure which is not out of line with that in other major OECD countries, but large compared both to private saving and to past experience. 1987 saw a major improvement, in the form of a 1½ per-centage point decline in the Federal deficit, due in part to the effects of the Tax Reform Act. But the general government deficit fell by somewhat less because the state and local sector recorded an unusually large deficit on operating and capital accounts. Overall, the growth in real government consumption decelerated from 3.8 per cent in 1986 to 2.5 per cent in 1987.

Real residential investment fell by nearly 2½ per cent throughout 1987, implying little change on average for the year. The housing sector was negatively influenced by

Diagram 4. **EMPLOYMENT PERFORMANCE**

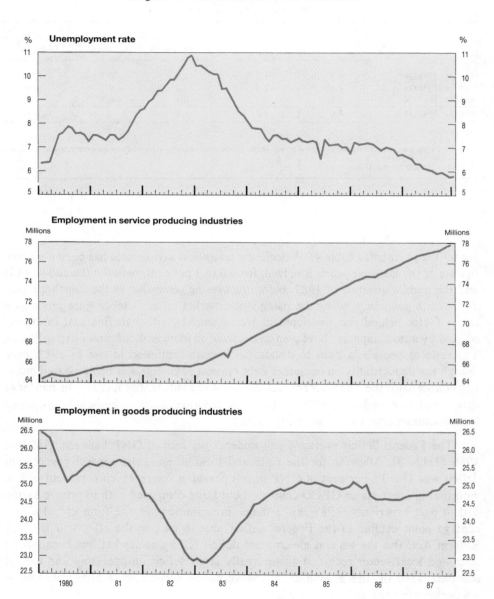

% **Unemployment rate**   %

Employment in service producing industries

Millions   Millions

Employment in goods producing industries

Millions   Millions

Source: Council of Economic Advisors, *Economic Indicators.*

18

rising interest rates, as mortgage rates rose from 9 per cent in early 1987 to 11.6 per cent by mid-October. Moreover, in the multi-family sector demand for housing was depressed by high vacancy rates and the reduced attractiveness of rental property resulting from the Tax Reform Act. However, the level of investment remained relatively high, and as a share of GNP was well above the average experience of the previous 20 years.

Labour market, productivity and inflation

Total employment grew quickly, by 2.8 per cent, in 1987, leading to a further decline in the unemployment rate to 5.7 per cent by year end (Diagram 4). Although the buoyancy of the service sector remained the main factor behind job creation, manufacturing employment, which had fallen between 1984 and 1986, reversed direction and began to expand. Employment in manufacturing accounted for an eighth (400 thousand out of 3 million) of jobs created during the course of the year, a contribution which rose to a fifth of all new jobs in the second half.

Wages (measured by total compensation per hour) have continued to grow slowly (Diagram 5). Despite the pick-up of activity in manufacturing, employment and capacity utilisation in the goods-producing sector remained below their previous cyclical peaks, probably helping to restrain wage demands. However, some areas of the service sector seem to have experienced an acceleration in wage increases, due to localised labour shortages. Overall, the employment cost index rose by only $3^{1}/_{4}$ per cent in 1987, almost the same rate as in 1986. Major collective bargaining settlements, including those in the auto industry, have remained a little below this, providing for a 2 per cent annual increase in wage rates over the life of the wage contract (usually three years). This moderation in wage growth has restrained the rise in unit labour costs, despite sluggish productivity growth in the non-farm business sector. (Output per hour rose only 0.9 per cent in 1987, down from 1.6 per cent the year before.) However, productivity performance in the manufacturing sector was considerably stronger – continuing the trend of recent years – and so international competitiveness was enhanced by falling unit labour costs.

Because of the fall in oil prices and the general softness in import prices, 1986 had been exceptionally favourable as far as inflation was concerned. The consumer price deflator rose by only $2^{1}/_{4}$ per cent. As oil prices rose and the effect of the dollar depreciation began to be felt on import prices, consumer price inflation accelerated to nearly 5 per cent in the first half of 1987, before falling back to $4^{1}/_{4}$ per cent in the second half. However, the GNP deflator, which does not incorporate import costs, increased more slowly – at about 3 per cent throughout the year – which was only

Diagram 5. **WAGE AND PRICE TRENDS**[1]

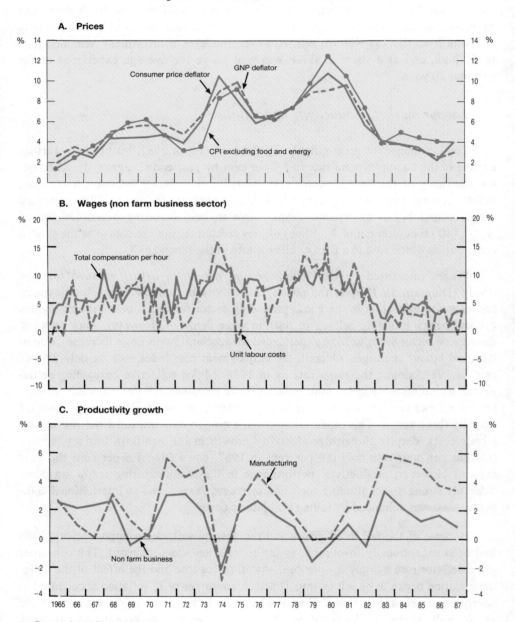

A. Prices

Consumer price deflator
GNP deflator
CPI excluding food and energy

B. Wages (non farm business sector)

Total compensation per hour
Unit labour costs

C. Productivity growth

Manufacturing
Non farm business

1965 66 67 68 69 70 71 72 73 74 75 76 77 78 79 80 81 82 83 84 85 86 87

1. Percent change from previous year.
Source: Department of Commerce, *Survey of Current Business.*

slightly up on the 1986 increase. This stability was partly a result of the swing towards goods in the composition of final output, and masked a marked difference between the performance of the service and manufacturing sectors. Whilst the price of manufacturing output has hardly risen since 1984, and the deflator for non-financial corporate business output has increased by less than 2 per cent a year, the price of services has been increasing at a 4 per cent average rate.

Corporate profits and the stock market

Between 1982 and 1986 the value of the stock market doubled (Diagram 6). The factors behind this rise are, of course, difficult to quantify directly, but probably relate to trends in after-tax profits, interest rates and inflation. Profits per unit of output rose sharply, partly because unit labour costs were better controlled, partly because the 1981 tax reform reduced company taxation (Table 5). Over the same period bond yields declined substantially, from about 13 per cent (AAA) in the first years of the decade, to 9 per cent in 1986. Inflation was also significantly reduced. Provided these changes were thought to be permanent, a significant rise in stock market values was justified.

The bull market continued into 1987 in the face of a reversal of at least some of the above fundamentals. In the first place, the Tax Reform Act (TRA) altered the structure of taxation in a way which was unfavourable to stocks: the average tax rate

Table 5. **Costs, profit margins and prices**

Non-financial corporate business	Total cost and profit[1]	Corporate profit margin[2]		Compensation of employees	Depreciation, etc.[3]
		Gross	After-tax		
	Current-dollar cost and profit per unit of output (in cents, 1982 = 100)				
1981	94.6	7.8	4.4	63.2	19.2
1985	107.3	10.7	7.4	70.2	19.0
1986	108.9	10.3	6.8	71.5	20.3
1987	111.4	11.0	6.1	72.8	21.7
	Annual average percentage change				
1981-1985[3]	3.2	8.2	13.9	2.7	0.2
1986	1.5	3.7	− 8.1	1.9	6.8
1987	2.1	1.9	− 11.0	1.9	6.9

1. Equal to the deflator for GDP in the non-financial corporate business sector.
2. Net of inventory valuation and capital consumption adjustments.
3. Capital consumption allowances with adjustments, net interest and indirect taxes.
Sources: Department of Commerce (Bureau of Economic Analysis), Department of Labor (Bureau of Labor Statistics) and OECD Secretariat estimates.

21

Diagram 6. **SHARE PRICES AND BOND YIELDS**

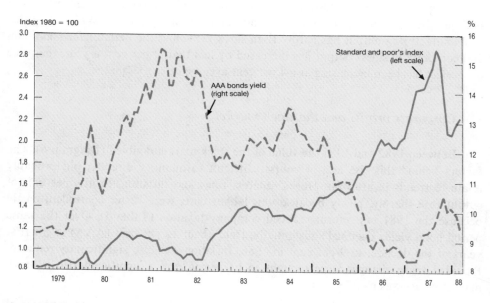

Source: Council of Economic Advisors, *Economic Trends.*

on corporate profits rose and the rate of income tax on capital gains increased. Second, and perhaps most important, bond yields were on a rising trend from the beginning of the year, partly because of rising inflation expectations. Stock market confidence began to ebb from mid-August onwards and on 19th October, after a string of large declines, the Dow Jones Industrial Average lost 22.6 per cent in a single day. The total value of the U.S. stock market had fallen by over $500 billion in the week of the crash, most of which represented the elimination of gains made in 1987: the index actually ended the year quite close to its year-earlier level. The damage to the financial system seems to have been relatively minor (see the chapter on financial markets), but because wealth effects stemming from the stock market rise were an important element in consumer confidence – which was at a peak just before the stock market crisis – the economic impact of the October fall was expected to be deflationary. The response of the economy to this wealth loss is discussed in the section on short-term prospects and risks.

22

The current expansion in perspective

Overview

The current expansion phase which follows the worst recession since the 1930s (in 1981 and 1982) has now become the longest in U.S. peacetime history. This has been accompanied by rapid increases in living standards, strong employment growth and a marked decline in the unemployment rate, to its lowest level since 1979. While productivity growth has remained below that achieved during the early post-war years, a substantial improvement over the period between the two oil shocks has been achieved. In contrast to past upturns prices and wages have shown little evidence of accelerating late in the expansion. Other important differences from earlier cyclical episodes have been the presence of large fiscal deficits, sharp fluctuations in the exchange rate of the dollar and the continued build-up of the current account deficit. In other words, the behaviour of saving and investment balances has considerably departed from normal patterns.

Output and living standards

Since the recovery began, real GNP has grown at an annual rate of 4.2 per cent, a performance broadly similar to that in previous U.S. post-war expansions, but significantly better than that of other large OECD countries, with the exception of Canada. During the current expansion, real manufacturing output has expanded faster than real GNP, offsetting the effects of the previous recession and bringing its share in real GNP close to its previous peak in 1973 (23 per cent). Viewed in a long-term perspective, manufacturing has not lost ground to other sectors of the economy and its share of total value added has remained remarkably stable. Rapid economic growth has gone hand in hand with rising living standards; real GNP per capita has grown at an average annual rate of 3.2 per cent during the current expansion, reflecting both accelerated productivity growth and increases in the proportion of the working age population employed.

Employment and unemployment

Employment growth has been faster in the current expansion (2.7 per cent annual rate) than the average in past cyclical upturns (2.5 per cent) and much stronger than in other major Member countries. In the five years to December 1987, total employment has increased by 15 million and the proportion of working-age population employed has risen to a record 62.3 per cent. Factors behind this good performance have been analysed in detail in the last OECD *Survey of the United States*

23

(November 1986). Gains have benefited all major demographic groups and have been particularly large for minority groups. They have also been widespread geographically, as total employment increased in all but three States. Contrary to popular assertions, there is no evidence that employment gains have taken place at the expense of job quality. Employment growth seems to have occurred in lower as well as higher paying occupations. Shifts in job opportunities across sectors have continued to take place, in line with post-war trends. The share of employment in service-producing industries has risen steadily to about 75 per cent in 1987, whereas that of the manufacturing sector has declined to 19 per cent.

Since the start of the current recovery, the unemployment rate declined by 4.9 percentage points to 5.7 per cent in December 1987, its lowest level since July 1979. Unemployment rates for men and women have fallen by 5.4 and 4.3 percentage points respectively, a greater reduction than in any other post-war expansion. Unemployment rates for black males and females have decreased by 9.9 and 6.1 percentage points respectively; nonetheless, those rates remained twice as large as the average for all civilian workers. Total youth unemployment declined by 8 percentage points to 16.1 per cent, its lowest level since 1979, but roughly one-third of black teenagers in the labour force were still without jobs. The average length of unemployment was also reduced, the mean duration declining from more than 20 weeks in 1983 to 14.2 weeks in December 1987. While unemployment has fallen across regions, substantial regional differences in unemployment rates still prevailed in 1987. Unemployment rates were relatively low along the east coast, especially New England, but were substantially above the national average in parts of the south and the west, particularly the oil-producing states.

Prices and wages

In spite of the substantial reduction in the unemployment rate, price inflation has shown little evidence of accelerating late in the expansion. The rise in the GNP deflator decelerated steadily from 1981 to 1985. If adjusted for fluctuations in energy prices, it probably stabilised at slightly below 3 per cent in the two years to 1987, a rate comparable to the average of other large OECD countries. Although the dollar has depreciated sharply since early 1985, underlying consumer price inflation has hovered at around 4 per cent, only slightly higher than the OECD average. Wage and earnings developments have also remained remarkably stable despite a decline in the unemployment rate. Over the last three years, average weekly earnings in private non-agricultural industries rose between 2 and 2½ per cent and the growth in total compensation per employee decelerated to less than 3 per cent. In regions with relatively low unemployment rates, wage increases have been somewhat higher, but no signs of significant acceleration have appeared. These developments, aided by favourable demographic trends, suggest that the unemployment rate could fall further from its present level without triggering an acceleration in the inflation rate[1].

Saving and investment balances

Typically, in a cyclical expansion phase the private saving-investment balance deteriorates as investment usually increases faster than saving. The government balance generally improves as revenues tend to grow more rapidly than expenditure. Overall, since the private saving-investment balance is generally more influenced by the cyclical upturn than the government position, the external balance tends to deteriorate somewhat, leading to an increase in net capital inflows (i.e. net foreign saving). In the current expansion, the behaviour has been somewhat atypical. As in the past, the private saving-investment balance deteriorated in the four years to 1986 but the government deficit did not decline in spite of the strong recovery. This situation was more than accounted for by the persistence of large Federal deficits. In 1987, the Federal deficit declined substantially (by over 1½ per cent of GNP). However, the private saving-investment balance also fell considerably, reflecting both a marked reduction in the personal saving ratio and an increase in gross private domestic investment, largely due to higher stockbuilding. Thus, despite the decline in the government deficit and improvement in the real trade balance, the current external deficit continued to widen. Balance of payments adjustment is the subject of the next section.

II.   The balance of payments

The rise and fall of the dollar

The trade-weighted value of the dollar reached a peak in early March 1985, at 45 per cent above its average 1980 level[2]. By February 1987, when the Louvre accord was announced, it had fallen back to its 1980 level – an effective depreciation of 31 per cent (Diagram 7). The accord (discussed more fully in the next section) did not

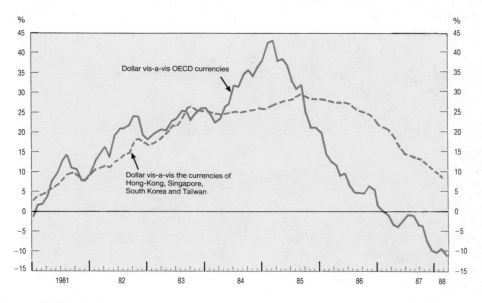

Diagram 7.   **EXCHANGE RATES OF THE DOLLAR**
Percentage variations from average 1980 levels

Source: OECD Secretariat.

halt the dollar's fall, but slowed it. The initial response was one of "wait-and-see" on the part of foreign investors; the second, beginning at the end of March, was a further bout of dollar weakness. There followed more than two months of relative strength, during the early summer, but downward pressure was renewed after the announcement of a record June trade deficit in mid-August. This pressure continued sporadically until mid-October, when the effective value of the dollar had fallen to 4 per cent below its Louvre level; pressure increased in the wake of the stock market fall and by year's end the dollar had declined 12 per cent from its Louvre parity and 40 per cent from its peak (Table 6).

Table 6. **Movements in the dollar**

| | Exchange rate as at 28th to 31st December 1987 Percentage changes since: | | | | | |
	Louvre Agreement[1]	End 1986	Plaza Agreement[2]	$ Peak[3]	End 1980	1973-1980 average
Dollar-effective	− 12.15	− 15.82	− 34.11	− 39.48	− 12.15	− 16.07
vis-à-vis YEN	− 19.93	− 22.97	− 49.16	− 52.82	− 39.88	− 52.67
vis-à-vis DM	− 12.78	− 17.86	− 45.08	− 53.18	− 18.74	− 44.64
vis-à-vis FF	− 11.10	− 15.91	− 38.99	− 48.27	18.84	19.07
vis-à-vis £	− 18.24	− 21.02	− 27.90	− 42.96	27.53	11.46
Memorandum item:						
Dollar effective rate, index 28th-31st December = 100	113.8	118.8	151.8	165.2	113.8	119.1

1. 16th to 20th February 1987.
2. 16th to 20th September 1985.
3. 4th to 8th March 1985.
Source: OECD Secretariat estimates.

Vis-a-vis the major currencies, the decline in the dollar has been greatest against the Yen and Deutschemark (its value more than halving from 261 Yen at the peak to 123 Yen at last year-end and from DM 3.40 to DM 1.59). Depreciation against the other EMS members has been a little less (a 48 per cent fall against the French franc, from over FF 10.43 to FF 5.39) with the rate against sterling easing by 43 per cent (from $1.07 to $1.87 to the pound). On the other hand, the dollar has depreciated only marginally against the Canadian dollar, while the currencies of Korea, Taiwan,

Hong Kong and Singapore, whose trade with the United States now accounts for a significant part of the external deficit, have collectively experienced a 15 per cent appreciation since early 1985[3].

Current account deterioration

Both the current account and the trade balance were in deficit by about $160 billion in 1987 (Table 7). This was equivalent to about 60 per cent of merchandise export receipts. Over one-third of the 1987 merchandise deficit was on trade with Japan; the newly industrialised economies in Asia (NICs) accounted for a fifth and Germany a further tenth. These economies, in aggregate, provide a market for a quarter of U.S. exports, while accounting for two-thirds of the trade deficit. Because of the uneven distribution of the deficit, there has been a tendency by some in the United States to blame unfair trading practices, American "deindustrialisation" or a shift in U.S. preferences towards certain types of consumer electronic goods and autos for its persistence. There is little doubt that bilateral imbalances of this order complicate the adjustment process. However, the *deterioration* in trade balances has been rather general in geographical terms (the deficit with Japan is a long-standing phenomenon) so that bilateral imbalances should not divert attention from the macro-economic fundamentals behind the generation of the trade deficit, which are both domestic and external.

Table 7. **Current account and bilateral trade balances**

	1981	1982	1983	1984	1985	1986	1987
				$ billion			
Balance of payments trends							
Current balance	6.3	− 9.1	− 46.6	− 106.5	− 118.4	− 141.4	− 160.7
Trade balance	− 28.0	− 36.4	− 67.1	− 112.5	− 122.1	− 144.3	− 159.2

	Total	Japan	Germany	Asian NICs	Canada	Rest of OECD	Other
				Percentage of total			
Bilateral trade in 1987[1]							
Trade deficit as percentage of total deficit	100.0	36.8	10.1	21.0	11.1	5.2	15.8
Share in U.S. exports	100.0	10.7	4.9	9.1	22.8	24.1	28.4
Share in U.S. imports	100.0	21.0	7.0	13.8	18.2	16.7	23.3

1. 1987, first half.
Source: Treasury, Office of Balance of Payments; Department of Commerce, and OECD Secretariat estimates.

The macroeconomic origins of the trade deficit

Between 1981 and 1985 the volume share of merchandise exports in GNP fell by 2 percentage points, while the import volume/GNP ratio rose by over 3 percentage points (Table 8). The nominal trade balance deteriorated by $92 billion and the real (merchandise) trade balance by $119 billion. Trade models, such as that embedded in the OECD's INTERLINK, ascribe the appearance of the deficit essentially to the appreciation of the dollar (which is not fully explained by such models) and to the

Table 8. **Export and import performance**[1,2]

Per cent of non-financial corporate sector GDP

| | Ratio to GDP | | | Change in volume ratio | | |
| | | | | | Due to: | |
	Value	Volume	Total	Market growth[3]	Market structure	Trade performance
Exports						
1981	13.7	13.0				
1985	9.7	10.9	− 2.1	+ 0.5	− 0.8	− 1.8
1986	9.5	11.2	+ 0.3	+ 0.2	− 0.1	+ 0.3
1987	10.2	12.4	+ 1.2	+ 0.1	—	+ 1.1
Imports						
1981	15.3	14.1				
1985	14.9	17.4	+ 3.3	+ 2.5	n.a.	0.8
1986	15.5	19.3	+ 1.9	+ 1.7	n.a.	0.1
1987	16.3	19.6	+ 0.3	+ 0.4	n.a.	− 0.1

Memorandum items:

| | Growth rates (annual averages, per cent) | | |
	1981 to 1985	1985 to 1987	1986 to 1987
Real total domestic demand			
United States	3.8	3.0	2.1
OECD *less* United States	2.0	3.6	3.5
Export market growth			
World exports	4.8	3.9	4.1
Market for U.S. exports[3]	3.1	3.5	4.5
Relative prices[4]			
Relative export prices	+ 19.1	− 22.3	− 9.4
Relative import prices	− 23.3	+ 2.6	+ 1.5

1. For methodology, see Annex II.
2. Merchandise trade, NIPA definition.
3. Based on the import growth in U.S. export markets, weighted by U.S. manufactured exports in 1981.
4. Relative export unit values and import unit values/domestic demand deflator, respectively.
Source: OECD Secretariat estimates based on NIPA data.

29

Diagram 8. **INDICATORS OF COMPETITIVENESS**

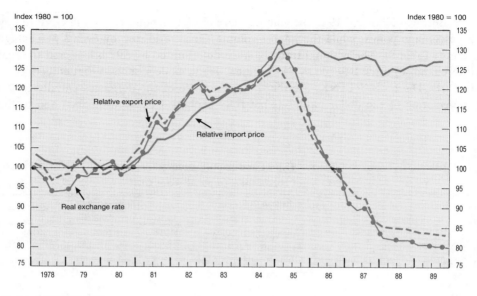

Index 1980 = 100

Index 1980 = 100

Source: OECD Secretariat.

fact that the U.S. grew faster than its trading partners[4]. The real exchange rate (expressed as relative unit labour costs measured in dollars) appreciated by 24 per cent from 1980 to 1985 (Diagram 8). Relative manufactured export prices rose by 19 per cent, which may have accounted for a deterioration of $49 billion in U.S. export performance according to the OECD INTERLINK model (Diagram 9). Relative import prices declined by 23 per cent, explaining about $15 billion of the increase in manufacturing import volumes[5]. Altogether, the OECD model attributes about $64 billion of the $119 billion increase in the real merchandise trade deficit to the effect of relative price changes on trade volumes. This leaves a further $55 billion due to other factors, including the fact that total domestic demand in the U.S. grew faster than in its main trading partners, as a result of the slow growth in the rest of the OECD and third world debt problems. An erosion of world agricultural markets may also have played a part[6].

Tables 8 and 9 provide a check on the model-simulation conclusions by analysing changes in U.S. manufactured trade shares. The fall in the share of manufactured exports in non-financial corporate sector GDP is allocated to three factors (see Annex II):

30

Diagram 9. **THE EFFECTS OF RELATIVE PRICE CHANGES ON MANUFACTURED TRADE**

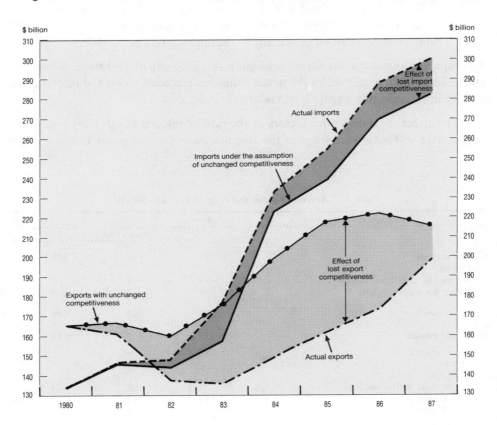

Source: OECD Secretariat estimates.

- *Market growth* (i.e. world trade expansion) would normally be expected to exceed U.S. and world GNP growth. This was the case in the 1981-85 period, but because the U.S. grew rapidly compared with the rest of the world, the expansion in world trade was not much greater than domestic output, and so this factor did not boost the export share of GNP by much (only $11 billion);
- *Market structure* (the relative concentration of U.S. exports on fast- or slow-growing markets) worked against the United States during the same period; the growth of markets which traditionally depend on the U.S. for supplies (such as Mexico) was slower than average. This had a negative impact on U.S. exports equivalent to an export loss of $18 billion;

31

- *Export performance* as measured by the difference between the growth of U.S. export markets and growth of U.S. exports to those markets accounted for a further, significant, export loss of $39 billion between 1981 and 1985, which can be ascribed principally to the appreciation of the dollar.

Although the loss of market share was significant, U.S. export performance was $10 billion better than predicted by the model estimates recorded above and incorporated in Diagram 9, so in this respect it was relatively good.

The effect of relative price factors on the ratio of imports to GNP are impossible to calculate without a knowledge of the relevant trade elasticities, so Tables 8 and 9

Table 9. **Accounting for the current account deficit**[1]

Contribution to deficit = (−)	1981 to 1985	1986	1987
	Change $ billion		
Current account	− 124	− 23	− 19
of which:			
Change in investment income	− 13	− 4	− 6
Other net service income	− 19	+ 3	− 3
Trade balance[2]	− 92	− 22	− 10
Real trade balance	− 119	− 7	+ 13
Volume effects			
due to:			
Exports:			
Export performance	− 39 ⎫	+ 9 ⎫	+ 23 ⎫
Export demand	+ 11 ⎬ − 46	+ 3 ⎬ + 8	+ 3 ⎬ + 27
Export market structure	− 18 ⎭	− 4 ⎭	+ 1 ⎭
Imports:			
Import performance	− 15 ⎫ − 70	− 3 ⎫ − 41	+ 1 ⎫ − 8
Import demand	− 55 ⎭	− 38 ⎭	− 9 ⎭
Price effects			
due to:			
Export price decline	− 46 ⎫ + 32	− 13 ⎫ + 15	− 2 ⎫ − 21
Import prices	+ 78 ⎭	+ 28 ⎭	− 19 ⎭
Level effect[3]	− 8	− 4	− 8
Memorandum items:			
Effect of competitiveness	− 54	+ 6	+ 24
Relative growth etc.	− 65	− 43	− 11
Prices	+ 27	+ 15	− 23

1. For methodology, see Annex II.
2. Merchandise trade, NIPA definition.
3. The effect on the deficit if exports and imports grew at the same rate. A negative indicates that imports exceeded exports in the base period.
Source: OCDE Secretariat estimates.

record the relative price and demand effects calculated from the INTERLINK model (as in Diagram 9):

- *Relative import price changes* accounted for an increase in import volumes of $15 billion, principally because of the long lags incorporated into the import equation and the relatively low import price elasticity incorporated in the OECD model;
- *Import demand*, measured by the extent to which import volumes grew faster than GNP, added $55 billion to the deficit.

Offsetting the effect of relative price changes during the 1981 to 1985 period were the favourable terms of trade effects resulting from the appreciation of the dollar. Although the ratio of import volumes to U.S. GNP increased significantly, the import share of current-dollar GNP actually fell slightly because of lower dollar import prices, so that the change in the value of imports, relative to GNP was negligible. On the other hand, deteriorating export performance was exacerbated by an unfavourable export price trend, so that the net negative contribution from the export side was $92 billion – exactly accounting for the overall deficit increase.

The persistence of the deficit

Explaining the persistence of the deficit in the dollar depreciation phase is somewhat more difficult. Although the U.S. has regained export shares, the import volume correction has been slower than expected, and the ratio of imports to GNP has continued to rise (Table 8). Forecasting models had tended to predict a faster turn-round than has occurred since the dollar began its fall. But for depreciation to affect trade volumes, relative prices have first to change and this stage of the adjustment may have been insufficient, or delayed. When price changes occur they may temporarily swamp the volume response (the so-called "J-curve" effect). And once the process of substituting domestic for foreign supplies has started, the income- and investment-generating effects of higher export earnings will have domestic demand effects which pull in more imports, muting the improvement in the trade balance.

Depreciation and the import price pass-through

The pass-through into import prices as the dollar has declined has been slow and incomplete, delaying the needed import volume adjustment and implying the persistence of attenuated "J-curve" effects well beyond their normal time scale. Foreign manufacturers appear to have absorbed a substantial part of the decline in the value

Table 10. "J-Curve" effects on the merchandise trade deficit

A. IMPORT AND EXPORT PRICES[1]

Index, 1985 Q1 = 100

		Non-oil imports			Exports		
		$ prices	Foreign currency prices	Exchange rate[2]	$ prices	Foreign currency prices	Exchange rate[2]
1985	Q1	100	100	100	100	100	100
	Q2	100.3	96.8	96.5	100	96.5	96.5
	Q3	100.7	94.2	93.6	99.0	92.8	93.8
	Q4	103.0	89.9	87.2	99.2	88.4	89.1
1986	Q1	106.6	87.7	82.2	99.5	84.8	85.3
	Q2	107.8	86.8	80.5	99.2	83.6	84.3
	Q3	110.9	85.6	77.2	97.5	79.9	82.0
	Q4	111.7	86.8	77.7	98.7	81.2	82.3
1987	Q1	114.4	84.1	73.5	99.7	77.8	78.1
	Q2	117.3	84.3	71.9	102.5	79.0	77.1
	Q3	118.8	84.5	71.1	102.8	78.4	76.3
	Q4	122.4	82.3	67.2	105.5	76.8	72.8

B. EFFECTS ON THE DEFICIT

$ billion, cumulated

[Contribution to deficit = (+)]

		Change in deficit	Price effects[3]		Volume effects		Rise in oil imports
			Non-oil import price increase	Export price decline	Rise in non-oil import volumes	Rise in export volumes	
1985	Q1	0.0	0.0	0.0	0.0	0.0	0.0
	Q2	21.7	− 0.8	1.8	9.9	1.6	9.2
	Q3	26.5	− 1.2	4.7	14.7	2.3	5.9
	Q4	46.7	0.5	7.2	26.9	− 0.8	12.9
1986	Q1	36.8	2.7	7.9	32.3	− 3.6	− 2.5
	Q2	40.0	7.0	9.5	42.3	− 5.9	− 12.9
	Q3	53.2	10.1	14.5	55.6	− 15.2	− 11.8
	Q4	54.6	13.9	16.3	58.8	− 23.0	− 11.4
1987	Q1	54.0	15.7	14.4	57.5	− 25.0	− 8.6
	Q2	57.9	20.6	13.5	63.1	− 35.9	− 3.4
	Q3	58.0	23.0	12.9	70.0	− 55.1	7.2
	Q4	56.3	27.2	14.3	80.9	− 69.4	3.3

1. Data relate to March, June, September and December.
2. Weighted respectively by import and export trade in each product category.
3. Based on national income accounts deflator (which differ from A).
Source: A. Bureau of Labour statistics; B. OECD Secretariat estimates.

of the dollar and, on average, have passed through only about one-half of the dollar's decline in higher prices for their U.S.-bound exports according to the Bureau of Labor Statistics[7]. Since the dollar began falling from its peak value in March 1985, dollar prices of imports (excluding fuels) have risen 22.4 per cent on average. If foreign manufacturers had attempted to compensate completely for the dollar's decline, and production costs had been unchanged, non-fuel import prices would have been raised by about 46 per cent. In the event foreign currency prices of foreign inputs (particularly raw materials) have fallen significantly; and even so foreign sellers have been willing to absorb a substantial part of the fall in the value of the dollar (Table 10)[8]. On the export side, the stability of the dollar-price index in conjunction with a sharp fall in foreign currency prices appears to imply that exporters have almost fully exploited the competitive advantage created by the depreciation of the dollar[9].

Table 10 examines the quarterly pattern of price and volume changes as they have affected the deficit since the beginning of 1985. On a simple accounting basis, it decomposes the quarterly change in the merchandise trade balance into five factors: non-oil import prices; export prices; non-oil import volumes; export volumes and the value of oil imports. The decomposition reveals that non-oil import prices boosted the trade deficit by only a small amount prior to the end of 1986, a slow and incomplete (40 per cent) passthrough, with a partial and delayed J-curve effect. However, non-oil import prices are only part of the story. Merchandise export prices (both total and non-agricultural) fell slightly until late 1986, adding, as in the 1981-85 period, to the external deficit. Together, export and import price changes account for about $40 billion of the trade deficit deterioration. Non-oil import volumes more than account for the rest, since increased export volumes and a lower oil bill have had a favourable influence.

The failure of both import and export prices to rise generated divergent trends in export and import competitiveness (Diagram 8). Depreciation has been fairly fully reflected in an improvement in the relative price of U.S. exports. But import prices rose by only 9 per cent, relative to domestic prices. To some extent, the behaviour of import prices may have reflected the growing importance of a small group of newly-industrialising economies – especially Taiwan and Korea – as major suppliers of manufactured goods, countries whose currencies collectively appreciated relatively little in relation to the dollar over the period (Diagram 7).

U.S. productivity and the real exchange rate

Even without the dollar's depreciation, importer's profit margins would have been under pressure because manufacturing unit labour costs have risen relatively

Table 11. **Productivity and labour cost increases in manufacturing**

Average annual percentage change 1984 to 1986

| | Hourly compensation | Output per hour | Unit labour costs | | Exchange rate change | |
			National currency	In dollars	Nominal[1] Vis-à-vis $	Real effective (Relative unit labour costs)
United States	**3.95**	**3.95**	**0**	**0**	**(−7.0)**	**−8.6**
Japan	4.2	5.05	−0.8	20.0	21.0	+13.5
Germany	4.9	3.15	1.7	18.4	16.4	+3.0
United Kingdom	7.6	3.25	4.2	9.6	5.2	−2.7
France	5.35	2.60	2.65	16.5	13.4	+1.9
Canada	3.75	0.85	2.85	−0.7	−3.45	−3.8

1. Change *vis-à-vis* the dollar, except for the dollar change, which is against a trade-weighted currency basket.
Source: Bureau of Labor statistics and OECD Secretariat estimates.

slowly in the United States (Table 11). This has meant that the real effective exchange rate has depreciated 1½ per cent a year faster than the nominal rate since 1984. Improved manufacturing productivity performance has been responsible. From 1979 to 1986, labour productivity in the U.S. manufacturing sector increased at an annual rate of 3.1 per cent: a return to the rate of increase registered in the 1960-73 period, whereas the recent trend in Europe has been towards lower productivity gains[10]. Productivity increases from 1984 to 1986 were second only to Japan. This improvement appears to be due to a large increase in total factor productivity (technological progress etc.) rather than additions to the capital stock or labour shedding; there has been an emphasis on improved management methods and production systems[11].

Export and import performance

Once allowance is made for the failure of dollar import and export prices to rise as expected, it appears that the volume effects of dollar depreciation have been fairly consistent with econometric evidence that U.S. manufactured goods elasticities (−0.8 for imports and −1.4 for exports) are high enough for depreciation to improve the current account[12]. The OECD INTERLINK model successfully "predicts" the trade balance outcome for the 1985 to 1987 period if actual import price and demand changes are used. According to the model, by 1987 a substantial part of the export share lost through appreciation had been recaptured; the larger fall in relative export prices is estimated to have generated an improvement in export volumes of about $30 billion between 1985 and 1987, which is close to the $32 billion export share gain noted in Table 9[13]. But because of the small rise in relative import prices and the lagged effects of the previous appreciation, the effect of currency adjustments should only have begun to raise import volumes in 1987 (Table 9).

Even so, the combination of small import volume gains and smaller than ex-pected rise in non-oil import prices could have been beneficial. It is sometimes argued that a higher pass-through into import prices was needed for depreciation to be effec-tive. This was probably the case for manufacturing output, but not necessarily for the current account. If, as suggested by INTERLINK estimates, import price elasticities are below unity and that for exports above, then the actual outcome of nearly full pass-through into foreign currency export prices and a relatively low import price pass-through into dollar prices has been favourable. If on the other hand (as es-timated by some other models) the "true" import price elasticity is actually above unity and that for exports only slightly lower than in the INTERLINK model, then a greater pass-through of the depreciation into import prices would have been ben-eficial.

Income effects

According to Table 9, the deterioration in the trade deficit between 1985 and 1987 is explained by the existing gap between imports and exports (which required that exports grew faster than imports in order to prevent the deficit getting worse) and a strong income-related growth of import volumes, amounting to $47 billion. Two factors were involved:

- The first was the unexpected buoyancy of domestic demand, which con-tinued to grow at the relatively robust rate of 3 per cent a year in real terms between 1985 and 1987 (and at a $3\frac{1}{2}$ per cent annual rate from the first quarter of 1985 to the end of 1987);
- The second was the relatively high income elasticity of demand for manufac-tured imports which seems to accompany U.S demand growth. According to some calculations this elasticity may be as high as 3, as compared to $1\frac{3}{4}$ to 2 for the other major seven economies.

Some of the reasons for the buoyancy of import demand are examined below, and in Annex III.

37

"Stock effects": growing external debt and debt interest

The external balance has also been negatively influenced by the "stock effects" of persistent deficits. The net investment position of the United States is estimated to have become negative by the end of 1985, foreign liabilities exceeding assets by $112 billion (Table 12). By the end of 1987, it may have reached a negative $400 billion – 9 per cent of GNP. However, the reported net foreign investment position of the United States may not accurately reflect the "true" position. There are two sources of potentially large errors. First, direct investment – ownership of a firm's equity in which the ownership share exceeds 10 per cent – is carried at historical value. Given the fact that the U.S. net direct investment position was until recently positive and large, valuation of the direct investment portion on a replacement cost basis is likely

Table 12.   **International investment position**

In billion dollars

	1980		1985		1986		1987	
	Official	Private	Official	Private	Official	Private	Official	Private
Net international investment position	106		− 112		− 264		− 403	
U.S. assets abroad	607		949		1 068		1 132	
	90	517	131	818	138	930	129	1 003
of which:								
Direct investment		215		230		260		298
Securities								
Bonds		44		73		80		} 135
Stocks		19		40		51		
Foreign assets in the U.S.	501		1 062		1 332		1 535	
	176	325	203	859	241	1 091	285	1 250
of which:								
Direct investment		83		185		209		250
Government securities	118	16	144	84	179	96	224	90
Corporate bonds		10		82		142		} 350
Stocks	—	65		124		167		
Memorandum items:								
Foreign holdings of public debt securities	16	1	8	6	9	6	11	5
(Percentage of total)	17		14		15		16	

Source: Department of Commerce (Bureau of Economic Analysis); OECD Secretariat estimates for 1987.

to produce estimates of the U.S. net investment position much higher than officially reported. Second, there have been sizeable statistical discrepancies in the balance-of-payments data which could represent unrecorded capital inflows. This would mean that the U.S. net investment position was more negative than recorded. Nevertheless, as a result of the accumulation of foreign debt, the traditional net interest surplus earned by the United States has been eroded, contributing $10 billion to the current account deterioration between 1985 and 1987. Although the full debt service cost depends on the way the current account is financed, as well as movements in the dollar (U.S. debt is, exceptionally, wholly denominated in domestic currency) a deficit of $100 billion gives rise to interest payments of about $6 billion a year at current average interest rates[14].

Fundamentals

The above analysis attributes the appearance of the deficit to the appreciation of the dollar and domestic demand growth differentials between the United States and its main trading partners, whilst its persistence is largely explained by a continued strong income-related demand for imports, together with an accumulating net interest burden. However, these are only proximate causes and a more complete understanding of the factors behind the deficit requires an analysis of the reasons for the saving and investment imbalance in the United States. According to a quite generally held view, the shift in fiscal policy in both the United States and abroad, together with the tightening of monetary policy that took place in the appreciation phase, can explain a substantial part (by some estimates, up to two-thirds) of the rise in the dollar and the widening of the external deficit[15]. However, holdings of U.S. corporate equities by non-residents more than doubled to around $125 billion, as did direct investment, so that it appears that capital inflows were also attracted by the enhanced investment opportunities available in the United States. No single factor was responsible for the dollar's appreciation[16]. In any case, a simplistic link between fiscal policy and the external deficit (the so-called "twin deficit" problem) has broken down since 1985, since the external deficit has risen as the federal deficit fell. This issue is returned to in the discussion on saving and investment balances in the section on fiscal policy.

III. The policy environment

Monetary and exchange rate policies

Monetary strategy

One of the attractions of monetary targeting from an operational point of view was that it offered to make interest rate adjustments less discretionary and more automatic. Moreover, given what was thought to be (by many analysts) a reliable link between monetary growth and nominal income growth, changes in demand for money balances were expected to trigger the correct interest rate responses, thus avoiding the defects of policy in the 1970s, when failure to adjust quickly and sufficiently to short-term economic pressures led to excessively low and even negative real interest rates. Experience has fallen short of expectation. From the beginning of the decade, monetary growth persistently exceeded nominal income growth (in contrast to the experience in the 1960s and 1970s), and fluctuations in the monetary aggregates became unreliable guides as to when and by how much interest rates should adjust (Diagram 10). M1 has tended to become highly sensitive to movements in rates on market instruments and on retail deposits not included in M1[17]. By the mid-1980s it had become very difficult to assess the implications of M1 growth for the future course of business activity and the rate of inflation, or to predict whether changes in money growth carried a correct message about the strength of economic activity. Operating procedures were altered in late 1982 to reduce interest rate volatility[18]; M1 targets had to be rebased because of overshooting in 1983 and again in 1985; and the FOMC finally elected not to set a target range for M1 in 1987.

Target ranges are still set for M2 and M3, and the Federal Open Market Committee (FOMC) also monitors the growth of domestic non-financial debt. Until 1987, the growth of such debt consistently exceeded both the Committees' expectations and the expansion of income by a wide margin, causing concern about potential fragilities in the nation's financial structure. (Where once the debt-to-GNP ratio had been remarkably constant at about 1.4, in the 1980s it has jumped to over 1.8.) However, there is no direct or immediate connection between either the broad aggregates or credit expansion and interest rate changes. The Federal Reserve has, instead, been

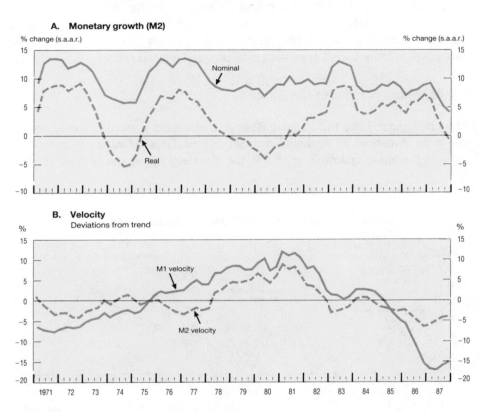

Diagram 10. **MONETARY GROWTH AND VELOCITY**

A. **Monetary growth (M2)**

% change (s.a.a.r.)

Nominal

Real

B. **Velocity**
Deviations from trend

M1 velocity

M2 velocity

1971 72 73 74 75 76 77 78 79 80 81 82 83 84 85 86 87

Source: Federal Reserve Board, *Federal Reserve Bulletin.*

forced back on a pragmatic approach, with reserve provision being decided in the light of a range of monetary and other economic indicators. Foremost among the latter have been information about the strength of the business expansion, indications of inflation and inflation expectations and more recently, developments in exchange markets.

Increased inflation, although to some extent anticipated, raised concern about further sharp declines in the dollar in 1987. Since 1985, conditions in the exchange market have been a more important factor in monetary policy decisions; but the exchange rate has not assumed the significance of a surrogate monetary rule (as for example in the United Kingdom). Attempts to stabilise the dollar imply that foreign

41

interest rates now play a role in determining U.S. rates and monetary conditions abroad affect the Federal Reserve's room for manoeuvre. But exchange rates are not viewed independently of business activity and inflation indicators. No automatic monetary tightening occurs when private capital inflows are insufficient to finance the current account deficit at existing exchange and interest rates.

Monetary policy and the dollar

Throughout 1986 the Federal Reserve maintained a relatively easy monetary stance, as evidenced by declining nominal interest rates, an easing of reserve pressures on the banks and rapid growth in the monetary aggregates (Tables 13 and 14,

Diagram 11.   **BANK RESERVES AND FEDERAL FUNDS RATE**

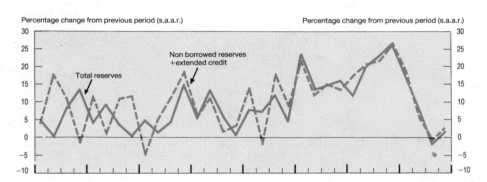

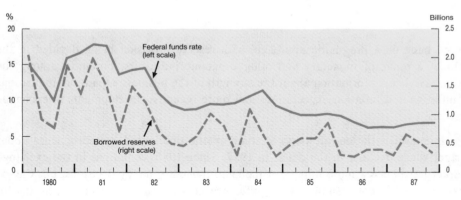

Source: Federal Reserve Board, *Federal Reserve Bulletin.*

Table 13. **Monetary and debt aggregates**

Target period (year to)	Date set	Target ranges (per cent per annum)			
		M1	M2	M3	Debt
1986 Q4	July 1985	4-7	6-9	6-9	8-11
	February 1986	3-8	6-9	6-9	8-11
	July 1986	(3-8)	6-9	6-9	8-11
	Outturn	15.3	8.9	8.8	13.2
1987 Q4	July 1986	(3-8)	5½-8½	5½-8½	8-11
	February 1987	(—)[1]	5½-8½	5½-8½	8-11
	July 1987	—	5½-8½	5½-8½	8-11
	Outturn	5.9	4.1	5.5	9.1
1988 Q4	July 1987	—	5-8	5-8	7½-10½
	February 1988	—	4-8	4-8	7-11

1. M1 targeting dropped because of uncertainty about its underlying relationship to the behaviour of the economy.
Source: Federal Reserve Board.

Diagram 11). The economy appeared in need of support, inflation was low, and a declining dollar was welcome on competitiveness grounds. The dollar underwent an orderly decline as monetary relaxation in the other major economies kept interest rate differentials from becoming too unfavourable on U.S. assets. Following a five-month pause, long-term interest rates resumed a downward trend from the autumn of 1985 with short-term rates following suit from March 1986 (Diagram 12). Prompted by discount rate cuts in July and August, short rates reached a trough in October 1986, with a Federal funds rate below 6 per cent and a three-month treasury bill rate of just

Table 14. **Interest rate trends**[1]

Per cent

	1986				1987			
	Q1	Q2	Q3	Q4	Q1	Q2	Q3	Q4
Money market								
Federal funds	7.83	6.92	6.20	6.30	6.22	6.65	6.84	6.92
Discount window borrowing	7.0	6.50	5.50	5.50	5.50	5.50	5.66	6.0
3-month Treasury bills	6.89	6.14	5.52	5.35	5.53	5.66	6.04	5.86
Bond yields								
30-year Treasury bonds	8.76	7.50	7.41	7.52	7.49	8.53	9.1	9.23
AAA corporate bonds	9.57	9.0	8.83	8.68	8.37	9.17	9.76	10.2

1. Average quarterly value, except for official discount rate, which is the end-of-quarter value.
Source: Federal Reserve Board.

Diagram 12. **INTEREST RATES AND THE TERM STRUCTURE**

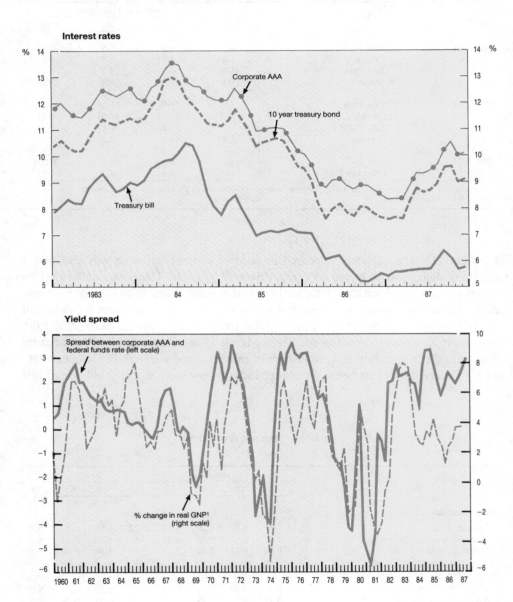

Interest rates

Corporate AAA

10 year treasury bond

Treasury bill

Yield spread

Spread between corporate AAA and
federal funds rate (left scale)

% change in real GNP[1]
(right scale)

1. 3 quarter centered moving average on (T + 1).
Source: Federal Reserve Board, *Federal Reserve Bulletin.*

44

over 5 per cent. Long-term treasury bonds then traded at about 7¼ per cent and corporate (AAA) bonds near to their cyclical low, at 8.4 per cent. M1 overshot its target range by a substantial margin, while both M2 and M3 ended the year very close to their 9 per cent growth ceiling.

The gradual fall in the dollar was accompanied by a steady reduction in nominal interest rate differentials throughout most of 1986 (Diagram 13). By late 1986, the foreign sector had become a net seller of fixed-income securities. This created a dilemma for the monetary authorities, since an apparent slackening of activity called for a more relaxed monetary stance while downward pressure on the dollar called for higher interest rates. Permitting further dollar depreciation appeared to entail greater risks in view of rising concern about inflation at the time; the extent of the depreciation was also beginning to cause worries among the major trading partners of the U.S., who were blaming appreciation of their currencies for sluggish investment and growth.

When the dollar came under major downward pressure in late January 1987, this was met by co-ordinated official intervention[19] – a development which paved the way for the Louvre accord in late February. The agreement contained a set of commitments covering both the conduct of economic policies and co-operation on exchange markets. The then prevailing exchange rates (Yen 140 and DM 1.80) were thought "broadly consistent with underlying economic fundamentals" and further substantial changes in exchange rates were considered likely to have adverse effects. Under these circumstances it was decided to "co-operate closely to foster stability of exchange rate around current levels". The communiqué said almost nothing about official intervention, although there appears to have been an understanding that concerted central bank action to stabilise currencies would, at times, be necessary. Although the Federal Reserve was worried about the potentially destabilising impact of a "self-generating cumulative process of currency depreciation and inflation", there was no commitment in the Louvre agreement to support the dollar through tighter U.S. monetary policy[20].

Monetary policy and the bond market

In the weeks before the Louvre accord, the bond market was marking time and monetary policy was relatively passive; the February 1987 FOMC meeting did not alter reserve provision. Subsequently, a divergence appeared between bond rates, which began to rise from March onwards, and money market rates, which increased more slowly (Diagram 12). In the face of declining private capital inflows, the central banks of the G7 countries intervened heavily to stabilise the dollar in late March and

Diagram 13. **YIELD DIFFERENTIALS ON DOLLAR ASSETS**

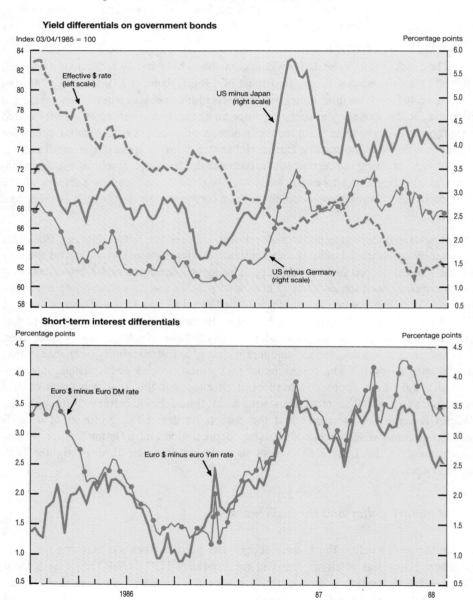

Yield differentials on government bonds

Index 03/04/1985 = 100

Percentage points

Effective $ rate
(left scale)

US minus Japan
(right scale)

US minus Germany
(right scale)

Short-term interest differentials

Percentage points

Percentage points

Euro $ minus Euro DM rate

Euro $ minus euro Yen rate

1986   87   88

Source: OECD, *Economic Outlook No. 42, December 1987.*

46

Table 15. **Financing of the current account deficit**

$ billion

	1984	1985	1986	1987 I	1987 II
United States					
Current account	− 107.0	− 116.4	− 141.4	− 78.2	− 82.4
Capital account, net[1]	79.5	92.7	84.1	44.2	37.8
Net transactions of monetary authorities[1]	0.7	5.8	33.3	32.3	24.4
(As a percentage of current account)	(1)	(5)	(23½)	(41)	(30)
Change in assets (increase = −)	− 3.1	− 3.9	0.3	5.4	3.8
Change in liabilities (increase = +)	2.4	− 2.0	33.0	26.9	20.6
Japan					
Net transactions of monetary authorities	2.4	− 1.5	13.7	42.3	
(As a percentage of current account)	(7)	(− 3)	(16)	(49)	
Germany					
Net transactions of monetary authorities	− 1.1	0.6	2.7	22.9	
(As a percentage of current account)	(− 13)	(4)	(7¾)	(52)	

1. Net increase in U.S. liabilities: + = capital inflow.
Source: Department of Commerce, Bureau of Economic Analysis, and OECD Secretariat estimates.

throughout most of April[21] (Table 15), but this did not prevent the differential in favour of U.S. bonds from widening appreciably, reflecting an increasing risk premium on dollar assets (Diagram 13 and Table 16). U.S. bond yields continued to rise steeply through April and May as private investors anticipated either further dollar depreciation or a tightening of U.S. monetary policy. Also, the inflation outlook worsened, as incoming data showed large price increases not only for energy and

Table 16. **Interest rate differentials**

Per cent

	1986 Q1	1986 Q2	1986 Q3	1986 Q4	1987 Q1	1987 Q2	1987 Q3	1987 Q4
Nominal differentials in favour of the $								
3-month term								
Vis-à-vis								
Japan	1.6	2.0	1.3	1.3	2.0	3.0	3.2	3.7
Germany	3.0	2.1	1.4	1.1	1.8	3.0	3.0	3.5
10-year term								
Vis-à-vis								
Japan	3.7	3.0	3.0	3.1	3.7	5.0	4.3	4.8
Germany	2.6	2.0	1.9	1.5	1.6	2.7	2.6	2.7

Source: OECD Secretariat estimates.

imported goods (which had been expected), but for many other items. To check these pressures, the Federal Reserve reduced reserve provision somewhat through April and May, but this move was a cautious one, since the FOMC remained rather sceptical about the strength of the recovery and the growth of the monetary aggregates was below target. The Federal Reserve still expected the growth of domestic demand to slow sufficiently to release resources to the external sector; consumer spending was expected to slacken, correcting the low saving ratio, and no capacity constraints or strong labour market pressures were expected to develop.

Conditions in the bond and exchange markets improved somewhat in the following months, as better trade figures, foreign monetary trends and the announcement of a Japanese fiscal package contributed to a strengthening of the dollar. An easing of monetary policy in Germany and Japan enabled interest rate differentials to widen in favour of dollar assets (Table 16 and Diagram 13). However, from July the bond market started weakening again, due to both foreign and domestic developments. On the foreign front, there was a tightening of monetary policy in Germany and Japan, where the monetary authorities were worried about the threat to longer-term price stability posed by the overshooting of monetary targets; the Bundesbank reacted to rapid monetary growth by increasing short-term rates slightly and the Bank of Japan tightened its "window guidance" on commercial bank lending. The dollar weakened again in mid-August, following disappointing trade figures, and this was met by further modest official intervention. Bond prices continued to fall, probably in anticipation of a tightening of monetary policy or heightened inflation fears, linked partly to the risk of further dollar depreciation. The Federal Reserve signalled such tightening by the announcement of a half-point discount rate increase in early September, a move accompanied by an increase in pressure on reserve positions.

Domestic considerations were also important in the discount rate increase. By late summer, the unemployment data were pointing to growing pressures in the labour market and the announced intention was to head off "potential inflation". With labour markets tightening more than expected, further dollar depreciation was thought likely to exacerbate inflationary pressures[22]. But there remained some doubt about the strength of the business expansion and the monetary aggregates were still undershooting. In laying down guidelines for the degree of reserve pressure acceptable in the inter-meeting period, these two factors were cited as possible reasons for allowing greater accommodation, if needed. In practice, however, there was mounting evidence that the economy was beginning to expand rapidly in the third quarter, partially explaining the failure of the trade balance to improve. In these circumstances, external and domestic objectives were increasingly pointing towards the need for a firm monetary policy.

The response to the stock market crash

As noted, bearish conditions in the bond market contrasted with the strength of the stock market in the first part of the year. With a few set-backs, shares posted major gains up to August (Diagram 6). The reasons for the decoupling of the bond and stock markets during this period are unclear, but it is noteworthy that foreign purchases of equities were substantial, as overseas investors switched from bonds to stocks. The stock market crisis brought a reversal of this trend, and bond yields fell and those on stocks rose. However, the portfolio shift to bonds was accompanied by a "flight to quality", which increased the gap between rates facing government and corporate borrowers. Long-term government bonds fell under 9 per cent, while corporate AAAs remained just below 10 per cent. Yields on low-grade bonds actually rose, because of fears about the future cash flow of highly-leveraged companies. Similarly, spreads between short maturity instruments of different quality increased, and the difference between the yield on commercial paper and treasury bills rose by over $1/2$ percentage point.

The spread between long and short-term rates also remained abnormally large, as pressure on the dollar persisted and the Federal Reserve sought to keep short rates down in the near term (in order to ensure that the financial system was sufficiently liquid to prevent any systemic weakness arising from the stock market crisis). The Federal Reserve eased pressures on reserve provision and shifted the focus of its operations towards maintaining stability in money market conditions. The Federal Funds rate fell from $7^{1}/_2$ to just under $6^{3}/_4$ per cent. As the threat of inflation receded (due to a downward adjustment in expected growth and the renewed weakness in the price of oil) the coalescence between domestic (anti-inflation) and exchange rate objectives, which had characterised monetary policy in the August to October period, disappeared. Against the background of a sharp rise in inventories in the fourth quarter of 1987, the System eased the pressures on reserve positions of depository institutions a bit further in the first months of 1988.

Monetary policy indicators

As measured by growth in the aggregates, monetary policy was, on average, relatively tight in 1987. M2 increased by only 4 per cent (as did non-borrowed reserves), well below the lower band of its $5^{1}/_2$ to $8^{1}/_2$ per cent annual growth range and the 9 per cent expansion of the preceding year (Table 13). M3 growth, though stronger, was at the bottom of its $5^{1}/_2$ to $8^{1}/_2$ per cent range, and M1 growth slowed sharply. However,

49

interpretation of the aggregates in terms of their impact on domestic demand is complicated by the sharp rise in velocity, which, in the case of M2, reversed part of the decline which occurred in 1985-86. The increase in velocity may have reflected a number of special factors, including the much-reduced rate of saving out of income and a preference for drawing upon liquid assets – rather than consumer credit – to finance purchases[23].

Some of the increase in velocity was also probably due to a strong, systematic sensitivity to changes in market rates of interest (which led the Federal Reserve to widen the target ranges in 1988)[24]. This sensitivity has led to large changes in money growth being associated with small interest rate adjustments, a combination which complicates the appraisal of monetary policy effects on the real economy. The marked deceleration in monetary growth which occurred in the first half was associated with a rise in the three month treasury bill rate of only ¾ per cent between its fourth quarter 1986 low and its peak in the first half of 1987 (Diagram 12). Movements in inflation and inflation expectations accentuate the contrast between trends in the aggregates and interest rates. Real money and reserve growth were slower than at any time since 1982, while real short term interest rates fell in the first half of 1987 (Diagram 11 and Table 17)[25]. Furthermore, the spread between short and long rates,

Table 17. **Real interest rate measures**[1]

	1984	1985	1986 I	1986 II	1987 I	1987 II
Short-term real rates[2]						
United States	**6.2**	**4.6**	**3.9**	**2.7**	**2.4**	**3.1**
Japan	4.7	4.7	3.7	5.3	4.3	3.1
Germany	4.1	2.6	1.6	1.8	2.5	2.7
France	5.8	4.4	4.5	5.0	5.3	5.3
United Kingdom	4.9	7.0	8.9	6.7	5.0	4.6
Long-term real rates[3]						
United States	**9.5**	**7.8**	**5.0**	**4.0**	**4.3**	**5.4**
Japan	5.2	5.6	4.8	4.5	2.8	3.5
Germany	5.3	4.3	4.1	4.3	4.4	4.9
France	8.2	8.1	6.5	6.1	6.9	7.9
United Kingdom	6.5	7.2	5.3	5.5	5.2	4.8

1. The short-term rates are for a three month term on the following assets: United States: Treasury bills; Japan: "Gensaki"; Germany, France, United Kingdom: inter-bank loans. The long-term rates are chosen in general to correspond to a ten year term to maturity: United States: U.S. government notes and bonds; Japan: central government bonds; Germany: public sector bonds; France: public and semi-public bonds; United Kingdom: government bonds.
2. Nominal short-term rate adjusted for actual or projected increases in GNP deflator two quarters after and one quarter before each observation.
3. Nominal long-term rate adjusted for actual or projected increases in GNP deflator two years after each observation.
Source: OECD Secretariat estimates.

which is often used as an inverse indicator of monetary tightness, widened appreciably in the first half, perhaps because policy was not tight enough to contain rising inflation expectations associated with accelerating commodity price increases and exchange rate weakness (Diagram 12)[26]. Monetary policy may thus not have been as tight as appears from the aggregates data. But against this has to be set the unpredictability of the lags between monetary policy action and effect and the fact that the decline in the Federal deficit implied a danger, *ex ante*, that policy could have become too restrictive.

Budgetary policy

Budgetary strategy

Deficit reduction has been a high priority of the present Administration, but it has always been linked to cuts in Federal non-defence spending. On this point there has been a difference between the Administration's view and other proponents of Federal deficit reduction, such as the OECD, who have taken the view that some combination of expenditure cuts and tax increases is necessary to achieve a reduction in the deficit[27]. The latter view is based on the ground that the Federal deficit imposes even greater costs than tax increases in the longer run, by raising interest rates and distorting trade. The Administration has tended to play down the effect of the fiscal deficit on interest rates[28]; it has also argued that if taxes were raised, the pressure to reduce Federal non-defence spending would be reduced. Because Congressional priorities have differed, particularly with respect to the balance of defence and non-defence spending cuts, there has been an impasse. The Budget decision-making process is decentralised in the United States, and it is this institutional unwieldyness which has been responsible for the deficit's persistence.

The relation between the Federal deficit and the imbalances of the U.S. economy is more complicated than would seem apparent from references to "twin deficits" – budget and current account. Viewed from the perspective of the national saving-investment imbalance, the federal deficit has obviously been a critical element in the U.S. demand for foreign capital. But private sector saving behaviour has also played a role: U.S. private savings have fallen to a low level and the U.S. Federal deficit is much higher in relation to domestic savings than in other major OECD countries. Moreover, the transmission mechanism by which the Federal deficit leads to a higher current account deficit (rather than to the "crowding out" of private spending) is a matter of controversy. According to one view, the appearance of the Federal deficit coincided with rising interest rates, capital inflows and appreciation of

51

the dollar. The latter helped engineer the current account deficit in the traded goods sector by making U.S. goods uncompetitive. But this "model" does not fit the 1985-87 period, when the dollar has fallen back to its late 1970's levels and private capital inflows have been insufficient to finance the current account deficit at then prevailing interest and exchange rate levels. In this period, the actions of the central banks (national and foreign), as residual sources of finance for the payments gap, also have to be taken into account.

The FY 1987 Budget

Significant progress towards a lower budget deficit was made in FY 1987. Total outlays rose by only 1.4 per cent, falling in real terms, and the deficit was reduced by $71 billion to $150 billion. This was very close to the original Gramm-Rudman-Hollings (G-R-H) target of $144 billion. Tax reform, which was intended to be revenue-neutral in the longer run, actually added about $22 billion to tax revenues in 1987, since higher corporate tax receipts were only partially offset by lower income tax proceeds (Table 18). Asset sales, loan prepayments, a one-day delay of the military

Table 18. **The impact of the Tax Reform Act on receipts**

$ billion	1987	1988	1989
Calendar years, NIPA basis[a]			
Tax Reform Act (TRA)			
Personal taxes	−5.5	−30.7	−41
Corporate profits tax	27.6	15.5	19
Net impact of TRA	**22.5**	**−14.6**	**−22**
Fiscal years, Unified Budget basis[b]			
Tax Reform Act	22	−10	−16
Budget summit agreement	—	11	17
Social Security (rate increase, effective 1st January 1988)	—	10	14
Net impact of legislation on receipts	**22**	**11**	**15**

Memorandum item:

	Implementation of Budget Agreement					
	Total	Taxes	Defence cuts	Other spending	Asset sales	Debt service
FY 1988	33½	11	5.1	8.2	7.7	1.3
FY 1989	42½	17	8.4	3.5	3.5	3.5

Source: a) Department of Commerce (Bureau of Economic Analysis), *Survey of Current Business,* February 1988;
b) CBO, *The Economic and Budget Outlook: FY 1989-93,* February 1988.

pay date and other one-time outlay savings took $15 billion off the 1987 deficit, but will add to the deficit from now on. Corrected for these two temporary items, the underlying deficit was $187 billion (Table 19).

The FY 1988 Budget

Because tax reform is expected to add to the deficit in 1988, the CBO baseline deficit published in October showed the deficit climbing back to $180 billion in FY 1988, before declining gradually towards $150 billion in 1992 (Table 19). Cuts of over $70 billion would have been needed to meet the Balanced Budget Act's target of $108 billion for 1988. This was considered unrealistic. Also, the original Act ran into a constitutional problem when the Supreme Court struck down the automatic sequestration provision. The Act was amended in September to correct these deficiencies. The FY 1988 target was raised to $144 billion and the goal of a balanced budget deferred to 1993. The Amendment specified the need for $23 billion to be cut from the baseline deficit in FY 1988. In the event of no compromise being reached between Congress and the President, the saving was to be achieved by across-the-board spending cuts, scheduled for 20th November, allocated equally to selected defence and non-defence programmes.

No negotiations took place between Congress and the Administration before 19th October, but subsequent to the financial crisis, negotiations did take place. A bipartisan agreement on a package of measures was reached on 20th November – the day of the sequestration deadline – which proposed to take $30 billion off the FY 1988 baseline and $46 billion off the FY 1989 deficit. As voted (on 21st December) the Budget incorporated cuts of $32 billion for FY 1988. Defence cuts were limited to $5 billion and revenues raised by $11 billion, the extra cuts, above the $23 billion called for under sequestration, being due chiefly to asset sales. The agreement can be seen as consolidating the temporary deficit reduction made in 1987.

The Administration now projects a current services deficit of $148 billion for FY 1988 ($4 billion above the revised G-R-H target) with a baseline ("current services") projection for FY 1989 of $139 billion (which is just above the G-R-H target of $136 billion) (Table 19). However, the projected rates of real GNP growth for FY 1988 and FY 1989, of 3.3 and 2.8 per cent respectively, year on year, are high in comparison with the CBO, which has projected a deficit of $176 billion for FY 1989. A suspension of the targets is allowed for under the Act if there is a cyclical weakening in the economy, but slippage of a structural nature, due to prolonged slower growth or sustained higher interest rates, would call for greater medium-term budgetary action than was provided by the November agreement.

53

Table 19. **Budget deficit projections**

	1987	1988	1989	1990	1991	1992	1993
	Fiscal year, $ billion (deficit = + ; reduction = −)						
Congressional Budget Office (CBO) projections							
Baseline projection for "Budget summit"							
(November 1987)	148	180	186	166	152	135	—
Subsequent legislation[1]	—	− 34	− 36	− 40	− 42	− 42	—
Adjusted baseline	148	146	150	126	110	93	—
Economic and technical changes	2	11	27	41	47	58	—
New CBO baseline	**150**	**157**	**176**	**167**	**158**	**151**	**134**
Adjusted for tax reform							
and one time outlay savings	(187)	(154)	(159)	(163)	(160)	(154)	(138)
Administration baseline	**150**	**148**	**139**	**111**	**86**	**63**	**39**
Balanced Budget Act							
Original target	144	108	72	36	0	0	0
Revised target		144	136	100	64	28	0
OECD projections[2]	**144**	**164**	**159**	**143**	**120**	**112**	**100**
Memorandum item:							
"Off Budget" (social security fund) surplus[3]	20	37	46	58	71	81	97

1. On 20th November, the President and Congress agreed on deficit cuts of $30 billion in 1988 and $46 billion in 1989. The CBO baseline incorporates these as legislated.
2. Based on CBO baseline Federal spending projections and OECD Secretariat projections of debt interest payments and revenues.
3. CBO estimate; the Administration projects a $93 billion surplus in 1993.
Source: Congressional Budget Office, *The Economic and Budget Outlook* FY 1989-93; Office of Management and Budget, *Special Analyses, Budget of the United States Government* FY 1989; and OECD Secretariat estimates.

Medium-term fiscal trends

The structural budget deficit

For 1989 and beyond, the outlook for the deficit depends quite critically on the expected long-run growth rate of the economy and the level of unemployment. The sensitivity of the deficit to economic activity is such that a ½ percentage point fall in the unemployment rate would reduce the deficit by about $10 billion in the first year and $25 billion after five[29]. A 1 per cent sustained increase in GNP growth, with unchanged unemployment, would reduce the deficit by $66 billion after five years[30]. Estimates of the "structural" (cyclically-adjusted) deficit are thus quite sensitive to the unemployment rate and growth rate chosen. The lower the rate of unemployment

Diagram 14. **STRUCTURAL BUDGET DEFICIT**

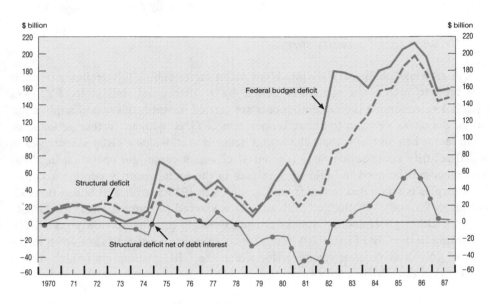

Source: Department of Commerce, *Survey of Current Business.*

towards which the economy is assumed to gravitate, the greater the contribution to deficit reduction which can be expected to come from economic growth and the less the need for discretionary fiscal restraint. The structural budget estimates given in Diagram 14 are based on a 6 per cent unemployment rate, which implies that the cyclical component of the deficit had disappeared by the last half of 1987. However, some recent calculations of the NAIRU put it lower than 6 per cent, and an optimis- tic assessment (based on a prime-age male unemployment rate of about 4 per cent) ascribes about $25 billion of the 1987 deficit to the effect of cyclical unemployment[31].

Differences in growth and interest rate assumptions make for a wide range of possible outcomes for the Federal deficit over the medium term. The Administration baseline now foresees the deficit falling to $39 billion by FY 1993. On more pessimis- tic growth assumptions, averaging 2¹/₂ per cent a year (the average of the last ten years), the CBO baseline is considerably higher, implying the need for cuts of $134 billion if the target of budget balance by FY 1993 is to be reached (Table 19). It could thus be misleading to assume that the economy can "grow" out of the Federal

55

deficit in its entirety. On the other hand, abstracting from possible short-term cyclical deterioration in the deficit, the underlying trend is generally agreed to be downward.

Growing social security surplus

A growing "off-Budget" surplus is the major factor behind this declining trend; it will tend to reduce the structural deficit by a further $60 billion by FY 1993 (Table 19). Assuming the December cuts are carried forward, this would imply a fall in the deficit/GNP ratio to about 1½ per cent of GNP without further action. The main factor behind this is the 1983 Social Security Act, which legislated increases in social security contribution rates (the latest of which came into operation in 1988) and specified the need to build up surpluses in the social security pension account. This surplus is scheduled to rise from $20 billion in 1987 to over $90 billion in 1993. Although formally "off-Budget", this surplus is allowed to count towards the G-R-H target[32]. Other government revenues are scheduled to grow more slowly than GNP according to the CBO (Table 20), but offsetting this is an assumed slow-down in the rate of growth of defence spending, for which the CBO assumption (which differs from that of the OMB) is one of zero real growth.

Table 20. **Accounting for the Federal deficit**

	Per cent GNP				Change (contribution to deficit = −)		
	1981	1985	1987	1993	1981-1985	1985-1987	1987-1993
Revenues	**20.1**	**18.6**	**19.4**	**19.4**	− 1.5	+ 0.8	0.0
Individual income taxes	9.6	8.5	8.9	8.8	− 1.1	+ 0.4	− 0.1
Corporate income tax	2.0	1.6	1.9	2.1	− 0.4	+ 0.3	+ 0.2
Social security	4.4	4.7	4.8	5.4	+ 0.3	+ 0.1	+ 0.6
Other social insurance contributions	1.7	2.0	2.1	1.7	+ 0.3	+ 0.1	− 0.4
Other	2.4	1.8	1.6	1.4	− 0.6	− 0.2	− 0.2
Expenditures	**22.7**	**24.0**	**22.8**	**21.5**	− 1.3	+ 1.2	+ 1.3
National defense	5.3	6.4	6.4	5.3	− 1.1	—	+ 1.1
Non-defense	4.4	3.2	2.5	2.3	+ 1.2	+ 0.7	+ 0.2
Social security	4.5	4.5	4.4	3.9	+ 0.0	+ 0.1	+ 0.5
Other entitlements	6.2	6.6	6.4	6.8	− 0.4	+ 0.2	− 0.4
Net interest	2.3	3.3	3.1	3.2	− 1.0	+ 0.2	− 0.1
Deficit ("on Budget")	**− 2.5**	**− 5.6**	**− 4.0**	**− 3.6**	− 3.1	+ 1.6	+ 0.4
Social security surplus ("off Budget")	**− 0.1**	**0.2**	**0.4**	**1.5**	+ 0.3	+ 0.2	+ 1.1
Total deficit	**− 2.6**	**− 5.4**	**− 3.6**	**− 2.1**	− 2.8	+ 1.8	+ 1.5

Source: Congressional Budget Office, *The Economic and Budget Outlook; FY 1989-1993;* February 1988.

Table 21. **Trends in Federal debt**

	1955	1975	1980	1985	1986	1987
	Per cent of GNP[1]					
Gross federal debt	71.0	35.7	34.2	46.3	50.8	53.4
Federal Government accounts	12.4	9.7	7.5	8.0	9.2	10.4
Debt held by the public[2]	58.6	26.1	26.8	38.3	41.6	43.0
of which:						
Domestic	n.a.	21.8	22.2	32.9	35.6	37.9
Overseas	n.a.	4.3	4.6	5.3	6.0	5.1
Interest on debt held by the public[3]	1.3	1.6	2.3	3.8	3.7	3.6
(Percentage of outlays)	(7.6)	(7.4)	(10.2)	(15.7)	(15.7)	(15.7)
Memorandum items:						
Average length of marketable debt (years, months)	n.a.	2.5	4.0	4.11	5.3	5.9

	Treasury Bills	Up to 1 year	1 to 2 years	2 to 10 years	Over 10 years
Debt by maturity (percentage of total at end of 1987)	18.9	14.6	16.2	34.6	15.6

1. Debt outstanding at the end of the financial year as a proportion of GNP during the financial year.
2. Includes Federal Reserve Banks.
3. Gross interest.
Source: Office of Management and Budget, *Special Analyses, Budget of the United States Government, FY 1989;* Department of the Treasury, *Treasury Bulletin.*

Federal debt and debt interest

Debt interest payments are also critical. Gross interest payments have doubled as a proportion of outlays since 1980, and interest charges have become the chief proximate source of the deficit (Table 20). The problem has become less acute with the fall in rates in recent years and net interest payments are assumed to stay in the region of 3 per cent of GNP. However, this ratio is highly sensitive to the course of interest rates. A sustained one per cent increase in interest rates raises the deficit by $5 billion in the first year and about $25 billion after five years. If long term interest rates were to remain at their current level, rather than fall towards 7 per cent as assumed in Table 20, the structural deficit would remain at $150 billion even on fairly optimistic growth assumptions.

Previous *Surveys* have argued that the growth of debt and debt service provide powerful *domestic* reasons for fiscal restraint in addition to those relating to external considerations. Federal debt held by the public rose by 15 per cent of GNP between 1980 and 1987, to 42 per cent (Table 21), and further increases in the ratio were in prospect in the absence of action to curb the deficit. According to the CBO's autumn baseline projection, the debt/GNP ratio would have continued to increase to 45½ per cent up to 1990. With a deficit of $150 billion (3 per cent of GNP), as now expected for 1988 and 1989, the debt/GNP ratio would stabilise near to its current level, at 43 per cent. To stabilise, the debt ratio has to equal the deficit/GNP ratio divided by the nominal growth rate (3 per cent/7 per cent = 43 per cent). If nominal income growth is slower than 7 per cent, the deficit/GNP ratio will continue to rise exacerbating the debt interest problem. Furthermore, there is some evidence, though not entirely conclusive, that a high debt/GNP ratio is itself a factor in higher interest rates[33]. In this case the problem of achieving budget balance becomes increasingly difficult and the need to reduce the debt/GNP ratio all the more important.

The Federal deficit, domestic saving and external adjustment

The budget deficit and the saving investment balance

In the light of the close links often drawn between the Federal and external deficit, it is something of a paradox that the stock market crisis should have occurred at a time when the Federal deficit had just fallen by $71 billion. Part of the fall was due to temporary factors, so that its direct impact on bond market confidence would have been expected to be small. But the coincidence of a lower budget deficit with a deteriorating nominal trade balance (one of the probable triggers for the stock market crash) tends to contradict the view that the Federal budget is the main source of the external deficit.

In reality, the links between the budget and external deficits are complex and indirect. In the first place, although the U.S. central government deficit is somewhat higher than the OECD average, the state and local sector is always in surplus. Incorporating this surplus, the general government deficit as a share of GNP is *below* the average for the major seven OECD countries (Table 22). Secondly, the availability of domestic private saving to finance the budget deficit varies with the business cycle. It is normal for the Federal deficit to rise in economic downturns, at the same time as private saving rises; it is the persistence of the Federal deficit well into the expansion which is an unusual feature of the present situation[34].

On average, however, Federal borrowing has been abnormally high in relation to domestic private saving during the 1980s, because of both Federal and private saving trends. Since the external account was last in balance, in 1979, gross private and Federal government saving have declined by about 3 per cent of GNP (Table 3), so

58

Table 22. **International comparison of budget deficits**

Surplus (+) or deficit (−) as a percentage of nominal GNP/GDP[1]

	1982	1983	1984	1985	1986	1987	1988[2]
Central government financial balances							
United States	**− 4.6**	**− 5.2**	**− 4.5**	**− 4.9**	**− 4.8**	**− 3.5**	**− 3.4**
Japan[3]	− 5.2	− 4.9	− 4.0	− 3.7	− 3.1	− 3.0	− 2.8
Germany	− 2.1	− 1.6	− 1.3	− 0.9	− 1.0	− 1.3	− 2.0
France	− 2.7	− 3.2	− 3.3	− 3.3	− 2.8	− 2.5	− 2.1
United Kingdom	− 2.8	− 2.8	− 3.1	− 2.4	− 2.3	− 1.3	− 0.9
Major 7[4]	− 4.7	− 5.0	− 4.5	− 4.6	− 4.3	− 3.5	− 3.4
General government financial balances[3]							
United States	**− 3.5**	**− 3.8**	**− 2.8**	**− 3.3**	**− 3.5**	**− 2.4**	**− 2.3**
Japan	− 3.6	− 3.7	− 2.1	− 0.8	− 1.1	− 0.2	− 0.3
Germany	− 3.3	− 2.5	− 1.9	− 1.1	− 1.2	− 1.7	− 2.6
France	− 2.8	− 3.2	− 2.7	− 2.9	− 2.9	− 2.3	− 2.5
United Kingdom	− 2.3	− 3.4	− 3.9	− 2.9	− 2.7	− 1.4	− 0.7
Major 7[4]	− 3.9	− 4.1	− 3.4	− 3.4	− 3.4	− 2.5	− 2.4
General government financial balances as a proportion of net private saving							
United States	**63.7**	**65.5**	**40.8**	**58.6**	**66.2**	**55.0**	**44.0**
Japan	25.4	26.6	15.2	6.0	7.7	1.3	2.3
Germany	45.2	32.6	24.5	15.4	13.4	17.2	23.6
France	42.2	48.2	37.2	41.9	34.6	27.4	28.7
United Kingdom	35.5	45.8	42.5	34.4	36.8	17.7	8.8
Major 7[4]	49.1	50.8	37.3	40.9	37.4	27.9	23.8

1. On an SNA basis except for the United States and the United Kingdom where the data are based on national accounts, and in France, where they are on an administrative basis.
2. OECD projections.
3. For the fiscal year beginning 1st April of the year shown.
4. 1982 GNP/GDP weights and exchange rates.
Source: OECD Secretariat estimates.

that either could be held responsible for the external deficit. (Because the relative cost of investment has fallen, investment has also declined, offsetting part of the declining saving ratio.) Moreover private saving has fallen by 2 per cent of GNP since 1985 at the same time as the Federal deficit has declined by 1½ per cent; it is this trend which has prevented the external deficit from being reduced.

Sectoral saving developments are especially interesting in 1987, since they help explain both the strength of activity in the third quarter and the failure of the trade balance to improve (Table 23). Two factors stand out: both the household saving ratio and the state and local surplus fell, partially offsetting the decline in Federal borrowing up to the second quarter. And domestic saving (in terms of new funds available for the corporate sector to borrow) became negative in the third quarter. It appears

Table 23. **Domestic saving flows**

$ billion

	1986 Q3	1986 Q4	1986 Q1	1987 Q2	1987 Q3	1987 Q4
Federal budget balance	− 203.7	− 188.7	− 170.5	− 139.2	− 135.8	− 158.8
State and local surplus	59.6	50.6	41.0	50.6	46.5	39.2
Personal saving	108.9	109.0	138.4	93.2	88.8	157.9
Net personal and government saving	− 35.2	− 29.1	8.9	4.6	− 0.5	38.3
Net foreign saving (= current account deficit)	150.7	156.5	147.7	154.5	159.0	167.7
Net domestic investment[1]	115.5	127.4	156.6	159.1	158.5	206.0

1. Net of capital consumption and retained profits.
Source: Department of Commerce, Bureau of Economic Analysis.

that Federal fiscal tightening was exactly offset by other domestic saving shifts between the third quarters of 1986 and 1987.

Saving behaviour in other OECD economies also enters the U.S. saving-investment picture. The 1981-86 period was one of slow growth and restricted investment abroad. The United States grew faster than its trading partners, and foreign capital (i.e. excess foreign saving) was attracted by the prospect of higher rates of return. The increased demand for credit on the part of the Federal Government was not the only factor driving interest rates, the dollar and the trade deficit up; the supply of

Table 24. **Average marginal tax rates on labour income, capital income and output**

	Pre-reform	Tax Reform Act
Labour income	41.6	38.0
Federal income tax	25.8	21.7
State and local income and sales tax[1]	4.9	5.4
Social security and medicare payroll tax[2]	10.9	10.9
Capital income[3]	34.5	38.4
Output[4]	39.8	38.1

1. Rate is the statutory tax rate (measured as State and local income and sales taxes divided by net national product in 1985) adjusted down in accordance with the deductibility of State and local taxes (except sales taxes under TRA) from the Federal income tax base.
2. Social security and medicare payroll tax rate, for both employees and employers, multiplied by the portion of total labour income earned by individuals who are subject to the payroll tax at the margin.
3. Includes taxes at all levels of government.
4. Tax rate on labour income multiplied by labour's share of income (0.75) plus the tax rate on capital income multiplied by capital's share of income (0.25).
Sources: Department of the Treasury (Office of Tax Analysis) and Council of Economic Advisers.

credit, related to the increasing mobility of international capital, may also have been a factor. In the depreciation phase, on the other hand, foreign central banks have financed a larger part of the external deficit, motivated by the possibly disruptive effects of a further dollar fall on export production. Without this support, U.S. interest rates might, by now, have been higher.

Tax reform and saving

The Tax Reform Act removed one saving incentive, by abolishing Individual Retirement Accounts (IRAs), but also removed a disincentive to save by eliminating interest deductibility for consumer instalment loans. It is too soon to assess the impact of the Act on saving, but it is noteworthy that many borrowers have switched to home equity loans, interest on which remains deductible. Tax reform, in general, has had two aims[35]:

- – Lower marginal tax rates on labour income;
- – More uniform tax rates on capital investments.

Although the combined effect is to lower the aggregate rate of tax on output, potentially increasing efficiency and longer-run saving, the reforms have meant a higher marginal tax rate on capital income, which will lower the net return on saving by 6 per cent (Table 24).

IV. Short-term prospects and medium-term adjustment

Short-term prospects

The stock-market crisis seems to have helped the U.S. economy to move towards better balance. The budget agreement reached after the crisis consolidated the improvement achieved in 1987 and the personal saving ratio recovered somewhat in the fourth quarter. At the same time, net exports continued to rise in volume terms, and as the monthly nominal trade figures improved, pressure on the dollar eased in the first quarter. Financial market confidence, though potentially quite fragile, returned to a considerable degree. Bond yields declined significantly from their October peaks; equities regained some of their October losses and the monetary authorities were able to maintain a cautiously accommodating stance. The monetary growth ranges of 4 to 8 per cent for both M2 and M3 adopted by the FOMC for 1988 should be consistent with moderate growth, acceptable price performance and continued external adjustment. Overall, the prospects for sustained and more balanced growth are somewhat better than might have been feared in the immediate aftermath of the stock-market crisis. Domestic demand growth is projected to slow, but with real net exports rising further, GNP may still expand by around 2½ to 2¾ per cent in both 1988 and 1989.

The reduction in household net worth resulting from the fall in the total value of the stock market since the late summer was of the order of $450 billion by the end of March. Econometric estimates suggest that this could raise the household saving ratio by 1 point (see Annex I). Real private consumption fell by 2½ per cent (annual rate) in the fourth quarter of 1987, partly reflecting the sharp decline in consumer confidence[36]. Although stock prices have recovered somewhat and confidence appeared to have rebounded in the early months of 1988, private consumption is likely to grow more slowly than personal disposable income in 1988.

Confidence effects on investment have been most noticeable in the housing sector. By January, housing starts were down by nearly a quarter on the year before, reflecting rising mortgage rates in the pre-crisis period, a larger stock of unsold houses, and increased uncertainty on the part of builders. However, business fixed investment has shown little sign of being affected by the crash[37]. Survey evidence

Table 25. **Household saving ratio**

Percentage changes from previous year

	1986	1987	1988	1989
Compensation per employee	3.0	2.9	4	5
Total compensation	5.7	5.7	6	6½
Income from property and other	8.1	7.3	8½	8½
Current transfers received	5.8	4.8	6½	7
less:				
Interest on consumer debt	8.7	4.0	5	6½
Total personal income	6.2	6.0	6½	7
less:				
Direct taxes	5.4	10.3	3	7½
Current transfers paid	6.0	5.3	9½	7½
Disposable income	6.3	5.3	7	6½
Real disposable income	4.0	1.3	3	2½
Private consumption (volume)	4.2	1.9	2	2
Personal savings ratio				
(as a percentage of disposable income)	4.3	3.8	5	5½

Source: Department of Commerce (Bureau of Economic Analysis), *Survey of Current Business,* and OECD Secretariat estimates.

gathered in October and November pointed to continued strength and new orders for capital equipment continued to climb briskly in the following months. Overall, businesses are expected to boost spending by roughly 9 per cent in real terms in 1988. Planned increases are especially large for those manufacturing industries with high capacity utilisation rates, such as paper and chemicals. This willingness of firms to invest, in the face of doubts about the strength of consumer demand and sluggish government purchases, is due in large measure to the expansionary effects of the past fall in the dollar, which has boosted international competitiveness and profitability in the traded goods sector. The post-crash decline in bond yields has probably been another supporting factor. Although the impact of the crisis on the cost and availability of capital is ambiguous and corporations could be dissuaded from raising funds through equity issues, U.S. firms typically rely more on capital markets and banks as a source of credit.

Under the recent budget agreement, real defence spending is projected to fall, and the growth in domestic Federal outlays has been curtailed. With no major initiatives for public investment planned at the state and local level, real government consumption should grow at a rate not much faster than 1½ per cent a year. As a result of the projected rise in household saving, continued restraint on public spending and weaker inventory accumulation, domestic demand should grow more slowly over the next two years. The strong employment gains of early 1988 suggest that the service

Table 26. **Demand and output projections**

Percentage changes from previous period, seasonally adjusted at annual rates, volume (1982 prices)

	1986	1987	1988	1989	1988 S1	1988 S2	1989 S1	1989 S2
Private consumption	4.2	1.9	2	2	1½	1¾	2	2¼
Government consumption	3.8	2.3	1	1½	−1	1½	1½	1½
Private fixed investment	1.8	0.7	6	2¼	6¼	2½	2¼	2½
Residential	12.5	0.0	−2	1	−2¾	¾	1	1½
Non-residential	−2.3	1.0	9½	2¾	10	3¼	2¾	2¾
Final domestic demand	**3.7**	**1.8**	**2½**	**2**	**1¾**	**1¾**	**2**	**2¼**
Change in stockbuilding[1]	0.2	0.8	−½	0	−¼	−1	0	¼
Total domestic demand	**3.9**	**2.5**	**2**	**2**	**1½**	**¾**	**2**	**2½**
Exports of goods and services	3.3	12.8	15¾	11¼	14½	14½	11	9
Imports of goods and services	10.5	7.3	6¾	5½	3½	4	5½	6
Change in foreign balance[1]	**−1.0**	**0.3**	¾	½	**1**	**1**	½	¼
GNP at market prices	**2.9**	**2.9**	**2¾**	**2½**	**2½**	**2**	**2¾**	**2¾**
GNP implicit price deflator	2.6	3.0	3¼	4	3¼	3¾	4	4½
Memorandum items:								
Consumer prices[2]	2.2	4.0	3¾	4¼	3½	4	4¼	4½
Industrial production	1.1	3.8	5¾	4¾	5¼	5½	4½	4½
Unemployment rate	7.0	6.2	5½	5½	5½	5½	5½	5¼

1. As a percentage of GNP in the previous period.
2. National accounts private consumption deflator.

Sources: Department of Commerce (Bureau of Economic Analysis), Survey of Current Business, and OECD Secretariat estimates.

sector could remain an important source of growth. Outside this sector, GNP growth will increasingly depend on net exports, which are projected to improve by some $30 billion in volume terms (3/4 per cent of GNP) this year. As the volume increase begins to outweigh the impact of import price rises, the nominal current account balance should improve by about $15 billion a year, bringing the deficit down towards $130 billion. But, under the technical assumption of unchanged exchange rates, the stimulus from net exports would gradually subside and the external improvement would tend to taper off.

With the unemployment rate projected to stabilise at around 5 1/2 per cent, inflation may remain around 3 1/2 to 4 per cent, as measured by the GNP deflator. The consumer price deflator, which will continue to be affected by rising import prices, will increase by somewhat more, but wage increases should remain moderate. According to many econometric models an unemployment rate of 5 1/2 per cent should give rise to wage pressures. However, the wage equations on which such models are based have recently tended to overpredict wage settlements, suggesting that wage

Table 27. **Balance of payments projections**

$ billion

	1986	1987	1988	1989
Exports	224	251	313	372
Imports	369	410	454	491
Trade balance	**− 144**	**− 159**	**− 141**	**− 119**
Services and private transfers, net	17	11	2	− 2
of which:				
Net investment income	21	14	− 2	− 11
Official transfers, net	− 14	− 12	− 11	− 11
Current balance	**− 141**	**− 161**	**− 150**	**− 132**
Memorandum items:				
Per cent changes in manufactured trade volumes				
Exports (customs basis)	7.5	16.2	24	17¼
of which[1]				
Market growth	2.4	7.4	11	8¼
Export performance	5.0	8.2	11¾	8¼
Imports (customs basis)	13.2	6.1	5¾	6

1. The calculation of market growth is based on the growth of import volumes in U.S. export markets, weighted by U.S. trade flows. The "export performance" effect measures the extent to which U.S. exports are expected to exceed market growth, leading to an increase in market share.
Note: Detail may not add, due to rounding.
Sources: Department of Commerce (Bureau of Economic Analysis), Survey of Current Business, and OECD Secretariat estimates and projections.

behaviour has changed. Deregulation, international competition, the trading off of wage increases against job security, and a higher proportion of prime-age participants in labour force may account for this reduced sensitivity of wage inflation to unemployment. Recent research tends to suggest that demographic trends alone may have lowered the non-accelerating inflation rate (NAIRU) by ½ percentage point from its mid-1970s level[38].

Risks to the outlook

The above projections are highly conditional on three main assumptions, namely: the impact of the stock market crash is restricted to the wealth effects outlined above; no generalised wage and cost pressures arise because of capacity constraints and the trade deficit continues to improve. However, there are risks to the forecast. Consumer spending may weaken more than expected, leading to a recession which could be exacerbated by certain vulnerabilities in the financial system. Alternatively, domestic demand could be stronger and in view of the probable strength in real net exports, upward pressure on wages and prices may arise. This could lead to downward pressure on the dollar particularly if there were to be a run of bad trade figures. Against such a backdrop, financial market turbulence could re-occur, seriously complicating the task of the monetary authorities.

The risk of recession

As consumer confidence has recovered, the possibility of a recession (due to weakening consumption and a run-down in inventories) seems to have receded. However, the gross indebtedness of the household and corporate sectors remains high and could be a source of vulnerability should the economy weaken. In the case of the household sector, debt-to-income ratios climbed from 76 to 90 per cent between 1980 and 1987 – a rise equivalent to 10 per cent of GNP (see Table 40 below). Concern about this growing debt burden – which has gone hand-in-hand with increased delinquency rates – has been qualified by the fact that household assets have also risen, so that debt-to-net worth ratios have increased only from 16 to 20 per cent over the same period (Tables 40 and 41). Nevertheless, the personal saving ratio could still rise more than implied by the OECD projections. If it were to return too quickly to the average level of the 1970s, an associated inventory correction could lead to a recession. Such an event could be exacerbated by developments in the business sector. Corporate

Table 28. **Bear markets and economic cycles**

Stock market			Recession	
Peak	Trough	Per cent decline	Peak	Trough
7th September 1929	1st June 1932	86.2	August 1929	March 1933
5th March 1937	31st March 1938	54.5	May 1937	June 1938
30th May 1946	13th June 1949	29.6	November 1948	October 1949
5th January 1946	14th September 1953	14.8	July 1953	May 1954
2nd August 1956	22nd October 1957	21.6	August 1957	April 1958
3rd August 1959	25th October 1960	13.9	April 1960	February 1961
12th December 1961	26th June 1962	27.9	—	—
9th December 1966	1st October 1966	22.2	—	—
30th November 1968	26th May 1970	36.1	December 1969	November 1970
28th April 1971	23rd November 1971	13.9	—	—
11th January 1973	3rd October 1974	48.2	November 1973	March 1975
21st September 1976	6th March 1978	19.4	—	—
13th February 1980	27th March 1980	17.1	January 1980	July 1980
28th November 1980	12th August 1982	27.1	July 1981	November 1982
25th August 1987	19th October 1987	33.2		

Note: A bear market is defined as a peak-to-trough drop in the S&P 500 Index of more than 10 per cent. The 1940-1945 period has been excluded.
Source: Data Resources Incorporated.

66

leverage has increased significantly, although a mitigating trend of recent years has been a somewhat better balance between long and short-term liabilities. However, companies whose working capital is based on the issuance of lower-grade bonds or bank bridge loans could find cash flow and retained profits squeezed. Furthermore, many of the sectoral weaknesses identified in previous *Surveys* – related to agricultural, energy prices and third world debt exposure – remain, even though they appear less serious now than before.

The inflation risk

If 1987 is any guide, the authorities would probably tighten monetary policy in circumstances where domestic costs were expected to accelerate. In this respect, there are two risks. The first is that the wealth effects of the stock market fall should prove insufficient to prevent a strengthening of growth in domestic demand and over-heating in the labour market, with the unemployment rate falling sharply below $5^1/_2$ per cent. Although rapid declines in stock prices have historically been associated with the onset of recession, on several occasions the emergence of a bear market has incorrectly signalled weak economic growth (Table 28). The second risk relates to

Table 29. **Recent trends in manufacturing capacity utilisation**

	Historical average	Previous cycle high	Recent trends			Exports as percent of total sales[1]	Planned change in investment (volume)
	1967 to 1986	1978 to 1980	Q4 1986	Q4 1987	Change		
Manufacturing	**80.6**	**86.5**	**79.8**	**82.0**	**0.2**	**17.0**	**8.9**
Durables	**78.6**	**86.3**	**77.0**	**80.0**	**0.3**	**24.0**	**6.5**
Primary metals	79.6	97.1	70.4	89.1	18.7	8.6	15.0
Fabricated metals	78.0	87.4	77.8	77.9	0.1	6.0	10.0
Non-electrical machinery	78.1	86.0	71.9	76.2	4.3	21.1	5.0
Electrical machinery	78.0	89.9	74.4	76.9	2.5	13.1	11.5
Motor vehicles	78.0	93.3	78.5	80.1	1.6	15.7	– 4.5
Other transportation equipment	77.0	87.1	89.2	88.5	– 0.7	15.7[2]	1.5
Instruments	83.2	88.9	78.2	80.4	– 2.2	17.4	10.0
Non-durables	**83.5**	**87.0**	**83.8**	**85.4**	**1.6**	**12.0**	**11.2**
Food	82.2	85.1	79.9	79.6	– 0.3	4.7	10.5
Textiles	84.9	88.3	89.7	93.3	3.6	5.3	4.5
Chemicals	78.7	87.9	80.2	84.5	4.3	13.0	8.0
Paper	88.7	92.7	92.8	96.1	3.3	6.4	26.0

1. Data for industrial sectors relate to shipments; data for sub-aggregates relate to GNP by product, measured in terms of final sales (cf. *Economic Report of the President*, 1988, Table B-7). The two are not directly comparable.
2. All transportation equipment (motor vehicles and other).
Sources: Federal Reserve Board; Department of Commerce (Bureau of Economic Analysis); OECD Secretariat estimates.

capacity constraints in the manufacturing sector as a result of rapid export volume growth. Manufactured exports are projected to grow at an annual average rate of 17 per cent over the next two years, implying a 3 per cent growth in manufacturing output. Some non-durable goods industries (textiles, chemicals and paper) are already operating close to, or even above the average utilisation rates recorded in the 1978/80 period (Table 29). For these industries, a substantially greater amount of foreign orders can only be filled if domestic demand softens and/or capacity is increased rapidly enough. Durable goods producers have ample unused capacity. Nevertheless, faster growth of export demand than forecast could imply an inflationary risk.

The exchange rate and financial market risks

Given the preoccupation of the markets with monthly trade figures, dollar and bond market stability partly depends on whether the improvement in the trade balance shown in the November to January figures can be re-established. According to OECD projections the monthly trade balance should trend down towards $11½ billion (seasonally adjusted) by the second half of the year, from its present level of

Diagram 15. **MONTHLY TRADE BALANCE**

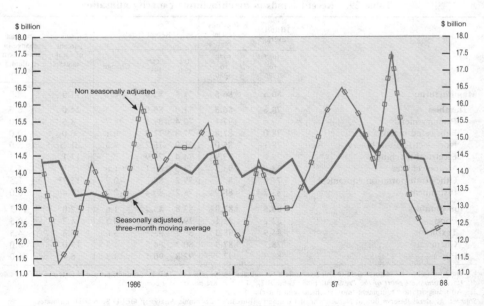

Sources: Department of Commerce, Bureau of the Census and OECD Secretariat estimates.

68

about \$13½ billion (Diagram 15). However, the dollar remains vulnerable to short-term fluctuations in the trade figures, and if these were to be less favourable than expected downward pressure on the exchange rate could re-emerge. This could lead to weakness in the bond market and renewed financial market turbulence, which would raise difficult problems for the conduct of monetary policy.

Medium-term adjustment

Medium-term trends

In the Secretariat's short-term projections, by 1989 the current account deficit falls by roughly \$30 billion from its value in 1987. Although the Federal deficit rises slightly, higher private sector saving allows the external deficit to decline. The following analysis explores the scope for smoothly unwinding remaining domestic and external imbalances over the medium term (i.e. until 1993). The aim is not to provide a set of medium-term projections, but rather to identify broad trends and assess the sensitivity of imbalances to various assumptions as to policy, growth performance and competitiveness.

The starting point for the analysis is a "reference case", built on the following assumptions:

  i) A restrictive *fiscal policy*, based on a real annual growth in Federal non-interest spending of about 1 per cent a year[39]. This would ensure a declining ratio of Federal spending to GNP (from 23 per cent in 1987 to about 21½ per cent in 1993, the exact figure depending on the interest rate assumption). The achievement of the revised G-R-H targets is not imposed at the outset, but is discussed in one of the scenarios;
 ii) Real *exchange rate* stability;
iii) An accommodating *monetary policy stance*, based on 6½ per cent M2 growth. This is taken to be consistent with interest rate stability, given nominal income growth of 6 to 7 per cent a year.

Estimates of U.S. potential growth used by Congress and the Administration for medium-term budgetary analysis vary between 2.5 per cent (CBO) and 3.1 per cent (Administration)[40]. Most of the difference concerns productivity growth, which the Administration puts at 1¾ per cent a year for GNP per employee and the CBO at 1.1 per cent. In the OECD "reference case", productivity and productive potential are assumed to grow at rates mid-way between the Administration and CBO estimates, giving an annual average real GNP growth of 2¾ per cent.

69

Total domestic demand in the rest of the OECD is assumed to grow by 2½ per cent a year, generating (with a recovery in non-OECD demand) a 6 per cent annual growth in the market for U.S. exports. However, in this reference case the current account balance still deteriorates gradually from 1990, because of the large existing difference between export and import levels (which implies that export volumes have to grow much faster than import volumes in order to prevent the gap from widening) and growing interest payments on foreign debt. Under this scenario, the current account deficit in 1993 amounts to 2 per cent of GNP, down from 3.5 per cent in 1987, and the net foreign investment position approaches a negative 15 per cent of GNP. The Federal deficit falls towards $100 billion in 1993 (Table 19), under the economic growth and Federal spending assumptions adopted, ensuring a gradual decline in the deficit/GNP ratio. The government debt/GNP ratio would increase in 1988 and 1989 but fall thereafter.

The risks from further dollar depreciation

The dollar came under severe downward pressure at the beginning of 1988, and this was met by concerted intervention to contain the fall before the boost provided by the publication of the November trade figures. The rationale for resisting such pressure is that a further significant dollar depreciation could be counterproductive by damaging world growth prospects. According to the INTERLINK model, a 10 per cent effective depreciation of the dollar from its mid-January level would improve the nominal trade balance after two years by $31 billion *ex ante* (i.e. before allowing for repercussions on domestic demand and prices) (Table 30). However, under currently prevailing conditions in the domestic economy an external stimulus of this magnitude could have inflationary consequences. In the depreciation simulation reported in Table 30, where nominal interest rates are held constant, improvement in the current account is eventually eroded because of a significant increase in price and wage inflation. But the combination of depreciation and inflation substantially reduces the ratio of overseas and government debt relative to U.S. GNP, again because of higher inflation.

In principle, the income- and inflation-generating effects of depreciation can be controlled through appropriate fiscal and monetary policies. However, in the very near term the U.S. budgetary system is likely to prove too inflexible to be an effective demand management instrument. If monetary policy alone were used to control domestic absorption and inflation, interest rates would have to rise more than if fiscal policy could help carry the load. Thus, in a simulation where a 10 per cent effective depreciation of the dollar is accompanied by a non-accommodating monetary stance

Table 30. **Effects of dollar depreciation**

| | "First round" impact[1] | Increments to reference case arising from a 10% dollar depreciation | |
| | | *Ex post* impact | |
		Monetary accomodation[2]	Monetary tightening[3]
		Annual average rates of change 1987 to 1993, per cent	
Export volumes[4]	+3.9	-0.20	+0.38
Import volumes[4]	-4.4	0	-0.40
GNP volume	+0.15	+0.2	-0.23
Total domestic demand volume	—	+0.2	-0.35
Inflation rate			
CPI	—	+2.0	+1.0
Wage rates	—	+2.1	+0.9
		Change from 1987 to 1993	
Current account balance ($ billion)	+31	-7	+20
Federal budget balance ($ billion)	—	+129	-34
Federal debt/GNP ratio (%)[5]	—	-9.7	-1.5
Net external debt/GNP ratio (%)	—	-2.7	-2.1
Interest rates (%)[6]	—	0	+2.4
Unemployment rate (%)	—	-0.6	+0.7

1. Trade sector simulation with prices and incomes exogenised, i.e. the substitution effects of depreciation, before allowing for repercussions on domestic demand and prices.
2. Real government spending and nominal interest rates assumed unchanged in the United States and overseas.
3. Real government spending and monetary growth assumed unchanged in the United States and overseas.
4. Goods and services.
5. Public debt securities held by the public (i.e. excluding social security and other government accounts). A negative sign shows a reduction.
6. Average of short and long rates.
Source: OECD Secretariat estimates.

(column 3 of Table 30) interest rates rise by over 2 percentage points and private spending is crowded out. This policy mix also has the disadvantage of raising the Federal deficit, principally because of higher interest payments.

Implementing the Balanced Budget Act

The elimination (or substantial reduction) of the structural Federal deficit is a key ingredient in the adjustment process. In this respect, the Balanced Budget Act (G-R-H), as amended, aims to balance the Federal budget by 1993. The possible consequences of such action for the current-account deficit and economic growth are analysed below. There are, however, problems in incorporating the G-R-H provisions into a simulation exercise, because neither the size nor the composition of the discretionary cuts needed to comply with the Act are known. The cuts would need to be larger, for instance, under the slower growth and higher interest rate assumptions used by the CBO than under the Administration's growth assumptions: according to the FY 1989 Budget, cuts of over $39 billion would be needed to balance the budget in 1993, while the CBO's baseline implies reductions of $134 billion. Consistent with its growth assumption, the OECD reference scenario would call for cuts of approximately $100 billion.

According to the OECD INTERLINK model, fiscal cuts of $100 billion over five years[41] would actually reduce the Federal deficit *ex post* by about $70 billion by 1993, a relatively favourable outcome partly due to the fact that as the deficit falls, debt and debt interest grow more slowly (Table 31). At the same time, the external deficit would improve by $36 billion. There would be some increase in unemployment, but because of the responsiveness of long-term interest rates to cuts in the deficit, and the interest-sensitivity of private spending, the long-run deflationary effect of budget cuts is considerably dampened.

Faster adjustment path

Although a cut in the budget deficit would benefit the internal and external balance of the economy, such action would have short-run costs in terms of growth and employment which might be avoided if it were accompanied by more favourable conditions in export and import markets. In Table 31 a number of additional simulations are reported, the objective being to evaluate the circumstances in which fiscal cuts could be compatible not only with a move towards balance in the Federal budget and a faster reduction of the external deficit but also with no deterioration in the employment and growth performance. The variants are:

   i) A sustained 1 per cent increase in total domestic demand abroad;

   ii) A further improvement in U.S. competitiveness of around 10 per cent over the 1990-1993 period, obtained for instance through a combination of greater nominal wage moderation, higher productivity growth and revaluation of the currencies of certain newly-industrialised countries;

   iii) A decline in the U.S. propensity to import as a result of structural change.

The simulations are intended merely to illustrate some circumstances in which the deficit could be eliminated while economic growth is maintained; no view is taken about the plausibility of these particular variants; nor do they encompass all the possible alternative paths around the reference case.

72

A 1 per cent sustained increase in total domestic demand in the rest of the world would be expected to improve the U.S. current account by $12 billion after six years (Table 31, column 2). In conjunction with the G-R-H package, this would bring the external deficit down to less than 1 per cent of GNP. With a deficit of that size, the net external debt/GNP ratio would begin to fall. But in view of the weaker growth in industrial output and employment, a further improvement in U.S. competitiveness might be useful to strike a better balance between current account and unemployment goals. In column 3 of Table 31, a further improvement of $3^1/3$ per cent per annum in U.S. relative prices from 1990 onwards has been described. This would bring the current account close to balance and would also lower the Federal deficit. If in addition an improvement were to occur in the U.S. trade elasticities (final column of Table 31), balance would be nearly achieved. However, an unavoidable feature of all strategies designed to correct the external deficit within a few years would be a very slow growth in U.S. domestic demand over that period. With investment needing to increase to underpin the swing to net exports, there will be little room for consumption to expand. Limits on public consumption could provide only part of the necessary restraint and private consumption growth would also have to be contained.

Table 31. **Reinforcing fiscal policy**

	Implementation of G-R-H cuts[1]	1% higher foreign demand	Improvement in U.S. relative prices[2]	More optimistic trade elasticities[3]
	Increments to reference scenario			
	Annual average rates of change 1987 to 1993, per cent			
Export volumes	− 0.4	0.4	0.6	0.4
Import volumes	− 1.2	0.2	− 0.8	− 0.1
GNP volume	− 0.15	0.05	0.05	0.05
Total domestic demand volume	− 0.3	—	0.25	0.10
Inflation rate				
CPI	− 0.4	0.2	0.9	0.25
Wage rates	− 0.5	0.3	0.7	0.25
	Change 1987 to 1993			
($ billion)				
Federal deficit	+ 74	+ 6	+ 29	+ 27
Current account	+ 36	+ 12	+ 36	+ 29

1. OECD reference case plus implementation of Balanced Budget Act with international linkages. Money growth assumed unchanged.
2. Amounting to 3.3 per cent per annum during the period 1990-1993.
3. Price elasticities of exports and imports increased 50 per cent, income elasticity of manufactured imports reduced from 2.0 to 1.8.
Source: OECD Secretariat estimates.

73

Trade liberalisation

The balance-of-payments adjustment process can operate effectively only in an environment of open and expanding international trade. Macroeconomic solutions have to be supported by trade initiatives aimed, not only at reducing protectionist tendencies in the United States and elsewhere, but also at expanding trade opportunities through multilateral negotiations. In pursuit of a larger market for U.S. exports, the Administration has continued to push for trade liberalisation within the context of the Uruguay Round and has been very aggressive in seeking concessions from its trading partners. It has been involved in a wide range of disputes with the European Community, Canada, and Japan, many of which have been settled (compensation for Spanish entry into the EC, the pasta agreement), and has reached agreement with Canada over the formation of a free-trade zone[42]. However, other issues remain in contention (access to telecommunication markets, government subsidies for the European Airbus). This fairly aggressive approach has been designed, in part, to head off protectionist sentiment in Congress, where the external deficit is often equated with unfair trading practices abroad.

Both houses of Congress passed their version of an omnibus trade bill in 1987, but these failed to reach the statute book, in part because of the need to reach a budget compromise. The two bills were very protectionist, but differed in significant details which were being reconciled as of mid-April. The original House version had tighter provisions for dumping and countervailing duties, while the Senate version provided more temporary protection from imports. Because current law already offers adequate protection from harmful dumping and subsidies, the expanded use of anti-dumping duties can be seen as protectionist. Although the Bills contain helpful features, such as "fast track" agreement authority, giving the President greater trade negotiation powers, any final Bill of a protectionist character is likely to be vetoed.

Summing-up

Analysis of some of the key issues involved in the external adjustment process underlines the fact that correcting the external deficit is likely to remain gradual and persistent. Implementation of the Balanced Budget Act is an essential factor, but can only be part of the adjustment process. Faster growth abroad would be needed to offset the adverse global growth effects of the inevitable restraints on U.S. domestic demand growth. External competitiveness will also have to evolve in a manner consistent with long-run current account balance. Overall, under a set of relatively favourable conditions, the task of unwinding the current external deficit will not be an intractable one over the medium term.

74

V. Financial markets: innovation and stability

Introduction

The changes in macroeconomic conditions that have occurred in the last two decades have had an important impact on the functioning of U.S. financial markets. The increased volatility of inflation, interest and exchange rates has caused lenders and borrowers to search for new ways to protect themselves against unexpected losses. High nominal and real interest costs have prompted borrowers to search for new sources and types of credit. The growth in world trade and income, movements in the value of the dollar and associated changes in the net external investment position of the United States, have boosted international linkages between financial markets and the role of foreign investors in the domestic economy.

Furthermore, there has been a technological revolution that has greatly reduced information and other financial transaction costs, and as a result has increased the ability of borrowers and lenders to meet directly in capital markets. Advances in computer technology and telecommunications, combined with the changes in the macroeconomic environment (Table 32), have spurred a widespread process of innovation that can be loosely summarised under three headings:

- Homogenisation. Broadly speaking, the 1970s and 1980s have seen many long-standing distinctions between institutions become blurred, and in some cases disappear altogether. Insurance companies have bought securities firms, retailers and manufacturers have become major suppliers of credit through finance subsidiaries, commercial banks have increased their investment banking activities, and thrift institutions now make commercial and industrial loans;
- Securitisation. The nature of credit granting has changed in important ways, and has shifted away from traditional bank loans. Increasingly, corporations raise short-term credit directly on securities markets, and not through intermediated deposits. Thrift institutions make home mortgages, but then sell

Table 32. **Macroeconomic forces and financial innovation**

Force/innovation	Advantages
Inflation	
Cash management techniques (e.g. sweep accounts)	Reduces average cash balances to minimise costs associated with foregone interest income
Bond market innovations (e.g. zero-coupon bonds)	Increases the attractiveness of fixed-rate securities to some investors (tax considerations important)
Home equity loans	Increases the effective liquidity of housing (wealth swelled by inflation); inflation also increases the value of the tax deductibility of mortgage interest
Money market and other mutual funds	Increases rate of return and widens investment opportunities on household transaction/savings accounts (interaction of inflation with bank deposit rate ceilings made such alternatives more attractive in the 1970s-early 1980s)
High real interest rates	
Mortgage passthroughs and other asset-backed securities	Increases the liquidity of mortgage assets, raising their price and widening the pool of potential investors
Bond market innovations (e.g. zero coupon)	Increases the attractiveness of fixed-rate securities to some investors (tax considerations important)
Home equity loans	Enables households to more easily tap a lower rate of credit
Eurobond, junk-bond markets	Exploits new sources of credit in order to reduce borrowing costs; junk bond market growth also associated with increase in merger activity
Adjustable rate mortgages and floating rate loans	Reduces interest costs by transferring price risk to borrower
Volatile interest and exchange rates	
Options and futures	Allows trading of price-risk separate from underlying assets or transactions
Adjustable rate mortgages and floating rate loans	Transfers price risk from lender to borrower
Note issuance facilities and credit enhancing guarantees	Increases the liquidity of securities markets by lowering credit-risk and providing limited insurance to borrowers against price risk
Growth in world trade and income	
Eurobond market and other foreign trading of dollar-denominated securities	Allows U.S. firms to take advantage of growing international sources of credit
Swaps	Enables borrowers to exploit imperfections/differences between national capital markets
Domestic trading of foreign securities	Allows U.S. investors to participate in world capital markets

Source: William Silber, "The Process of Financial Innovation", *American Economic Review* (May 1983), and OECD Secretariat.

them to other institutions which convert them into bond-like securities to be sold to other investors. New types of bonds and a variety of risk-hedging devices are used to increase the appeal of securities to investors;
- Internationalisation. National capital and banking markets have become much more integrated; U.S. firms are important participants in markets abroad, as are foreign institutions in the intermediation of domestic funds. Disturbances in one market are rapidly transmitted across international borders.

These innovations have increased the options available to borrowers and lenders, and have improved the quality and efficiency of financial intermediation.

In addition to promoting innovations, changes in the economic climate have placed strains on different sectors of the economy. Disinflation, high real interest rates and swings in many commodity prices undercut the economic rationale of many ongoing investment projects in the first half of the 1980s. As a result, export earnings of many LDCs have been squeezed, agricultural land values have fallen, many energy firms have gone bankrupt, and real estate development projects in certain parts of the country have failed. These and other troubles have caused a deterioration in the financial position of many businesses. Associated loan losses have reduced the profitability of the banking sector, and have created capital problems for some institutions. The stability of banks, and the financial system in general, may also have been affected by the ongoing process of innovation, to the extent that the adequacy of the existing institutional and regulatory structure has been called into question, leading to various proposals for its reform. On top of these developments there has been a marked increase in the general indebtedness of all non-financial sectors. All these factors together have increased the potential vulnerability of the financial system and the economy as a whole to further shocks, such as those discussed in the previous chapters.

In the sections that follow, these developments and issues are reviewed in greater detail. The discussion begins with an overview of the financial system. It then turns to the competitive position and profitablity of the banking sector, and how depository institutions (and regulatory agencies) have coped with the increased strains of recent years. Next, the review examines the growth in non-depository financial institutions, the role of foreign institutions and markets, and the increase in securities issuance and trading. A discussion follows of the effect that recent innovations have had on the efficiency and stability of the financial system, and on the role of government financial supervision. Finally, the ways in which the conduct and transmission of monetary policy has changed is considered, along with the growth in aggregate debt, and their possible implications for macroeconomic stability.

Diagram 16.   **FINANCIAL SAVINGS AND INVESTMENT**
(As a percentage of GNP)

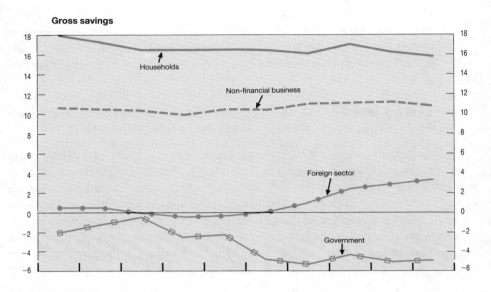

Gross savings

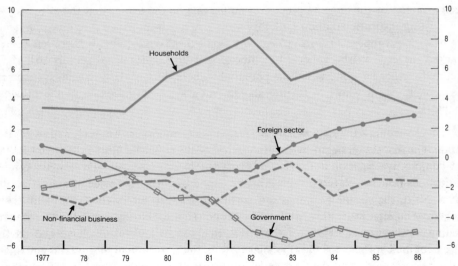

Net financial investment

Source: Federal Reserve Board, *Flow of Funds.*

Overview of the financial system

In its broad features, the U.S. financial system is similar to that of other OECD Member economies. Households are the primary savers and ultimate source (along with foreigners in the 1980s) of credit to other domestic sectors (Diagram 16). Roughly 25 per cent of household financial assets are held as bank deposits, and about 30 per cent takes the form of direct holdings of market securities, a large percentage in comparison to other countries (Table 33). Households also have indirect stock and bond holdings in the form of pension fund and life insurance company reserves. Household liabilities are mostly made up of long-term mortgage debt. Unlike households, non-financial businesses are net financial borrowers despite being large gross savers. (This arises from high capital expenditures.) Outside of trade credit, their net holdings of financial assets are relatively small, and important liabilities include loans from banks and finance companies, mortgages, bonds, and trade debt. The Government dissaves in the aggregate, although this masks approximate balance (net of contributions to pension funds) at the state and local level. Governments at all levels issue substantial amounts of debt, though only the Federal Government has a large outstanding volume of obligations with a maturity under one year. On the asset side, State and Local Governments are important participants in short-term wholesale money markets, and both Federal and State Governments lend to individuals, farmers, and business.

The flow of funds between and within these non-financial sectors follows many channels, and involves a number of different types of financial intermediaries. The most important of these are *commercial banks*, who control one-third of all private intermediated assets (Table 34). These institutions raise funds primarily through retail depository liabilities (household and small business accounts), but they also rely heavily on large denomination certificates of deposits and other wholesale money markets instruments[43]. Their liabilities are in turn invested in loans to consumers and business, in mortgages, and in government securities. Aside from commercial banks, the banking system includes *thrift institutions* (savings and loan associations, mutual savings banks, and credit unions), which are also insured depository institutions. These differ from banks by mainly holding portfolios of home mortgages and mortgage-backed securities[44]. Outside the banking system are a number of other financial institutions, which together control about half of all intermediated assets. The liabilities of these firms are not insured by the government and for the most part are long-term, e.g. *pension fund* and *life insurance company* reserves and shares in *open-end mutual funds*. This characteristic enables them to hold long-maturity assets such as corporate equities, bonds, and non-residential mortgages. *Money market*

79

Table 33. **Assets and liabilities of non-financial sectors**

1986 end-of-year outstandings

	Households	Non-financial business	Federal government[1]	State and local governments[1]	Households	Non-financial business	Federal government[1]	State and local governments[1]
	$ billions				Per cent of total assets			
Total financial assets	11 203.9	1 616.5	383.2	523.5	100.0	100.0	100.0	100.0
Deposits and currency	2 881.1	288.3	39.6	126.1	25.7	17.8	10.3	24.1
Securities	1 008.3	218.7	—	—	9.0	13.5	—	55.1
Corporate equities	2 350.3	—	—	—	21.0	—	—	—
Pension fund and life insurance reserves	2 234.6	—	—	—	20.0	—	—	—
Equity in non-corporate business	2 404.3	—	—	—	21.5	—	—	—
Trade credit	—	646.8	33.8	—	—	40.0	8.8	—
Other	475.6	462.7	309.8	108.9	4.2	28.6	80.8	20.1
	$ billions				Per cent of total liabilities			
Total financial liabilities	2 741.0	3 423.1	2 041.9	575.0	100.0	100.0	100.0	100.0
Mortgages	1 690.6	869.4	—	—	61.7	25.4	—	—
Consumer credit	723.0	—	—	—	26.4	—	—	—
Loans, ex consumer credit	139.9	1 032.6	1.2	27.5	5.1	30.2	0.1	4.8
Securities	82.0	775.9	1 813.5	523.3	3.0	22.7	88.8	91.0
Trade debt	31.2	526.5	27.3	24.2	1.1	15.4	1.3	4.2
Other	74.3	218.7	199.9	—	2.7	6.4	9.8	—
Net financial assets	8 462.9	−1 806.6	−1 658.7	−51.5	308.8	−52.8	−81.2	−9.0

1. Government accounts exclude off-budget financial agencies.
Source: *Flow of Funds*, Federal Reserve Board.

80

mutual funds (MMMFs), by contrast, issue demand deposit-like instruments and invest in short-term securities. Other non-bank intermediaries include *finance companies* (which make loans to consumers and business funded in part by commercial paper issuance), and *security dealers* which trade stocks, bonds and other financial instruments on behalf of individuals and firms, as well as on their own account. Alongside these private intermediaries are the government financial agencies. Aside from the Federal Reserve System, these include federal and state regulatory and deposit insurance agencies, and federally-sponsored corporations that are important in housing finance. (See Annex IV for a glossary of financial market terms.)

The broad similarity of this institutional structure with that existing in other countries masks some important differences. Foremost among these is the size and depth of U.S. financial markets, which are rivalled only by those in the United Kingdom and Japan. Total credit market debt outstanding, excluding corporate stock, stands at almost $10 trillion, and the market value of corporate equity adds an additional $3 trillion. Treasury obligations alone constitute the largest single market in the world, worth about $2 trillion. This tremendous volume of paper has given rise to large secondary markets in many different securities, allowing trading across a wide range of maturities and borrowers. Another difference from other financial systems is the relatively small share of total intermediation that takes place through the banking system. The percentage of financial intermediation occurring via monetary institutions (commercial banks, thrifts and money market mutual funds) has only averaged about 35 per cent since the mid-1970s; comparable figures for Germany, Canada and the United Kingdom were around 90 per cent, 50 per cent, and 50 per cent, respectively[45]. This low percentage exists for many reasons, but partly reflects another characteristic of the U.S. financial system: the existence of markets for the trading of a large number of non-traditional instruments, such as loan-backed securities and financial futures and options. The creation of these markets – along with economies of scale in financial operations – has increased the options available to borrowers and lenders alike, and has helped to draw business away from the banking sector. Finally, direct lending by the Government plays only a minor role in total finance. Outstanding government loans and mortgages are only equal to about 5½ per cent of the total liabilities of households and non-financial business, although for certain groups, such as farmers and students, government credit is important. Instead, the chief credit role of government has been in the guarantee and securitisation of home mortgage credit (see the Securitisation and capital markets section, below).

Like every country, the U.S. financial system has evolved subject to its own particular set of economic, political and social forces. Via inherited legal and institutional structures, these forces continue to affect the economy long after they have

81

Table 34. Assets and liabilities of financial institutions

1986 end-of-year outstandings, $ billion

	Commercial banks	Savings banks[1]	Pension funds	Insurance companies[2]	Finance companies	Mutual funds	Security brokers	Federal credit agencies
Assets								
Total financial assets	2 580.0	1 563.3	1 329.0	1 218.6	412.1	715.9	79.2	874.9
Deposits[3]	2.5	116.2	65.8	31.8	7.0	80.0	3.7	34.8
Government securities[4]	519.6	256.6	262.4	289.7	—	306.8	1.3	11.5
Corporate and foreign bonds	47.3	16.1	253.6	352.9	67.5	46.9	9.6	—
Mortgages	502.5	801.2	20.4	201.4	—	—	—	679.2
Consumer credit and loans	319.6	147.7	—	54.0	162.8	—	—	14.7
Business bank loans[5]	718.8	24.0	—	—	174.8	—	—	18.1
Corporate equities	0.1	7.0	616.9	155.8	—	161.2	12.2	0.1
Open market paper	11.1	36.1	32.3	33.2	—	114.7	—	—
Other	458.5	158.4	80.2	97.2	—	6.3	52.3	116.5
Liabilities								
Total financial liabilities	2 535.7	1 514.9	1 329.0	1 089.0	436.5	715.9	72.2	866.9
Deposits[3]	2 008.5	1 289.9	—	—	—	228.3	—	—
Government securities	—	—	—	—	—	—	—	800.2
Corporate and foreign bonds	74.9	12.0	—	1.7	115.6	—	—	—
Mortgages	—	—	—	2.8	—	—	—	—
Bank loans[5]	—	23.9	—	0.8	11.4	—	—	—
Open market paper	101.9	—	—	1.0	181.8	—	—	—
Insurance and pension reserves	—	—	1 329.0	725.5	—	—	—	—
Mutual fund shares, ex money market	—	—	—	—	—	487.6	—	—
Other	350.4	189.1	—	357.2	127.7	—	72.2	66.7
Memorandum item:								
Share of total private intermediated assets	32.7	19.8	16.8	15.4	5.2	9.1	1.0	n.a.

1. Savings and loan associations, mutual savings banks, and credit unions.
2. Includes real estate investment trusts.
3. Currency, checkable deposits, time and savings deposits, federal funds and security RPs, and inter-blank credit.
4. Includes federal mortgage pool securities.
5. Includes bank loans not classified elsewhere.
Source: Flow of Funds, Federal Reserve Board.

disappeared. For example, a widespread fear of financial concentration led to a rejection of a centralised banking system in the early 1800s, and the adoption of a state-centred structure. The federal nature of government, the power of local interests, and southern and western mistrust of eastern banks, all combined to produce a system where interstate bank activity was effectively prohibited[46]. As a result, the U.S. today has over 13 000 commercial banks, with the largest ten controlling only 20 per cent of total commercial bank assets, as compared to much higher percentages in other countries (Table 35). Another event that had major long-term institutional effects was the Great Depression. The stock market crash of 1929 and the widespread bank failures of the early 1930s prompted an overhaul of the Federal regulations governing finance. Public disclosure rules for trading in corporate securities were strengthened, and the Securities and Exchange Commission was created to regulate bond and equity markets. The Federal deposit insurance programmes were started to restore faith in the safety of the banking system. Investment banking was largely separated from commercial banking by the *Glass-Steagall Act*, on the grounds that the soundness of the banking system had been compromised by imprudent security dealings.

Table 35.   **International comparisons of bank concentration**

United States (1985)	Out of 13 739 commercial banks, the largest five control 12.8 per cent of total assets, the largest ten control 20.3 per cent, and the largest 100 control 57.5 per cent. Adding the assets of thrift institutions to those of the commercial banks reduces these percentages to 7.5 per cent, 11.8 per cent, and 33.5 per cent, respectively.
Japan (1986)	Out of 87 commercial banks, thirteen city banks control 56.7 per cent of total assets.
Germany (1987)	Out of 316 commercial banks, the largest six control 37.9 per cent of total assets. Adding the assets of 4 232 other banking institutions reduces this percentage to 8.8 per cent, but an additional 17 per cent of assets are controlled by the postal and regional Giros.
France (1986)	Out of 367 banks, three control 41.7 per cent of all assets. If one excludes foreign-affiliated banks, this percentage increases to 62.2 per cent. Adding the assets of mutual and savings banks to those of banks reduces these percentages to 29.5 and 44.0, respectively.
United Kingdom (1986)	The five largest banks control 45.6 per cent of the total assets of the monetary sector.
Canada (1985)	The four largest banks control 51.2 per cent of all deposits, and seven banks account for over 80 per cent of all deposits.

Source: "Interstate Banking Developments", *Federal Reserve Bulletin,* February 1987; Federation of Bankers Associations of Japan, *Analysis of Financial Statements of All Banks* (1st April 1986 to 31st March 1987); Deutsche Bundesbank, *Monthly Report,* Vol. 39, No. 8, August 1987; Commission Bancaire, *Rapport 1985,* France; *Abstract of Banking Statistics,* Committee of London and Scottish Bankers, Vol. 3, May 1986; and Economic Council of Canada, *Competition and Solvency* (1986).

Henceforth, direct access to the safety net of deposit insurance and central bank credit would be denied to almost all institutions engaged in corporate securities underwriting, real estate development, or insurance[47]. Commercial banks and thrift institutions also were made subject to stricter prudential supervision, and the payment of interest on demand accounts was prohibited[48]. Thrift institutions specialising in housing finance were retained alongside the commercial banks, and interstate banking continued to be effectively prohibited. After extensions and modifications provided by subsequent legislation[49], this structure was more-or-less the one in place at the start of the 1980s.

Strains in the banking system

The past few years have been difficult for depository institutions. The net income after taxes of commercial banks fell to .64 per cent of average net assets in 1986, down from much higher levels in the 1970s (Diagram 17). Incomplete data for 1987

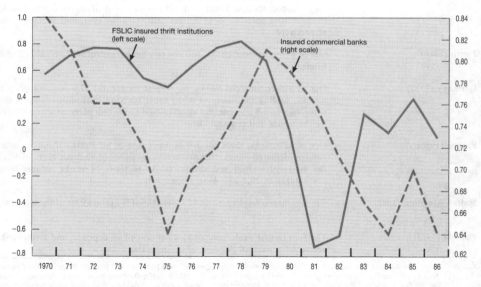

Diagram 17. **PROFITABILITY OF DEPOSITORY INSTITUTIONS**
(Per cent of total assets)

Sources: Federal Reserve Board, *Federal Reserve Bulletin* and Federal Home Loan Bank Board, *Savings and Home Financing Source Book.*

suggests a further worsening, and it is likely that average profitability approached zero last year. A decline in loan quality has been a primary factor in these difficulties, as loss provisions have more than tripled from the beginning of the decade. These asset quality problems have afflicted both small and large banks, although losses at the largest banks were especially great in 1987, due to ongoing problems with LDC loans. The fall-off in earnings has affected investors' perceptions of the worth of commercial banks: bank stocks, especially money centre ones, have underperformed the general market by a significant amount. Nevertheless, most commercial banks have been able to improve their capitalisation, and the ratio of primary capital (which includes reserves for loan losses) to assets has risen from below 6 per cent in 1980 to 7.6 per cent in 1986. Large money centre banks have been particularly successful in their efforts to increase primary capital, but these banks face large potential losses on loans to some Latin-American countries. (For a more extended discussion of recent developments in the banking system, see Annex V.)

Thrift institutions have fared even more poorly than commercial banks in the 1980s. Net after tax earnings at savings and loan associations (S&Ls) fell from .77 per cent of assets in 1977 to −.73 per cent in 1981. This precipitous decline occurred because S&Ls and mutual savings banks (MSBs) had portfolios dominated by fixed-rate long-term mortgages: as the Federal Funds rate jumped from 5.5 per cent to 16.4 per cent over this period, thrifts found it impossible to offset the resultant increase in their cost of funds. Since 1982 earnings have recovered somewhat – largely due to a decline in interest rates and turnover of the mortgage portfolio – but average profitability remains low because of loan losses on real estate development projects. This continued poor performance has threatened the viability of many of these institutions. Currently, 20 per cent of all S&Ls have negative earnings, and almost 10 per cent are insolvent.

Many of these problems have stemmed from changes in macroeconomic conditions, such as the rise and then rapid decline in inflation in the 1970-1983 period, the 1980s' increase in real interest rates and the value of the dollar, and the drop in commodity prices. These developments undercut the economic value of many ongoing investment projects. As a result, loans made to many developing countries, farmers, energy producers, and real estate developers became uncollectable, or were renegotiated in a way that left the banks with large capital losses. Although large losses were unavoidable in the face of such shocks, other factors exacerbated the situation. For example:

- Insufficient prudential supervision, combined with legislation granting thrift institutions expanded investment powers, allowed many S&Ls to pursue imprudent strategies in the mid-1980s. Using large-scale wholesale money market borrowings and aggressively priced insured retail deposits, a significant minority of the industry expanded rapidly and invested in high-risk projects, such as commercial real estate. Default rates proved higher than expected, leading to large capital losses and insolvency in many cases;

– Limitations on interstate branching created commercial banks and thrifts which were insufficiently diversified across regions, and tied too closely to the fortunes of the energy or agriculture sectors. Also, in view of branching restrictions, some banks expanded by relying heavily on money markets for raising funds. Such dependence can complicate bank portfolio management because wholesale deposit rates are more volatile than retail ones. Moreover, since wholesale deposits are only partially covered by Federal insurance, large deposits tend to be especially responsive to changes in institutional investors' assessment of the financial health of individual banks;

– Other financial institutions continued to make inroads into the traditional markets of commercial banks, aided by restrictions on bank activities and a general freedom from regulatory requirements. This increased competition actually began well before the 1980s: from 1975 through the early 1980s bank assets grew significantly more slowly than those of other financial institutions (Table 36). Adding to these competitive pressures was an increase in the issuance of securities, which reduced the relative importance of traditional bank intermediation. Moreover, restrictions on the securities activities of banks limited their ability to profit from these expanding markets.

Commercial banks have responded to these pressures by improving operations in traditional fields and finding new sources of income. Continuing a process begun in the inflationary 1970s, banks have increased the attractiveness of holding deposits through improvements in cash-management services provided to customers. Overseas operations have been expanded (by money centre and large regional banks) in order to take advantage of both the growth in international trade and foreign income, and the absence of Glass-Steagall restrictions in many foreign markets. Earnings have also been augmented through fee income derived from a variety of sources, including the provision of back-up credit for commercial paper and tax-exempt industrial revenue bonds, arranging currency and interest rate swaps, and trading in interest rate futures and forward rate agreements. Because many of these new activities are off-balance sheet, they have been attractive to banks trying to improve both earnings and capitalisation. Their importance to bank profitability has grown substantially, and the ratio of non-interest income to assets stood at 1.40 in 1986, up from .78 in 1979.

Unlike commercial banks, thrift institutions have by and large concentrated on improvements in their traditional field of home finance, the most important being the

Table 36. **Asset growth of financial institutions**

Per cent change, annual rate

	1965-1970	1970-1975	1975-1980	1980-1986
	Current dollars			
Commercial banks	7.85	10.14	9.83	9.43
Thrift institutions[1]	6.48	12.68	11.92	10.44
Finance companies	7.48	9.10	15.65	12.37
Investment companies[2]	7.68	8.60	21.07	40.48
Memorandum items:				
Bank loans	8.21	11.18	9.40	8.60
Commercial paper	28.90	7.58	20.58	17.91
GNP	7.57	9.50	11.32	7.58
	Constant dollars[3]			
Commercial banks	3.27	2.80	3.03	4.26
Thrift institutions[1]	1.96	5.17	3.97	5.23
Finance companies	2.91	1.83	7.44	7.06
Investment companies[2]	2.19	− 6.02	13.08	20.75
Memorandum items:				
Bank loans	3.61	3.77	1.63	3.47
Commercial paper	23.42	0.41	12.02	12.34
GNP	2.97	2.21	3.41	2.58

1. Savings and loan associations, mutual savings banks, and credit unions.
2. Mutual funds, money market mutual funds, and security brokers.
3. Deflated using GNP implicit deflator.
Source: Flow of Funds, Federal Reserve Board, and the Bureau of Economic Activity, *Survey of Current Business.*

use of adjustable rate mortages (ARMs). Like traditional mortgages these are typically 30 year loans, but their interest rate is pegged to a shorter-term market rate, such as the yield on one-year Treasury securities. By transferring price risk to households, and decreasing the sluggishness of the mortgage portfolio yield, these instruments partially insulate thrifts from swings in income caused by fluctuations in market interest rates. Over half of all new mortgage loans made now carry such terms, and ARMs accounted for 43 per cent of all outstanding mortgage debt in 1986. Thrifts have also increased the liquidity of their portfolios by substituting mortgage-backed securities for individual mortgage loans. These instruments, extensively traded in secondary markets, enhance the ability of institutions to adjust to deposit flows, and to participate in wholesale money markets via repurchase agreements. The share of mortgage-backed securities in S&L portfolios has risen from 4.4 per cent in 1980 to over 13 per cent today (Table 37). In addition to increased liquidity, this form of securitisation has boosted portfolio diversification – by replacing local mortgages with securities backed by nation-wide mortgage pools – and has

Table 37. **Composition of thrift institution portfolios**

	1980	1981	1982	1983	1984	1985	1986
FSLIC insured thrift institutions							
Mortgage assets	84.1	83.0	77.2	74.7	72.3	71.1	69.9
Residential loans	72.4	70.7	61.3	54.8	50.3	48.6	44.7
Non-residential loans	7.3	7.3	7.4	8.8	10.9	12.1	12.2
Mortgage-backed securities	4.4	5.0	8.5	11.1	11.1	10.4	13.0
Real estate holdings	0.4	0.5	0.8	1.0	1.2	1.6	4.7
Cash and securities	9.8	10.1	12.0	13.4	13.8	13.9	14.5
Non-mortgage loans	3.0	2.8	2.9	3.4	} 12.7	} 13.4	6.2
Other assets	2.8	3.8	6:8	7.0			4.7
Total assets	100.0	100.0	100.0	100.0	100.0	100.0	100.0
Mutual savings banks							
Mortgage assets	66.3	64.8	62.1	59.7	59.9	60.0	60.0
Loans	58.2	56.9	54.0	50.3	50.5	51.0	50.2
Mortgage-backed securities	8.1	7.9	8.1	9.4	9.4	9.0	9.8
Non-mortgage loans	6.8	8.4	9.7	9.9	12.2	14.2	15.5
Cash and securities	24.0	23.6	23.7	25.4	22.3	19.8	18.2
Other assets	2.9	3.2	4.5	5.0	5.6	6.0	6.3
Total assets	100.0	100.0	100.0	100.0	100.0	100.0	100.0

Source: Federal Reserve Bulletin, Federal Reserve Board; *Savings and Home Financing Source Book*, Federal Home Loan Bank Board.

enabled thrifts to earn off-balance sheet income by originating and servicing mortgages held by other investors. Thrifts have also begun to diversify away from housing finance, and non-mortgage loans at S&Ls rose from around 2 per cent of assets in 1978 to 6½ per cent in 1987. Increases at MSBs have been even more pronounced, and consumer and business loans now account for 14½ per cent of their portfolios, up from 4½ per cent ten years earlier.

Government regulation of the banking sector has also undergone important changes in the 1980s. Legislation passed in 1982 started a gradual process of deposit rate decontrol, which by 1986 left commercial banks and thrifts free to set their own rates on essentially all categories of deposits. These changes have improved the ability of the regulated banking sector to compete for funds. (For example, the 1983 decontrol of bank rates on close substitutes for money market mutual fund shares led to a large flow of funds from MMMFs to banks in the succeeding months.) The permitted investment activities of S&Ls have been expanded to include consumer, commercial and industrial lending[50]. As noted above, many institutions have used these new powers to diversify somewhat out of housing financing, but others have entered unfamiliar fields and suffered large losses. The barriers separating commercial and investment banking have been weakened. For example, bank holding companies are now allowed to control discount brokerage firms (low fee brokers that do not dispense investment advice or research) and separate investment advisory services. Beyond this, the major bank regulatory agencies have issued independent reports proposing various modifications to the Glass-Steagall Act (see the Stability and prudential regulation section, below), and legislation that would repeal the Act's restrictions on bank securities activities has recently been introduced in Congress. There have also been major moves in the direction of interstate banking, initiated by the individual states. Forty states and the District of Columbia currently allow out-of-state holding companies to own in-state banks, although most do not allow equal entry to firms from all states. This movement has given rise to large regional banks, which should prove to be formidable competitors to the large money centre banks.

Banking system competitors: institutions and securitisation

Finance companies and investment firms

Reflecting the diversion of credit flows away from the banking system, non-depository financial intermediaries have grown rapidly in the last ten years. Measured in constant dollars, the assets of finance companies have been expanding at a rate in excess of 7 per cent per annum, while the rate at commercial banks has averaged only 3 or 4 per cent since 1975 (Table 38). In addition, the assets of investment companies (mutual funds and security brokers) have mushroomed in the 1980s. Although much of this growth was fuelled by a trend towards securitisation (see below), part grew out of a competitive advantage granted by earlier deposit rate ceilings and other restrictions on bank activities. This phenomenon is illustrated by the effect decontrol had on the assets of money market mutual funds. These funds issue shares that are uninsured substitutes for bank time and savings deposits, which pay a market rate of interest. As market rates rose in the late 1970s and early 1980s, the volume of these shares ballooned from $10.8 billion in 1978 to $206.6 billion in 1982. The introduction by banks at the beginning of 1983 of money market deposit accounts (MMDAs) paying competitive rates (see Annex V) eliminated much of the competitive advantage of these funds, and so the outstanding volume of shares fell to $162.5 billion that year.

Non-depository financial institutions have also profited from economies of scale and scope denied banks. For example, because mutual funds are typically grouped into "families", where each individual member has special investment characteristics, investors can conveniently move funds between different accounts, including money market mutual fund accounts, on which they can write cheques. In the consumer lending field, some companies – such as Sears and General Motors – benefit from a mixing of commerce and finance denied banks[51]. These commercial institutions are also potent competitors to banks because they have extensive distribution networks that cross state lines and engage in capital market transactions on a scale that only the largest banks can match[52]. Non-depository institutions are increasingly important in business lending as well: the ratio of finance company loans to bank loans made to non-financial firms has risen from 13.4 per cent in 1970 to 27.1 per cent in 1986; insurance companies are the largest individual commercial mortgage lenders; and industrial firms dominate the equipment-leasing business[53]. Super financial institutions have begun to emerge – such as American Express and Prudential-Bache – that combine brokerage, investment banking, insurance, and other financial services on a large scale, in hopes of achieving economies of scope. Because the addition of commercial banking powers to these other operations offers the potential for even further economies – as well as direct access to the Federal safety net and the payments mechanism – some of these institutions, as well as some bank holding companies, have gone so far as to open non-bank banks. These are institutions that evade Federal bank holding company regulations by not accepting demand deposits and making commercial loans, but are still able to obtain FDIC deposit insurance[54].

Foreign competition

At the same time that U.S. banks were expanding overseas, foreign financial institutions also increased their presence in the domestic economy. The share of domestic banking system assets controlled by foreign banks rose from 2.9 per cent in 1970 to about 9 per cent in 1985, a faster rate of foreign penetration than in the OECD area as a whole (Table 38). (Although this percentage is low compared to most European nations, this primarily reflects their dependence on foreign trade; a more comparable country might be Japan, which has a foreign penetration ratio of less than 6 per cent.) Japanese and European financial institutions have become important players in domestic equity and security markets, either through direct participation or by buying into established firms. For example, Yasuda Mutual Life Insurance owns 25 per cent of Paine Webber Group, and Nippon Life Insurance owns 13 per cent of Shearson Lehman Hutton. In recent years a number of Japanese firms have joined the small group of primary dealers in government securities. This penetration is a natural result of the growth in world trade and income outside the U.S., as well as the absence of barriers to entry into domestic financial markets. The United States places almost no restrictions on foreign ownership of banks, brokerage firms or other financial entities, nor is domestic ownership and trading of foreign securities controlled. The only exception to this rule are restrictions on the right of

Table 38.   International comparisons of foreign share of domestic banking

Per cent of total assets

		1970	1980	1985
Australia	B	0.6	0.4	2.0
Austria	A	10.7	23.0	29.8
Belgium	A	36.6	52.7	63.3
Canada	C	19.8	19.7	20.2
Denmark	A	6.7	24.5	39.6
Finland	A	4.3	8.9	16.9
France	A	15.8	30.1	34.5
Germany	A	8.7	9.7	11.5
Greece	D	3.5	6.2	8.9
Iceland	E	1.0	2.9	3.3
Ireland	A	35.7	42.7	14.3
Italy	D	12.6	9.6	13.5
Japan	A	3.7	3.5	5.8
Luxembourg	A	84.5	96.7	97.8
Netherlands	A	27.0	35.1	38.3
New Zealand	F	7.2	7.2	7.1
Norway	A	7.4	2.1	8.4
Portugal	E	5.6	9.2	13.5
Spain	A	3.5	7.2	9.8
Sweden	A	4.9	8.8	13.8
Switzerland	A	37.6	35.5	33.2
Turkey	A	0.7	2.3	12.9
United Kingdom	A	46.1	64.6	68.9
United States	**A**	**2.9**	**12.1**	**9.1**
OECD Average[1]		13.1	18.2	20.8

Legend: A   =   Deposit money banks
B   =   Trading banks and savings banks
C   =   Chartered banks
D   =   Commercial banks
E   =   Commercial banks and savings banks
F   =   Trading banks

1.   Excluding Luxembourg.
Source: IMF, *International Financial Statistics.*

foreign banks to engage in domestic investment banking activities (i.e. a national treatment policy), but even these are weakening as the wall between commercial and investment banking falls[55].

Another factor in the growth of foreign competition has been the large and rising current account deficit of the United States in recent years, which has increased net foreign ownership of domestic securities, and thus the role of foreign institutions in the trading of these assets. For example, foreign holdings of Treasury obligations, corporate bonds and other credit market instruments have climbed from $165.2 billion in 1980 to $456.6 billion in 1986. Similarly, the value of corporate equities held by non-residents grew from $64.6 billion to $204.4 billion. Nevertheless, even these examples understate the growth in foreign competition. Because of the integration of national capital markets, a large percentage of the world's credit transactions can be only arbitrarily broken down by market location: banks in New York compete with their counterparts in London and Tokyo for the same business, as do security exchanges worldwide. For this reason, the standardisation of financial supervision across countries has become an important issue, because national differences in capital requirements and allowed activities can lead to non-economic shifts in the location of transactions (and financial market employment), and complicate prudential supervision. To help reduce these problems, the G-10 countries under the auspices of the Bank for International Settlements recently agreed on a proposed set of uniform capital requirements for banks.

Securitisation and capital markets

As noted above, traditional bank credit has increasingly been replaced by the issuance of securities, either directly by borrowers or indirectly through loan-backed instruments. The commercial paper market is one of the earliest examples of this phenomenon: the outstanding paper of non-financial corporations in the early 1960s was equal to only $1\frac{1}{2}$ per cent of their bank and finance company loans combined, but this ratio jumped to 6 per cent in 1970 and to almost 11 per cent in 1985 (Diagram 18). At the same time, a rising percentage of business and consumer loans have represented intermediated commercial paper (in the sense that lending institutions have raised funds through paper issuance), and outstanding commercial paper liabilities of bank holding companies and finance companies doubled as a per cent of loan assets between the early 1970s and 1986. This circumvention of deposit intermediation arose from many factors. For example, technological advances reduced information and transaction costs, making it easier for ultimate lenders and borrowers to meet directly in capital markets. The institutionalisation of savings via pension and mutual funds also decreased the relative value of bank expertise in investing – since institutional managers have a similar knowledge of financial markets – and boosted the demand for securities[56]. Rising inflation and interest rates increased the incentives to minimise borrowing costs, and led to a search for alternatives to bank loans. More generally, the strong growth of finance companies and other non-bank competitors increased the relative size of the commercial paper market, as it is a traditional source of funds for these institutions. However, banks themselves began to issue substantial amounts of paper (via their holding companies), at first to avoid reserve requirements, but later as a standard funding tool. Overall, these factors underlying the

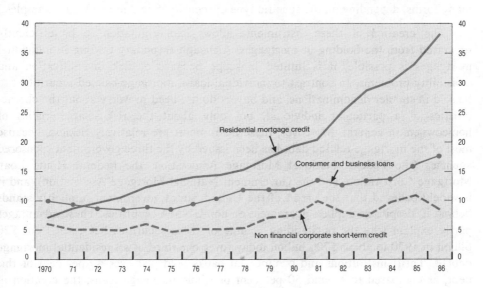

Diagram 18. **THE GROWTH OF SECURITISATION**
(Per cent of outstanding credit held in the form of securities)

Residential mortgage credit

Consumer and business loans

Non financial corporate short-term credit

1970 71 72 73 74 75 76 77 78 79 80 81 82 83 84 85 86

Source: Federal Reserve Board, *Flow of Funds.*

growth of the commercial paper market probably gave rise to a further increase in its competitive position *vis-à-vis* deposit-intermediated lending, because the efficiency and flexibility of securities markets may have grown as the volume of issues and trading increased[57].

Securitisation has also occurred in such areas as new car loans, life insurance policy loans, and credit card and lease receivables. (In all these cases, individual payment streams from the underlying assets are pooled and sold on the open market. The original owner usually continues to service the individual loans for a fee.) The cumulative gross issuance of car loan-backed securities, first offered in 1985, now stands at $15.5 billion, or about 6 per cent of all outstanding car loans. However, the largest growth in securitisation has come in the area of housing finance through home mortgages which have been bundled into bond-like instruments. Such mortgage-backed securities begin by the issuance of conventional mortgage credit to homebuyers, by S&Ls or other financial institutions. The mortgages are then resold to another institution which finances the purchase by selling conventional bonds, or by pooling the mortgages and selling the rights to the pool's income stream. (The conversion of the income stream into a payout schedule for the pool's owners takes many forms, depending on the specific type of security. See Annex IV for examples.)

The creation of these instruments allows loan-origination to be efficiently separated from the holding of mortgages. Although secondary trading in individual mortgages is possible, it is limited in scope because of risk diversification and divisibility problems. In contrast to individual loans, mortgage-backed securities can be sold in smaller denominations, and buyers do not need to worry about the characteristics of a particular individual, but only about the risk characteristics of homeowners in general. Moreover, these instruments are relatively riskless, because most of the mortgage-related debt has been issued by the three government-sponsored agencies (the Federal National Mortgage Association, the Federal Home Loan Mortgage Corporation, and the Government National Mortgage Association), and it is widely believed that the credit of the United States government implicitly stands behind it, despite no explicit guarantees on non-GNMA securities. These advantages partly explain why the outstanding volume of these securities has risen from $20 billion in 1970 to about $700 billion today (over one-third of all residential mortgage debt)[58]. Thrift institutions and commercial banks hold just over 40 per cent of this debt, as compared to around 50 per cent of whole mortgage loans; the creation of these instruments has boosted the flow of housing credit that bypasses the banking system.

Mortgage-backed securities are traditional financial instruments that have been transformed into new instruments to better meet the preferences of investors. Innovations have occurred in other capital markets as well. Floating rate notes and corporate bonds with put options (i.e. ones that can be sold back to corporations at fixed prices) were introduced to protect lenders from rising interest rates. Stripped bonds (where the coupon and final payments are sold separately) were created to allow investors to lock in high yields, and to take advantage of certain tax rules. In addition, firms seeking alternative sources of credit in the face of high interest rates have looked abroad, and increased international linkages have facilitated the exploitation of differences between national capital markets. New instruments have been the result, not only in the form of Euroborrowings, but also interest and currency swaps. In fact, swaps and Eurobonds are often linked, in that the two can be combined to convert borrowings in a market in which a firm enjoys a comparative advantage, into a more preferred form. This type of contract can also be used as a hedging instrument by firms to protect against interest and exchange rate volatility. The market in swaps is not only quite large – around $50 billion were issued in 1986 – but it has been a profitable source of off-balance sheet income for banks, the typical broker in such transactions.

Diagram 19. **VOLUME OF TRADING ON SECURITIES MARKETS**

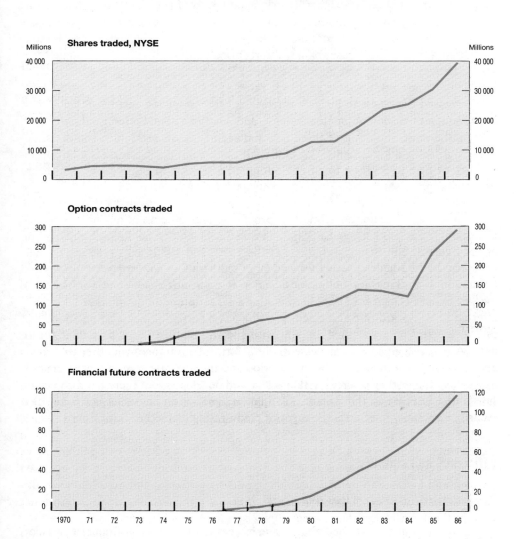

Shares traded, NYSE

Option contracts traded

Financial future contracts traded

Sources: Securities and Exchange Commission, *Monthly Statistical Review* and Commodity Futures Trading Commission, *Annual Report.*

The growth in securitisation has been accompanied by the increased use of instruments designed to manage the risk exposure of firms and individuals. This phenomenon is partly due to securitisation itself, since this direct form of credit extension leaves borrowers more exposed to price risk than traditional deposit-intermediation. (In the latter case, banks absorb price and credit risk in exchange for a spread between lending and borrowing rates.) Beyond this, high and volatile rates of inflation and interest, unstable exchange rates, and swings in commodity prices have also increased the desire to hedge positions, and the associated cost has fallen due to improvements in computer technology and mathematical pricing algorithms[59]. Among the most important of these risk management tools are future contracts, options, and forward agreements. Generally, all these contingent contracts allow an individual or firm to contract to purchase (or sell) a security or other claim at a future date, at a price set today. Such agreements have been used for many years for agricultural products and other commodities, because these goods have traditionally seen major price fluctuations, making producers and processors anxious to reduce uncertainty and protect against capital losses on inventory holdings. Similarly, increased volatility in financial markets in the 1970s and 1980s led to the use of their counterparts for financial securities, and large-scale trading now exists for futures and options in U.S. Treasury obligations, major foreign currencies, and various stock market indices (Diagram 19). There is also a large international market (primarily interbank) in forward rate agreements, in which two parties agree today on an interest rate to be paid on a specified amount with specific maturity at a particular future date. All these agreements are essentially a form of insurance, which enable firms and individuals to transfer some or all price and interest rate risk to other parties[60]. Markets in the trading of credit risk are less well developed, but there has also been a substantial increase in the issuance of financial guarantees, in which an issuer of a security essentially purchases the superior credit rating of another institution[61].

Efficiency and stability

Intermediation services and costs

The innovations described above have increased the variety of financial services, but it is difficult to quantify their effect on efficiency. Unlike manufacturing or some service industries, the output of banks and other intermediaries is not clearly defined. At best, there are only indirect measures of production, and many innovations that increase investor welfare (e.g. securities that more closely match individual preferences) are by necessity neglected when decomposing nominal value-added into price and quantity. Nevertheless, while this measurement problem makes productivity estimation difficult, there is evidence that transaction costs have declined sharply. The demand deposit turnover rate (aggregate debits to accounts divided by average balances) for all commercial banks leaped from 63 in 1970 to over 600 in 1987. Technological innovations at banks have thus enabled each dollar held in demand deposits to do ten times more work, but at a declining unit cost: total operating costs of commercial banks declined from .12 per cent of debits to under .05 per cent over the same period. Similar increases in activity have occurred in other financial markets. For example, the volume of trading on the New York Stock Exchange has risen twelvefold since 1970, as has futures trading on all exchanges combined. These gains were obtained with much less than a proportional increase in workers, but in spite of rapid productivity growth the financial sector's share of non-farm employment rose from 4.2 per cent in 1970 to 5.2 per cent in 1986[62].

A high degree of competition exists in almost all areas of finance, and most services are probably provided at near to minimum cost. For example, the cost of bond issuance in the U.S. is lower than in any other country, reflecting competition, the absence of minimum brokerage fees, and economies of scale (Table 39). This is true even for small issues, where the inherent advantage of large U.S. capital markets is less. Moreover, costs for securities underwriting and trading domestically are held down by competition from foreign financial centres such as London and Tokyo. However, repeal of the Glass-Steagall Act may reduce costs in non-banking finance further, since a small number of large investment banks have carved out niches in certain specialised areas of corporate and municipal finance. Currently, the five largest underwriters of commercial paper account for around 95 per cent of the

Table 39. **Costs of bond issues**[1]

Country	Bond maturity (years)	Cost by issue size (per cent of total issue)		
		Small	Medium	Large
United States	**20**	**1.45**	**1.08**	**0.98**
Australia	5	1.57	1.61	1.60
Belgium	8	4.2	4.15	4.10
Canada	10	2.5	2.1	1.75
France	10	3.3	3.2	3.2
Germany	10	3.6	3.6	3.6
Japan	10	3.5+	3.5+	3.5+
Netherlands	10	2.7	2.5	2.4
Switzerland	10	2.85	3.0	3.0
United Kingdom	20	1.83	1.15	1.08

1. Domestic market issues during 1982-1983.
Source: J.R. Hakim, *Securities Markets,* IFC Occasional Papers, Capital Markets Series, Washington D.C., 1985.

market, and the five largest underwriters of all domestic corporate debt account for almost 70 per cent of such business. Because many commercial banks probably have expertise in these areas, their entry into investment banking could reduce existing profits and costs[63]. In contrast, the erosion of the prohibition on interstate banking probably should not have a pronounced effect on costs in the banking sector, because of significant intra-state competition in most areas, and because the economies of scale in banking appear limited[64]. Rather, the gains from interstate branching are likely to come in the form of stability through diversification, although regulations limiting intra-state operations in some states may have kept competition at a point that affects efficiency.

Risk management

Intermediation efficiency has also been increased by the use of risk-hedging instruments, which can yield a more optimal distribution of risk across individuals and firms. Although the existence of large-scale trading in futures and options clearly suggests that they enhance individual welfare, the implication for efficiency and social welfare is more complex. Contingent contracts are useful to firms that wish to reduce the level of risk embodied in their normal business operations. This function of futures and options clearly enhances the quality of financial services. Moreover, to the extent that these instruments have helped to redistribute price risk to those best able to bear it, aggregate stability may also have increased.

However, there have been difficulties with the use of these instruments in practice, as evidenced by the role of the futures and options markets in the October stock market crash. According to many recent commission reports on the causes and implications of the crash[65], a breakdown in the linkages between the primary market in equities and those in derivative securities helped to destabilise trading and put downward pressure on prices. Usually, prices in these various markets move sympathetically, which is to be expected because in practice they function as one market. (Large institutional investors can adjust their position in various stocks via purchases of index futures, and hedging via futures and options are an integral part of many investment strategies.) On 19th and 20th October though, normal relationships broke down, partly because the volume of trading was so huge that it overwhelmed the capacity of the clearance and settlement system. As a result, trading orders were not executed promptly, which caused stock prices to lag behind current desires to buy and sell, and created difficulties in the pricing of stock index futures[66]. Computer-assisted arbitraging operations therefore became ineffective. Furthermore, in the view of some (including the SEC) portfolio insurance programmes (PIPs) may have exacerbated the situation, not only by generating a large volume of sell orders for stocks and index futures directly, but by prompting earlier selloffs by others who anticipated the triggering of automatic PIP sales. Options markets suffered from extreme volatility, order imbalances, and trading halts[67]. Altogether, while the existence of markets in derivative securities did not cause the crash, future and options markets and the primary stock market did not perform normally: in the face of extreme conditions, arbitrage and hedging strategies broke down.

Securitisation and stability

Securitisation, like the development of risk hedging tools, represents an increase in intermediation efficiency; similarly, it too has changed the allocation of risk among financial market participants. Part of the efficiency gain associated with this trend has been a narrowing of the spread between borrowing and lending rates. As noted above, the growth of the commercial paper market appears to have reduced the relative cost of funds for large corporations: the spread between the prime lending rate (the loan rate charged by banks to their best medium-sized business customers) and the commercial paper rate has increased over the past twenty-five years (Diagram 20). Securitisation's effect on mortgage markets is less clear – the spread

Diagram 20. **SECURITISATION GAINS: CHANGES IN INTEREST RATE SPREADS**

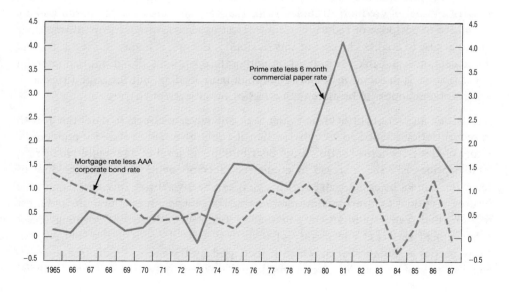

between mortgage rates and bond yields displays no clear trend – but this may be due to the influence of other factors[68]. Securitisation has also increased the range of options available to lenders and borrowers alike, allowing firms and individuals to more closely tailor the characteristics of investment or funding strategies (return, risk, maturity, diversification, *et cetera*) to their particular needs. This latter gain has benefited financial institutions as well, including depository institutions, by improving portfolio liquidity and diversification, and by creating new sources of income. Thrift institutions have used mortgage-backed securities to reduce their vulnerability to interest rate movements and changes in local and national economic conditions. Commercial banks have benefited in a similar manner, although gains to date have been limited by restrictions on their ability to participate in these markets.

Securitisation has given investors a broader range of instruments from which to choose, allowing them to increase the liquidity and diversity of their portfolios. However, individual securities tend to entail more price and credit risk for ultimate lenders than do deposits. Although portfolio diversification and hedging techniques can reduce these risks, deposits are inherently safer because bank profits and capital (and if necessary deposit insurance) protect against capital losses. Lenders forgo the safety of bank deposits only if they can earn compensating higher rates of return elsewhere: increased securitisation illustrates that the return/risk tradeoff has swung against banks in recent years. On the borrowing side, too, businesses have given up certain advantages of conventional bank finance in order to reduce overall interest expenses. Banks probably are more able than securities holders to be forbearing when a firm runs into financial difficulties. Because debt renegotiations are easier with a smaller number of creditors, troubled firms that rely on bank finance are more likely to be able to postpone or reduce current interest expenses, without jeopardising their future access to credit. The cost of this flexibility, though, is higher interest rates and the acceptance of bank restrictions on corporate operations. Bond and commercial paper finance is in some ways more rigid than bank lending, but for large firms such disadvantages appear to be more than offset by lower interest charges.

Although there is little or no evidence of any adverse effects to date, the growth in securitisation has led to speculation that it could give rise to stability problems[69]. Many of these concerns centre on the distribution and level of aggregate credit risk. Unlike price risk, the increase in credit risk accompanying the direct holding of securities cannot be easily hedged, although it can be diversified. Investors cannot use futures or options to insure against moral hazard or other sources of default, and must rely on their own capitalisation, and that of financial institutions providing credit enhancement services. The quality of a security thus depends on the behavior of many parties – the number of which is increased by the use of credit insurance[70] – and the risk of default involves complicated linkages between different financial players. The unexpected chain reactions that sometimes result from isolated disturbances illustrate these risk estimation problems: for example, the 1985 failure of a small securities firm in Florida triggered the closure of many small state-insured thrifts in Ohio and Maryland, and temporarily unsettled securities markets. Beyond this, securitisation has the potential for complicating prudential supervision and, perhaps, monetary policy. The rapid growth in bank-supplied credit enhancements has made traditional capitalisation rules inadequate, because they do not fully take into account such risk exposure; in response capital regulations have recently been revised. More generally, at the level of the banking system (and the financial system as a whole), increased securitisation could complicate regulatory oversight, because a smaller percentage of credit is closely supervised. Given that the trend towards securitisation is likely to continue, this suggests that regulatory policies and procedures (inside and outside the United States) must be periodically reviewed to ensure that the maximum efficiency gains from innovation are retained, consistent with adequate protection of financial market stability.

Prudential regulation and stability

Such a review is now taking place in the U.S. for the banking system, where the institutional and regulatory structure has increasingly become outmoded. As noted earlier, the growth of commercial banks has been held back by restrictions on their ability to compete fully with other financial institutions. Banks have lost market shares not only to securities firms and other domestic competitors, but also to foreign banks. In certain ways these regulatory limitations have weakened the banking industry, by restricting its sources of income and making it more difficult for it to attract new capital. Thus the original purpose of legislation such as the Glass-Steagall Act – to promote aggregate stability by protecting banks from certain types of losses – has to some degree been compromised. Glass-Steagall and similar laws have also been weakened by attempts by banks and other institutions to expand their powers, through loopholes or new court interpretations of the law. This process has the potential for weakening prudential supervision, and it has created oddities whereby a bank with a particular charter can enter some market, but another with a different legal structure cannot. The piecemeal breakdown of Glass-Steagall also has prevented the economy from fully reaping the benefits of competition in the supply of financial services: as mentioned above, there remain portions of the securities market which are highly concentrated, and in which commercial banks have already demonstrated their expertise abroad.

However, the debate over possible reforms to the banking system also has recognised the need to safeguard its special economic role. Depository institutions provide a safe and liquid form of savings, a stable source of credit for small to medium-sized borrowers, and are the backbone of the payments mechanism. Because these services are vital to the functioning of the economy, and because banks are vulnerable to lapses in public confidence (in the sense that panics can undermine the health of even sound institutions), banks are closely supervised, and have access to government deposit insurance and Federal Reserve credit. Such safety net coverage is by and large denied to other institutions, because of its potential effect on efficiency. Coverage may also adversely affect the efficiency of the banking system, but these losses are deemed acceptable because of the gain in aggregate stability. With these considerations in mind, many of the specific proposals for modifying the system have carefully tried to remove the barriers between commercial banking and other financial activities, without threatening the financial health of the banking system itself. For example, a bill recently passed by the Senate would permit the mixing of commercial and investment banking, by allowing holding companies to own commercial banks, securities firms, and possibly other financial institutions. However, the operations and capital of these subsidiaries would be segregated, and strict "firewalls" would be maintained by not allowing commercial bank subsidiaries to loan to, nor purchase assets from, their securities affiliates. Likewise, commercial banks would not be permitted to guarantee nor extend letters of credit to back securities issued or underwritten by affiliates. The bill contains other provisions against actions that might threaten the capital or otherwise undermine public confidence in the bank subsidiary[71]. Although concerns have been expressed in the past that legal firewalls might prove to be insufficient in practice[72], the bill appears to have gone far in allaying such fears, and it has met with the general approval of most of the government regulatory community[73].

Other actions for reforming the financial system have also been proposed or undertaken. For example, the FDIC and the Federal Reserve Bank of New York have issued separate studies concerning the structure of commercial banking and its general role in the financial system. These proposals imply more far-reaching changes than embodied in the legislation discussed above, and address the question of whether commerce and banking should be allowed to mix[74]. In other areas, the Federal Savings and Loan Insurance Corporation (FSLIC), which is presently insolvent[75], has been authorised to improve its capitalisation through the issuance of bonds. This infusion of funds will enable the corporation to liquidate or otherwise close many bankrupt S&Ls, and thus increase the overall health of the thrift industry. Coupled with this refunding is a major expansion of supervisory staffs at FSLIC (and the FDIC), and a tightening of capital requirements for S&Ls. It has also been proposed that depository institutions should face risk-based capital requirements, and that deposit insurance premiums should be a function of the riskiness of a bank's portfolio

102

and its off-balance sheet activities. These two proposals are attractive, in that banks pursuing an aggressive investment strategy – and therefore the possibility of large loan losses – would be required to both reduce the risk of insolvency (via higher capital requirements) and increase the funding of the insurance pool (via higher premiums). However, their implementation raises some practical problems, particularly as regards the accurate determination of a bank's portfolio risk[76].

The commission reports issued in the wake of the stock market crash contained a number of proposals for various changes in the operations of securities markets[77]. Unfortunately, while the various studies agreed on the broad details of how the markets performed in mid-October, there was not a similar consensus on how such events should be prevented from reoccuring. All parties generally agreed that inter-market coordination needs to be improved, and that futures and options trading should not be viewed as separate from the primary stock market. In particular, it was felt that clearance and settlement procedures need to be improved, and that decisions on special opening and closing hours, or other limits on trading, should be coordinated across exchanges. Who should take on this task is the subject of debate. The SEC has recommended that regulation of futures trading should be transferred from the CFTC to itself, while the Presidential commission has proposed that the Federal Reserve oversee the operations of all financial markets. The Federal Reserve has expressed its extreme reluctance to take on this task, it being outside its traditional area of expertise, and carrying the risk that markets might perceive an extention of the Federal safety net. Other studies recommended that an interagency council might be created, with the possible participation of the representatives of the different exchanges. Some of the reports proposed the use of circuit breakers, such as daily price limits or trading halts, in the event of extreme price movements; others argued that such restrictions were potentially destabilising, and that an increase in the processing capacity of the system would be sufficient to prevent a repeat of many of October's problems. It was also suggested that margin requirements on options and futures markets should be increased, and that the specialist system be strengthened by increasing the capitalisation of brokerage firms carrying out market-maker functions. At the moment all these suggestions are under review by the appropriate congressional bodies.

International linkages

The financial system has also been affected by the growing linkages between national capital markets. Markets for U.S. Treasury securities, inter-bank lending and borrowing, and other forms of credit operate worldwide, making it more likely that disturbances arising in one location can quickly affect other markets. As a result, investors and other market participants have less time to digest the implications of new foreign and domestic developments, and such speed has decreased the available lead time for national authorities to deal with financial crises. An example of how quickly shocks can ripple across national borders occurred during the October stock market crash, when the initial drop in prices in New York triggered similar responses in Asia and Europe. In the days following, large movements in Tokyo prompted sympathetic movements in Europe a few hours later (when exchanges opened), which in turn affected trading in New York with a lag, leading back to Tokyo when their markets began their new trading day. Interestingly, because exchanges were not completely linked due to staggered trading hours, shocks travelled through the system in jolts, perhaps increasing the day-to-day volatility of prices. These linkages have also increased the need for international co-ordination in economic policy and financial supervision. As mentioned above, important steps have recently been taken along these lines under the auspices of the Bank for International Settlements. More will have to be done in the future, especially as regards the collection of data on the income, assets, and risk-exposure of international financial institutions.

Innovation and monetary control

One of the side effects of changes in financial markets since the mid-1970s has been an alteration in the manner in which monetary policy influences economic activity. Whereas a strong credit rationing mechanism formerly existed, there is now a greater reliance on interest rate movements to clear markets. In the 1960s and early 1970s, any rise in short-term interest rates above deposit ceilings initiated an outflow of funds from depository institutions. Lenders responded to this drop in their deposit base by rationing credit, especially new mortgage lending. Through this mechanism, monetary policy could damp overall economic activity by causing a sharp (and disruptive) cutback in construction activity, engineered through modest increases in short-term rates. Because of the decontrol of deposit rates, widespread use of wholesale money markets, and growing access to foreign capital markets, domestic credit flows are no longer as sensitive to changes in short-term interest rates. As a result, the incidence of monetary policy has changed, and is no longer so concentrated on the housing sector. The foreign channel especially has become more important. With the growing openness of the economy (both financially and in terms of trade), changes in monetary and fiscal policy now have a greater effect on the manufacturing output, through the competitiveness effects of exchange rate movements. In contrast, financial innovations may have reduced the direct interest rate sensitivity of other sectors. For example, business investment may now be less sensitive due to the use of hedging techniques to protect against a rise in interest rates[78]. Capital investment may also have become less sensitive in the short run to changes in bond yields, due to their increased volatility: a jump in current rates is no longer as good a predictor of a sustained increase in borrowing costs[79]. In the case of housing, the end of credit rationing has meant that fluctuations in activity are accompanied by larger movements in real short-term interest rates (Diagram 21), although it is not clear that there has been a corresponding shift in the sensitivity to real mortgage rates[80].

The conduct of monetary policy has also been influenced by a change in the behaviour of the monetary aggregates. (For a discussion of recent policy, see The

Diagram 21. **HOUSING CYCLES AND REAL INTEREST RATES**

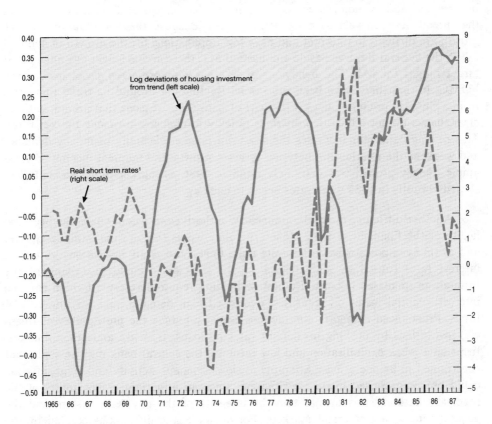

1.   Three-month treasury bill rate minus current inflation rate for consumer prices.
Sources: Federal Reserve Board, *Federal Reserve Bulletin* and Department of Commerce, *Survey of Current Business*.

policy environment, above.) M1 velocity in the 1980s has deviated sharply from its trend growth path of the 1960s and 1970s, although M2 velocity appears more stable (Diagram 10). While part of this shift can be explained by conventional demand-for-money equations[81], much of the increased demand for M1 is due to the decontrol of deposit rates and a resultant change in the character of M1 transaction accounts. Now that a major portion of M1 pays an explicit rate of return that is not much below that available on many non-transaction accounts, households use M1 deposits as both checking accounts and as a vehicle for savings. Similarly, because some non-M1 components of M2 have limited check writing privileges, consumers can use savings balances to pay bills. With the functional difference between M1 and M2 blurred by decontrol, the demand for M1 balances has on average been stronger in the 1980s than would have been expected on the basis of historical behaviour. More importantly, the growth in M1 has been erratic in recent years, due in part to large shifts between M1 and the non-M1 components of M2 that have been caused by changes in the spread between various bank deposit rates. Because these fluctuations in M1 growth are difficult to interpret and have few implications for the growth in nominal GNP, the Federal Reserve has de-emphasised M1: there are no longer any announced target ranges for M1. The behaviour of M2 has also presented problems for the FOMC, in that there have been substantial fluctuations around its trend that arise from a sluggish pricing policy on the part of banks. For reasons that are not entirely clear, banks do not adjust deposit rates quickly to changes in money market rates. This pricing behaviour increases the short-run interest elasticity of money demand, and weakens the relationship between reserves growth and nominal income. For example, money growth was extremely rapid in 1986 as market rates fell, but then slowed abruptly in 1987 when rates began to back up.

Another difficulty facing the monetary authorities in recent years has been the health of the financial system. Monetary policy works through the banking system, and at times imposes substantial costs upon banks and thrift institutions. A rise in interest rates caused by a decreased supply of reserves could hurt bank profits through an increased opportunity cost of holding required reserves (which earn no interest), capital losses on securities, decreased loan demand, and a rising cost of funds. Pronounced monetary contractions can also reduce the profitability of financial institutions by pushing up default rates on loans. If banks and other financial firms have weak capitalisation and low earnings, the central bank may be somewhat constrained in its operations. Attempts to slow economic activity and fight inflation could be compromised in such a situation, since an important responsibility of the monetary authorities is to maintain the integrity of the payments system and the general functioning of credit markets. For example, the difficulties created by the Latin American debt situation, combined with the weakness of some banks in agricultural and energy-producing regions, probably has influenced the conduct of monetary policy. More recently, the stance of monetary policy was adjusted in the face of the stock market crash.

Debt, savings and investment

Growth of debt

An important feature of financial markets in the 1980s has been a sharp increase in borrowing by households, firms and the government. Although the ratio of total non-financial sector debt to GNP remained remarkably stable at about 1.4 during the 1960s and 1970s, in the past few years it has climbed rapidly to above 1.8 (Table 40). All non-financial sectors have contributed to this rise, but the bulk of it is attributable to the Federal government, households, and non-financial corporations. Since 1980, large budget deficits have boosted the outstanding credit market debt of the Federal government by well over $1 trillion. Household debt has risen by about the same amount, as consumers have borrowed heavily to purchase homes, cars, and other durable goods. Corporate non-equity liabilities jumped about $800 billion over the

Table 40. **Debt of the non-financial sectors**[1]

	1970	1980	1981	1982	1983	1984	1985	1986	1987
Debt/GNP ratios									
Total debt	1.42	1.44	1.41	1.48	1.54	1.59	1.71	1.81	1.86
Households	0.47	0.53	0.52	0.52	0.54	0.55	0.59	0.63	0.64
Corporations	0.35	0.33	0.33	0.34	0.34	0.36	0.38	0.40	0.42
Non-corporate business	0.15	0.19	0.19	0.19	0.20	0.21	0.22	0.23	0.24
State and local Governments	0.15	0.11	0.10	0.10	0.11	0.10	0.12	0.13	0.12
Federal Government	0.30	0.27	0.27	0.31	0.35	0.36	0.40	0.43	0.44
Debt-to-net worth ratios									
Households	0.15	0.16	0.16	0.16	0.16	0.18	0.18	0.19	0.20
Corporations	0.46	0.35	0.35	0.37	0.37	0.42	0.47	0.53	—
Non-corporate business	0.25	0.24	0.24	0.26	0.29	0.33	0.36	0.39	—
Memorandum items:									
Household debt-to-income ratio	0.67	0.76	0.74	0.73	0.76	0.78	0.84	0.89	0.90
Corporate debt-to-equity ratio (market value)[2]	0.48	0.60	0.70	0.72	0.64	0.75	0.70	0.69	—

1. End-of-year outstandings.
2. Unpublished Federal Reserve estimate.
Source: Federal Reserve Board, *Flow of Funds.*

same period, fuelled by large outlays for capital goods during the recovery, and by a wave of corporate buyouts in which debt-finance played a prominent role (see below). Partly due to this increase in merger activity, rising gross corporate indebtedness has led to a decline in net worth relative to GNP, and the aggregate debt-to-equity ratio (par basis) for non-financial corporations rose from .35 in 1980 to .53 in 1986. (On a market-value basis the rise is smaller, even after allowance for the recent fall in stock prices.) Non-corporate businesses also experienced a deterioration in their balance sheets, partly due to a 40 per cent decline in the value of farmland, and partly due to a boom in office and other commercial construction that was financed by mortgage lenders. (The recent end of this boom, combined with an excess supply of office space in many cities, has worsened the situation further.) In contrast, increased borrowing by consumers was not been matched by a decline in household net worth. Sustained in part by capital gains on holdings of corporate equities and land, personal net wealth in the mid-1980s was little changed (as a percentage of GNP or income) from the late 1970s. By and large, growth in household debt has not outpaced the accumulation of financial assets. The stock market crash worsened the financial position of households, but it came after a very large run-up in prices over the first eight months of 1987; as a result, household net worth at the end of 1987 was still greater than it had been one year before.

Debt and stability

An important question raised by this increase in general indebtedness is the effect, if any, on the stability of the economy. In this regard, it is noteworthy that higher borrowing has been accompanied by a fall in the quality of debt, which is of particular concern because it has occurred during a period of strong economic growth. For example, loan loss provisions at commercial banks have more than doubled as a per cent of assets since the late 1970s, reflecting rising default and delinquency rates in all categories (Table 41). Although the vast majority of losses have been taken on business and foreign loans, the decline in quality also includes home mortgages and consumer instalment loans, which have historically been among the safest of investments. The deterioration (albeit limited) in the quality of consumer debt is due to many factors, but probably includes: a rising debt service burden; reduced homeowners' equity in economically depressed regions; and an increase in the number of heavily-indebted families[82]. The quality of corporate securities has also fallen. Reductions and omissions in dividend payments by corporations have been trending upwards, and 176 major firms had investment ratings on their corporate bonds downgraded in 1987, as opposed to only 69 upgradings. In general, annual net downgradings are up substantially from the average pace of the late 1970s. A portion

Table 41. **Debt quality**

	Average 1976-1980	1981	1982	1983	1984	1985	1986
Commercial bank loan loss provisions (per cent of net assets)	0.29	0.26	0.40	0.47	0.57	0.67	0.77
Delinquency rate on commercial bank consumer instalment loans (per cent)[1]	—	—	—	2.65	2.59	3.01	3.27
Delinquency rate on S&L mortgage holdings (per cent)[2]	1.09	1.28	1.90	2.20	2.13	2.80	4.19
Net corporate downgradings, Moody's Investor Services (number)	18	34	88	53	8	73	107

1. Banks with at least $300 million in assets.
2. Includes non-residential mortgage loans.
Source: Federal Reserve Bulletin; Federal Home Loan Bank Board, *Savings and Home Financing Source Book* and Moody's Investor Services.

of these downgradings have been due to industry-specific factors, such as difficulties associated with the construction and operation of nuclear power plants. Others are the result of broader-based trends, such as increases in corporate indebtedness associated with merger and takeover activities, or a squeeze on earnings caused by high interest rates and strong foreign competition. These problems have partly manifested themselves in a decline in the average investment grade of new bond issues. Until the late 1970s the percentage of issues below investment grade (Baa by Moody's or BBB by Standard and Poor's) never rose above 10 per cent, but in the last few years it has consistently been above 20 per cent, and reached 29 per cent in 1986[83].

Whether this decline in debt quality could become a significant problem is an open question, especially as it is limited, somewhat transitory (the agricultural sector has stabilised and the LDC debt situation appears to be slowly improving), and in part reflects an increased acceptance/demand for low-quality high-yield debt. Many low-grade securities have been issued by well-known firms that were once more highly rated, and therefore are probably regarded more favourably by investors; in addition such securities have often taken innovative and attractive forms, e.g. warrant or commodity-indexed bonds. Similarly, the general rise in indebtedness is also not necessarily a threat to economic stability. Aggregate debt will increase if two parties issue financial claims to each other, but such a transaction has no effect on the net worth of either party, nor does it increase either's net debt service burden. Such a phenomenon may characterise the growth in household debt, where the increase in liabilities has been matched by the accumulation of financial assets.

However, even if at the aggregate level the household sector's financial health is relatively good, many households whose debt has risen relative to income may not have benefited from an offsetting rise in the value of their gross assets. Data are lacking to determine whether or not this has been the case, but the slow growth in real wages in the 1980s suggests that workers who did not own houses or corporate stock may have seen their relative net worth decline. If this is indeed true, then a large percentage of the population could experience difficulties if interest rates rose significantly: heavily indebted families with few assets would be strained by a rise in their debt service burden. Furthermore, the greater use of adjustable rate mortgages means that debt servicing will be more sensitive to movements in market rates than was true in the past. Such concerns must be balanced against the many households for whom interest payments are a significant source of income; innovation has caused their income to be more responsive to increases in interest rates.

The business sector has experienced a significant decline in its capitalisation in recent years. As a result, many firms are now more highly leveraged, making the sector more vulnerable to a rise in interest rates. In addition, the share of corporate debt that is short-term is historically high at about 50 per cent – a potential source of trouble since these firms hold long-lived and relatively illiquid assets – and some highly leveraged firms have recently experienced difficulties in trying to convert bank bridge loans into more stable bond liabilities. Partially offsetting these developments, though, has been a reduction in debt service burden accompanying the general decline in bond yields since the early 1980s.

Corporate finance and control

The increase in corporate indebtedness noted above is somewhat surprising, because profits have been strong during the recovery, enabling firms to finance the bulk of their capital expenditures through internal financing (Diagram 22). Moreover, a strong bull market in stocks has been an incentive to raise funds through new equity issues, and high real interest rates should have discouraged borrowing from banks or on capital markets. Nevertheless, net equity issues were strongly negative in 1984-1986, and have drained almost $250 billion from the market (Diagram 23). This reduction in capitalisation was primarily a result of equity retirements associated with a wave of mergers, acquisitions, leveraged buyouts, and share repurchases, and not a failure of firms to take advantage of higher stock prices. Indeed, the *gross* issuance of equity has been running at record levels in recent years. The roots of this surge in takeover activity are not totally clear, but unlike earlier waves, mergers in the 1980s have taken place in an environment of high and volatile nominal and real interest

Diagram 22. **NET SOURCES OF FUNDS FOR CORPORATE BUSINESS**

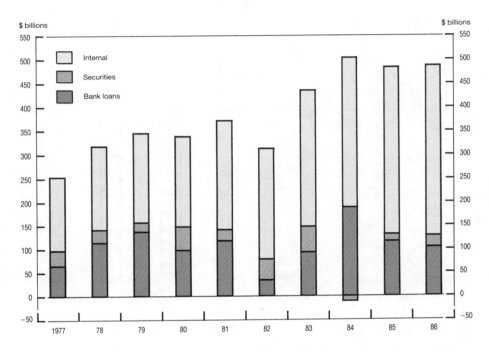

Source: Securities and Exchange Commission, *Small Business Financing Trends (1977-1986).*

rates, as well as major swings in commodity prices and exchange rates. These conditions have increased the difficulty of assessing the present value of firms, because the appropriate choice of a longrun discount rate is less clear, and because of greater uncertainty surrounding estimates of future earnings. Such uncertainty may have led in many cases to a divergence between management and outside investors as to the value of the firm and appropriate corporate strategies, leading to a takeover bid[84]. These valuation problems are particular great for companies with very long-lived assets or resources, which may explain why oil companies have been attractive takeover targets.

The implications of this merger activity for economic stability and efficiency are complex. The financing methods used to fund many acquisitions – stock purchases have in many cases been financed through bank loans, commercial paper and junk

Diagram 23. **NET EQUITY ISSUES FOR NON-FINANCIAL CORPORATIONS**
1980-1986

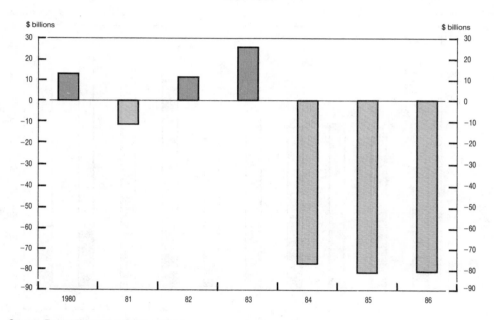

Source: Federal Reserve Board, *Flow of Funds.*

bond issuance, and the sale of assets of the acquired company – have left many firms in a financially weakened position. Management strategies to fend off hostile takeover bids have often achieved the same result, due to deliberate attempts to increase the cost of acquiring the firm to outsiders wishing to take control. Some techniques appear to be designed more for the benefit of the existing management than for the company's shareholders, as in the case of "golden parachutes". Balanced against these negative factors, though, are potential gains in the performance of the merged firms. The presumed goal of most acquiring firms is to improve management, enter new lines of activity, or achieve economies of scale or scope more cheaply than is possible through their own independent efforts. (Increased profitability through a reduction in market competition may be another goal, but such combinations can be blocked through the enforcement of antitrust laws.) Beyond this, the threat of takeovers works as an incentive for existing management to operate companies for the

112

maximum benefit of their shareholders. Studies of the stock market's appraisal of firms targeted for takeover provide clear evidence that such activity increases their market value. However, the effect on the value of acquiring firms is less clear, as is the degree of improvement in the long-run profitability of merged firms[85].

Financial innovation, savings and investment

Financial innovation helps to explain some of the growth of debt in the 1980s, in that changes in financial markets have partially shielded firms and individuals from the effects of an historically high level of real interest rates. Improved access to foreign markets through eurodollar borrowings, along with the development of new forms of corporate debt, have lowered interest expenses for large firms, and reduced the extent to which business investment has been crowded out by the Federal deficit and the low personal saving rate. Risk management techniques have possibly increased capital expenditures by reducing the uncertainty surrounding the finance costs of long-term investment projects. Households have benefitted from mortgage securitisation, which has made lending to homeowners more attractive to traditional

Diagram 24.   **CHANGES IN CONSUMER RATE SPREADS**
Loan rates minus yield on AAA corporate bonds

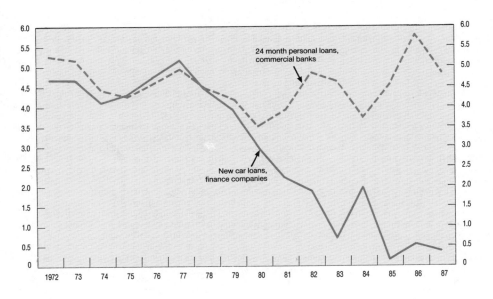

113

lenders, and has brought new sources of credit into the housing market. The use of ARMs has also boosted housing investment, in that the supply of mortgage credit would certainly fall if lenders could not transfer price-risk to borrowers. Liberalised terms in certain areas of consumer finance have also been important in boosting consumption expenditures. For example, the spread between the yield on bonds and the rate charged on auto loans has fallen by over 4 percentage points since the early 1970s (Diagram 24). The average maturity of car loans has also lengthened considerably; combined with the relative decline in auto rates, these innovations have decreased monthly car payments by about 40 per cent. The use of credit cards has expanded, facilitating spending, and the development of home equity loans – lines of credit advanced by banks and thrift institutions based on the market value of a house net of outstanding mortgage debt – has enabled homeowners to tap existing resources more easily. This latter innovation has certain tax advantages (interest on such loans is tax deductible under the new tax law, unlike consumer lending), and so has become popular as a source of general purpose credit for homeowners.

VI. Conclusions

The present Administration came to office in 1981 with a four-part programme:

- To cut the rate of growth in Federal spending;
- To reform the tax system;
- To bring down inflation by slowing the rate of money creation;
- To deregulate the economy.

The programme has been largely successful in accomplishing the four above objectives. The economy has now entered its sixth year of sustained recovery, making it the second longest U.S. expansion in the post-war era. The country has been in the forefront of tax reform and there has been substantial deregulation which has improved the competitive environment. Underlying inflation has been brought down substantially and employment creation has been vigorous, more so than elsewhere, reflecting strong economic growth and labour-market flexibility. However, the emergence of a large Federal budget deficit and a declining national saving rate, together with a large and rising current external deficit, has complicated the conduct of macroeconomic policy. Although, during the 1981 to 1984 period, the Federal deficit helped sustain growth in the rest of the OECD area, by 1985 it had become a cause of domestic and international concern.

When the United States was last examined by the Committee in September 1986, forces making for growth were on balance thought likely to prevail over the subsequent eighteen months or so. With a progressive reversal of fiscal stimulus and other contractionary influences expected to be more than offset by the combined effects of lower oil prices, reduced interest rates and the weaker dollar, real GNP was projected to continue to expand at a rate of around 3 per cent. In spite of some anticipated tightening of labour markets and a pick-up in oil prices, the outlook for inflation was not seen as posing a serious threat to stability. However, the large domestic and external imbalances were expected to persist. The Federal deficit was still projected to amount to around $160 billion in 1987, with virtually no further improvement in 1988. The current external deficit was projected to remain at its peak 1986 level of around $135 billion. Against this background, the risk of financial tensions appeared considerable. In particular, doubts were raised as to the medium-term sustainability of the U.S. external deficit, namely, whether, at the then prevailing interest rate differentials and exchange rate levels, dollar denominated assets would remain sufficiently attractive to allow a smooth financing of the current external deficit.

In the event, the real economy evolved almost as expected in 1987. Reflecting improved external competitiveness in the wake of the steady dollar depreciation since early 1985, there was a sustained expansion of activity, accompanied by a shift in the pattern of growth. For the first time since 1980, real net exports became an element of strength whereas domestic demand slowed from the rapid rates of growth experienced in the previous three years. Unemployment fell sharply, spurred by rapid growth in service sector jobs and a subsequent pick-up in manufacturing employment. Although underlying inflation remained moderate, by mid-year the tightening of the labour market was raising concern in some quarters about future price and wage performance. These concerns were intensified by periods of weakness of the dollar.

Substantial progress was made in reducing the budget deficit in 1987. The improvement was greater than initially expected, due in part to a temporary boost to revenue. But reduced Federal dissaving was insufficient to prevent a renewed deterioration of the already large imbalance between domestic saving and investment. As a result, despite rapidly rising real net exports, the nominal trade balance deteriorated further. The dollar came under downward pressure, due in part to disappointing nominal trade figures, the continued build-up of foreign indebtedness, and the perceived lack of progress in implementing policies liable to foster the adjustment process, both in the United States and abroad. To a large extent, this pressure was met by official exchange-market intervention.

Tensions in the world economy, including rising bond rates, to which the persistence of large international imbalances made a contribution, were probably an important factor behind the sharp world-wide falls in equity prices in mid-October. Unsettled stock market conditions and the volatility of exchange markets have added to uncertainties about the short-term outlook of the U.S. economy. The fall in the stock market is expected to have a deflationary impact, since the loss of financial wealth resulting from lower equity prices should reduce private consumption. Somewhat weaker domestic demand growth should be compatible with a more favourable pattern of output growth and progress in unwinding imbalances. With household saving expected to rise and the Federal budget deficit to stabilise, as a result of the agreement reached between Congress and the Administration in late 1987, prospects for an improvement of the current account balance have been enhanced. Increased net export volumes should lead fairly quickly to an improvement in the nominal current account. Under such a scenario, contained in the Secretariat's short-term conditional projections, pressure on the dollar may abate giving policy-makers in the United States and abroad more time to adopt the needed policy actions.

However, there are, as always, risks to the forecast in the short-run. On the one hand, consumer spending may weaken more than projected, which, together with inventory adjustment, could tip the economy into recession. On the other hand, the personal saving rate may rise less than expected and, in view of the need to add capacity to meet demand for exports and import substitutes, non-residential fixed investment may display greater strength. With stronger domestic demand growth than embodied in the Secretariat projections, the expected improvement in the nominal trade balance could be delayed and inflationary tendencies may start to appear. Under such circumstances, financial and exchange market turbulence could re-emerge, seriously complicating the task of monetary policy.

Over the medium term, the U.S. economy thus remains faced with the critical task of maintaining non-inflationary growth, while unwinding domestic and external imbalances. In this respect, the recent budget agreement is welcome, but it may do little more than stabilise the Federal deficit at about $150 billion up to the end of the decade. For the external adjustment to be completed over the medium term, a sustained reduction in the Federal budget deficit is necessary. As a share of GNP, the general government deficit is not abnormal; nor is the Federal debt and debt interest burden exceptional, especially when measured in terms of government and private sector net worth. However, government credit demands are large in relation to private saving. In this context of a continuing demand for world savings, the further build-up of dollar liabilities could weaken confidence in the dollar and contribute to exchange-rate instability and interest rate volatility. On the real side, the growth of U.S. domestic demand will have to be reduced if the transfer of real resources from the domestic to the external sector is to take place.

In these circumstances, it is essential that the provisions of the Balanced Budget Act be implemented, and that Federal budget balance be broadly achieved by 1993. Given the importance of the Federal deficit for financial market confidence, the momentum of deficit reductions has to be maintained and seen to be maintained. Such reductions would be beneficial in their own right, but it is also essential that they be accompanied by increased efforts to raise the U.S. private saving ratio, faster growth of domestic demand abroad, continued structural adjustment in the United States and its main trading partners as well as progress in world trade liberalisation. Specifically:

117

i) The repeal of interest deductibility on consumer loans, incorporated in the Tax Reform Act and still being phased in, has been unsuccessful in increasing the personal saving rate as consumers have been able to take out second mortgages to finance consumption, interest on which still qualifies for interest relief. At a minimum, efforts should be made to close this loophole;

ii) Faster domestic demand growth in the main trading partners of the United States is necessary to achieve a more sustainable international pattern of current account balances and to support world economic growth;

iii) U.S. manufacturing industry must continue to adjust in order to meet the rapidly changing pattern of world demand. This implies a rate of investment sufficient to increase both productivity and capacity, as well as efforts to cut costs, diversify products and improve quality standards. Structural adjustment in other countries is equally important to foster stronger world economic growth without raising risks of inflation;

iv) Administration policy has, appropriately, been to seek greater openness in world trade and resist protectionist tendencies at home. Reducing distortions to international trade through the progressive removal of barriers that prevent the free play of market forces would allow both the United States and other countries to exploit more fully their comparative advantage.

In the immediate future, the interests of the U.S. economy and those of other countries would seem to be best served by a period of relative exchange rate stability. The advantages and disadvantages of dollar depreciation depend quite crucially on the degree of capacity utilisation and labour market tightness in the U.S. economy, both of which have shown significant increases recently. With real net exports and manufacturing output expected to expand rapidly as a result of previous dollar depreciation, additional external stimulus could risk being inflationary. There is a significant possibility that the household saving ratio will rise further in coming months and that domestic demand will slacken. This may be accompanied by an improvement in the monthly trade data, reassuring currency markets on the viability of the current dollar exchange rate. However, if downward pressures on the dollar were to continue, these should be resisted. Indeed, as agreed by the Finance Ministers and Central Bank Governors of the seven major industrial countries in their December statement, a further decline of the dollar could be counterproductive.

Monetary policy will have to remain pragmatic and flexible. Given the particular uncertainties attaching to the short-term outlook the appropriateness of changes in the policy stance should continue to be assessed in the light of the strength of aggregate demand, the potential for inflationary pressure and conditions in financial and exchange markets. In this regard, the strategy followed immediately after the 19th October crisis in equity markets – namely, announcing and supplying liquidity to meet the needs of the economy – was essential, as it contributed to maintaining orderly conditions in credit markets. Given current economic conditions, the relatively cautious accommodating stance of monetary policy would seem appropriate. However, the monetary authorities must remain alert to signs of inflationary tendencies or excessive weakening of the economy.

The stress of an outdated regulatory structure in the presence of changes in the macroeconomic environment has spurred a process of innovation in U.S. financial markets. This process, aided by improvements in computer and telecommunication technology, has diminished many long-standing distinctions between various financial institutions and increased the level of competition in many financial markets. This rise in competition has extended beyond domestic markets, as U.S. intermediaries, businesses and even households have become increasingly linked to foreign markets and institutions. Along with internationalisation, innovation has also involved a diversion of funds away from the banking sector and into security issuance. With information and other transaction costs falling, ultimate borrowers and lenders are now often able effectively to dispense with bank intermediation and meet directly in capital markets. These changes, along with the increased use of risk-management tools and other innovative instruments, have increased the range and quality of financial services. These improvements have been augmented by the decontrol of interest rates, and the easing of the few remaining restrictions on competition, such as the prohibition on interstate bank branching and the separation of commercial and investment banking.

Maintaining stable financial and monetary conditions appears all the more desirable since the vulnerability of the economy to shocks may have increased. The profitability and, in some cases, the capitalisation of depository institutions has declined in the 1980s in the face of large loan losses. There has been a large increase in the indebtedness of the non-financial sectors, and in the case of the business sector, a decline in net worth. The quality of outstanding debt has fallen. However, these changes do not seem to have seriously compromised the stability of the economy – so far the October fall in stock prices has been absorbed with remarkably few problems. Nevertheless, many households and firms could have difficulties servicing existing debt in the event of a large increase in interest rates or a recession. Coupled with lingering nervousness resulting from the stock market crash, this vulnerability makes it especially important that the stability of the financial system be protected and enhanced.

Overall, the task of smoothly unwinding the existing large domestic and external imbalances is bound to take time but does not appear intractable over the medium-term. It is essential that the substantial adjustment currently under way in the real trade balance continues and translates into a steady reduction of the nominal deficit. To sustain this process, two key domestic requirements will have to be fulfilled: external competitiveness will have to evolve in a manner consistent with long-run current account balance, and the U.S. Federal deficit will have to be progressively eliminated. Given the nature of the imbalances and the sheer size of the U.S. economy, an increase in domestic saving is clearly crucial, not only for a soft landing of the U.S. economy but also for maintaining stable world economic conditions. In this respect, domestic demand growth in other industrial countries will have to be strong enough to offset the decline in their net exports associated with the U.S. current account adjustment. It is also essential for the future of the world economy that protectionist tendencies in the United States and elsewhere be resisted and that progress in expanding trade opportunities be made under the ongoing Uruguay Round negotiations of GATT. Finally, for co-operative action to improve market confidence, policies will have to be seen as credible and internationally-consistent, both with respect to macroeconomic action and micro structural reforms.

Notes and references

1. For a discussion of potential output and the NAIRU, see *The Economic and Budget Outlook: An update*, Appendixes B and C, Congressional Budget Office (August 1987).

2. On a weekly basis, according to the OECD dollar effective rate measure; the actual daily peak occurred in the last days of February.

3. There have, however, been quite big differences; the Taiwan currency has appreciated by nearly 40 per cent while that of Hong Kong has been tied to the dollar.

4. For a review of the literature on this subject see P. Hooper and C.L. Mann, "The U.S. external deficit: its causes and persistence", *International Finance Discussion Papers*, No. 316, Federal Reserve Board, November 1987. For a report of comparative simulations involving changes in exchange rates and U.S. and foreign growth, see Bryant R., and G. Holtham, "The U.S. Deficit: Diagnosis, prognosis and cure", *Brookings Discussion Papers in International Economics*, 55, Washington, March 1987.

5. In Diagram 9, the trade sub-model of U.S. INTERLINK has been used to simulate the partial equilibrium path of *manufactured* export and import volumes under the assumption of unchanged relative export and import prices (set at 1980 II values). The deterioration in the manufactured trade balance more than accounted for the increase in the overall trade deficit between 1981 and 1985.

6. Between 1981 and 1985 the value of U.S. exports of agricultural products declined by $14 billion.

7. This is based on a newly-developed series of U.S. export and import price indexes measured both in dollar and foreign currency terms. A specially designed series of average exchange rate indexes, weighted by the relative importance of a given country's trade with the U.S. in each product category, was used in the construction of the foreign currency price series. A description of the methodology underlying the new series appeared in the December 1987 issue of the *Monthly Labor Review*.

8. Changes in the exchange value of the dollar, as well as the rate at which it is passed through or absorbed, vary widely by product area. For instance, in the category of motor vehicles and parts, the trade-weighted value of the dollar has declined about 31 per cent since March 1985 and about 55 per cent of this decline has been passed through into higher dollar prices for these imported products. However, to the extent that dollar depreciation has reduced raw materials and energy costs in U.S. trading partners' economies, it is normal to observe a less than a full pass-through of dollar depreciation into U.S. import prices, all the more since efforts have also been made

121

abroad to reduce production costs. In general, to be completely accurate, measurements of "pass-through" require information on unit labour and other input costs in export- and import-competing industries, which are not available.

9. However, the price of exports at the time of final sale in foreign markets (which is unobserved), may not have fallen by as much as implied by the measured export price indices. Foreign distributors, which in some cases are subsidiaries of U.S. corporations, may have preferred to boost profit margins somewhat, rather than increase the volume of sales as much as possible.

10. United States Department of Labor (Bureau of Labor Statistics), *International comparisons of manufacturing productivity and labor cost trends*, Washington, June 1987.

11. Bank of Japan, *U.S. Competitiveness in Manufacturing*, September 1987 and *OECD Economic Outlook no. 42*, pp. 39 *et seq.*

12. The operative constraint, known as the "Marshall-Lerner" condition, is that the sum of the absolute values of the export and import elasticities should exceed unity. However, this standard condition applies only if exports equal imports initially.

13. For the period 1981 to 1987 as a whole, the model overpredicts somewhat the loss in export share ($19 instead of $7 billion), suggesting that U.S. exporters performed relatively well in the circumstances.

14. The rate of return on foreign assets (excluding direct investment) held in the United States was about 6 per cent in 1987, having fallen from $8\frac{1}{2}$ per cent in 1984. The return on United States private holdings of foreign assets (also excluding direct investment) was $6\frac{1}{2}$ per cent in 1987, having declined from $10\frac{1}{2}$ per cent in 1984.

15. See Hooper and Mann, *op.cit.*

16. *Economic Report of the President*, February 1988, p. 114.

17. The sensitivity to movements in market rates reflects in part the slow adjustment of M1 deposit rates to changes in market rates and the tendency for demand deposits to be increasingly composed of business holdings, which have been increasingly dominated by compensating balances: when interest rates rise, businesses are permitted to reduce the amount of balances held with the banks as compensation for services provided but not paid with fees – a factor which helps to explain a high interest elasticity for demand deposits.

18. Under the former system, in which non-borrowed reserves were the operating target, deviations of money from its specified growth path were allowed to show through automatically in changed levels of banks' borrowings at the discount window. This tended to lead to changes in the Federal funds rate and hence to other market rates, as banks were forced to alter their borrowings. By contrast, under the more recent procedure, an operating target is established for borrowed reserves and – until that operating target is changed, which may occur between meetings of the FOMC – non-borrowed reserves are allowed to vary to accommodate changes in required reserves. There may be a tendency for the Federal funds rate to be less variable in the short-run under the new system, because changes in borrowing levels are no longer so directly linked to short-run fluctuations in monetary growth.

19. Concerted intervention on 28th January followed a consultation between Secretary Baker and Finance Minister Miyazawa on the 21st January in which the commitment to co-operate on exchange rate issues was reaffirmed.

20. See Statement by Mr. Volcker before the Joint Economic Committee, 2nd February 1987 and Testimony before the Committee on the Budget, U.S. Senate, 24th February 1987.

21. As noted above, the U.S. authorities intervened for the first time in 1987 in support of the dollar by selling yen on 28th January. The bulk of the official intervention in 1987 comprised purchases of dollars by the G7 central banks (Table 15), although the U.S. authorities did undertake significant yen and DM sales in March/April and from October onwards:

Dollar purchases by the U.S. Authorities in 1987

	Jan./Feb.	March/April	May/June	July/mid-Aug.	mid-Aug/mid-Oct.	mid-Oct./5th Jan.	Total
Millions of dollars equivalent :	50	3 965	123	− 85	390	2 165	6 608
Japanese yen Deutschemark	Nil	66	703	− 631	50	3 500	3 688
Total	50	4 031	826	− 716	440	5 665	10 296

Source: Federal Reserve Bank of New York, *Quarterly Review*, Spring and Autumn 1987 and Winter 1987/88.

22. At its meeting in September the FOMC justified somewhat greater reserve pressure by the prospect that any pick-up in prices could be expected to push up labour costs in 1988, given that the unemployment rate was projected to edge lower.

23. Monetary Policy Report to Congress Pursuant to the Full and Balanced Growth Act of 1978, 22nd February 1988, p. 12.

24. *Ibid.*, p. 2.

25. Calculations of real rates depend on price expectations, which are difficult to measure accurately – an important reason why monetary policy does not rely on them as indicators. But it is through changes in real interest rates that monetary factors enter into most macro-economic models (including that of the Federal Reserve Board staff).

26. For a discussion of the term structure as a short-run predictor of activity change see *Economic Perspectives*, January/February 1988, Federal Reserve Bank of Chicago. The yield spread tends to narrow, or even turn negative during periods of severe monetary restraint. See also *Economic Report of the President*, February 1988, p. 39.

27. Calls for revenue increases have often been linked with an extension of expenditure taxation, particularly specific taxes. For example, the Chairman of the Federal Reserve Board has urged consideration of a sizeable increase (15 cents) in the gasoline tax. An increase of 25 cents would yield $25 billion in revenue, while returning real gasoline prices to their levels of the early 1980s. Restraint on energy use would be a side benefit. See Statement by Alan Greenspan before the Committee on the Budget, United States Senate, 2nd March 1988, p. 6.

28. For an exposition of the U.S. government view see U.S. Treasury Department, *The Effects of Deficits on Prices of Financial Assets: Theory and Evidence* (Washington D.C., U.S. Government Printing Office, March 1984).

29. See CBO, *The Economic and Budget Outlook, Fiscal years 1988-92*, pp. 52-55. This estimate assumes that a ½ point decrease in the unemployment rate is associated with a 1 ¾ per cent level increase in GNP. Interest savings are also incorporated.

30. Office of Management and Budget, *Budget of the United States Government, FY 1989*, p.3b-16.

31. U.S. Department of the Treasury, *Accounting for the Deficit*, October 1987; see also CBO., *The Economic and Budget Outlook: an Update*, August 1987.

32. As was pointed out in the last OECD *Economic Survey of the United States* (p. 51) the social security surpluses will eventually be drawn down when the baby boom generation retires.

33. For a discussion, see CBO, *The Economic and Budget Outlook: Fiscal years 1988-1992*, January 1987, pp. 98 *et seq.*

34. For a discussion of this issue, see *Economic Report of the President*, February 1988, pp. 109 *et seq.*

35. For a discussion of tax reform in the United States see *Economic Report of the President*, January 1987, pp. 79-96.

36. The monthly survey on consumer sentiment conducted by the University of Michigan Institute for Social Research revealed a sharp decline of more than 10 per cent in the aggregate index between the early-October and late-October post-crash responses. A similar monthly survey by the Conference Board declined by more than 17 per cent from October to November.

37. The Dun and Bradstreet business expectations survey for the first quarter of 1988 noted that any reduction in planned manufacturing output as a result of the stock market crash was expected to be small, "because the manufacturing sector is currently driven by export orders".

38. See *OECD Economic Outlook no. 42*, pp. 30-34 for a discussion of this issue, as well as the reference cited in note 1.

39. Consistent with a rise in nominal spending by about 5 per cent a year, as in the CBO's October 1987 baseline, adjusted for the 21st December budget agreement.

40. Officially published estimates of labour force and productivity growth are as follows (annual average growth rates):

	U.S. Department of Labor			Congressional Budget Office	Council of Economic Advisers
	1986-2000			1988-1993	1988-1993
	Low	Moderate	High		
Civilian labour force	1.0	1.2	1.3	1.3	1.4
GNP per employee	.7	1.2	1.5	1.1	1.7
Potential GNP growth	1.7	2.4	2.8	2.5	3.1

Sources: U.S. Department of Labor, *Monthly Labor Review*, September 1987, p. 16; Congressional Budget Office, *The Economic and Budget Outlook: Fiscal Year 1989-1993; Economic Report of the President*, February 1988, p. 52.

41. The cuts have been implemented by imposing the following expenditure shocks, equal to the difference between the Balanced Budget Act's targets and the deficit in the reference case:

1989	1990	1991	1992	1993
– 22	– 43	– 56	– 83	– 100

Public expenditure cuts have been used to implement the simulation package; if tax increases were used, the financial market affects would be similar, but allocative effects markedly different.

42. For a description of the Agreement, see *Economic Report of the President*, February 1988, pp. 128-136. The United States also signed an understanding with Mexico on a framework of principles and procedures for consultation regarding trade and investment relations.

43. However, most large money centre banks have relatively few retail deposits, and rely on wholesale money markets.

44. The small credit union portion of the thrift sector is an exception, as it holds mainly consumer loans.

45. *Financial Accounts of OECD Countries* (1986, part 2).

46. Many states went further and did not allow state-wide branching, and this prohibition still exists in some areas. Illinois, a large banking centre, is currently phasing out such restrictions.

47. Grandfather provisions allowed some banks to retain non-bank financial operations, such as limited insurance activities. Also, underwriting of general obligation municipal securities by banks was permitted.

48. This latter restriction was imposed because of the belief that an excessive competition for funds had undermined the health of the banking system, and that the prohibition of interest on demand accounts, along with interest-rate ceilings on time and savings accounts, would make the system more stable.

49. Among such legislation was the Bank Holding Company Act of 1956, which was subsequently amended in 1970. This law established the permissible activities of the parent companies of commercial banks, allowing them to operate subsidiaries such as finance companies or data processing facilities. The BHC Act also made the Federal Reserve the chief regulator of bank holding companies, with oversight responsibilities for all corporate activities.

50. State chartered MSBs have had these powers for some time, but it was not until interest rate volatility increased in the early 1980s that these thrifts began to rapidly diversify away from housing finance. Their long-term experience in such lending may help to explain why they have been able to diversify to a much larger extent than S&Ls.

51. For example, goods are often sold as part of a package that includes financing (e.g. auto sales incentive programmes that offer subsidised interest rates), and financial services (insurance or stockbrokering) are sold under the same roof with merchandise.

52. They are also not small from an aggregate prospective, since 10 of the 15 largest consumer lenders are non-banks, and account for about 25 per cent of consumer instalment credit outstanding. See Pavel and Rosenblum, "Financial Darwinism: Nonbanks – and Banks – are Surviving", *Federal Reserve Bank of Chicago Working Paper* SM-85-05.

53. See Pavel and Rosenblum, *op. cit.*.

54. The Competitive Equality Banking Act (CEBA) of 1986 outlawed new non-bank banks and grandfathered existing ones; grandfathered institutions have only limited access to the payments system. CEBA's non-bank provisions expire in 1988.

55. Until ten years ago, foreign banks based in countries without Glass-Steagall restrictions could operate securities subsidiaries in the U.S., but this was prohibited in 1978 by the International Bank Act; existing subsidiaries were allowed to continue operating.

56. This institutionalisation partly arose out of a strong growth in employment and labour force participation, which raised the share of household net worth held in the form of pension fund reserves from 7.5 per cent in 1970 to 14 per cent in 1986. In addition, the success of deposit insurance programmes and the perceived stability of the financial system may have (paradoxically) increased institutionalisation, by raising individuals' willingness to hold uninsured forms of savings, especially in light of rising levels of per capital wealth.

57. For a further discussion of this topic – and securitisation in general – see "The Economics of Securitization", *Federal Reserve Bank of New York Quarterly Review*, Volume 12, No. 3 (Autumn 1987).

58. The growth in the market for these and other asset-backed securities has also been fuelled by the increased desire of commercial banks and thrifts to move assets off of their balance sheets, as mentioned above.

59. The pricing of these contingent contracts can be quite complicated, and much mathematical and statistical research has been carried out to determine the appropriate pricing of derivative assets. For a non-technical review of the subject, see M. Rubinstein "Derivative Assets Analysis", *The Journal of Economic Perspectives*, Vol. 1, No. 2 (Fall 1987); this review has a useful bibliography of technical papers.

60. Option contracts represent the purest form of such insurance: by allowing one party to purchase the right, but not the obligation, to buy or sell from another party a block of securities at an agreed upon price (before a specified future date), the ownership of a security is completely decoupled from speculation in changes in its price.

61. For a recent review of this subject, see "The Growth of the Financial Guarantee Market", *Federal Reserve Bank of New York Quarterly Review*, Vol. 12, No. 1 (Spring 1987). Commercial banks have been an important element in the growth of this market: Outstanding standby credit issued by commercial banks grew from $50 billion in 1980 to $250 billion in 1986. Moreover, some commercial bank holding companies have equity stakes in financial guarantee insurance companies.

62. The rising proportion of resources devoted to the provision of financial services in the U.S. and other OECD economies has led some to argue that aggregate productivity has suffered from "excessive" intermediation. However, such arguments represent subjective value judgements, and cannot prove that the market-generated composition of final

output is undesirable. For an interesting essay that argues this position, though, see James Tobin "On the Efficiency of the Financial System", *Lloyds Bank Review* No. 153 (July 1984).

63. Evidence for this statement comes from various studies of the municipal bond market that show underwriting costs are significantly lower for general obligation bonds than for revenue bonds. A primary reason for this difference appears to be that commercial banks have long been allowed to underwrite the former, but not the latter.

64. For a general review of this subject see Stephen Rhoades, "Interstate Banking and Product Line Expansion: Implications from Available Evidence" *Loyola of Los Angeles Law Review*, Vol.18, p. 4, 1985. A recent study on economies of scale and scope in banking, which includes a useful bibliography, is Berger, Hanweck, and Humphrey, "Competitive Viability in banking", *Journal of Monetary Economics*, Vol. 20, No. 3 (December 1987). It should be noted that studies on this subject generally exclude the largest money centre banks, due to data availability problems.

65. These include the following: the Presidential Task Force on Market Mechanisms (the Brady Report); the testimony of four government regulatory agencies, the Federal Reserve Board, the General Accounting Office, the Commodity Futures Trading Commission, and the Securities and Exchange Commission, delivered to the Senate Banking Committee in early February 1988; the reports issued by the New York Stock Exchange (the Katzenbach Report, released in late December) and the Chicago Mercantile Exchange (the Miller-Hawke-Malkiel-Scholes report, released in late December); and the testimony before the Senate Banking Committee in early February of Leo Melamed of the CME and John Phelan, Chairman of the NYSE.

66. For example, trading in S&P 500 futures was suspended at one point when buyers no longer appeared on the New York Stock Exchange for many of the component stocks. Furthermore, during the entire week of 19th October index future prices were below their equivalent on primary stock exchanges, in spite of the fact that theoretically (and historically) such prices should trade at a slight premium.

67. The behaviour of options prices before and after the crash raises another interesting issue: the difficulties surrounding the pricing of these instruments. Option prices have roughly doubled since the crash, showing that the market has significantly increased its estimate of the variance in stock prices, on the basis of one new (admittedly extreme) observation on price movements. While this revision can be seen as simply the incorporation of new information into prices, it shows the difficulty of estimating the probability distribution of security prices. Unlike the mortality distribution for major population groups, or the probability of harsh weather conditions in a given area, the future variance of stock prices is poorly understood, and may very well shift over time in unknown ways. It is even possible that the variance may be a function of one's own actions, if one is a large institutional investor engaging in programmed trading along with other large investors.

68. See *The Effect of Mortgage-Related Securities on Corporate Finance*. Study prepared by the staff of the Board of Governors of the Federal Reserve System (August 1986).

69. For example, see *Recent Innovations in International Banking*, Bank of International Settlements (April 1986), Chapter 10.

70. In the case of a private collateralised mortgage obligation (CMO), for example, these include the agents that service the underlying mortgages, the institution that manages the aggregate mortgage pool, and banks or other financial institutions that provide credit-enhancement services. Furthermore, others not directly involved in the transaction are important: if the party providing credit guarantees is involved in other security dealings, its ability to perform depends on the behaviour of additional firms.

71. The bill is entitled the Financial Modernization Act. See the 20th November 1987 statements of Senators Proxmire and Garn, the bill's sponsors, for an overview of its provisions and purposes. In addition to the provisions already noted, the bill attempts to promote equal regulatory conditions across institutions in the same field, whether or not they are affiliated with other types of institutions, via functional regulation. Securities affiliates would be subject to SEC regulation alone, and would be treated the same as independent brokerage houses; commercial bank subsidiaries would have their deposits insured by the FDIC; and the operations of the holding company would be subject to review by the Federal Reserve. The bill also contains a provision that would prevent mergers between the largest commercial and investment banks. Similar legislation has been introduced into the House of Representatives, and there are a number of other bills under consideration that address the general question of financial market reform.

72. Careful legislation can eliminate most of the concerns about the strength of firewalls, but it remains true that the management of a bank or its holding company, if so determined, can breach any legal barrier. The temptation to call on the full resources of a corporation to save a troubled affiliate can be strong: the experience of real estate holding trusts during the early 1970s is instructive in this regard. (These subsidiaries of bank holding companies sustained major losses in this period, and even though not legally obligated to do so, the commercial bank affiliates assumed their debt.) However, regular supervision should prevent occasional violations from developing into major problems.

73. See the testimony of Alan Greenspan, Chairman of the Federal Reserve Board, and Gerald Corrigan, President of the New York Federal Reserve Bank, on the bill before the Senate Banking Committee, 20th November 1987. Also see earlier testimony at similar hearings conducted by the House Banking Committee in mid-November 1987, including the comments by the following: Alan Greenspan; Willian Seidman, Chairman of the FDIC; Robert Clarke, Comptroller of the Currency; and George Gould, Undersecretary for Finance, U.S. Department of the Treasury.

74. See "Mandate for Change: Restructuring the Banking Industry" *FDIC Staff Study* (draft, 18th August 1987); and Gerald Corrigan, President of the New York Federal Reserve Bank, *Financial Market Structure: A Longer View*, Federal Reserve Bank of New York (January 1987).

75. According to the General Accounting Office, FSLIC's present net worth is −$6.3 billion. See the Federal Home Loan Bank Board's *1986 Annual Report*.

76. For a review of the literature on this topic, see Arthur Murton, "A Survey of the Issues and the Literature concerning Risk-Related Deposit Insurance", *Banking and Economic Review* (September/October 1986).

77. See note 65 for a list of references.

78. On the other hand, a gain or loss on a futures contract is a sunk profit or loss, which should not affect economic decision making. Individuals and firms may not be fully rational in this regard, however; also, there may be other reasons why such gains or losses are not irrelevant. For a discussion of this issue, see D. Small, "Investment Demand and Financial Futures Markets", in *Financial Futures and Options in the U.S. Economy*, Myron Kwast (ed.) Federal Reserve Board, 1986.

79. The poor performance during the 1980s of many econometric models of business investment is perhaps evidence of this phenomenon. The business investment equations of the Federal Reserve Board staff's MPS model actually perform *better* over the 1980s if interest rate and tax variables are exogenised at their 1980 levels. A similar phenomenon occurs with the OECD's INTERLINK model.

80. For a formal econometric analysis of this subject, see M. Akhtar and E. Harris, "Monetary Policy Influence on the Economy – An Empirical Analysis", *Quarterly Review*, Federal Reserve Bank of New York (Winter 1986-87). Interestingly, the authors find that the *long-run* sensitivity of aggregate demand (including net external demand) to interest rates may actually have increased in the 1980s.

81. See R. Porter, P. Spindt, and D. Lindsey, "Econometric Modeling of the Demand for the U.S. Monetary Aggregates: Conventional and Experimental Approaches", Federal Reserve Board, *Special Studies Working Papers*, No. 217 (March 1987).

82. See "Changes in Consumer Installment Debt: Evidence from the 1983 and 1986 Surveys of Consumer Finances", *Federal Reserve Bulletin* (October 1987).

83. See "Recent Developments in Corporate Finance", *Federal Reserve Bulletin* (November 1986).

84. See F.M. Scherer, "Takeovers: Present and Future Dangers", *The Brookings Review*, (Winter/Spring 1986), and a recent symposium on takeover activity published in the *Journal of Economic Perspectives* Vol. 2, No. 1 (Winter 1988).

85. However, these studies of profitability do not examine the results of the latest wave of merger activity. See D. Ginsburg and J. Robinson, "The Case Against Federal Intervention in the Market for Corporate Control", *The' Brookings Review*, (Winter/Spring 1986); also note 84.

Annex I

Stock market wealth and the personal saving ratio

The decline in the personal saving ratio can be partially explained by rising stock prices and other increases in household wealth. According to the life-cycle theory of consumer behaviour, individuals plan their consumption in accordance with expected lifetime resources, which include both the present value of the stream of future income and the market value of current assets[1]. This theory, on certain simplifying assumptions, suggests an aggregate consumption function of the form:

$$C_t = (c_0 + c_1 r)YL^*_t + (c_2 + c_3 r)W^*_t$$

where C is real consumption; YL is real after-tax labour income; r is the real after-tax rate of interest; W is the real market value of current net household assets and * denotes expected values. The coefficients c_0 and c_2 should be positive, while c_1 and c_3 should be negative insofar as an increase in the interest rate increases the incentive to save (by raising the value of postponing consumption to a later period). However, the coefficient c_3 may in practice be positive, because a rise in interest rates will increase property income and hence purchasing power. Identification of interest rate effects is the more complicated because the market value of wealth will also vary with changes in interest rates (see Diagram 6).

A version of the above equation was estimated using quarterly data over the 1961Q4 to 1985Q4 period. Following the Federal Reserve's MPS model, consumption was defined as non-durable goods and services plus the imputed flow of services from the stock of housing and consumer durable goods[2]. This differs from the NIPA definition of personal consumption, which includes the purchase of durables rather than their use. Wealth was defined as net household worth, including land and physical assets. Income was disaggregated into two components, transfer income (YT) and other personal income net of taxes. (The propensity to consume out of transfer income should be high relative to other income sources, since it is more stable and continues after retirement; labour and property were aggregated because their individually estimated coefficients were quite close.) Expressing the variables in real, per capita terms, the following long-run equation was obtained[3]:

$$C = 0.524 (Y - YT) + 1.085 YT + 0.069 W$$

The coefficient of 0.07 on wealth compares with a coefficient of 0.05 in the the MPS model, which distinguishes between stock market and other types of wealth.

Rising stock prices increased real household net worth by about $1100 billion between the end of 1981 and the end of 1986, so that the equation would suggest that capital gains increased consumer spending by about \$75 billion – equivalent to a reduction of 3 per cent in the saving ratio.

The equation has a number of disadvantages from the point of view of analysing the effects of the stock market crash on consumption, because the definition of consumption is not the standard national accounts one and because the comprehensive nature of the wealth variable makes it difficult to incorporate in a standard model such as US/INTERLINK. An alternative version of the equation was therefore estimated, with total NIPA consumption expenditures as the dependent variable and wealth effects restricted to stock prices. The equation partially controls for the effects of innovations in consumer finance, by including the average maturity of new car loans and the spread between auto loan rates and bond yields as additional explanatory variables. (See the section on Debt, savings and investment in the financial markets chapter for a discussion of these factors.) This yields the following long-run relationship[4]:

$$\ln (C/Y) = -.498 - .0049R + .0895WSTK + .0916 \ln(MAT) + .0095 \, UNR$$
where

C	=	real consumption expenditures plus consumer interest payments to business (deflated by the implicit consumption deflator);
Y	=	real disposable in come;
R	=	real after-tax interest rate, defined to equal (l-TRM)*(RCB+MARKUP) - INFLA, where TRM is the average marginal federal personal income tax rate (as calculated by the CBO), RCB is Moody's AAA corporate bond rate, MARKUP is the difference between the rate charged by finance companies on new car loans and RCB, and INFLA is a six-semester moving average of the percentage change in the personal consumption deflator;
WSTK	=	the ratio of the value of household corporate equities (Flow of Funds definition) to disposable income;
MAT	=	average maturity on new car loans made by finance companies;
UNR	=	civilian unemployment rate.

The ratio of stock market wealth to income rose from .49 in 1982 to .89 just prior to the crash, sufficient to explain almost a 2½ percentage point fall in the personal saving rate by mid-1987, all other things equal. Due to the lagged response of consumption to changes in wealth, the savings ratio would have fallen an additional ½ percentage point in 1988 if stock prices had remained unchanged from their 1987Q3 levels. However, the sharp decline in prices late last year should do much to reverse the realised and projected stimulus to consumption: the direct wealth effects stemming from the crash will probably increase the rate (relative to what it would have been otherwise) by about 1½ per cent by the end of 1989. This static analysis ignores second-round effects that mute the effect of the decline in wealth on household savings and the economy as a whole, though. Taking into account the probable decline in interest rates and other factors, a full model simulation of US/INTERLINK suggests that the crash should boost the personal saving rate by just under 1 percentage point by 1989.

131

Notes

1. See Ando, A., and Modigliani F., "The life-cycle hypothesis of saving", *American Economic Review*, 53, 1963.
2. See "The structure and uses of the MPS quarterly econometric model of the United States", *Federal Reserve Bulletin*, February 1987.
3. The estimation results were as follows (t - statistics in parenthesis):

$$C_t = \sum_{s=0}^{8} a_s \, (Y_{t\text{-}s} - YT_{t\text{-}s}) + \sum_{s=0}^{8} b_s \, W_{t\text{-}s} + \underset{(8.1)}{1.085} \sum_{s=0}^{8} YT_{t\text{-}s}/4$$

$$\sum_{s=0}^{8} a_s = .524 \,(6.3)$$

$$\sum_{s=0}^{8} b_s = .069 \,(4.1)$$

a_s, b_s constrained to lie on a second degree polynomial with a zero end point restriction

Autoregressive coefficient: .94 (31.6)
Standard error: .052
Adjusted R-squared: .999
Estimation period: 1961Q4 to 1985Q4.

4. The estimation results were as follows (t-statistics in parenthesis):

$$\ln(C/C_{\text{-}1}) = \underset{(-3.0)}{-.182} + \underset{(6.5)}{.560 \ln(Y/Y_{\text{-}1})} + \underset{(3.7)}{.366 \ln(Y_{\text{-}1}/C_{\text{-}1})} \underset{(-1.8)}{-.0018R}$$

$$\underset{(4.4)}{+.033 \, WSTK} + \underset{(2.4)}{.033 \ln(MAT)} + \underset{(3.8)}{.0035 \, UNR}$$

$$\underset{(-4.2)}{-.0051 \,(UNR\text{-}UNR_{\text{-}1})} \underset{(-4.1)}{-.0037 \,(UNR_{\text{-}1}\text{-}UNR_{\text{-}2})} \underset{(-1.7)}{-.0024 \,(UNR_{\text{-}2}\text{-}UNR_{\text{-}3})}$$

Standard error: .0056
Adjusted R-squared: .69
Estimation period: 1960S2 to 1987S2

Accounting for the real trade deficit

Export volumes

The change in the ratio of exports to GDP can be expressed in terms of the respective growth rates of export volumes (x) *and* real GDP (g), such that $\Delta (X/GDP) = (X(x-g)/GDP(1+g))$, where g is the growth rate of volume GNP and x the growth rate of volumes exports. The growth rate of exports can, in turn, be split into three factors, giving the following decomposition of the change in export share:

$$\Delta (X/GDP) = \underset{\substack{export \\ demand}}{sx(w-g)} + \underset{\substack{trade \\ structure}}{sx(u-w)} + \underset{\substack{export \\ performance}}{sx(x-u)}$$

where $sx = X/GDP(1+g)$;
               w = the growth rate of world markets;
               u = the U.S. trade-weighted growth rate of world markets.

If world export demand grows faster than GNP (w>g), as is the norm, exports will increase as a ratio of GDP; however, a concentration of trade on slower-growing markets (u<w), which has characterised the U.S., would lead to a falling share in world exports, offsetting part of the impact of expanding world demand. Where x<u, U.S. export share would be falling because of declining competitiveness, and vice versa.

Import volumes

The decomposition of changes in the ratio of import volumes to GNP $(\Delta (M/GDP) = M(m-g)/GDP(1+g))$ is based on simulations with the INTERLINK model, distinguishing relative price and demand factors:

$$\Delta (M/GDP) = \underset{\substack{import \\ demand}}{sm.g(\gamma-1)} + \underset{\substack{import \\ performance}}{sm(\varepsilon p)} + error$$

An income elasticity of demand for imports above 1 ($\gamma > 1$) raises the ratio of imports to GNP; *import performance* depends on relative price effects, deriving from the import price elasticity (ε) and the relative price change (p).

The trade balance

In Table 9, changes in share are translated in dollar terms, using the same method, such that the change in the trade balance is defined as

$$Xx - Mm = X(x-g) - M(m-g) + (X-M)g.$$

The last item on the right hand side is a "level effect" deriving from the difference between X and M in the base period.

Annex III

Import elasticities

The OECD INTERLINK model currently uses an income elasticity of 2.0 for manufactured imports, with a price elasticity of –0.8. These compare with average elasticities of 1.75 and –1.1 respectively for the other major economies. Moreover, preliminary updates of the U.S. estimates, yield an income elasticity of imports of around 3, with roughly the same relative price elasticity.

One possible explanation for such a high income elasticity is that in the standard specification, where the volume of imports is regressed on an activity and a relative price variable, the estimated "income" coefficient tends to pick up some structural trend variable. There have been major structural changes in the world economy over the past 25 years, including the rise of the east Asian economies (first Japan, later the NICs) as major competitors. Helkie and Hooper[1], add two additional variables to their export and import volume equations to control for these factors: *i)* the ratio for the U.S. business capital stock to the stock outside the U.S.; and *ii)* the ratio of domestic capacity utilization to foreign, which acts as a proxy for short-run supply constraints. Export and import equations containing these variables both have income elasticities of slightly above 2.

Alternatively, the high import elasticity may reflect short-run cyclical responses rather than long-run income effects. Demand for goods is much more variable than total domestic demand (the variance of goods-GNP growth is over three times that of GNP)[2]. When both a moving average of aggregate demand and deviations from the moving average are incorporated in U.S. import equations (estimated in logarithmic form, using semi-annual data from 1970I to 1987I), the long-run income elasticity falls to 2.4[3]:

$$M = -44.6 + 2.44D^* + 3.12(D - D^*) - 0.8RP$$

where   M   =   manufactured import volumes;
          D   =   total domestic demand, less government wage expenditures;
        D*   =   a four-semester moving average of D;
       RP   =   the ratio of the total domestic demand deflator to import unit values

The coefficients of 2.4 and –0.8 compare with an average income elasticity of 2 and price elasticity of –0.7 for the other major economies under this specification.

Import prices enter the equations in relative terms and the usual procedure is to deflate them with an aggregate price index. This would tend to bias the estimated price elasticities downwards, since higher productivity growth would generally mean that the implicit price deflator for the output of the traded goods or manufacturing sector would tend to increase more slowly than the aggregate measure. Incorporating manufacturing producer prices into the relative price measure, the manufacturing import equation becomes:

$$M = -43.9 + 2.42D^* + 3.00(D - D^*) - 1.3RPP$$

where   RPP = the ratio of producer prices in manufacturing to import unit values.

The increased price elasticity is still associated with an income elasticity of 2.4, suggesting that the coefficient on income may be picking up the influence of other omitted variables, which may be correlated with income because of long adjustment lags. Not including *expected* price changes may be one source of bias:

- Trade patterns are determined by location decisions, which are mainly a function of long-term expected costs in different countries. For these goods, exports and imports depend on expected relative unit labour (and other) costs. If unit costs rise in the U.S., this will prompt a slow transfer of production abroad. For such goods, an increase in relative costs above some equilibrium level, would result in a continuing loss of market share while equilibrium is being restored;
- From the demand side, expectations of further import price rises may encourage imports at a time when import prices are rising; as suggested in the main text (paragraph 31), expectations of future dollar depreciation could be important in sustaining import demand, even where the currency has fallen and real income increases are slowing. The latter effect might be especially strong during periods when the authorities are intervening to support the currency.

Implications

The important point is that standard specifications may not adequately model longer-run import behaviour. And the possibility that the income elasticity of demand for imports may be overstated and the price elasticity under-stated has important implications for external adjustment in the medium-term. If long-term income elasticities are nearer to 1 and the price elasticity below −1, the exchange rate mechanism may be more powerful than it has seemed up to now. A limited experiment with higher price elasticities and lower income elasticities has been undertaken in the section on medium-term adjustment. The effect on the external balance is a powerful one. As reported in Table 33, a simulation of a staged 20 per cent depreciation under more optimistic elasticity assumptions shows that if the price elasticities of imports and exports were raised by 50 per cent and the income elasticity reduced to 1.8, the improvement in the current account would nearly double. Viewed another way, if incorporated in the medium-term baseline, more optimistic assumptions would mean that the underlying adjustment process might be more rapid, and the need for further dollar depreciation would be reduced.

Notes

1. Helkie W and P. Hooper, "The U.S. External Deficit in the 1980s: An Empirical Analysis", *Federal Reserve Board International Finance Discussion Paper 304.*
2. This hypothesis that the short-run elasticity is greater than the longer-run is supported by the fact that lagged values of GNP enter import demand equations with significant negative coefficients.
3. The research underlying these results has been undertaken by the Balance of Payments Division. All the coefficients are highly significant.

137

Annex IV

Glossary of financial market terms

Adjustable rate mortgages (ARMs): home mortgages, typically of 20 to 30 years maturity, with a fixed nominal principle, whose interest rate is adjusted periodically (every one to five years) according to movements in some specified market interest rate.

Bank holding companies (BHCs): any corporation owning one or more bank subsidiaries. The activities of the parent and all subsidiaries (bank and non-bank) are restricted and subject to Federal regulation (mainly by the Federal Reserve System), under the provision of the Bank Holding Company Act.

Certificates of deposit: insured time deposits at commercial banks and thrift institutions. Large deposits ($100 000 and up) have negotiable terms, and are traded in secondary markets.

Collateralised mortgage obligation (CMOs): a bond-like security backed by the cash flow from a pool of home mortgages. CMOs differ from other derivative mortgage securities in that the bonds issued on a pool are divided into payout classes in order to create securities of different effective maturities. (Principle in the first class is retired before the pool's cash flow is used to pay principle in the second class, and so on.) These maturity classes reduce the variability of cash flow on mortgage-backed securities arising from the prepayment options on the underlying mortgages.

Commercial paper: short-term (less than one year) unsecured obligations issued by large private corporations. The contract specifies that a fixed amount is to be paid at a particular future date. There is large-scale secondary trading in such securities.

Commodity Futures Trading Commission (CFTC): the Federal government supervisory body regulating trading in futures, financial or otherwise.

Commodity-indexed bonds: a bond whose return depends on movements in the price of some commodity or basket of commodities, by pegging coupon or final payments to a specified commodity price index.

Conventional mortgage: a residential mortgage made by a private lender without governmental guarantees or insurance.

Credit risk: the risk faced by a lender that a borrower will fail to fulfil the provisions of a debt contract, such as occurs in the case of default.

Daylight overdrafts: generally, any excess of debits over available funds in an account occurring in the course of a business day, that are made up prior to the end-of-day settlement.

Large overdrafts of this type are frequent in the interbank electronic settlements system operated by the Federal Reserve: the Federal Reserve guarantees all fund transfers without requiring that senders continuously maintain positive balances.

Deposit insurance: insurance, provided by a government-backed organisation (usually Federal), guaranteeing deposits in the event of bank insolvency. In the U.S., such insurance is granted on individual accounts only up to a specified amount, e.g. $200 000; the surplus in an account in excess of this ceiling is not formally protected. Insured depository institutions must pay premiums and comply with supervisory restrictions.

Discount brokerage firms: securities dealers that charge low commissions on small security transactions made by individuals. They are distinguished from other dealers by primarily dealing with the general public (as opposed to large institutional investors), and by offering few services, such as investment advice.

Federal Deposit Insurance Corporation (FDIC): the government-backed corporation which insures the deposits of member commercial banks and mutual savings banks.

Federal funds rate: the rate charged on unsecured interbank borrowings (usually overnight), used by banks to adjust their reserve positions. Movements in this interest rate mirror changes in the stance of monetary policy, and many other short-term money market rates move closely with it.

Federal Home Loan Bank Board: the oversight body charged with the regulation of federally-insured savings and loan associations. It is the parent organisation to FSLIC.

Federal Home Loan Mortgage Association (Freddie Mac): a private corporation which purchases home mortgages and converts them into derivative securities. It holds only a small portfolio – rights to the income stream from pooled mortgages are typically sold outright to investors – but its sponsored securities are widely believed to have the implicit backing of the Federal government.

Federal National Mortgage Association (FNMA, Fannie Mae): a private corporation which purchases home mortgages, and funds its acquisitions through the issuance of debentures and short-term notes. It holds a very large portfolio of mortgages, and its obligations are widely believed to have the implicit backing of the Federal government. FNMA also packages pools of mortgages.

Federal Open Market Committee (FOMC): The chief body determining monetary policy, composed of the seven members of the Federal Reserve Board and six of the twelve presidents of the regional Federal Reserve District Banks. (Except for the president of the New York Federal Reserve Bank, the non-Board members are chosen on a rotating basis).

Federal Reserve System: the central bank of the United States, composed of the Board of Governors and twelve District Banks. The members of the Board are appointed by the President and approved by the Senate; the District Banks are private (they are owned by the regional commercial banks) but their presidents are appointed by the President subject to Congressional approval. Although many supervisory and monetary control questions can be decided by the Board alone, monetary policy is the province of the FOMC.

Federal Savings and Loan Insurance Corporation (FSLIC): the government sponsored insurer of Savings and Loan Associations. It is under the direction of the Federal Home Loan Bank Board.

Floating rate notes (FRNs): a medium-term security carrying a floating rate of interest which is adjusted periodically subject to some reference rate, usually the LIBOR.

Forward rate agreements: an agreement made by two parties (often banks), that specifies an interest rate to hold over a particular future period, based on an agreed principle amount. When the start day of the specified period arrives, no principle is exchanged; the two parties only exchange the difference between the interest payment based on the earlier agreed upon rate, and the payment based on the current spot rate.

Futures contract: a traded contract calling for delivery of a specified amount of a particular commodity or financial instrument at a fixed date in the future. Contracts are highly standardised: traders need to only agree on the price and number of contracts traded.

Glass-Steagall Act: the Federal statute governing the permitted investment banking activities of commercial banks.

Golden parachutes: contract provisions for corporate managers that provide generous benefits in the event of job loss resulting from a merger or other specified causes.

Government National Mortgage Association (GNMA, Ginnie Mae): a corporation wholly owned by the Federal government, that guarantees privately-issued securities backed by pools of federally insured or guaranteed mortgages.

Home equity loans: loans collateralised by the borrower's equity in a residential property. The loan often takes the form of a line of credit advanced at a specified rate of interest. The interest charges on such borrowing are tax-deductible.

Industrial revenue bonds: obligations issued by municipalities and states to fund private business projects. Until recently, the interest income earned by investors in such securities was exempt from federal taxation.

Junk bonds: high-yielding bonds that are below investment grade, which have been used at times to finance corporate takeovers or buyouts.

Leveraged buyouts: the financing strategy used in many corporate takeovers, in which the purchase of a corporation is funded through the issuance of debt, such as short-term bank loans or junk bonds.

Market maker securities dealers: securities firms who facilitate trading in particular stocks. This is done by acting as temporary sellers or buyers on their own account when there is a mismatch between the volume of buy and sell orders.

Money centre banks: the nine largest commercial banks in the United States.

Money market deposit accounts: savings accounts paying a market rate of interest, with limited cheque-writing privileges. These accounts are subject to reserve requirements, and typically have some minimum balance restrictions.

Money market mutual funds: institutions which issue deposit-like equity shares which have limited cheque-writing privileges. Their liabilities are uninsured, and depositors share directly in the capital gains and losses of the funds' portfolios.

Mortgage-backed securities: any of a number of securities derived from an underlying block of residential mortgages. These include the obligations of certain corporations, such as FNMA, and instruments such as CMOs and pass-through securities.

Mortgage pools: individual mortgages whose income stream has been aggregated together.

Off-balance sheet activities: banking business, often fee-based, that does not involve holding assets or issuing deposit liabilities.

Open-end mutual funds: institutions which invest in corporate equities and other securities, whose portfolio is funded through the issuance of equity shares to the general public.

Option contracts: a traded instrument which gives the right, but not the obligation, to buy or sell a specified amount of a given commodity or financial instrument at a fixed price before a specified future date. A call option grants the right to buy the instrument, a put option grants the right to sell.

Pass-through securities: certificates representing ownership in a pool of mortgages. The monthly cashflow of the pool is passed through directly to the holders of the certificates. They differ from CMOs (see above) in that each certificate is identical.

Portfolio insurance: a short-term investment strategy used by institutional investors that attempts to limit losses in a falling stock market through the purchase of future contracts. When the traded price of the stocks held in an investor's portfolio drops below a specified threshhold, a computerised trading programme automatically attempts to sell future contracts representative of the portfolio basket, in order to lock in future prices.

Price risk: the risk of capital losses (or gains) on a portfolio resulting from changes in interest rates or other prices.

Primary capital: legally, the net capital of a commercial bank as defined by the regulatory authorities. Capitalisation is defined in bookvalue terms, and includes loan loss reserves.

Prime lending rate: the interest rate charged on loans by commercial banks to their most credit-worthy business customers.

Retail deposits: non-negotiable deposit liabilities of commercial banks and thrift institutions, including most household and small business accounts. They are distinguishable from wholesale money market borrowings in that banking institutions take these deposits passively, and do not bid for them in organised markets.

Securities and Exchange Commission (SEC): the government agency responsible for the regulation of securities markets.

Stand-by letters of credit: an obligation on the part of a bank to the holders of a customer's securities that it will redeem the securities if the customer defaults.

Stripped bonds: bonds which have had their coupon payments removed and transformed into a separate instrument, leaving a zero-coupon bond.

Swaps, currency and interest: a transaction in which two parties exchange specific amounts of two different currencies (currency swap), which is then repaid over time according to a specific schedule reflecting interest and amortisation charges; alternatively, the exchange of interest payment streams of differing character (interest rate swap). In the latter case, the swap can be fixed rate debt for floating, either within or across currencies.

Warrants: tradeable instruments giving holders the right to purchase from, or sell to, their issuer fixed-income or equity securities under specified conditions for some period of time. Warrant bonds, for examples, give investors the right to purchase additional debt from the issuer at a predetermined price.

Wholesale money market instruments: instruments actively traded in secondary markets that are used to raise short-term funds. These include commercial paper, large negotiable CDs, repurchase agreements, and Federal Funds.

Zero coupon bonds: single-payment long-term securities which do not pay periodic interest payments.

Annex V

Recent developments in the banking system

Profitability

As discussed in the main text, commercial bank profitability has declined sharply in the 1980s[1]. The net income after taxes of banks fell to .64 per cent of total assets in 1986, down from an average of about .77 per cent during the 1970s; profitability fell by a similar amount when measured by the return on net equity. Incomplete data for 1987 suggests that conditions worsened further, and large loan loss provisions of money centre banks may have reduced aggregate profitability to zero last year. Excluding 1987, small banks suffered the greatest erosion in earnings. Historically, these institutions have been very profitable due to an entrenched position in uncompetitive local markets, but the slump in the farm and energy sectors has dropped the rate of return on their assets (and equity) well below the industry average. In part the decline in their earnings arose from their dependence on local conditions: medium-sized banks ($100 million to $1 000 million in assets) experienced a similar increase in loan losses, but a greater diversification in both their balance sheets and overall operations enabled them to partially offset the decline in asset quality. Large banks were even more successful in this regard. As with all banks, loan losses jumped during the 1980s, as a result of LDC debt problems as well as increased default rates on domestic loans. However, until 1987, large money centre banks managed to almost completely offset these losses through an increased investment in high yielding loans and securities, a decreased dependence on expensive wholesale deposits, and by a major effort to boost fee income. Provisions for anticipated losses on LDC loan portfolios overwhelmed other sources of income last year, and most major banks reported large losses in the course of 1987. These earnings declines have not yet affected capitalisation – loss reserves are counted in primary capital – but point to a probable future drop in capital once the losses are actually realised. Large regional banks have profited from a smaller exposure to LDC debt problems, and new opportunities created by the relaxation of interstate branching prohibitions (along with other measures to boost income) have enabled them to increase their profitability.

Losses at thrift institutions have been more extreme than those faced by commercial banks, with the result that 10 per cent of all S&Ls have negative capitalisation[2]. These severe problems began when interest rates in the early 1980s rose rapidly, causing large losses because of the importance of fixed-rate long-term mortgages in thrift institutions' portfolios. With the decline in market rates since 1982, and the increased use of ARMs and the turnover of the mortgage portfolio, these strains on earnings gradually eased. However, insufficient

143

prudential regulation led to a second round of losses in the middle of the decade. Many S&Ls, pressed by negative income and rapidly declining net worth, sought high rates of return by investing outside their traditional sphere of home finance. Direct investment in real estate rose from 0.4 per cent of assets in 1979 to 4.7 per cent in 1986, and over the same period the percentage of mortgage assets based on non-residential projects doubled from 8.7 per cent to 17.5 per cent. Much of this increase represented investments in real estate development projects with a high degree of credit risk. Many institutions funded these invest-ments through large-scale purchases of managed liabilities and aggressively-priced retail deposits, a strategy that greatly reduced capitalisation, but that promised substantial profits if the projects succeeded and market rates did not rise. Unfortunately, default rates proved to be high, in part because of problems associated with depressed activity in the energy and agricultural sectors, and in part because lenders were insufficiently prudent in their credit standards. Of the 20 per cent of the thrift industry which is now unprofitable, about half are so because of such loan losses, and these institutions are largely responsible for the decline in aggregate profitability in the 1980s. Much of this problem could have been avoided if the regulatory authorities had required capital ratios to remain at prudent levels, and had more closely inspected the credit-worthiness of lending.

Liberalisation measures

Partly in response to declining competitiveness and problems created by high inflation and market interest rates, the government initiated a gradual process of deposit rate decontrol, beginning in May 1982. Although some liberalisation of controls had begun earlier (e.g. the nationwide introduction of interest bearing household transaction accounts in 1980), the lifting of ceilings on any time deposit with an original maturity of at least 3½ years marked the first complete decontrol of a retail depository instrument. By October 1983, all controls on time deposits with an original maturity of 32 days and over were lifted. These changes were accompanied by the introduction in January 1983 of money market deposit accounts and super NOW accounts, household transaction deposits that pay a market rate of interest. (Initially these instruments had minimum denominations of $2 500, but this was decreased to $1 000 in January 1985, and eliminated altogether at the beginning of 1986.) The remaining category of retail deposits, passbook savings accounts, were decontrolled in April 1986. These changes have improved the ability of banks to compete for funds, as illustrated by the large shift in liabilities from money market mutual funds to banks that occurred in 1983.

Aside from the measures taken by regulatory authorities that have weakened some of the barriers separating commercial and investment banking (see the main text), there were also major moves in the direction of interstate banking[3]. However, these were undertaken by the individual states and not the Federal Government. One of the federal statutes governing interstate banking, the Bank Holding Company Act of 1956, contains a provision that al-lows states to permit out-of-state holding companies to acquire in-state firms. Until 1975 no state exercised this option, but in that year Maine passed a law allowing general entry. Since then 40 states and the District of Columbia have passed similar laws, except that most do not allow equal entry to firms from all states. (For example, the southeastern states have formed a compact that denies reciprocal entry to states outside the region.) The chief force behind this movement was a concern that the old system was hindering economic development by being too fragmented and inefficient. By allowing out-of-state entry, it was hoped that more funds could be attracted into particular regions, and that bigger banks could provide improved financial services. A desire to maximise the number of potential bidders for failing in-state institutions was another motive, along with a recognition that the branching restrictions had penalised banks relative to other financial institutions. Finally, some states have hoped to preserve local financial decision-making through the creation of large regional banks, who will be powerful competitors of the money centre banks once full interstate banking is in place.

Notes

1. See "The Profitability of U.S. Chartered Insured Commercial Banks in 1986", *Federal Reserve Bulletin* (July 1987)
2. See "The Thrift Industry in Transition," *Federal Reserve Bulletin* (March 1985)
3. See "Interstate Banking Developments," *Federal Reserve Bulletin* (February 1987)

STATISTICAL ANNEX

Selected background statistics

	Average 1978-86	1978	1979	1980	1981	1982	1983	1984	1985	1986	1987
A. Percentage change from previous year at constant 1982 prices											
Private consumption	3.0	4.1	2.2	-0.2	1.2	1.3	4.6	4.8	4.6	4.2	1.9
Gross fixed capital formation	3.3	9.8	3.7	-7.9	1.1	-9.6	8.2	16.8	5.5	1.8	0.6
Residential	3.2	5.9	-4.0	-19.8	-7.6	-16.9	42.0	14.5	2.2	12.5	0.0
Non-residential	3.8	11.8	7.5	-2.6	4.2	-7.2	-1.5	17.7	6.8	-2.3	0.9
GNP	2.6	5.3	2.5	-0.2	1.9	-2.5	3.6	6.8	3.0	2.9	2.9
GNP price deflator	6.1	7.3	8.8	9.1	9.6	6.4	3.8	3.7	3.2	2.6	3.0
Industrial production	2.6	6.5	3.9	-1.9	2.2	-7.2	5.9	11.6	1.6	1.1	3.7
Employment	2.0	4.4	2.9	0.5	1.1	-0.9	1.3	4.1	2.0	2.3	2.6
Compensation of employees (current prices)	8.8	13.0	12.2	9.8	10.3	5.5	6.0	9.6	7.1	5.6	5.7
Productivity (GNP/employment)	0.6	0.9	-0.4	-0.6	0.8	-1.7	2.2	2.5	1.0	0.6	0.3
Unit labor costs (compensation/GNP)	6.1	7.3	9.5	10.0	8.2	8.3	2.3	2.6	3.9	2.6	2.7
B. Percentage ratios											
Gross fixed capital formation as % of GNP at constant prices	16.6	17.3	17.6	16.2	16.1	14.9	15.6	17.0	17.4	17.2	16.9
Stockbuilding as % of GNP at constant prices	0.4	1.2	0.5	-0.2	0.7	-0.8	-0.2	1.8	0.2	0.4	1.1
Foreign balance as % of GNP at constant prices	-0.7	-0.9	0.1	1.8	1.5	0.8	-0.6	-2.4	-3.0	-3.9	-3.5
Compensation of employees as % of GNP at current prices	59.4	59.1	59.5	60.0	59.2	60.2	59.3	58.7	59.1	59.1	59.0
Direct taxes as percent of household income	14.8	14.4	15.0	15.1	15.6	15.3	14.5	14.2	14.6	14.5	15.1
Household saving as percent of disposable income	6.2	7.1	6.8	7.1	7.5	6.8	5.4	6.1	4.5	4.3	3.8
Unemployment as percent of total labour force	7.5	6.1	5.8	7.2	7.6	9.7	9.6	7.5	7.2	7.0	6.2
C. Other indicator											
Current balance (billion dollars)	-47.5	-15.4	-1.0	1.9	6.9	-8.7	-46.2	-107.0	-116.4	-141.3	—

Table A. National product and expenditure

Seasonally adjusted, percentage changes from previous period, annual rates, 1982 prices

	1977-1987 % p.a.	1977	1978	1979	1980	1981	1982	1983	1984	1985	1986	1987
Private consumption	3.0	4.4	4.1	2.2	-0.2	1.2	1.3	4.6	4.8	4.6	4.2	1.8
Public expenditure	2.7	1.5	2.6	0.8	1.9	1.5	1.9	1.1	4.4	7.3	3.8	2.5
Gross fixed investment	4.0	14.1	9.8	3.7	-7.9	1.1	-9.6	8.2	16.8	5.5	1.8	0.4
Residential	4.4	19.4	5.9	-4.0	-19.8	-7.6	-16.9	42.0	14.5	2.2	12.5	-0.1
Non-residential	4.2	11.5	11.8	7.5	-2.6	4.2	-7.2	-1.5	17.7	6.8	-2.3	0.7
Final domestic demand	3.1	5.3	4.7	2.2	-1.2	1.2	-0.4	4.5	6.6	5.3	3.7	1.7
Stockbuilding[1]	0.1	0.2	0.3	-0.7	-0.7	1.0	-1.5	0.6	2.1	-1.6	0.2	0.8
Total domestic demand	3.1	5.5	4.9	1.5	-1.8	2.2	-1.9	5.1	8.7	3.6	3.9	2.5
Exports of goods and services	4.3	2.6	11.0	14.1	9.1	0.9	-7.8	-3.8	6.8	-1.7	3.3	12.8
Imports of goods and services	6.6	11.1	7.0	4.1	-6.0	3.4	-2.2	9.6	23.9	3.9	10.5	7.1
Foreign balance[1]	-0.3	-0.9	0.3	1.0	1.7	-0.2	-0.7	-1.5	-1.9	-0.7	-1.0	0.3
GNP	2.8	4.7	5.3	2.5	-0.2	1.9	-2.5	3.6	6.8	3.0	2.9	2.9

	1987 levels (1982 $ billions)	1985 Q3	1985 Q4	1986 Q1	1986 Q2	1986 Q3	1986 Q4	1987 Q1	1987 Q2	1987 Q3	1987 Q4
Private consumption	2 495.2	5.3	4.5	4.1	4.2	4.3	4.1	2.7	2.2	1.7	0.6
Public expenditure	773.2	15.7	8.4	-8.3	7.8	3.0	7.9	-6.2	3.8	2.6	12.6
Gross fixed investment	643.0	0.4	10.5	-3.5	-1.0	0.8	4.2	-12.5	6.9	15.0	-0.8
Residential	196.2	8.9	11.4	14.5	24.8	9.7	2.2	-7.7	-2.8	-6.5	5.9
Non-residential	446.8	-2.7	10.1	-9.9	-10.3	-3.0	5.1	-14.6	11.6	25.8	-3.6
Final domestic demand	3 911.4	7.4	4.1	0.5	4.0	5.3	2.5	-3.8	3.1	6.4	-0.2
Stockbuilding[1]	42.4	-0.6	0.1	1.0	-0.2	-0.6	-0.6	1.7	-0.2	-0.4	0.9
Total domestic demand	3 953.8	4.7	4.6	4.5	3.2	3.0	0.4	2.5	2.1	4.8	3.2
Exports of goods and services	425.8	-4.5	6.8	5.6	-1.4	10.6	9.5	10.2	17.9	23.7	16.2
Imports of goods and services	560.1	2.6	18.3	-1.1	19.6	20.1	-0.8	-5.2	11.1	22.4	6.3
Foreign balance[1]	-134.3	-0.2	-0.4	-0.2	-0.6	-0.4	0.3	0.4	0.1	-0.1	0.2
GNP	3 819.5	4.1	3.1	5.3	0.6	1.4	1.5	4.4	2.5	4.3	4.1

1. Changes as a percentage of previous period GNP.
Source: *Survey of Current Business,* US Department of Commerce.

149

Table B. Labour market (s.a.)

	1978	1979	1980	1981	1982	1983	1984	1985	1986	1987	1987 Q1	1987 Q2	1987 Q3	1987 Q4
1. Numbers of persons, millions														
Population of working age[1,2]	161.9	164.9	167.7	170.1	172.3	174.2	176.4	178.2	180.6	182.7	182.0	182.5	183.0	183.5
Civilian labour force[1]	102.2	105.0	107.0	108.7	110.2	111.5	113.5	115.5	117.8	119.8	119.2	119.6	120.0	120.6
Unemployment[1]	6.2	6.1	7.7	8.3	10.7	10.7	8.5	8.3	8.2	7.4	7.9	7.5	7.2	7.1
Employment[1]	96.0	98.8	99.3	100.4	99.5	100.8	105.0	107.2	109.6	112.4	111.3	112.1	112.9	113.5
Employment[3]	86.7	89.8	90.4	91.2	89.6	90.2	94.5	97.5	99.6	102.1	101.1	101.7	102.3	103.3
Federal government	2.8	2.8	2.9	2.8	2.7	2.8	2.8	2.9	2.9	2.9	2.9	2.9	2.9	3.0
State and local	12.9	13.2	13.4	13.3	13.1	13.1	13.2	13.5	13.8	14.1	14.0	14.1	14.1	14.2
Manufacturing	20.5	21.0	20.3	20.2	18.8	18.4	19.4	19.3	19.0	19.1	19.0	19.0	19.1	19.3
Construction	4.2	4.5	4.4	4.2	3.9	3.9	4.4	4.7	4.9	5.0	5.0	5.0	5.0	5.0
Other	46.3	48.3	49.4	50.7	51.1	52.0	54.7	57.1	59.0	61.0	60.2	60.7	61.2	61.8
2. Percentage change from previous period (s.a.a.r.)														
Population of working age[1,2]	1.8	1.8	1.7	1.4	1.3	1.1	1.2	1.0	1.3	1.2	0.3	0.3	0.3	0.3
Civilian labour force[1]	3.3	2.7	1.9	1.6	1.4	1.2	1.8	1.7	2.1	1.7	0.5	0.3	0.3	0.4
Employment[1]	4.4	2.9	0.5	1.1	-0.9	1.3	4.1	2.0	2.3	2.6	3.0	3.2	2.5	2.3
Employment[3]	5.1	3.6	0.7	0.8	-1.7	0.7	4.8	3.2	2.1	2.5	3.0	2.3	2.2	3.9
Federal government	0.9	0.7	3.4	-3.3	-1.2	1.3	1.2	2.4	0.8	1.5	2.3	2.4	1.6	3.7
State and local	4.2	2.0	1.5	-0.9	-1.2	0	0.9	2.3	2.2	2.2	1.0	1.9	-0.2	4.6
Manufacturing	4.2	2.6	-3.6	-0.6	-6.9	-1.9	5.1	-0.6	-1.4	0.6	0.6	0.7	2.5	4.0
Construction	9.8	5.6	-2.4	-3.7	-6.8	0.9	11.0	6.7	4.9	2.7	7.8	-2.0	-0.8	7.2
Other	5.5	4.3	2.3	2.6	0.6	2.0	5.2	4.4	3.3	3.4	4.1	3.4	3.3	4.0
3. Unemployment rates														
Total	6.1	5.9	7.2	7.6	9.7	9.6	7.5	7.2	7.0	6.2	6.6	6.2	6.0	5.9
Married men	2.8	2.8	4.2	4.3	6.5	6.4	4.6	4.3	4.4	3.9	4.1	4.0	3.7	3.5
Females	7.2	6.8	7.4	7.9	9.4	9.2	7.6	7.4	7.1	6.2	6.6	6.2	6.1	6.0
Youths	16.4	16.1	17.8	19.6	23.2	22.4	18.9	18.6	18.3	16.9	17.8	17.0	16.1	16.6
4. Activity rate[4]	59.3	59.9	59.2	59.0	57.7	57.9	59.5	60.1	60.7	61.5	61.1	61.4	61.7	61.8

1. Household survey.
2. Non-institutional population aged 16 and over.
3. Non-agricultural payroll.
4. Employment as percentage of population aged from 16 to 64.
Source: Monthly Labor Review, Department of Labor.

150

Table C. Costs and prices
Percentage changes from previous period, s.a.a.r.

	1978	1979	1980	1981	1982	1983	1984	1985	1986	1987	1987 Q1	Q2	Q3	Q4
Rates of pay														
Major wage settlements[1]	8.0	8.9	9.7	9.7	6.7	3.9	3.7	3.2	2.3	3.1	1.6	4.0	3.6	3.2
Hourly earnings index[2]	8.2	8.0	9.0	9.1	6.9	4.6	3.3	2.9	2.5	2.5	2.1	2.5	2.7	3.5
Wages and salaries per person	7.9	8.7	9.1	8.9	5.9	4.3	5.3	5.3	3.4	3.2	3.5	2.0	3.8	5.8
Compensation per person	8.2	9.1	9.3	9.1	6.4	4.6	5.2	4.9	3.3	3.0	2.9	2.0	3.6	5.3
Productivity														
Hourly, non-farm business	0.8	-1.6	-0.5	1.0	-0.6	3.4	1.6	1.6	1.7	0.8	0.4	1.5	4.1	0.4
Per employee, non-farm business	0.7	-1.7	-1.8	0.9	-1.6	4.2	3.3	0.5	1.0	–	0.8	0.8	2.0	–
Per employee, whole economy	0.9	-0.4	-0.6	0.8	-1.7	2.2	2.5	1.0	0.6	0.3	1.3	-0.7	1.8	2.1
Unit labour costs														
Hourly, non-farm business	8.0	11.2	11.0	8.3	8.4	1.0	1.9	3.2	2.2	2.0	0.7	1.6	-0.7	3.8
Whole economy	7.3	9.5	10.0	8.2	8.3	2.3	2.6	3.9	2.6	2.7	1.6	2.7	1.8	3.4
Prices														
GNP deflator	7.3	8.8	9.1	9.6	6.4	3.9	3.7	3.2	2.6	3.0	4.0	3.7	2.8	2.7
Private consumption deflator	7.2	9.2	10.8	9.2	5.7	4.1	3.8	3.5	2.2	4.0	5.8	5.1	3.8	4.3
Consumer price index	7.6	11.3	13.5	10.4	6.2	3.2	4.3	3.6	1.9	3.7	4.5	5.3	4.7	3.4
Food	10.1	10.9	8.5	7.8	4.0	2.1	3.9	2.3	3.2	4.2	3.9	4.3	2.7	3.1
Wholesale prices	7.8	12.5	14.1	9.1	2.0	1.3	2.4	-0.5	-2.9	2.6	4.8	6.5	4.6	1.8
Crude products	7.0	12.8	18.8	14.0	-2.9	1.3	2.2	-7.5	-8.4	6.7	13.3	21.0	8.6	-5.6
Intermediate products	6.8	12.6	15.4	9.3	1.4	0.6	2.5	-0.4	-3.5	2.4	4.5	6.3	6.4	4.0
Finished products	7.8	11.1	13.5	9.3	4.0	1.6	2.1	0.9	-1.4	2.1	2.2	4.7	2.0	0.8

1. Total effective wage adjustment in all industries under collective agreements in non-farm industry covering at least 1 000 workers, not seasonally adjusted.
2. Production or non-supervisory workers on private non-agricultural payrolls.
Sources: Monthly Labor Review, Bureau of Labor Statistics, Department of Labor; *Survey of Current Business,* US Department of Commerce.

Table D. Household income and expenditure

OECD definitions

	1978	1979	1980	1981	1982	1983	1984	1985	1986	1987
$ billion										
Wages and salaries	1 119	1 252	1 372	1 510	1 586	1 677	1 837	1 975	2 089	2 213
Other labour income	210	239	266	297	321	344	375	396	416	434
Compensation of employees	1 329	1 491	1 638	1 807	1 907	2 021	2 212	2 371	2 505	2 647
Property income, etc.	411	467	512	597	623	666	763	819	885	950
Current transfers received	244	273	325	368	411	443	457	490	518	543
less: Consumer debt interest	37	44	47	52	56	62	72	83	90	93
Total income	1 947	2 187	2 428	2 720	2 885	3 068	3 360	3 597	3 818	4 047
less: Direct taxes	434	503	558	646	680	703	767	841	888	961
Disposable income	1 513	1 684	1 870	2 074	2 205	2 365	2 593	2 756	2 930	3 086
Consumers expenditure	1 404	1 567	1 733	1 915	2 051	2 235	2 430	2 629	2 800	2 966
Savings	109	117	137	159	154	130	163	127	130	120
Percentage changes from previous period (s.a.a.r.)										
Wages and salaries	12.6	11.9	9.6	10.1	5.0	5.7	9.7	7.4	5.8	5.9
Other labour income	14.9	14.0	11.3	11.6	8.0	7.2	9.1	5.5	5.0	4.3
Compensation of employees	13.0	12.2	9.8	10.3	5.5	6.0	9.6	7.1	5.7	5.7
Property income, etc.	15.9	13.6	9.6	16.5	4.4	6.9	14.6	7.3	8.1	7.3
Current transfers received	8.0	11.9	18.9	13.4	11.5	7.8	3.2	7.2	5.8	4.8
Total income	12.8	12.3	10.9	12.1	6.0	6.3	9.6	7.0	6.2	5.9
less: Direct taxes	14.5	16.1	10.9	15.7	5.3	3.3	9.1	9.7	5.7	8.2
Disposable income	12.3	11.3	11.0	11.0	6.3	7.3	9.7	6.2	6.3	5.3
Consumers expenditure	11.6	11.6	10.6	10.5	7.1	9.0	8.8	8.2	6.5	5.9
Savings ratio[1]	7.3	7.0	7.3	7.7	7.0	5.5	6.3	4.6	4.5	3.9
Consumer price deflator	7.2	9.2	10.8	9.2	5.7	4.1	3.8	3.4	2.2	4.0
Real disposable income	4.7	1.9	0.1	1.6	0.5	3.0	5.7	2.7	4.0	1.2
Real consumers expenditure	4.1	2.2	-0.2	1.2	1.3	4.6	4.8	4.6	4.2	1.6
Non-durables	3.1	1.7	-0.5	0.2	0.9	3.8	3.2	2.9	3.3	-0.2
Services	4.6	3.3	2.1	1.7	1.8	3.5	3.5	4.5	3.4	3.5
Durables	5.3	-0.3	-7.7	2.0	0.8	12.0	14.1	9.2	8.7	1.2

1. Savings as percentage of disposable income.
Source: *Survey of Current Business*, US Department of Commerce.

Table E. Monetary indicators

	1978	1979	1980	1981	1982	1983	1984	1985	1986	1987	1987 Q1	Q2	Q3	Q4
Monetary aggretates (percentage changes from previous period s.a.a.r.)														
M1	8.2	7.7	7.5	5.2	8.7	10.2	5.3	12.0	15.6	6.2	13.2	6.6	0.8	3.9
M2	8.5	8.2	8.9	9.3	9.1	12.1	7.6	8.9	9.4	4.0	6.5	2.6	2.8	4.0
M3	12.0	10.4	9.5	12.3	9.9	9.8	10.4	7.7	9.1	5.4	6.5	4.7	4.5	5.6
Velocity of circulation														
GNP/M1	6.4	6.6	6.8	7.1	6.9	6.7	6.9	6.7	6.3	6.0	5.9	5.9	6.0	6.1
GNP/M2	1.7	1.7	1.7	1.8	1.7	1.6	1.7	1.6	1.6	1.6	1.5	1.6	1.6	1.6
GNP/M3	1.4	1.5	1.4	1.4	1.3	1.3	1.3	1.3	1.3	1.2	1.2	1.2	1.2	1.3
Federal Reserve Bank reserves ($ billion)														
Non-borrowed	26.7	26.6	28.3	30.3	32.0	34.8	37.3	42.5	50.1	57.2	56.6	57.3	57.3	57.6
Borrowed	1.0	1.4	1.4	1.5	1.0	0.8	0.6	0.7	0.3	0.4	0.3	0.7	0.5	0.4
Total	27.7	28.0	29.7	31.8	33.0	35.6	37.9	43.2	50.4	57.6	56.9	58.0	57.8	58.0
Required	27.5	27.9	29.5	31.4	32.6	35.1	37.2	42.3	49.5	56.7	55.8	57.0	56.9	56.9
Excess	0.2	0.1	0.2	0.4	0.4	0.5	0.7	0.9	0.9	0.9	1.1	1.0	0.9	1.1
Free (excess – borrowed)	-0.8	-1.3	-1.2	-1.1	-0.6	-0.3	0.1	0.2	0.6	0.5	0.8	0.3	0.4	0.7
Interest rates (%)														
Federal funds rate	7.9	11.2	13.4	16.4	12.3	9.1	10.2	8.1	6.8	6.7	6.2	6.6	6.8	6.9
Discount rates[1]	7.5	10.4	11.8	13.4	10.9	8.5	8.8	7.7	6.2	5.7	5.5	5.5	5.7	6.0
Prime rate[2]	9.1	12.7	15.3	18.9	14.9	10.8	12.0	9.9	8.3	8.2	7.5	8.0	8.4	8.9
3 month Treasury Bills	7.2	10.1	11.4	14.0	10.6	8.6	9.5	7.5	6.0	5.8	5.5	5.7	6.0	5.9
AAA rate[3]	8.7	9.6	11.9	14.2	13.8	12.0	12.7	11.4	9.0	9.4	8.4	9.2	9.8	10.2
10 year Treasury Bonds	8.4	9.4	11.5	13.9	13.0	11.1	12.4	10.6	7.7	8.4	7.2	8.3	8.9	9.1

1. Rate for Federal Reserve Bank of New York.
2. Prime rate on short-term business loans.
3. Corporate Bonds, AAA rating group, quoted by Moody's Investors Services.
Sources: Federal Reserve Bulletin, Board of Governors of the Federal Reserve System.

153

	1974	1975	1976	1977	1978
Exports, fob[1]	98 310	107 090	114 740	120 810	142 060
Imports, fob[1]	103 820	98 180	124 230	151 910	176 000
Trade balance	−5 510	8 910	−9 490	−31 100	−33 940
Services, net[2]	14 650	13 820	18 690	21 220	23 620
Balance on goods and services	9 140	22 730	9 200	−9 880	−10 320
Private transfers, net	−1 020	−900	−910	−870	−850
Official transfers, net	−6 160	−3 700	−4 080	−3 760	−4 270
Current balance	1 960	18 130	4 210	−14 150	−15 440
Long-term capital					
(excluding special transactions)	−5 030	−16 950	−11 780	−11 030	−10 750
a) Private[3]	−5 700	−15 000	−12 220	−8 740	−8 570
b) Official	670	−1 950	440	−2 290	−2 180
Basic balance	−3 070	1 180	−7 570	−25 540	−26 190
Non-monetary short-term private capital[4]	−767	1 130	−2 030	−2 330	−2 130
Non-monetary short-term official capital	−	−	−	−	−
Errors and omissions	−1 433	5 940	9 460	−2 460	13 920
Balance on non-monetary transactions	−5 270	8 250	−140	−30 330	−14 400
Private monetary institutions short-term capital	−3 490	−12 900	−10 380	−4 710	−17 530
a) Assets[5]	−19 510	−13 540	−21 370	−11 430	−33 670
b) Liabilities[5][6]	16 020	640	10 990	6 720	16 140
Net transactions of monetary authorities	−8 760	−4 650	−10 520	−35 040	−31 930
Liabilities to foreign official monetary agencies[7][8]	10 230	5 500	13 080	35 410	31 190
Use of IMF credit	−	−	−	−	−
Special transactions	−	−	−	−	−
Miscellaneous official accounts	−	−	−	−	−
Allocation of SDR's	−	−	−	−	−
Change in reserves (+ = increase)	1 470	850	2 560	370	−740
a) Gold	−	−	−	120	70
b) Currency assets	40	320	270	−160	4 690
c) Reserve positions in IMF	1 260	480	2 220	300	−4 240
d) Special drawing rights	170	70	90	120	−1 250

1. Excluding military goods.
2. Services include reinvested earnings of incorporated affiliates.
3. Including:
   a) Direct investment financed by reinvested earnings of incorporated affiliates;
   b) Investments by foreign official agencies in US corporate stocks and in debt securities of US Government corporations and agencie
      private corporations and State and local governments.
   c) Investment by international financial institutions and private foreign residents in US Treasury bonds and notes.
   d) Until 1977, US banks' long-term assets and liabilities.
   e) Until 1978, US non-banking concerns' long-term assets and liabilities to unaffiliated foreigners.
4. Including investments by international financial institutions and private foreign residents in US Treasury bills and certificates an
   since 1979, US non-banking concerns' long-term assets and liabilities to unaffiliated foreigners.
5. Including US banks' long-term assets and liabilities since 1978.
6. Excluding liabilities held by foreign official monetary agencies.
7. Excluding liabilities to IMF and investments by foreign official agencies in US corporate stocks and in debt securities of U
   Government corporations and agencies, private corporations and State and local governments.
8. Including liabilities to BIS.
Source : Survey of Current Business, US Department of Commerce.

dollars

1979	1980	1981	1982	1983	1984	1985	1986	1987
184 470	224 270	237 090	211 200	201 810	219 900	215 930	224 360	250 820
212 010	249 760	265 070	247 650	268 890	332 410	338 090	368 700	410 020
−27 540	−25 490	−27 980	−36 450	−67 080	−112 510	−122 160	−144 340	−159 200
32 180	34 440	42 340	36 720	30 320	17 650	21 060	18 650	11 990
4 640	8 950	14 360	270	−37 760	−94 860	−101 100	−125 690	−147 210
−920	−1 050	−950	−1 200	−980	−1 440	−1 910	−1 660	−1 280
−4 720	−6 030	−6 520	−7 760	−8 510	−10 740	−13 390	−14 000	−12 190
1 870	6 890	−8 690	−46 250	−107 040	−116 400	−141 350	−141 350	−160 680
−19 360	−3 920	12 750	9 730	11 720	46 090	64 180	73 850	34 530
−15 570	630	18 200	15 250	16 120	50 980	66 180	74 050	36 540
−3 790	−4 550	−5 450	−5 520	−4 400	−4 890	−2 000	−200	−2 010
−20 360	−2 050	19 640	1 040	−34 530	−60 950	−52 220	−67 500	−126 150
−2 540	4 130	1 230	10 300	−1 260	11 780	410	−8 050	3 170
–	–	–	–	–	–	–	–	–
30 140	26 140	19 960	36 090	11 320	27 170	17 900	23 950	21 890
7 240	28 220	40 830	47 430	−24 470	−22 000	−33 910	−51 600	−101 090
6 390	−36 090	−42 040	−45 420	20 410	22 730	39 730	18 310	44 430
−26 210	−46 840	−84 840	−111 070	−29 930	−11 130	−1 320	−59 040	−33 430
32 600	10 750	42 130	65 650	50 340	33 860	41 050	77 350	77 860
13 630	−7 870	−1 210	2 010	−4 060	730	5 820	−33 290	−56 660
−13 630	14 880	5 300	2 950	5 250	2 410	−1 960	32 970	47 520
–	–	–	–	–	–	–	–	–
–	–	–	–	–	–	–	–	–
1 140	1 150	1 090	–	–	–	–	–	–
1 140	8 160	5 180	4 960	1 190	3 140	3 860	−310	−9 150
70	–	–	–	–	–	–	–	–
−250	6 460	860	1 040	−3 310	1 160	3 880	950	−7 590
190	1 660	2 500	2 550	4 440	990	−910	−1 500	−2 070
1 130	10	1 820	1 370	60	980	890	240	510

BASIC STATISTICS :

INTERNATIONAL COMPARISONS

	Units	Reference period[1]	Australia	Austria
Population				
Total	Thousands	1986	15 974	7 565
Inhabitants per sq.km	Number		2	90
Net average annual increase over previous 10 years	%		1.3	0.0
Employment				
Total civilian employment (TCE)[2]	Thousands	1986	6 946	3 235 (85
of which: Agriculture	% of TCE		6.1	9.0
Industry	% of TCE		26.8	38.1
Services	% of TCE		67.1	52.9
Gross domestic product (GDP)				
At current prices and current exchange rates	Billion US$	1986	167.3	93.8
Per capita	US$		10 473	12 403
At current prices using current PPP's[3]	Billion US$	1986	193.0	85.1
Per capita	US$		12 084	11 254
Average annual volume growth over previous 5 years . . .	%	1986	2.9	1.8
Gross fixed capital formation (GFCF)	% of GDP	1986	23.3	22.4
of which: Machinery and equipment	% of GDP		11.2 (85)	9.8
Residential construction	% of GDP		5.2 (85)	4.6 (85
Average annual volume growth over previous 5 years . . .	%		−0.1	0.5
Gross saving ratio[4]	% of GDP	1986	18.6	24.3
General government				
Current expenditure on goods and services	% of GDP	1986	18.8	19.0
Current disbursements[5]	% of GDP	1986	35.3 (85)	45.7 (85
Current receipts	% of GDP	1986	33.5 (85)	48.1 (85
Net official development assistance	% of GNP	1986	0.47	0.21
Indicators of living standards				
Private consumption per capita using current PPP's[3] . . .	US$	1986	7 199	6 299
Passenger cars, per 1 000 inhabitants	Number	1985	. .	306 (81
Telephones, per 1 000 inhabitants	Number	1985	540 (83)	460 (83
Television sets, per 1 000 inhabitants	Number	1985	. .	300 (81
Doctors, per 1 000 inhabitants	Number	1985	. .	1.7 (82
Infant mortality per 1 000 live births	Number	1985	9.2 (84)	11.0
Wages and prices (average annual increase over previous 5 years)				
Wages (earnings or rates according to availability)	%	1986	7.7	5.0
Consumer prices	%	1986	8.2	3.8
Foreign trade				
Exports of goods, fob*	Million US$	1986	22 536	22 428
as % of GDP	%		13.5	23.9
average annual increase over previous 5 years	%		0.7	7.3
Imports of goods, cif*	Million US$	1986	23 916	26 724
as % of GDP	%		14.3	28.5
average annual increase over previous 5 years	%		0.1	4.9
Total official reserves[6]	Million SDR's	1986	6 202	5 778
As ratio of average monthly imports of goods	Ratio		3.7	3.0

* At current prices and exchange rates.
1. Unless otherwise stated.
2. According to the definitions used in OECD *Labour force Statistics*.
3. PPP's = Purchasing Power Parities.
4. Gross saving = Gross national disposable income *minus* Private and Government consumption.
5. Current disbursements = Current expenditure on goods and services *plus* current transfers and payments of property income.
6. Gold included in reserves is valued at 35 SDR's per ounce. End of year.
7. Including Luxembourg.
8. Included in Belgium.
9. Including non-residential construction.

Belgium	Can	Spain	Sweden	Switzerland	Turkey	United Kingdom	United States	Yugoslavia
		38 688	8 369	6 533 (85)	49 841 (85)	56 618 (85)	239 283 (85)	23 120 (85)
9 858 (85)	25 67	77	19	158	64	231	26	89
323		0.7	0.2	0.2	2.1	0.1	1.0	0.8
0.1	1.							
		10 959	4 269	3 196	15 290 (85)	24 239	109 597	..
3 607 (85)	11 63	15.6	4.2	6.5	57.1	2.6	3.1	..
2.9	5	32.4	30.2	37.7	17.5	31.1	27.7	..
29.7	25	52.1	65.6	55.8	25.4	66.4	69.3	..
67.4	69							
		229.1	131.1	135.1	58.0	547.8	4 185.5	44.2 (85)
112.2	363	5 945	15 661	20 587	1 142	9 651	17 324	1 913 (85)
11 377	14 1'	310.8	109.7	..	199.7	652.7	4 185.5	..
111.2	413	8 065	13 111	..	3 927	11 498	17 324	..
11 276	16 1(	2.1	2.1	1.6	5.5	2.6	2.9	
1.5								
		19.7	18.2	24.3	23.6	17.2	17.8	21.8 (85)
16.1	2(	6.6 (85)	8.5	8.4	9.1 (82)	8.1	7.8	..
5.2 (85)	(	4.6 (84)	3.8	15.9 (9)	2.6 (82)	3.8	5.2	..
3.2 (85)	(	1.4	2.1	4.0	7.6	4.4	4.4	..
0.7	(							
		22.2	18.3	31.1	22.2	18.3	15.0	..
18.4	1!							
		13.8	27.2	12.9	8.8	21.3	18.6	13.8 (85)
16.7	2	36.7	59.9	30.4	..	44.9 (85)	35.6	..
52.0 (85)	4	35.8	61.5	35.0	..	43.7 (85)	31.3	..
46.2 (85)	3	0.09	0.85	0.30	..	0.32	0.23	..
0.49	0							
		5 113	6 804	12 326 *	2 713	7 156	11 500	953 (85)*
7 172	9	240	377	402	18 (82)	312 (83)	473 (84)	121 (83)
335 (84)		369	890 (83)	1 334	55 (83)	521 (84)	650 (84)	122 (83)
414 (83)		256 (82)	390	337	76 (79)	336 (84)	621 (80)	175 (83)
303 (84)		3.3	2.5	1.4 (84)	1.5 (83)	0.5 (83)	2.3 (83)	1.6 (82)
2.8 (84)		7.0 (84)	6.8	6.9	..	9.4	10.6 (84)	31.7 (83)
9.4								
		17.4	8.0	..	..	9.1	4.0	
4.4		11.1	7.4	3.1	37.2	5.5	3.8	56.3
5.7								
		27 132	37 200	37 248	7 428	107 016	217 308	7 188
68 652[7]	86	11.8	28.4	27.6	12.8	19.5	5.2	16.3
61.2		5.8	5.4	6.7	9.3	0.7	-1.4	-3.1
4.4		34 920	32 484	40 860	11 124	126 156	369 960	8 196
68 544[7]	81	15.2	24.8	30.2	19.2	23.0	8.8	18.5
61.1		1.7	2.4	6.0	4.5	4.2	7.2	-7.5
2.1		12 581	5 568	20 726	1 332	15 726	39 790	1 259
5 724[7]		5.1	2.4	7.1	1.7	1.8	1.5	2.2
1.2								

Sources:
Population and Empl...
GDP, GFCF, and G...
Historical Statistics.
Indicators of living s...
Wages and Prices: O...
Foreign trade: OECI...
Total official reserve...

EMPLOYMENT OPPORTUNITIES

Economics and Statistics Department
OECD

A.   **Administrator.**   A number of economist positions may become available in areas such as monetary and fiscal policy, balance of payments, resource allocation, macroeconomic policy issues, short-term forecasting and country studies. *Essential* qualifications and experience: advanced university degree in economics; good knowledge of statistical methods and applied econometrics; two or three years experience in applied economic analysis; command of one of the two official languages (English and French); some knowledge of the other official language. *Desirable* qualifications and experience also include: familiarity with the economic problems and data sources of a number of Member countries; proven drafting ability; experience with the estimation, simulation and implementation of computer-based economic models.

B.   **Principal Administrator.**   A number of senior economist positions may become available in areas such as monetary and fiscal policy, balance of payments, resource allocation, macroeconomic policy issues, short-term forecasting and country studies. *Essential* qualifications and experience: advanced university degree in economics; extensive experience in applied economic analysis, preferably with a central bank, economics/finance ministry or institute of economic research; good knowledge of statistical methods and applied econometrics; command of one of the two official languages (English and French) and proven drafting ability; working knowledge of the other official language. *Desirable* qualifications and experience also include: experience in using economic analysis for formulating policy advice; familiarity with a number of OECD economies; experience in using econometric models.

These positions carry a basic salary from FF 202 200 or FF 249 480 (Administrator) and from FF 292 416 (Principal Administrator), supplemented by further additional allowances depending on residence and family situation.

Initial appointment will be on a two- or three-year fixed-term contract.

Vacancies are open to both male and female candidates from OECD Member countries. Applications citing reference "ECSUR", together with a detailed curriculum vitæ in English or French, should be sent to:

Head of Personnel
OECD
2, rue André-Pascal
75775 PARIS CEDEX 16
FRANCE

WHERE TO OBTAIN OECD PUBLICATIONS
OÙ OBTENIR LES PUBLICATIONS DE L'OCDE

ARGENTINA - ARGENTINE
Carlos Hirsch S.R.L.,
Florida 165, 4º Piso,
(Galeria Guemes) 1333 Buenos Aires
Tel. 33.1787.2391 y 30.7122

AUSTRALIA - AUSTRALIE
D.A. Book (Aust.) Pty. Ltd.
11-13 Station Street (P.O. Box 163)
Mitcham, Vic. 3132　　　Tel. (03) 873 4411

AUSTRIA - AUTRICHE
OECD Publications and Information Centre,
4 Simrockstrasse,
5300 Bonn (Germany)　　Tel. (0228) 21.60.45
Gerold & Co., Graben 31, Wien I　Tel. 52.22.35

BELGIUM - BELGIQUE
Jean de Lannoy,
avenue du Roi 202
B-1060 Bruxelles　　　　Tel. (02) 538.51.69

CANADA
Renouf Publishing Company Ltd/
Éditions Renouf Ltée,
1294 Algoma Road, Ottawa, Ont. K1B 3W8
Tel: (613) 741-4333
Toll Free/Sans Frais:
Ontario, Quebec, Maritimes:
1-800-267-1805
Western Canada, Newfoundland:
1-800-267-1826
Stores/Magasins:
61 rue Sparks St., Ottawa, Ont. K1P 5A6
Tel: (613) 238-8985
211 rue Yonge St., Toronto, Ont. M5B 1M4
Tel: (416) 363-3171
Federal Publications Inc.,
301-303 King St. W.,
Toronto, Ontario M5V 1J5
Tel. (416)581-1552

DENMARK - DANEMARK
Munksgaard Export and Subscription Service
35, Nørre Søgade, DK-1370 København K
Tel. +45.1.12.85.70

FINLAND - FINLANDE
Akateeminen Kirjakauppa,
Keskuskatu 1, 00100 Helsinki 10　Tel. 0.12141

FRANCE
OCDE/OECD
Mail Orders/Commandes par correspondance :
2, rue André-Pascal,
75775 Paris Cedex 16
Tel. (1) 45.24.82.00
Bookshop/Librairie : 33, rue Octave-Feuillet
75016 Paris
Tel. (1) 45.24.81.67 or/ou (1) 45.24.81.81
Librairie de l'Université,
12a, rue Nazareth,
13602 Aix-en-Provence　　Tel. 42.26.18.08

GERMANY - ALLEMAGNE
OECD Publications and Information Centre,
4 Simrockstrasse,
5300 Bonn　　　　　　Tel. (0228) 21.60.45

GREECE - GRÈCE
Librairie Kauffmann,
28, rue du Stade, 105 64 Athens　Tel. 322.21.60

HONG KONG
Government Information Services,
Publications (Sales) Office,
Information Services Department
No. 1, Battery Path, Central

ICELAND - ISLANDE
Snæbjörn Jónsson & Co., h.f.,
Hafnarstræti 4 & 9,
P.O.B. 1131 – Reykjavik
Tel. 13133/14281/11936

INDIA - INDE
Oxford Book and Stationery Co.,
Scindia House, New Delhi 110001
Tel. 331.5896/5308
17 Park St., Calcutta 700016　Tel. 240832

INDONESIA - INDONÉSIE
Pdii-Lipi, P.O. Box 3065/JKT.Jakarta
Tel. 583467

IRELAND - IRLANDE
TDC Publishers - Library Suppliers,
12 North Frederick Street, Dublin 1
Tel. 744835-749677

ITALY - ITALIE
Libreria Commissionaria Sansoni,
Via Lamarmora 45, 50121 Firenze
Tel. 579751/584468
Via Bartolini 29, 20155 Milano　　Tel. 365083
Editrice e Libreria Herder,
Piazza Montecitorio 120, 00186 Roma
Tel. 6794628
Libreria Hœpli,
Via Hœpli 5, 20121 Milano　　Tel. 865446
Libreria Scientifica
Dott. Lucio de Biasio "Aeiou"
Via Meravigli 16, 20123 Milano　Tel. 807679
Libreria Lattes,
Via Garibaldi 3, 10122 Torino　　Tel. 519274
La diffusione delle edizioni OCSE è inoltre
assicurata dalle migliori librerie nelle città più
importanti.

JAPAN - JAPON
OECD Publications and Information Centre,
Landic Akasaka Bldg., 2-3-4 Akasaka,
Minato-ku, Tokyo 107　　　Tel. 586.2016

KOREA - CORÉE
Kyobo Book Centre Co. Ltd.
P.O.Box: Kwang Hwa Moon 1658,
Seoul　　　　　　Tel. (REP) 730.78.91

LEBANON - LIBAN
Documenta Scientifica/Redico,
Edison Building, Bliss St.,
P.O.B. 5641, Beirut　　Tel. 354429-344425

**MALAYSIA/SINGAPORE -
MALAISIE/SINGAPOUR**
University of Malaya Co-operative Bookshop
Ltd.,
7 Lrg 51A/227A, Petaling Jaya
Malaysia　　　Tel. 7565000/7565425
Information Publications Pte Ltd
Pei-Fu Industrial Building,
24 New Industrial Road No. 02-06
Singapore 1953　Tel. 2831786, 2831798

NETHERLANDS - PAYS-BAS
SDU Uitgeverij
Christoffel Plantijnstraat 2
Postbus 20014
2500 EA's-Gravenhage　　Tel. 070-789911
Voor bestellingen:　　　Tel. 070-789880

NEW ZEALAND - NOUVELLE-ZÉLANDE
Government Printing Office Bookshops:
Auckland: Retail Bookshop, 25 Rutland Stseet,
Mail Orders, 85 Beach Road
Private Bag C.P.O.
Hamilton: Retail: Ward Street,
Mail Orders, P.O. Box 857
Wellington: Retail, Mulgrave Street, (Head
Office)
Cubacade World Trade Centre,
Mail Orders, Private Bag
Christchurch: Retail, 159 Hereford Street,
Mail Orders, Private Bag
Dunedin: Retail, Princes Street,
Mail Orders, P.O. Box 1104

NORWAY - NORVÈGE
Tanum-Karl Johan
Karl Johans gate 43, Oslo 1
PB 1177 Sentrum, 0107 Oslo 1 Tel. (02) 42.93.10

PAKISTAN
Mirza Book Agency
65 Shahrah Quaid-E-Azam, Lahore 3 Tel. 66839

PHILIPPINES
I.J. Sagun Enterprises, Inc.
P.O. Box 4322 CPO Manila
Tel. 695-1946, 922-9495

PORTUGAL
Livraria Portugal,
Rua do Carmo 70-74, 1117 Lisboa Codex
Tel. 360582/3

**SINGAPORE/MALAYSIA -
SINGAPOUR/MALAISIE**
See "Malaysia/Singapor" Voir
« Malaisie/Singapour »

SPAIN - ESPAGNE
Mundi-Prensa Libros, S.A.,
Castelló 37, Apartado 1223, Madrid-28001
Tel. 431.33.99
Libreria Bosch, Ronda Universidad 11,
Barcelona 7　　Tel. 317.53.08/317.53.58

SWEDEN - SUÈDE
AB CE Fritzes Kungl. Hovbokhandel,
Box 16356, S 103 27 STH,
Regeringsgatan 12,
DS Stockholm　　　　Tel. (08) 23.89.00
Subscription Agency/Abonnements:
Wennergren-Williams AB,
Box 30004, S104 25 Stockholm Tel. (08)54.12.00

SWITZERLAND - SUISSE
OECD Publications and Information Centre,
4 Simrockstrasse,
5300 Bonn (Germany)　　Tel. (0228) 21.60.45
Librairie Payot,
6 rue Grenus, 1211 Genève 11
Tel. (022) 31.89.50
United Nations Bookshop/
Librairie des Nations-Unies
Palais des Nations,
1211 – Geneva 10
Tel. 022-34-60-11 (ext. 48 72)

TAIWAN - FORMOSE
Good Faith Worldwide Int'l Co., Ltd.
9th floor, No. 118, Sec.2
Chung Hsiao E. Road
Taipei　　　Tel. 391.7396/391.7397

THAILAND - THAILANDE
Suksit Siam Co., Ltd.,
1715 Rama IV Rd.,
Samyam Bangkok 5　　　Tel. 2511630
INDEX Book Promotion & Service Ltd.
59/6 Soi Lang Suan, Ploenchit Road
Patjumamwan, Bangkok 10500
Tel. 250-1919, 252-1066

TURKEY - TURQUIE
Kültur Yayinlari Is-Türk Ltd. Sti.
Atatürk Bulvari No: 191/Kat. 21
Kavaklidere/Ankara　　　Tel. 25.07.60
Dolmabahce Cad. No: 29
Besiktas/Istanbul　　　Tel. 160.71.88

UNITED KINGDOM - ROYAUME-UNI
H.M. Stationery Office,
Postal orders only:　　　(01)211-5656
P.O.B. 276, London SW8 5DT
Telephone orders: (01) 622.3316, or
Personal callers:
49 High Holborn, London WC1V 6HB
Branches at: Belfast, Birmingham,
Bristol, Edinburgh, Manchester

UNITED STATES - ÉTATS-UNIS
OECD Publications and Information Centre,
2001 L Street, N.W., Suite 700,
Washington, D.C. 20036 - 4095
Tel. (202) 785.6323

VENEZUELA
Libreria del Este,
Avda F. Miranda 52, Aptdo. 60337,
Edificio Galipan, Caracas 106
Tel. 951.17.05/951.23.07/951.12.97

YUGOSLAVIA - YOUGOSLAVIE
Jugoslovenska Knjiga, Knez Mihajlova 2,
P.O.B. 36, Beograd　　　Tel. 621.992

Orders and inquiries from countries where
Distributors have not yet been appointed should be
sent to:
OECD, Publications Service, 2, rue André-Pascal,
75775 PARIS CEDEX 16.

Les commandes provenant de pays où l'OCDE n'a
pas encore désigné de distributeur peuvent être
adressées à :
OCDE, Service des Publications. 2, rue André-
Pascal, 75775 PARIS CEDEX 16.

71602-03-1988

OECD PUBLICATIONS
2, rue André-Pascal
75775 PARIS CEDEX 16
No. 44297
(10 88 02 1)   ISBN 92-64-13093-4
ISSN 0376-6438

•

PRINTED IN FRANCE